Annals of Entrepreneurship Education and Pedagogy – 2021

ANNALS IN ENTREPRENEURSHIP EDUCATION

Series Editor: *The United States Association for Small Business and Entrepreneurship, USA*

The *Annals in Entrepreneurship Education* chronicles the state of the art in entrepreneurship education and pedagogy, both in terms of research and practice. This comprehensive source provides a focused review of top contributions delivered at USASBE's annual conference and allied activities. Invited contributions are included from scholars in the field who provide critical perspectives on methodological approaches, practices and future directions. Scholars, educators, practitioners and policy makers will find this publication to be an invaluable resource for thought leadership in entrepreneurial education.

The *Annals in Entrepreneurship Education* curates the latest and best thinking. Original material includes outcomes assessment and its impact on learning and teaching, experiential methods of learning, and methodologies that use emerging and digital tools and platforms in the classroom. This is a 'must-read' for those involved and passionate about the transformation of entrepreneurship education. Please visit the website for more information about the launch of this invaluable addition to the entrepreneurship education library: www.usasbe.org.

Titles in the series include:

Annals of Entrepreneurship Education and Pedagogy – 2014
Edited by Michael H. Morris

Annals of Entrepreneurship Education and Pedagogy – 2016
Edited by Michael H. Morris and Eric W. Liguori

Annals of Entrepreneurship Education and Pedagogy – 2018
Edited by Charles H. Matthews and Eric W. Liguori

Annals of Entrepreneurship Education and Pedagogy – 2021
Edited by Charles H. Matthews and Eric W. Liguori

Annals of Entrepreneurship Education and Pedagogy – 2021

Edited by

Charles H. Matthews

Distinguished Teaching Professor of Entrepreneurship and Strategy, Lindner College of Business, University of Cincinnati, USA

Eric W. Liguori

Rohrer Endowed Chair of Entrepreneurship and Executive Director of the Center for Innovation and Entrepreneurship, Rohrer College of Business, Rowan University, USA

ANNALS IN ENTREPRENEURSHIP EDUCATION

Edward Elgar
PUBLISHING

Cheltenham, UK • Northampton, MA, USA

Published by
Edward Elgar Publishing Limited
The Lypiatts
15 Lansdown Road
Cheltenham
Glos GL50 2JA
UK

Edward Elgar Publishing, Inc.
William Pratt House
9 Dewey Court
Northampton
Massachusetts 01060
USA

Paperback edition 2022

A catalogue record for this book
is available from the British Library

Library of Congress Control Number: 2020950846

This book is available electronically in the **Elgar**online
Business subject collection
http://dx.doi.org/10.4337/9781789904468

ISBN 978 1 78990 445 1 (cased)
ISBN 978 1 78990 446 8 (eBook)
ISBN 978 1 0353 0026 6 (paperback)

Printed and bound by CPI Group (UK) Ltd, Croydon, CR0 4YY

Contents

Editorial review board

Contributors

Dennis Barber III is Assistant Professor in the Miller School of Entrepreneurship at East Carolina University, USA.

Jarlyne Batista Monzon is Community Manager of the Hynes Institute for Entrepreneurship and Innovation at Iona College, USA.

Josh Bendickson is Associate Professor of Entrepreneurship at the University of Louisiana at Lafayette, USA.

Andrew Bunoza supervises Studio 231, an experiential learning lab and makerspace, at Rowan University, USA.

Peter M.W. Burley is Graduate Assistant in the School of Business and Public Administration at California State University, Bakersfield, USA.

Daniel Cliver is Broadcast Television Instructor at Delsea Regional High School District, USA.

Sara L. Cochran is Clinical Assistant Professor in the Kelley School of Business at Indiana University, USA.

Dan Cohen is Professor of Practice and Executive Director of the Center for Entrepreneurship at Wake Forest University, USA.

Sílvia Costa is Assistant Professor of Entrepreneurship at the University of Groningen, the Netherlands.

Birton Cowden is Assistant Professor and Research Director of the Shore Entrepreneurship Center at Kennesaw State University, USA.

Robert D'Intino is Professor of Management and Entrepreneurship in the William G. Rohrer College of Business at Rowan University, USA.

Saskia De Klerk is Senior Lecturer of International Business at the University of the Sunshine Coast Business School, Australia.

Michael Dominik is Lecturer of Management and Entrepreneurship in the William G. Rohrer College of Business at Rowan University, USA.

Bronwyn Eager is Lecturer in Management at the University of Tasmania School of Business and Economics, Australia.

Katarina Ellborg is Lecturer in the Department of Organization and Entrepreneurship at the Linnæus University School of Business and Economics, Sweden.

Robert Fanuzzi is Associate Provost for Academic Affairs and Director of Civic Engagement and Public Programs at St. John's University, USA.

Alain Fayolle is Professor in the EMLYON Business School, France.

James Fiet is the Brown Forman Chair of Entrepreneurship at the University of Louisville, USA.

Susan Fiorito is the Jim Moran Professor and Dean of the Jim Moran College of Entrepreneurship at Florida State University, USA.

Robert S. Fleming is Professor of Management and Entrepreneurship in the William G. Rohrer College of Business at Rowan University, USA.

Dennis Foley is Professor of Indigenous Entrepreneurship at the University of Canberra, Australia.

Arjan Frederiks is Assistant Professor of Entrepreneurship at the University of Groningen, the Netherlands.

Katie Gallagher is Community Planner for the Mad River Valley Planning District in Vermont, USA.

William B. Gartner is the Bertarelli Foundation Distinguished Professor of Family Entrepreneurship at Babson College, USA and a Visiting Professor in Entrepreneurship at Linnaeus University in Sweden.

Michael Glauser is Executive Director of Entrepreneurial Programs in the John M. Huntsman School of Business at Utah State University, USA.

Thomas Haines is Professor of Commercial Music Production at the University of Cincinnati, USA.

Michael Harris is Professor and Director of the Miller School of Entrepreneurship at East Carolina University, USA.

James Hart is Director of Arts Entrepreneurship at Southern Methodist University, USA.

Andrew Heise is Instructor and Assistant Director of the Regnier Institute for Entrepreneurship and Innovation at the University of Missouri – Kansas City, USA.

Mark Hiatt is Associate Professor of Management, Entrepreneurship and Hospitality in the Coles College of Business at Kennesaw State University, USA.

Daniel Holland is Associate Professor of Entrepreneurship and Strategy at Utah State University, USA.

Deborah Hoover is President and Chief Executive Officer of the Burton D. Morgan Foundation, USA.

Jeffrey Hornsby is Professor, Department Chair, and Director of the Regnier Institute for Entrepreneurship and Innovation at the University of Missouri – Kansas City, USA.

Colin Jones is an Associate Professor of Academic Development at the University of Southern Queensland, Australia.

Paul Jones is Professor of Entrepreneurship and Innovation and Head of the Business Department at Swansea University, UK.

Jerome Katz is the Robert H. Brockhaus Endowed Chair in Entrepreneurship at Saint Louis University, USA.

Tina Kiefer is Professor of Organizational Behavior at Warwick Business School, UK.

Eric W. Liguori is the Rohrer Endowed Chair of Entrepreneurship and Executive Director of the Center for Innovation and Entrepreneurship at Rowan University, USA. He served as President of USASBE in 2019.

Yanxin Liu is Assistant Professor of Management at Eastern Washington University, USA.

Michela Loi is Assistant Professor at University of Cagliari, Italy.

Federico Mammano is Co-Founder and Product/Market/Entrepreneurship Hacker of TeachingEntrepreneurship.org, Italy.

Alex Maritz is Professor of Entrepreneurship, Management Sport and Tourism at La Trobe University, Australia.

Charles H. Matthews is Distinguished University Teaching Professor and Professor of Entrepreneurship and Strategic Management at the University of Cincinnati, USA. He served as President of USASBE in 2004.

Maimouna Mbacke is a senior marketing and entrepreneurship student at Iona College, USA.

Anthony Mendes is Managing Director of the Regnier Institute for Entrepreneurship and Innovation at the University of Missouri – Kansas City, USA.

Nada Miljkovic is Instructor at Crown College, University of California Santa Cruz, USA.

Xaver Neumeyer is Assistant Professor of Entrepreneurship and Management in the Cameron School of Business at the University of North Carolina Wilmington, USA.

Quan Nguyen is Lecturer of Entrepreneurship, Management Sport and Tourism at La Trobe University, Australia.

Lendynette Pacheco-Jorge is Assistant Director of the Hynes Institute for Entrepreneurship and Innovation at Iona College, USA.

Sharon Paynter is Assistant Vice Chancellor for Economic and Community Engagement at East Carolina University, USA.

Whitney Peake is Associate Professor of Entrepreneurship and Center Director at Western Kentucky University, USA.

Luke Pittaway is the O'Bleness Professor of Entrepreneurship and Associate Dean for Undergraduate Programs in the College of Business at Ohio University, USA.

Wendy Plant is Director for the InNOLEvation® Center for Student Engagement in the Jim Moran College of Entrepreneurship at Florida State University, USA.

Jeffrey Pollack is Associate Professor of Management, Innovation, and Entrepreneurship in the Poole College of Management at North Carolina State University, USA.

Gregory Quinet is Associate Professor and Executive Director of the Entrepreneurship Center at Kennesaw State University, USA.

Jeff Reid is Professor of the Practice of Entrepreneurship and Founding Director of the Georgetown Entrepreneurship Initiative in the McDonough School of Business at Georgetown University, USA.

William Reisel is Professor in the Department of Management at St. John's University, USA.

Susana C. Santos is Assistant Professor of Entrepreneurship in the Rohrer College of Business at Rowan University, USA.

Julienne Shields is Chief Executive Officer of USASBE and former Executive Director of the Center for Entrepreneurship at Millikin University, USA.

Otis Solomon, Jr. is employed at Sandia National Laboratories in the Primary Standards Laboratory, a subsidiary of Honeywell International, USA.

Shelby Solomon is Assistant Professor of Management at the University of West Florida, USA.

James Swaim is Clinical Assistant Professor of Management, Entrepreneurship and Hospitality in the Coles College of Business at Kennesaw State University, USA.

Bruce Teague is the EWU Foundation Distinguished Professor of Entrepreneurship at Eastern Washington University, USA.

Pedro Tonhozi de Oliveira is Professor of Management at FGV Sao Paulo School of Business Administration, Brazil.

Caroline Vanevenhoven is Visitor Services Manager at the Milwaukee School of Engineering's Grohmann Museum, USA.

Jeff Vanevenhoven is the Irvin L. Young Professor of Entrepreneurship at the University of Wisconsin, Whitewater, USA.

Rasheda Weaver is Assistant Professor of Entrepreneurship and Innovation at Iona College, USA.

Rebecca White is the Walter Chair of Entrepreneurship and Director of the Lowth Entrepreneurship Center at the University of Tampa, USA.

Justin Wilcox is Founder of TeachingEntrepreneurship.org, USA.

Doan Winkel is the John J. Kahl, Sr. Chair of Entrepreneurship at John Carroll University, USA.

Christoph Winkler is the Hynes Endowed Professor of Entrepreneurship and Innovation at Iona College, USA.

Jeremy Woods is Associate Professor in the School of Business and Public Administration at California State University, Bakersfield, USA.

Lee Zane is Associate Professor of Entrepreneurship in the Rohrer College of Business at Rowan University, USA.

Andrew Zimbroff is Assistant Professor and Extension Specialist of Textiles and Apparel Entrepreneurship at the University of Nebraska-Lincoln, USA.

Acknowledgments

The editors would like to thank the following individuals and/or groups:

- USASBE CEO Julienne Shields and the USASBE Board of Directors for their continued support of the *Annals of Entrepreneurship Education and Pedagogy* and for all the work they do year-round to ensure the vibrancy of the USASBE community.
- Dr. Susana C. Santos, forthcoming Co-Editor of Vol. V of the *Annals of Entrepreneurship Education and Pedagogy*, for her support in helping this volume come to fruition.
- USASBE's Longenecker Fellows for their thought leadership, past, present, and future.
- Alan Sturmer and the team at Edward Elgar Publishing for being great partners in this effort.

Preface: entrepreneurship education – what is it we need to know?

Charles H. Matthews, Eric W. Liguori and Susana C. Santos

Welcome to Volume IV of the *Annals of Entrepreneurship Education and Pedagogy* published in partnership between the United States Association for Small Business and Entrepreneurship and Edward Elgar Publishing. As noted in the preface of Volume III, the state of the art and science of entrepreneurship education is good. Yet, despite the continued advances in content, delivery, evaluation, review, and feedback developed, there remains work to be done. This is not unexpected. After all, we teach ideation, innovation, experimentation, design thinking, customer discovery, and more, so our knowledge base continues to evolve and develop as do the needs of our students, and thus so too must our approach to entrepreneurship education itself. If nothing else became apparent in the year leading up to the release of Volume IV, it is the realization that as educators we need to be prepared to adapt rapidly to changing, and often complex, conditions that require us to be innovative in our pedagogical approaches.

A case in point is the value of experiential learning in entrepreneurship education. Morris and Liguori (2016) note, "a large percentage (perhaps as much as 60 percent) of the [entrepreneurship] education program should center on experiential learning." In this sense, the majority of the contemporary entrepreneurship education is prescribed as being experiential in nature, a defining characteristic most model programs across the globe embrace and advertise to prospective students. The prevalence of experiential learning in entrepreneurship education is widespread and evidenced by the majority of content published in the previous three volumes (e.g., Choi, 2014; Neck, Greene, & Brush, 2014; Schindehutte & Morris, 2016; Morland & Thompson, 2016). It is also a prevalent theme in much of the contemporary entrepreneurship research in the field (e.g., Heriot, Cook, Matthews, & Simpson, 2007; Neck & Greene, 2011; Morris, Kuratko, & Cornwall, 2013; Vanevenhoven & Liguori, 2013).

Yet, despite the proliferation of "experiential learning" in entrepreneurship education, a review of the tools available to entrepreneurship educators reveals that nearly all of the "experiential learning" activities, assignments, role-plays, and exercises are designed for face-to-face instruction. In short, as entrepreneurship educators we have honed our craft for primarily in-person environments. While the advent of the Internet and its adaptation in higher education in general and entrepreneurship education in particular has and continues to be impactful (Pittinsky, 2003), by and large entrepreneurship educators tend to use it as a supplement or complement to face-to-face content delivery rather than more widely embracing it as a more *complete* mode of delivery. While this is certainly not true in the absolute sense (e.g., there are 100 percent online entrepreneurship and other courses), it is true for the majority of courses and the majority of entrepreneurship degree programs.

Like most things, the delivery mode was not a challenge or problem for the majority of educators, especially given that in general, we do not typically fix what does not appear to be broken. The spring 2020 semester, however, witnessed an unprecedented change. It began much like every prior semester for the past few decades. Students filled classrooms, engaged in classroom exercises, field case exercises, and started attending startup events in local, regional, national, and international venues. As the semester progressed, students continued to engage in a plethora of experiential learning approaches offered through their programs (exercises, community events, competitions, internships, apprenticeships, and more).

Then the COVID-19 pandemic dramatically changed everything, first in the short term and likely in the long term as well (Liguori & Winkler, 2020). As the preface to Volume IV goes to press, we are looking at the conclusion of a semester which started very typically and abruptly became 100 percent virtual. It was at this point the realization set in that most of our high-impact and experiential learning approaches and opportunities required face-to-face interaction for delivery. Moreover, the awareness emerged that very little research on, and pedagogical approaches for, experiential learning beyond face to face have been developed.

Reflecting back, the last ten weeks have been a period of learning, adapting, satisficing, salvaging, and triaging the semester. Very little time was available for developing new and impactful online learning tools and approaches; instead, best-case scenario was the mindset "how can I adapt this face-to-face activity to fit an online environment?" As a new term dawns, we find ourselves in an evolving world of face-to-face, hybrid, synchronous, and asynchronous teaching and learning environments, tools, and techniques. In short, we exist in an ever evolving complex system, with external factors that impact the "what" and the "how" of entrepreneurship education. Looking forward, we must continue to address and consider three fundamental questions: (1) what is it we need to know, (2) why is it important to know, and (3) how are we going to know it?

WHAT IS IT WE NEED TO KNOW?

Today, new challenges arise as we still struggle with the core definition of entrepreneurship and the hijacking of the discipline by just about everyone. In the preface of Volume III, it is noted:

> I know of no other academic (or non-academic for that matter) discipline that has allowed itself to be so abused and ultimately hijacked by others when it comes to what that discipline actually is. As a result, the word "entrepreneurship" continuously suffers a definitional crisis, which in turn, systematically obscures the core element of entrepreneurship education, and all that it encompasses. (Matthews, 2018, p. xvii)

This begs the question, as an academic discipline and practice, what is it that is important to know? Interestingly, it is not about the ever expanding entrepreneurship literature, per se, that has evolved over multiple decades. Too often, researchers note the goal of their work is "to advance the literature." Not surprising given the often misguided notion that published work is the best measure and subsequently our goal, rather than advancing knowledge. In reality, it is about advancing what we know or, more precisely, what we don't know. The literature exists to inform our quest for knowledge, not the other way around. What are the compelling questions surrounding what we need to know to advance both the theory and practice of entrepreneurship and subsequently entrepreneurship education?

WHY IS IT IMPORTANT TO KNOW?

Which brings us to the second question, "Why is it important to know?" Simply, the discipline of entrepreneurship itself, and subsequently entrepreneurship education, cannot advance without identifying why we need to know something. Are we asking the important questions and why each is important? Or are we just going with the flow? Why is it important to know a core definition of entrepreneurship? Why is it important to know how ventures differ in terms of growth aspirations? Why is it important to know how artificial intelligence, machine learning, blockchain, the Internet of Things, the Industrial Internet of Things, venture funding, and more will impact entrepreneurship and, subsequently, entrepreneurship education? At what point do we see the relevance of theory and the intersection with practice? That the pedagogy of entrepreneurship education was caught so flat-footed by the seismic shift from face-to-face to all online instruction is a clarion call to focus on these first two questions more expansively. It is not just about the literature. What is it we need to know and why is it important to know it?

HOW ARE WE GOING TO KNOW IT?

Given the pursuit of knowledge and its importance, how are we going to know what it is we need to know? That is, how do we know something? How is it measured? What are the standards by which an assessment is made? Which brings us squarely into the realm of entrepreneurship education. As a discipline, what topics are important to be covered? Which are the best pedagogies to use in that pursuit? What metrics are best to use in given circumstances? Where are "one-size-fits-all" tools appropriate and where do we need highly customizable frames to illuminate the content of entrepreneurship?

As noted in Volume III, "as a discipline, we need to integrate our research more closely with entrepreneurship education. That is, we need to engage more in the scholarship of entrepreneurship education" (Matthews, 2018, p. xxi). It has, is, and continues to challenge us entrepreneurship educators. Are you up for the challenge?

IN THIS VOLUME

Even a cursory read of Volume IV reveals that the authors in this volume have risen to the challenge of advancing entrepreneurship education on multiple fronts. Moreover, Volume IV comes out at a time when the world is dealing with the ravages of the COVID-19 pandemic and all the challenges it has presented to every occupation and lifestyle. While only a few articles in this volume touch directly on the impact of the pandemic, its aftershock will continue to play a role in entrepreneurship education for some time to come. Time-tested and timely topics from brainstorming to the role of experiential learning to gender and equity inclusion evolve in and out of the classroom. The challenges of undergraduate and graduate entrepreneurship education follow similar yet divergent paths. From classroom-tested practices, five master entrepreneurship educators (viz., Dan Cohen, Paul Jones, Jerry Katz, Jeff Pollack, and Rebecca White, Chapter 1) share key insights. In addition, five model university programs (viz., Florida State University, Georgetown University, Iona College, Millikin University, and University of Missouri – Kansas City) highlight the ever evolving landscape of entrepreneurship education from programmatic and ecosystem perspectives. Finally, an incredibly impressive collection of thought leaders shares a variety of best practices, including a piece on the impact of the COVID-19 pandemic on small businesses. In the chapters ahead, you will be enlightened and challenged in thought and practice. Here is just a sampling of the contributors' individual and collective insight and wisdom.

When it comes to new venture creation, brainstorming is a valuable technique for ideation both in the classroom and practice. In Chapter 4, Zane and

Zimbroff introduce various ways that brainstorming and other ideation techniques can be applied in the classroom to facilitate entrepreneurship education. Three exercise examples show how to introduce brainstorming in the classroom and provide insights into content, process, and outcomes from time well spent working with entrepreneurship students. More than just a step-by-step guide, the authors share key insights into the value added for the students, instructor, and ultimately, the startup experience.

In Chapter 13, Sara Cochran presents a compelling thesis on the experiences of women in entrepreneurship education. It is a complex environment, but Cochran frames the essential question around which to pursue this well-crafted qualitative study: *What role does gender play in the academic experience of women participating in an entrepreneurship program?* The results of her work are a must-read as we continue to move forward to develop an entrepreneurship education environment that is inclusive and diverse and ultimately contributes to a better world.

In universities and colleges around the world, entrepreneurship education continues to evolve both within business schools as well as across campuses. Katarina Ellborg takes a close look at the role and use of visual artifacts from a student-centered perspective. In Chapter 6, Ellborg takes a deep dive into the theory and practice, shedding light on how visual artifacts play a role in didactic analysis in order to approach students' contemporary meaning of entrepreneurship in the beginning of the learning process.

MBA programs across the country strive to remain current, identify meaningful curricula for the future, and translate theory into practice. At the same time, companies across the industrial and commercial spectrum struggle to avoid complacency, search for ways to be creative and innovative, and face increasing pressure from a changing competitive landscape. It is this perfect storm that propels Birton Cowden, Mark Hiatt, James Swaim, and Gregory Quinet to explore the intersection of the past, present, and future of MBA core curricula and the role of managerial mindset versus an entrepreneurial mindset. Using effectuation as a focal point, Chapter 5 outlines the need and process for making MBA education in general and the core curriculum valuable into the twenty-first century.

In Chapter 22, Shelby Solomon and Otis Solomon, Jr. tackle a very timely and important question in our classrooms today. How do we deal with classroom diversity in our pursuit of entrepreneurship education? They note that to date many routine attempts at encouraging diversity are based upon student majors or some other readily observable difference. They outline an interesting perspective on how to respect individual autonomy while encouraging diversity via a game based on MTV's reality series "Are You the One." The game encourages diversity through the use of group incentives, thereby preserving autonomy and inspiring social exploration.

The future of entrepreneurship education relies on many factors, and perhaps chief among them is preparing doctoral qualified scholars to rise to the challenge of pursuing both theory and practice. In Chapter 2, James Fiet explores the development of theory and provides a keen insight into the often little understood world of the state of the art of doctoral-level entrepreneurship education. He notes that although "doctoral programs vary in length from three to as many as five years and more, this short, intensive period of study has a much larger, ongoing influence on a scholar's career." The impact of blending and balancing the ever evolving landscape of theory and practice for these future scholars cannot be overstated, yet is often underestimated. A must-read for faculty engaged in mentoring, coaching, and preparing the next generation of entrepreneurship scholars.

"Philanthropy is almost the only virtue which is sufficiently appreciated by mankind" (Henry David Thoreau). There is no stronger connection between the success of entrepreneurs and their willingness to give back than the foundation of philanthropy in the United States. While not totally unique to America, charitable giving is a potent element for positive change in the world of entrepreneurship moving forward. In Chapter 9, Deborah Hoover provides a comprehensive overview of the role of philanthropy in identifying, initiating, developing, and growing entrepreneurship ecosystems in both community and university settings. Skillfully drawing out examples of philanthropic development from the past and present, she gives the reader a full view into the future of the transformative role of philanthropy across multiple constituencies. "If we don't transform the world, who will? If not now, when?" (Anonymous).

"We shape our buildings; thereafter they shape up" (Winston Churchill). As the field of entrepreneurship continues to gain momentum into the twenty-first century, it is inevitable that we more fully consider how we shape it and it shapes us. Luke Pittaway builds an intriguing case in Chapter 3 that explores the role and impact of universities building new infrastructure for entrepreneurship and innovation activities. He does a deep dive into the extant literature to reveal the extent to which the role of physical infrastructure influences the entrepreneurship and innovation educational process. Effectively using multiple case studies of universities that have built new space, "the critical parameters that enable creativity and innovative behavior in on-campus entrepreneurship education spaces" are explored, analyzed, and discussed.

Of course, this is just a sampling of the many thought-provoking insights offered in this volume for your consideration, debate, use, and more. The chapters which follow contain a compendium of best practices, ideas, insights, and more from an incredibly diverse group of thought leaders from around the world. Read it from cover to cover or pick and choose a chapter here or there. Either way, you will not be disappointed. Enjoy!

REFERENCES

Choi, D. Y. (2014). Bringing design capability into entrepreneurship: LMU and Otis. In M. H. Morris (Ed.), *Annals of Entrepreneurship Education and Pedagogy – 2014*. Cheltenham, UK and Northampton, MA, USA: Edward Elgar Publishing.

Heriot, K. C., Cook, R. G., Matthews, C. H., & Simpson, L. (2007). Creating active and high-impact learning: Moving out of the classroom with field-based student consulting projects. *Industry and Higher Education, 21*(6), 427–34.

Liguori, E., & Winkler, C. (2020). From offline to online: Challenges and opportunities for entrepreneurship education following the COVID-19 pandemic. *Entrepreneurship Education and Pedagogy*. https://doi.org/10.1177/2515127420916738

Matthews, C. (2018). Preface. In C. H. Matthews & E. W. Liguori (Eds), *Annals of Entrepreneurship Education and Pedagogy – 2018*. Cheltenham, UK and Northampton, MA, USA: Edward Elgar Publishing.

Morland, L., & Thompson, J. (2016). New venture creation as a learning agenda: Experiences, reflections and implications from running a venture creation programme. In M. H. Morris & E. Liguori (Eds), *Annals of Entrepreneurship Education and Pedagogy – 2016*. Cheltenham, UK and Northampton, MA, USA: Edward Elgar Publishing.

Morris, M. H., Kuratko, D. F., & Cornwall, J. R. (2013). *Entrepreneurship Programs and the Modern University*. Cheltenham, UK and Northampton, MA, USA: Edward Elgar Publishing.

Morris, M. H., & Liguori, E. (2016). Preface: Teaching reason and the unreasonable. In M. H. Morris & E. Liguori (Eds), *Annals of Entrepreneurship Education and Pedagogy – 2016*. Cheltenham, UK and Northampton, MA, USA: Edward Elgar Publishing.

Neck, H. M. & Greene, P. G. (2011). Entrepreneurship education: Known worlds and new frontiers. *Journal of Small Business Management, 49*(1), 55–70.

Neck, H. M., Greene, P. G., & Brush, C. (2014). Practice-based entrepreneurship education using actionable theory. In M. H. Morris (Ed.), *Annals of Entrepreneurship Education and Pedagogy – 2014*. Cheltenham, UK and Northampton, MA, USA: Edward Elgar Publishing.

Pittinsky, M. S. (2003). *The Wired Tower: Perspectives on the Impact of the Internet on Higher Education*. Upper Saddle River, NJ: FT Press.

Schindehutte, M., & Morris, M. H. (2016). The experiential learning portfolio and entrepreneurship education. In M. H. Morris & E. Liguori (Eds), *Annals of Entrepreneurship Education and Pedagogy – 2016*. Cheltenham, UK and Northampton, MA, USA: Edward Elgar Publishing.

Vanevenhoven, J., & Liguori, E. (2013). The impact of entrepreneurship education: Introducing the entrepreneurship education project. *Journal of Small Business Management, 51*(3), 315–28.

PART I

Leading edge research perspectives

1. What I have learned about teaching entrepreneurship: perspectives of five master educators

Dan Cohen, Paul Jones, Jerome Katz, Jeffrey Pollack and Rebecca White

INTRODUCTION FROM CHARLES H. MATTHEWS AND ERIC W. LIGUORI

As editors, it is our privilege to serve the USASBE community by coordinating the assembly of this biennial volume showcasing the high-impact scholarship and pedagogy of so many talented individuals. While we are inspired by each and every entry in this volume, a true highlight is the thoughtful reflections which follow, where five master educators share their thoughts on the question, "What I have learned about teaching entrepreneurship." Their perspectives are insightful and inspiring; challenging us all to do better. Moreover, they illustrate the collective passion that exists within the USASBE community for what we are charged with doing every day – inspiring the next generation of entrepreneurs. Many of these contributions were written during the 2020 COVID-19 pandemic, the largest mass intervention on education (and entrepreneurship education) ever experienced (Liguori & Winkler, 2020). As such, these contributors rose to a special challenge; one where they had to balance deep reflection over many decades of cumulative experience against a very different look and feel in their classrooms today that could not have been predicted even three months earlier. They did this knowing that for this contribution to be useful it also needed to help inform the future, one that may be very different to what we have experienced in the past or are experiencing now. What follows from these five master educators is thought leadership in its most pure form. We thank Dan Cohen, Paul Jones, Jerome Katz, Jeffrey Pollack, and Rebecca White, as well as the ten individuals who have contributed to answering the same question in prior volumes (viz., Heidi Neck, Jerome Engel, Minet Schindehutte, Ray Smilor, Bill Rossi, Bill Aulet, Andrew

Hargadon, Luke Pittaway, Candida Brush, and Sharon Alpi), for their vulnerability, candor, and passion for entrepreneurship education.

DAN COHEN

I am honored to share my thoughts on what I have learned about teaching entrepreneurship over the last 15 years. Since I transitioned to academia from a career as an entrepreneur, I have had the good fortune to teach and conduct research on entrepreneurship at three excellent, albeit different, universities during my career (Iowa, Cornell, and Wake Forest). I've had varying roles at each institution (teaching at Iowa, teaching, researching, and venture creation as founder of Cornell's eLab Startup Acceerator program, and teaching, researching, and leading the program at Wake Forest). As I think about my experiences at these institutions and the differing roles I played as a faculty member, some common themes have emerged throughout my career which I believe are worth sharing.

Focus on Skill Development Rather Than Traits

Research indicates that entrepreneurs possess certain skills and traits. Traits such as the need for achievement, tolerance for risk, and tolerance for ambiguity are certainly valuable for entrepreneurs to possess. However, traits are hard to alter. Skills, on the other hand, can be vastly improved. In my experience, three key skills are vital for developing nascent entrepreneurs: ideation, passion for entrepreneurship, and learned optimism. These three skills are important because they are conduits to building resilience—in my opinion, a key to negotiating the entrepreneurship experience. Taken together, skill development also helps nascent entrepreneurs form an entrepreneurial identity. While critics of entrepreneurship education may deem us somehow "less than" because our discipline is skill-based rather than purely theoretical, I embrace the practicality of our field and am quite passionate about developing skills in my students that they will use throughout their careers.

IDEATE

I developed a method of teaching ideation called IDEATE and have presented this method at conferences in recent years. When I present IDEATE, I ask fellow entrepreneurship educators how they go about teaching ideation in the classroom. At one teaching-oriented conference, approximately 100 professors attended the session. When I asked how many taught a course with an ideation component, about 80 hands raised. When I asked if they felt underwhelmed by the quality of their students' ideas, almost 100 hands went up! When I asked their methods of teaching ideation, two approaches were mentioned most frequently. One was to ask students to keep a log of problems encountered in daily activity and then brainstorm possible solutions with classmates and the second was to assign students the task of generating their own ideas, which they would bring back to the classroom. Experienced entrepreneurs rely on pattern recognition—the constellation of domain expertise, industry experience, and a robust professional network to create ideas (Baron, 2006). Student entrepreneurs do not typically have any of these resources to draw upon (Hägg & Kurczewska, 2018). By focusing on their own problems or lives, ideas are often generated which are myopic and reflective of college students' experience; ideas we have all encountered such as the app that tells us when the laundry machine is available, or if the gym is crowded, or the coffee service that delivers to class.

There are many issues associated with developing ideas that are not so valuable. First, on some level, the students know that the ideas are not so great and they often "go through the motions" of customer discovery and experimentation when seeking to validate their ideas. "Going through the motions" is not typically a good prescription for most entrepreneurial endeavors. Nor is it a good behavior to teach students. Second, these ideas often identify problems of a minor inconvenience rather than real migraine headache problems and, as such, prospective customers are less likely to be concerned about solving the problem. Third, and potentially most damaging, is that poor-quality ideas usually do not get any meaningful traction in the market and this can lead to nascent entrepreneurs concluding that they are not "cut out" to be entrepreneurs. In truth, this may not be the case at all—they may be working with a poor idea—however, they can easily reach this conclusion. This might explain why research findings show that most nascent entrepreneurs do not become entrepreneurs.

The above issues led me (ably partnered by colleagues Greg Pool and Heidi Neck on the IDEATE book published recently by Sage, and by Dan Hsu and Rachel Shinnar on the IDEATE academic paper published recently in *Small Business Economics: an Entrepreneurship Journal*) to create the IDEATE method, an empirically proven method that helps students spot, evaluate, and select high-potential venture ideas. IDEATE is an acronym. Identify teaches students what makes ideas valuable, Discover focuses on where to find valuable ideas, Enhance teaches how to make good ideas even better, Anticipate focuses on how change is the progenitor of new ideas, Target helps entrepreneurs answer the question "to whom am I selling and why should they buy from me," and Evaluate teaches entrepreneurs how to select the highest potential idea. Armed with better-quality ideas, students are more likely to engage in customer discovery to validate their ideas more robustly. Students who believe in the ideas on which they are working are significantly more engaged in the classroom.

Unleash Their Anticipatory Passion for Entrepreneurship

Passion for entrepreneurship has been a hot topic in literature over the past ten years. It makes sense because passion drives sustained effort and helps entrepreneurs persist when adversity inevitably occurs. Passion for entrepreneurship is an intense desire or longing to engage in activities (in this case entrepreneurship) that are meaning to the self-identity of the entrepreneur (Cardon, Wincent, Singh, & Drnovsek, 2009). In a sense, you cannot separate the venture from the venturer, which explains why entrepreneurs persist. They quite literally would be quitting on themselves. I, along with co-authors Jagdip Singh and Melissa Cardon, am currently finalizing a study on how passion for entrepreneurship develops and what causes an entrepreneurial identity to form (Cohen, Cardon, & Singh, 2019). In this study, we examined nascent entrepreneurs using a longitudinal design, curious to see how passion and role identities relevant to entrepreneurship are formed. Each week we would collect data immediately after entrepreneurs met with their mentors and garnered feedback on the previous week's progress and then set goals for the coming week. Sometimes the feedback is positive and encouraging, while other times the feedback can be negative and discouraging. Without delving into too much detail, the feedback the entrepreneurs received from mentors mattered significantly to the passion and identity formation (or not) of the entrepreneur. When passion formed (it did not in all cases), it had a significant effect on other important outcome variables. We, as faculty, along with prospective customers and investors are "meaningful others" and, as such, we play a strong role in potentially validating or invalidating nascent entrepreneurs' emerging passion and identity (Markowska, Härtel, Brundin, & Roan, 2015). As such, in addition to giving specific advice and feedback on how to best develop their current venture, we should also be talking to them more broadly about skill development, strengthening their entrepreneurial mindset, and socializing them to the field of entrepreneurship. We should go beyond just providing tactical feedback regarding their ventures (which is important) and realize that we are nurturing the next generation of entrepreneurs by talking about things that are salient to their overall development as budding entrepreneurs.

Help Them Become the Eternal Optimist

Optimism is an important skill for nascent entrepreneurs to develop. I admit that I began reading Martin Seligman's great work to help teach my children to be more optimistic. After I learned of the important results Seligman had found about optimism's positive effects on anxiety and depression, I incorporated it into my teaching. I gave my students the Entrepreneurial Mindset Profile and was surprised at the pervasiveness of pessimism that existed among them. This cemented the importance of incorporating optimism into my teaching. I recently collected data on an experiment designed to test the efficacy of optimism as a mechanism to overcome the fear of failure. We have not yet analyzed the results, however, and as a sneak preview of coming research, we believe that optimism helps nascent entrepreneurs frame adversity (failure) in a healthier, less personal, and less permanent manner. Further, we predict that optimism helps nascent entrepreneurs frame failure in a way that preserves their budding passion for entrepreneurship and perceived fit with an entrepreneurial career. Here are some key differences, gleaned directly from Seligman's work, which differentiates optimists from pessimists when it comes to handling adversity (Seligman, 2006).

Humans have an explanatory style to make sense of adverse happenings in life. Three continuums help frame explanatory style:

1. Permanent to Temporary (pessimists think adverse situations are permanent while optimists think they are temporary).
2. Pervasive to Specific (pessimists believe adversity will impact many situations while optimists think the adversity will only affect a few situations).
3. Personal to Impersonal (pessimists think they are the cause of the adversity and optimists tend to think other people or circumstances caused the adversity).

Two mechanisms that can turn pessimistic thinking into optimistic thinking are distraction and disputation. Pessimists tend to focus on the worst-case scenario outcome, despite the knowledge that it is a low-probability outcome. Distraction can be an effective tool to switch focus away from worst-case thinking. Disputation, according to Seligman, is more effective (Seligman, 2006). Disputation occurs when one looks for evidence to dispute their worst-case scenario thinking. Specific to entrepreneurship, optimism is the belief that things will turn out well in the future. Entrepreneurship is uncertain, challenging, and chock full of adversity. Optimism is a skill that can help nascent entrepreneurs proactively frame challenges in order to handle adversity in their stride. On the other hand, pessimism, according to Seligman's research, leads to giving up and a lack of resilience. While admittedly in a very early stage of inquiry, I believe that learned optimism is a mechanism for coping with failure, for developing resilience while enduring challenges, and for mustering up the courage necessary to pursue an entrepreneurial initiative—whether it be starting a venture, solving a social problem, or simply being entrepreneurial in a larger organization.

Conclusion and Some Thoughts on the Future of Entrepreneurship Education

To recap, I have learned over my career that strengthening key skills of ideation, passion for entrepreneurship, and learned optimism has yielded lasting value for my students. I believe these particular skills are important because they foster resilience. I also know from my research that strengthening these skills aids entrepreneurs in developing an entrepreneurial identity.

From a philosophical standpoint, I have used two guiding principles throughout my academic career that have served me well and I will share them here. One is to practice what I preach. I teach my students about evidence-based entrepreneurship and experimentation. I practice that by creating new teaching methods and ways to build skills in my students. I also practice by experimentation and by subjecting new methods to rigorous empirical testing and the peer-reviewed journal process. This helps me share my methods with able colleagues around the world. I also practice what I preach by continuing to engage in entrepreneurial endeavors. The second is to remain true to my entrepreneurial roots. I started as an entrepreneur in my mid-20s by co-founding a startup and building up for a successful exit 15 years later. When I create a new teaching method or write a book, or conduct a peer-reviewed study, I ask myself if entrepreneurs would be interested in the topic. Would it capture their interest enough to make them want to sacrifice their precious time (entrepreneurs are busy!) to read it? Keeping in touch with my entrepreneurial roots has always served as a barometer for me whether it be in determining the value of a new line of research inquiry, the creation of a new teaching method, or the building of a new program.

I conclude with a challenge to the field. Most programs, including mine at Wake Forest, tout that we help our students develop an entrepreneurial mindset. There are a few issues, in my opinion, with this proclamation. First, as much as an entrepreneurial mindset is talked about, it is not so well studied or understood. Therefore, the first challenge is to know more about the entrepreneurial mindset. The second is that if we tout it, we should vigorously assess and test whether or not we are developing an entrepreneurial mindset. This is one reason why I have completed or am working on completing empirical studies on ideation, anticipatory entrepreneurial passion, and learned optimism. I encourage all of my colleagues to join me in researching the entrepreneurial mindset and its antecedents to test whether or not we are helping develop an entrepreneurial mindset in our students.

PAUL JONES

To reflect on the question "What I've learned teaching entrepreneurship" is particularly challenging when one considers the current global Covid-19 pandemic and its likely impact on the higher education sector and national economic performance globally. The pandemic and its short-, medium-, and long-term impacts are likely to have significant implications regarding how we teach entrepreneurship in coming years. Practically overnight, all universities have changed their pedagogical delivery model to an online-only strategy. This has enormous implications for the entrepreneurship discipline, which has evolved towards an experiential practice-based student experience. Now the entrepreneurship discipline must effectively embed an e-learning peda-gogy into its teaching delivery and potentially move away from experiential elements of its previous delivery at least in the short term. There are also sig-nificant implications for graduate startups in specific industries which may no longer be viable entities in the short term due to the lock down enforced by the virus. To survive, the entrepreneurship discipline must rapidly adjust, evolve, and disseminate best practice across the sector.

I can reflect on my 28 years of experience in the education sector and the entrepreneurship discipline. I offer multiple perspectives to this reflection as an entrepreneurship educator, an active researcher, and as journal editor of the *International Journal of Entrepreneurial Behavior and Research*. When I began teaching in the further education sector in the early 1990s, entrepreneurship was an afterthought with limited consideration in the aca-demic curriculum. Delivery and assessment typically took the form of the development of a business plan without any attempt to test or implement its value. However, over the last two decades in the United Kingdom (UK), this gradually changed with the evolving nature of the employment market, techno-logical evolution, and the decline of the public sector realizing the requirement for more business startups. Societal attitudes towards entrepreneurship have also changed in the media with entrepreneurs becoming widely recognized and regarded as "economic heroes" with programs such as *Dragons' Den* and *The Apprentice* encouraging entrepreneurship career choices. This trend has also been reflected globally with a gradual and now increasingly accelerated move towards embracing entrepreneurship education in the higher education sector. The exception to this is the United States, which has been at the forefront of entrepreneurship education for several decades.

Since the early 2000s, the delivery of entrepreneurship has proliferated both in UK universities and globally. In many countries, for example Nigeria, this is driven through necessity with endemic graduate unemployment levels driving the need for change. I have been fortunate enough to work in several UK universities, plus deliver entrepreneurship programs and training throughout Europe and Africa. I have witnessed, and I hope supported, the evolution of entrepreneurship programs and pedagogy. Initially, there was a belief that one could simply teach entrepreneurship to hundreds of students in traditional ways (e.g., through traditional lectures and seminars). This rapidly proved a fallacy. Whilst students typically wanted to study for entrepreneurship modules only a minority wanted to pursue a dedicated entrepreneurship program and fewer still undertake a startup. In recent years, there has been a significant growth of experiential non-traditional programs and modules including the team enterprise degree with no formal curriculum delivery, two-year venture creation degree programs, and use of information technology software for modelling business simulation. In the UK, sector-wide change for an entrepreneurship curriculum has been recognized by the development of quality assurance Enterprise and Entrepreneurship[1] guidelines. This has included the definition of key variables such as entrepreneurship and enterprise and the clear discernment between what constitutes these behaviors. Thus, UK educators can now effectively design entrepreneurship programs with the appropriate design and content. This has been mirrored in Europe with the development of the Entrecomp[2] framework which has been designed to act as a reference for any initiative aiming to foster entrepreneurial capacity of European citizens and used for the development of curricula and learning activities enabling entrepreneurship as a competence. I reflect on the requirement for entrepreneurship programs having to justify their value and existence more so than any other academic discipline in terms of enabling viable business startups. I call on colleagues to evaluate the impact of their provision with rigorous cross-institutional longitudinal research. In the age of social media, we can track our graduates' progress long after graduation. Such evidence is required to provide validation for our discipline.

Alongside the development of an entrepreneurship curriculum has seen the widespread creation of university entrepreneurship ecosystems. This is a recognition that an entrepreneurship education curriculum alone is not sufficient. Typically, these include creating a culture to enable entrepreneurship behavior within the university including incubation facilities for business startups, financing for business startups, capture of intellectual property, creation of entrepreneurship centers to enable research and income generation projects and cross-university curricula. There are several stories of successful examples of entrepreneurship ecosystems in the UK such as Coventry, Leeds, Strathclyde, Lancaster, and Swansea universities. However, there are also several instances of closure of entrepreneurship centers and educational programs whereby institutions have lost patience in the immediate returns achieved. As noted previously, dedicated venture creation programs require high levels of student support to enable successful graduate startups. Venture creation programs should seek to select elite graduate students suited to entrepreneurship career choices. Such programs require relatively small cohort sizes and specialist student support. A further issue is the location of entrepreneurship education within the university and that business graduates are not necessarily the ideal candidates for an innovative startup. This has resulted in entrepreneurship being offered across the university to capture potential candidates with different skills and knowledge. As both a researcher and teacher, I reflect on the need to further research this issue. Entrepreneurship education needs to learn and embrace best practice from a range of disciplines, for example, use of design thinking in the construction of its pedagogy.

A further trend has seen the emergence of specialist ecosystems focusing on specific forms of innovations such as medical technologies or technology-focused startups. I believe the specialism and identity of entrepreneurship education is important. The headlong rush by many countries to embrace entrepreneurship offers the threat of creating homogenous ecosystems and universities that are not differentiated across a country. I would describe this as a "vanilla"-flavored approach. The danger of vanilla entrepreneurship education is the creation of low-value graduate startups with minimal chance of long-term economic viability. My preference would be for each university to create an ecosystem that supports particular entrepreneurship activity, for example, technology entrepreneurship, tourism entrepreneurship, etc. In this way, individual universities could create specific and specialized ecosystems that truly enable effective startups that support the requirements and needs of the local community that the university supports. I also reflect on the need for social enterprise to be used to support disadvantaged communities. Universities must lead such initiatives and embrace environmentally sustainable business startups that enable sustainable and localized supply chains. There is a clear need to work with local and national governments to enable long-term change and create more entrepreneurship identity for communities which the university supports.

The growth of the research community supporting entrepreneurship has been dynamic with the emergence of entrepreneurship-learned societies and communities globally such as Babson, International Council for Small Business, USASBE, European Council for Small Business and Entrepreneurship, and Institute for Small Business and Entrepreneurship. As a journal editor, I have tried to facilitate this growth by increasing the number of published issues and manuscripts annually within the *International Journal of Entrepreneurial Behavior and Research*, whilst seeking to maintain quality. I reflect on the need for the entrepreneurship discipline to continue to grow and prosper. In terms of the number of academic journals, there is a necessity for further journals to emerge and grow. The entrepreneurship discipline remains a poor relation in terms of number of available journals in comparison to virtually all other business disciplines.

In conclusion, I refer back to the current situation with the Covid-19 pandemic. The entrepreneurship discipline must in the short term rapidly reposition itself to absorb the changes that this will bring on the student experience. The use of virtual learning environments embellished with business stimulation software and synchronous media such as Zoom must be rapidly embraced to reflect the new reality. In the mid-term, I urge universities to work with local and national policy makers to develop entrepreneurship activity that supports the locality and provides an entrepreneurship identity to the region in which the university operates. I urge all entrepreneurship educators to reflect on the teaching and academic practice and seek to report the value that they create in their communities. In the long term, I urge the entrepreneurship discipline to continue to grow but in a responsible manner to reflect the requirement for environmental sustainability and social enterprise that supports all communities.

JEROME KATZ

Entrepreneurship's appeal is universal because it can offer people a path to better ways to do things or live—what Saras Sarasvathy (2012) calls world-making. In the midst of the worst situations people face, entrepreneurship is often one of the first seeds of hope to be planted. I grew up in a community of Second World War concentration camp survivors from Europe, and for almost all of them the American Dream included a place free of hatred and a business of their own.

Teaching at Wharton in 1985, my office was 2 miles from a poor neighborhood where 60-plus homes burned down after a police bombing (Demby, 2015; Norward, 2019). Within a week a few professors from local colleges were running programs in the devastated community. I was part of a program helping residents find entrepreneurship opportunities. In 1993, in the months before the signing of the Oslo Accords ending the First Intifada, I was in a trailer in the no-man's land between Jerusalem and Bethlehem teaching how to organize bi-national sales (Katz, Hazboun, & Toren, 1995). In 2014, as the first wave of the Ferguson Protests were happening at night, I joined others a few hundred feet down the street to teach entrepreneurship in the afternoons at a local church.

As other contributors to this series in *Annals* have pointed out, teaching our classes in colleges and universities is a remarkable privilege, one of tremendous importance. But given that universality, which I believe is real, there is an even larger calling for us, and that is to teach to the larger world outside of our classrooms. That is such a broad mandate, I can readily imagine those of you reading this might find the prospect daunting, but it's actually easier than you think and closer than you might imagine. Let me share my thoughts on how, what, and where to do that.

How: Advice for Potential First-Time Speakers

If you find yourself asked to speak to a group of entrepreneurs, potential entrepreneurs, or just people seeking some insight, always follow Adams' (1979) universally acclaimed advice, "Don't panic." The skills you've used in the classroom still work. Perhaps unexpectedly, your freedom in pursuing a public lecture, seminar, workshop, or class is even greater than what you face (or imagine you face) in the classroom. Even having experience with TED talks, people can still get entranced and excited by a remarkably broad range of topics and styles. So, consider the following basics.

Know your audience
Find out all you can about the potential audience members. Ask about major subgroups. Ask about what they've responded well to in the past. Run your ideas by the host. My worst speech ever was a talk I gave in Stockholm where I focused on ethical techniques for obtaining financial information on private businesses. The applause was ever so polite, but I knew I blew it. I asked my host, and he explained that in Sweden at that time, tax returns were public records, so any entrepreneur can see their competitors' actual tax returns. Who knew? The Swedes did, but sitting in St. Louis, I didn't. Think of it as the speaker's version of the customer discovery process.

Keep it simple
Aim for no more than three ideas in a talk. My colleague Patricia Bagsby sets a tough bar for public talks—any idea has to be explained in 100 words or less. Think in terms of take-aways like a tweetable moment or image, a catchy meme, phrase, or acronym as a great goal for any idea you want to have live past the talk. Consider similes—Doordash is like Uber for food. Ideas should be simple enough that notes don't need to be taken, though if you're using visual models or slides, make them big enough to read and leave them up long enough for the most interested listeners to be able to snap usable pictures of the slides with their smartphones.

Know your voice and work it
Some speakers are at their best as the voice of authority. Others are storytellers. Some are preachers, while others are comedians. All of these, and a lot more styles, are completely legit. Knowing which style is the voice you are most comfortable with and able to easily bring the most energy to is what is

important to setting the tone and model of your talk. You are at your best when you're using your preferred voice.

What: Enduring Topics for Public Talks

There are a multitude of topics of interest to entrepreneurs in the field and those who support them. Many of them are variants of what we teach in our classes, while other topics can be truly different. Over the years some of the most enduring or recurring topics include:

* *How-to talks*: Teaching a basic skill in a few minutes is always appreciated. This can be something as simple as using Facebook's Audience Insights to get a sense of the size of markets with particular interests in a focused or national geography.
* *First-step talks*: When new to something, people look for an idea of the first steps on the path. This article is a first-step example telling the how, what, and where of public speaking in entrepreneurship.
* *What's new talks*: One of the things that makes our lives interesting is the constant array of new ideas we're exposed to. Consider sharing some of those like the valuations.com website which provides multiple ways to assess a company's valuation from general sales, growth rate, and industry information.
* *Best practices*: Academics are often the ones determining what are best practices, so your opinion is probably welcome, especially if you explain the hows and whys of the practice so others can understand and begin to apply it.
* *Heroes*: Academics have the power of anointment. Not just of best practices, but of best performers. When we say someone did exceptionally well in innovation, making money, giving back, or any of a hundred valuable contributions, people listen. Your former "C" student who had three failed startups, but persevered, made number four into a rousing success and has hired a hundred dropouts, and encouraged them to finish high school, hopefully knows she's done good, but a local professor who tells her story conveys a *gravitas* that garners the entrepreneur instant respect. You have the power to make heroes. Use it.
* *What's next*: Generating and observing new knowledge means you're positioned to know what's coming. Thoughtful entrepreneurs appreciate having a glimpse of the future and an idea of what to prepare for.
* *Hidden Gems*: While a graduate student, I astounded my father (an entrepreneur) when I used the RMA volume in the library to find the typical expense percentages for stores like his. He was shocked to know that sort of information was "out there" and available at most libraries. You proba-

bly have dozens of go-to sources to accomplish all sorts of business-related research. Share them.

• *Ecosystems*: In the old days we talked about local and government resources, but today those and the infrastructure of startup communities are called the ecosystem. Even with a grander and more encompassing name, few are as exposed to as many parts of the ecosystem as academics. Breaking down silos letting entrepreneurs know about the opportunities for help or giving back reflects the best part of your path of academic discovery.

• *Be a responder*: Consider doing a very short talk, like the story of a local hero or resource, and open the floor for Q&A where you can connect attendees to the people and organizations you know about. Where you don't know the answer, write down their question and their contact info (or that of the organizer), and when you get home, find them an answer. Ask your host to share the answer with the other attendees.

• *Telling the story of entrepreneurship*: Knowing the ecosystem, the heroes, the new and coming ideas, the relevant resources in academia and the Internet, and the troves of data available, you are probably uniquely positioned to be able to talk about the state and future of entrepreneurship in your locality and in the larger society and economy. Your opinion as to the strengths, weaknesses, opportunities, and threats of and to entrepreneurship is based on your continuing immersion in all the above, and your commitment to prepare the next generation of entrepreneurs. What you see and how you feel about it is important, and a lot of people around you want to hear that story about entrepreneurship today and into the future.

Where: Settings Entrepreneurship Educators Can Contribute

My first non-academic talk was in 1980 to a United States Department of Agriculture Extension Service conference in Gainesville, Florida, over 1,000 miles from my doctoral student office at the University of Michigan. Since then I've found myself asked to speak in all sorts of situations. Obvious examples include entrepreneur-focused organizations like the NFIB, Entrepreneurs' Organization, YPO, or Vistage, entrepreneur organizations focused on demographic niches (e.g., National Association of Women Business Owners, the Black MBA Association, newly arrived Syrian refugees, or local veterans organizations), or functional niches (e.g., GlobalHack, Inventors' Association, FFA, makerspaces, fashion designers, musicians, shared use kitchens), local chambers of commerce, the vast range of trade and professional associations (check http://directoryofassociations.com/ for 35,000 to start with).

How do you find places to talk? Make the offer to the organizations you belong to, to your students, family, and friends, to the entrepreneurs you involve in your classes. Let your department chair, dean, and alumni and development offices know you're willing to go out into the community. Offer occasionally on your social media accounts and ask your school to retweet it. Contribute a column or letter to the local press on a topic you think would be of interest.

Do not assume entrepreneurship is only for entrepreneurs. Over the past 20 years entrepreneurship has become a staple of leadership training. In fact, entrepreneurship is more universal that it has ever been. Managers in for-profit and non-profit situations want to know how to become sensitized to new opportunities, business models, and riding the waves of disruption. Topics like dealing with failure and sustaining passion over the long term which came out of entrepreneurship are now seen as relevant to nearly all organizations. With so many great new insights being developed by researchers and practitioners of entrepreneurship, there is likely to be years of opportunity to share entrepreneurship's message with the larger world.

Think beyond different groups, think different geographies. These days, the world beckons. Speaking to entrepreneurship classes and programs around the world is happening widely on a daily basis. I have keynoted in Brazil, China, and Croatia among other places and have loved every minute of those trips, maybe excepting that one Swedish talk, but even that trip taught me a valuable lesson.

Even knowing that, it seems to me more and more that the greatest need for our ideas is closer to home, just beyond our immediate neighborhood's or campus' borders. Rural America is facing the consequences of a half-century of increasing neglect and a steady drain of people (Acs & Malecki, 2004; Ajilore & Willingham, 2019). As economic inequality grows, poorer rural and urban communities everywhere are struggling harder than ever to find paths to economic, and even food, security, and I sincerely believe that the most enduring answers are those of self-sufficiency that entrepreneurship can provide. Given how hard structural change is, it often seems to me that the best path available to us as individuals in the face of daunting challenges is often that individual path, putting yourself, your head, heart, hands, and health (as 4-H taught me) to the task of making things better. And as entrepreneurship educators you are uniquely capable of doing that.

JEFFREY POLLACK

"Half the World Is under Stay-Home Order; White House Debates Face Masks"

I started writing this at the beginning of April 2020. The day I started, in particular, was April 3 and the headline in the *New York Times* was: "Half the

World Is under Stay-Home Order; White House Debates Face Masks." This is what is on my mind today. I am thinking about the millions of people who filed for unemployment, many of whom are entrepreneurs, and who have seen their revenues disappear in a matter of days (Huddleston, 2020). Also, I am about to email students an article about how the Covid-19 pandemic will fuel the next wave of innovation (Mudassir, 2020).

It is with the pandemic as the milieu that I reflect on the potential value I provide to students. I am very honored to be considered a "Master Educator" in entrepreneurship and I am grateful to Eric Liguori and Charles Matthews for asking me to contribute to this volume of *Annals of Entrepreneurship Education and Pedagogy*. I will say that it is difficult, given the calamity of the Covid-19 pandemic, to consider myself a master at anything since everything we once did, personally and professionally (as recently as two weeks ago), is potentially outdated.

Here are some of my current thoughts, shaped by the question of whether, and how, I can create value with the students with whom I work given the backdrop of the Covid-19 pandemic.

Be an entrepreneur—the students are the customers

I email students ten days before any class starts. I send the following email to small undergraduate classes of 25 students as well as classes that have more than 400 students enrolled, to MBA classes with 45 students enrolled, to online classes I teach (some have more than 200 students), and to PhD students:

> Hello and welcome to our class [insert class title] for the [insert term and year] semester! I am thrilled to work with you all and have tons I want to share. However, you are paying money to be in this class…so, I am an entrepreneur and you are my customers. Overall, I want to know what interests you most about this class. What can I do to enable you to get the most out of this experience? Call/email me anytime. Best, Jeff

I list my cell phone number on the syllabus. I change the syllabus based on what students tell me they want to learn; and, I adapt to changes that occur during the semester—so, naturally, Covid-19 has been on my mind. Put simply, the "product" (i.e., my entrepreneurship class) that I started teaching this semester in January 2020 is going to end up being different than planned. Overall, the structure is the same—it was an online class to begin with, and so minimal change happened there. But, as the pandemic took hold, I pondered what students might need and made additional changes.

Everyone teaching anything from K-12 to college has had to change their classes in response to the Covid-19 pandemic. But, prior to the pandemic, I sought to adapt my classes based on constantly evolving student needs. That, in my mind, is one of the most important things I do—I think of myself as an academic entrepreneur who pivots the product based on customer interests. Taking this approach, especially in the semester when the Covid-19 pandemic struck, has enabled me to better connect with the students—they know (and have known) from the beginning of the semester (i.e., before the virus shut down the world) that I will change the class as needed.

Enable the students to keep their eye on the ball
In the first class of the semester (or in the first activity of an online class), I ask the students to watch a video.[3] Many of you may be familiar with this—it is a selective attention test in which students are asked to watch six people passing a basketball amongst themselves. The students try to count the number of passes that the people in white shirts make (half of the people passing have black shirts, half have white shirts). There is a correct answer to the number of passes, but that is not the point. The point is that the students focus so carefully on counting the passes that the people in white shirts make that they miss what's really going on—and, what's really going on is that, in the middle of the video, a person dressed up as a gorilla walks into the middle of the circle of people passing the ball, beats its chest, and then strolls off the other side of the screen. Most students who see the video for the first time do not see the gorilla. Then, when I replay the video, it is so amusing to see the students' reactions! This exercise has been replicated tons of times across classrooms all over the world, and it is described in a book by Chabris and Simons (2010) as well as in multiple journal publications (e.g., Drew, Võ, & Wolfe, 2013).

Put simply, I bring attention to the notion that students (and all of us) sometimes focus so intently on one task that we miss opportunities. I make the assertion that, even though we have to do tasks that are asked of us—e.g., by professors, employers, friends, parents—we should not lose sight of the bigger picture. For them, and for me, "keeping their eye on the ball" means focusing on the activities in the class I am teaching while also being cognizant of where they want to be in the future. I invite (and encourage and perhaps demand) them to use the class to help them reach their goals. Can they use the ideation portfolio we do in the class in the job application process as a point of differentiation? Can they use the customer discovery activities we do to help them in their current role at work (most of the students have outside employment)? Can they use the interview activity to get an introduction to someone with whom they want to work in the future? My most sincere hope is that they use the activities in the class to get closer to where they want to be in the future—simply put, I want them to do the activities in the class (i.e., counting the number of passes that the people in white make) while also making sure the class is useful to them (i.e., not missing the gorilla). I aim to create a class in which students envision their future (we do a Dreamlining activity that Tim Ferriss designed[4]) and they work towards making it a reality.

Be vulnerable—also titled "Professor finds out what a juul is"

It is tempting as a professor to act like you know everything. I know that being a professor puts me in a role that is very visible and the things that I say can influence how the students feel, think, and act. But, I have never felt comfortable with the "sage on the stage" approach (King, 1993). So, I share a lot about myself in my classes. I make it clear that I do not know everything. And, overall, I make myself vulnerable. Recently, in a class of 422 students, I was leading a class discussion on new technologies that disrupt industries and products. I asked for some examples and we talked about a few. One student yelled "juuls and vapes." I asked for clarification and for an example—an "actual" example. So, another student in the back of the class (stadium seating for a large auditorium class) raised one (a juul) up in the air—so, I walked on up the aisle…and, he demonstrated it for me. The moment—much to my surprise was captured on Instagram (I found this out a week later) and it had gotten 230,000 views![5]

My first thought was: "Wow, I am glad I did not do something any more embarrassing." My second thought was to ask the students why the video seemed so compelling. Overwhelmingly, they said that it was fun to see a professor learn something and be willing to admit that it was new. We laughed and laughed some more and I shared with them that I learn as much from them as they learn from me. My approach here enables students to share things with me that they may not ordinarily share—and, it enhances my ability to create value for them in the class setting.

"Think and do"

"Think and do" is the motto at North Carolina State University. This resonates with me as a person as well as an educator—and, it serves nicely as a framework for what I do in the entrepreneurship classroom. Yes, we *think* about entrepreneurship, but we also *do* entrepreneurship. Everyone in all the classes I teach envisions and evaluates an opportunity to create value. My approach is rooted in the clinical model of entrepreneurship teaching and research that was described in an earlier volume of *Annals of Entrepreneurship Education and Pedagogy* (Pollack et al., 2018). Put succinctly, I aim to *engage* students with experiential activities. This serves to *embed* students in the startup community. This, in turn, helps students *execute*—achieve their goals more effectively and efficiently. For me, entrepreneurship classes are about where the students are now and where they want to go—it's not about starting ventures, it's about helping them approach the future more effectively and efficiently by identifying opportunities for value creation and being able to communicate those ideas to the right people.

Concluding Thoughts

Right now, there is tragedy all around us, and all focus seems to be on that (remember the people in white shirts passing the ball). Yet, if we also notice other things (remember the gorilla), we can also see opportunity (and hope). So, I did send the students (via email) an article about how the Covid-19 pandemic will fuel the next wave of innovation (Mudassir, 2020). Everything is different now. And, I hope the students see that—both the tragedy, and the opportunity and hope.

Overall, my most sincere wish is that students—my customers—find value in the classes I teach. My approach to teaching entrepreneurship, in short, is as a vulnerable academic entrepreneur who wants the students to use the class to reach their full potential. As I reflect on the value I create with the students, in the midst of the Covid-19 pandemic, I am grateful that I am able to pivot, as needed, and make the product (the class) valuable in such a difficult time.

REBECCA WHITE

As I considered the content for this brief section, I was reminded of a coffee mug I purchased a few years ago on a visit to the National Gallery of Art. I seldom purchase items in museum stores, and never buy coffee mugs, but this one spoke to me. It had a simple quote—"I am still learning," attributed to Michelangelo. What I love about this short sentence is that it sums up most of what I believe about education in general and entrepreneurship education specifically. That is, an education is transformative in that it provides the foundation for lifelong learning. And, since I also believe that learning is at the core of the entrepreneurship journey, the goal of an entrepreneurship education is first and foremost to help students develop the skills associated with being effective and efficient learners.

What does the goal of preparing students to be lifelong learners mean? For me, like the quote, I am still learning and probably the most important lesson I have gotten is that in order to remain relevant and to provide my students with the tools they need to succeed, I must remain open and humble. Since change is constant and inevitable, what I have learned will likely be at least somewhat modified before this goes to print. However, I have been asked to share some lessons I have gleaned through the years, and so I will.

Entrepreneurship Competencies

I have long believed that opportunities to study entrepreneurship should not be limited to business majors. In fact, my focus from the late 1990s has been to bring entrepreneurship to students across campus. I quickly found that while this provided great opportunities for innovative outcomes, it led to challenges in the classroom. With this model, the fact that students do not enter the classroom at a common level of knowledge and that they will not leave with the same degree of mastery is often magnified. Moreover, if students are learning through both classroom and co-curricular experiences, how do we assess learning? As I considered the dilemma of how to assess learning, I then began to consider what it means to be a graduate of entrepreneurship. What should our students know, demonstrate, and be able to do with a degree in entrepreneurship? I found that when I looked a bit further, our discipline had not satisfactorily answered that question and so I looked around to see what I could learn from other fields and found the concept of identifying and measuring competencies. The length of this section does not afford the opportunity to elaborate on the application nor the full content of a comprehensive entrepreneurship competency model. However, for the purpose of this piece it is important to at least note that the application of a competency model to courses and programs allows for a design that can measure whether students are gaining knowledge, experiencing application, and, in some cases, developing mastery of subject matter.

Opportunity Exploitation

Entrepreneurship is also a verb. Successful entrepreneurs take the steps required to exploit an opportunity. If our goal is to prepare nascent entrepreneurs, then entrepreneurship courses and programs must include the opportunity for students to develop business acumen. These topics should include, at a minimum, the study of business models, resource acquisition, finance, leadership, business law, marketing, strategy, operations, and sales. However, I believe the study of these business topics is necessary, but not sufficient.

Opportunity Recognition and Creative Problem Solving

When I first began teaching entrepreneurship, most classes were focused on how to execute on a business concept. While this is important, I found that students who had a meaningful opportunity to which they could apply their studies were more engaged and, therefore, likely to learn more. Yet, I would often have students who had not yet gathered enough life experience to be able to recognize an opportunity. They didn't know enough about any industry or the world around them to generate feasible business concepts. Thus, I realized that entrepreneurship programs cannot start at the point of customer discovery or validation, they must begin at the creative problem-solving level. When students realize that opportunity exists in virtually any problem, and they develop skills associated with creative problem solving, they can begin to generate viable business opportunities. This process starts with requiring students to do the research necessary to understand themselves and the context in which they exist. In addition to business acumen, entrepreneurship education must include the skills associated with gathering raw material (conducting research) and creative problem solving.

Intellectual Honesty

Over the past 25+ years I have had the chance to learn from many of the pioneers in our field. One such trailblazer was Jeffry Timmons. Recently I wrote a blog posting where I talked about his regard for intellectual honesty as a key characteristic necessary for success as an entrepreneur. Intellectual honesty can simply be defined as a focus on seeking the truth even when it doesn't agree with your own personal beliefs. It involves four basic practices: not lying to oneself, not pretending to know the truth when one doesn't, not omitting relevant facts purposely, and giving credit to sources of information where possible. For Professor Timmons, intellectual honesty was one of the key components in a coachable entrepreneur. And a coachable entrepreneur, he argued, is more likely to succeed and, therefore, present an opportunity for an investor. His guidelines suggested that an entrepreneur who knows what they don't know is better prepared for the entrepreneurial journey than one who doesn't know what they don't know. I agree. Thus, I have learned over the years that the four key tenets of intellectual honesty should be a foundation for entrepreneurship education programs and courses.

Coachability

Intellectually honest entrepreneurs collaborate and seek input. They ask questions and listen not only for confirmation but more importantly for contradiction. An intellectually honest entrepreneur is one who is coachable. Coachability requires the ability to listen and to remain open to input while maintaining the ability to balance that input against what is already known. Coachability doesn't mean taking every suggestion offered, nor does it mean ignoring everyone else to pursue a passion. In their classes and programs, many entrepreneurship educators include options to work with coaches and mentors and the requirement of talking to prospective customers. However, I have learned that without discussion and lessons on being coachable many of our students are not able to take full advantage of these opportunities.

Resilience

One challenge for us as entrepreneurship educators is that intellectual honesty and coachability require a level of resilience many of our students have not yet attained. A few years ago, I had an experience that magnified this fact for me. One of my graduate students angrily walked out of class and dropped out of the entire graduate program during a lively class discussion on the role of failure in entrepreneurship. While I wasn't able to confirm that it was that experience that led to his withdrawal, based on his remarks during the conversation, I was fairly certain it had played a pivotal role in his decision. This experience left me feeling that I had somehow *failed* in my attempts to better prepare my students for the rough and tumble world of entrepreneurship where failure is so often a part of the pathway to success. This experience left a strong impression on me and ultimately influenced me to look more closely at resilience as a competency of successful entrepreneurship.

Those of us who are familiar with entrepreneurship—either because we have lived it or studied it—know that entrepreneurship is a verb. Entrepreneurs are successful because they take action. We also know that every new venture is an experiment. We are making and testing assumptions along the way to some desired outcome. And the path to something we can define as a successful outcome is quite frequently littered with failure. At the same time, we know that for entrepreneurs, failure is not an option. Entrepreneurs persevere. So, how do we reconcile that paradox and how do we teach this to our students?

The answer, I have learned, lies in the combination of two concepts: equifinality and resilience. The first, equifinality, can simply be thought of as the belief that there are many paths to the same end. A fatal flaw among many founders is an assumption that the solution they have created to address a problem in the marketplace is the most effective, efficient, or is desired by the marketplace. The second, resilience, the capacity to recover quickly from difficulties, is required of a founder when they learn through trial and error that what they thought was true is not. This is the essence of the entrepreneurship theory "fail early and fail fast." The less invested the easier to pivot or adapt. Thus, failure may come along the way, but the final outcome can still be success. Reframing failure reminds us that we have options and we can change the way we think about this concept and that each failure is a learning process. While maybe not welcome at the time, it can lead to ever greater success than imagined. I have learned that it is critical to spend time helping students reframe the role of failure in success.

Entrepreneurship Is a Practice

After many years of teaching entrepreneurship, I have come to believe that entrepreneurship is a practice. I often tell my students that entrepreneurship is like yoga. One should not expect to perfect it, but to be successful one must show up every day to practice and learn. I have also learned that traditional teaching styles of lecturing and tests are not as effective as experiential learning techniques. To better understand experiential learning, I turned to research in education and found that models of situated cognition (Brown, Collins, & Duguid, 1989) were a good fit for our discipline. Much like yoga this model suggests that experiential education should include opportunities for multiple practice as well as collaboration, coaching and mentoring, reflection, and apprenticeship. For this reason, I have dedicated a significant portion of my academic career to building both in-class and co-curricular experiences that afford students with opportunities to collaborate with peers, to be coached and mentored, to reflect, and for apprenticeships, to shadow and intern with entrepreneurs. I have come to believe that entrepreneurship education programs should offer learners the chance to "practice" what they are learning. To give them the chance to fail and learn from that failure. I have learned that as educators, our role is to help curate this process of experiential learning.

As I conclude, it is impossible to ignore the massive changes occurring now in our discipline and in higher education. I began teaching entrepreneurship during the dotcom bubble and continued through the subsequent busting of the bubble, 9-11, the great recession, the great economic recovery, and now the Covid-19 pandemic. In between there have been massive changes worldwide that have provided great opportunities for both learning and for business start-ups. Likewise, the changes we are now experiencing are providing our students with experiential education opportunities like never before as they apply what they are learning during this seismic shift.

For those of us who are educators, there will be lasting change. While our industry has been undergoing disruption for some time, this most recent experience has accelerated those changes significantly. Initial evidence is demonstrating that we all value the tradition of the college community but that there is also great opportunity in the changes we have been required to make. As we move forward, we may try to reduce anxiety by returning to the familiar. But I believe education as we knew it cannot be recovered. It must be reinvented. Everything is on the table now. There has never been a more exciting time to be an entrepreneurship educator and to create positive, productive, and lasting change.

What have I learned after more than several decades of teaching entrepreneurship? The primary responsibility of higher education is to prepare students for future success. The key lessons of an entrepreneurship education—creative problem solving, seeing problems through an opportunity lens, intellectual honesty, resilience, and coachability—provide a powerful foundation for that success. In a world defined by Industry 4.0, a gig economy, excessive information and complexity, uncertainty, rapid change, environmental challenges, the forces of globalization, and yes, pandemics, that means we help them develop a passion for lifelong learning.

NOTES

1. www.qaa.ac.uk/scotland/news-events/enterprise-and-entrepreneurship-new -advice-for-universities
2. https://ec.europa.eu/jrc/en/publication/eur-scientific-and-technical-research -reports/entrecomp-entrepreneurship-competence-framework
3. http://theinvisiblegorilla.com/gorilla_experiment.html
4. https://tim.blog/lifestyle-costing/
5. https://www.instagram.com/p/BnZGsoMn0HD/?utm%20source=igsharesheet& igshid=1gd6z8z0o6bpo

REFERENCES

Acs, Z. J., & Malecki, E. J. (2004). Entrepreneurship in rural America: The big picture. In Center for the Study of Rural America (Ed.), *Main Streets of Tomorrow: Growing and Financing Rural Entrepreneurs* (pp. 21–9). New York: Books for Business. https://citeseerx.ist.psu.edu/viewdoc/download?doi=10.1.1.194.4285&rep=rep1& type=pdf

Adams, D. (1979). *The Hitchhiker's Guide to the Galaxy*. London: Pan.

Ajilore, O., & Willingham, Z. (2019). Redefining rural America. Center for American Progress. www.americanprogress.org/issues/economy/reports/2019/07/17/471877/ redefining-rural-america/

Baron, R. A. (2006). Opportunity recognition as pattern recognition: How entrepreneurs "connect the dots" to identify new business opportunities. *Academy of Management Perspectives, 20*, 104–19.

Brown, J. S., Collins, A., & Duguid, P. (1989). Situated cognition and the culture of learning. *Educational Researcher, 18*(1), 32–42.

Cardon, M. S., Wincent, J., Singh, J., & Drnovsek, M. (2009). The nature and experience of entrepreneurial passion. *Academy of Management Review, 34*(3), 511–32.

Chabris, C. F., & Simons, D. J. (2010). *The Invisible Gorilla: And Other Ways Our Intuitions Deceive Us*. New York: Random House.

Cohen, D., Cardon, M., & Singh, J. (2019). A developmental framework for anticipatory entrepreneurial passion and its consequences for affect and effort for nascent entrepreneurs. Paper accepted to 2019 Annual Proceedings of Academy of Management.

Cohen, D., Hsu, D. K., & Shinnar, R. S. (2020). Identifying innovative opportunities in the entrepreneurship classroom: a new approach and empirical test. *Small Business Economics: an Entrepreneurial Journal*, 1–25.

Demby, G. (2015). Why have so many people never heard of the MOVE bombing? *NPR Code Switch Podcast*, May 18. www.npr.org/sections/codeswitch/2015/05/18/ 407665820/why-did-we-forget-the-move-bombing

Drew, T., Võ, M. L. H., & Wolfe, J. M. (2013). The invisible gorilla strikes again: Sustained inattentional blindness in expert observers. *Psychological Science, 24*(9), 1848–53.

Hägg, G., & Kurczewska, A. (2018). Who is the student entrepreneur? Understanding the emergent adult through the pedagogy and andragogy interplay. *Journal of Small Business Management.* https://doi.org/10.1111/jsbm.12496

Huddleston, T. (2020). How small business owners are coping with Covid-19 pandemic: "It was my civic duty to be a part of the solution." *CNBC.com*, March 23. www.cnbc.com/2020/03/23/how-small-businesses-across-us-are-coping-with-covid -19-pandemic.html

Katz, J. A., Hazboun, S., & Toren, B. (1995). Palestinian manufacturers: Age of firm, individual vs. family ownership and implications for policy. Presented at the 1995 Family Firm Institute National Convention, St. Louis, MO, October 13.

King, A. (1993). From sage on the stage to guide on the side. *College Teaching, 41*(1), 30–5.

Liguori, E., & Winkler, C. (2020). From offline to online: Challenges and opportunities for entrepreneurship education following the COVID-19 pandemic. *Entrepreneurship Education and Pedagogy.* https://doi.org/10.1177/2515127420916738

Markowska, M., Härtel, C. E. J., Brundin, E., & Roan, A. (2015). A dynamic model of entrepreneurial identification and dis-identification: An emotions perspective. *Research on Emotion in Organizations.* https://doi.org/10.1108/S1746 -979120150000011009

Mudassir, H. (2020). How COVID-19 will fuel the next wave of innovation. *Entrepreneur.com*, March 16. www.entrepreneur.com/article/347669

Norward, L. (2019). The day Philadelphia bombed its own people. *Vox.* www.vox.com/ the-highlight/2019/8/8/20747198/philadelphia-bombing-1985-move

Pollack, J. M., Barr, S. H., Michaelis, T. L., Ward, M. K., Carr, J. C., Sheats, L., & Gonzalez, G. (2018). The North Carolina State University entrepreneurship clinic model of teaching and research. In E. Liguori & C. Matthews (Eds), *Annals of Entrepreneurship Education and Pedagogy*, 3rd ed. Cheltenham, UK and Northampton, MA, USA: Edward Elgar Publishing, pp. 247–55.

Sarasvathy, S. (2012). Worldmaking. In A. C. Corbett & J. A Katz (Eds), *Advances in the Study of Entrepreneurship Firm Emergence and Growth, Volume 14: Entrepreneurial Action* (pp. 1–24). Bingley: Emerald Group Publishing.

Seligman, M. E. (2006). *Learned Optimism: How to Change Your Mind and Your Life.* New York: Vintage.

2. Doctoral programs in entrepreneurship

James Fiet

INTRODUCTION

Universities rely on doctoral programs to train future entrepreneurship scholars and their students. It is through training future scholars that these programs are able to provide the most systematic opportunity to understand why entrepreneurs are successful and what they do when they are not successful. Of course, research into why entrepreneurs succeed is ongoing and likely to follow previous research, as well as the rules, suggestions, and protocols that aspiring scholars learn as doctoral students. To the extent that scholars share their knowledge of entrepreneurs with other scholars later in their careers, a large part of what they share will be influenced by their initial doctoral training. Thus, although doctoral programs vary in length from three to as many as five years and more, this short, intensive period of study has a much larger, ongoing influence on a scholar's career. Most notably, this begins with the research questions he or she asks and how they are answered. It extends to the contributions that can be derived from the resulting research, as well as how this knowledge is ultimately conveyed to students in the classroom.

Given their influence, it is surprising that more study has not been devoted to them. In 2002, when I launched the entrepreneurship doctoral program at the University of Louisville, there were between three and five programs in the world, depending on the classification criteria. Today, Jerry Katz (2020) at Saint Louis University reports that there are more than 85 programs world-wide, which is an astonishing rate of growth. All of the views expressed in this chapter are a reflection of a careful study of these programs.

Nor does there appear to be any noticeable cessation in the growth of these programs. Two obstacles that could curtail the growth include: (1) the saturation of the market for new entrepreneurship professors; or (2) a reduction in the number of qualified students seeking a doctorate because of alternate opportunities. However, with the growing development of a world-wide informational infrastructure, it is highly likely that it will facilitate even more rapid interest and growth in entrepreneurship, which will then have a multiplicative effect on the demand for additional, doctorally trained scholars. It may be that this high rate of growth is the reason that the field has not yet developed a global consensus about what should be taught. This chapter analyzes the issues involved with reaching such a consensus and what that consensus could be.

A PARTIAL CONSENSUS ABOUT PROGRAM CONTENT

Based on my study of the 85 doctoral programs, there seems be a partial consensus that research methods, including experimental design and statistics, are important (Katz, 2020). They are a common requirement of nearly every known doctoral program. Research methods include everything from the philosophy of science and analysis of variance to factor analysis, multiple regression, hierarchal linear modelling, covariance structure modelling, panel studies, and event history analysis. Also suggested by some programs are qualitative research methods, but these are definitely a minority recommendation. Another growing consensus is that it is impossible to take too many courses in research methods. Programs typically require three or four courses in this area with many students adding a couple of additional methods electives.

THE BIAS OF ACADEMIC AUTOBIOGRAPHY

Another area of partial consensus in the field is that the theoretical content of the seminars taught is often a reflection of academic autobiography (Fiet, 2020). That is, the theories that are emphasized in a program resemble the theoretical persuasion of the professors supervising the doctoral seminars and dissertations in each program. So far, the field has not conceded that this sort of theory selection could create theoretical biases.

Another related danger of academic autobiography to provide a theoretically balanced exposure is that a student may select a research topic prior to enrolling in a program, after which at every opportunity he or she is relating the theoretical topics covered back to that original research interest.

Exacerbating academic autobiography is a concomitant trend to save credit hours by providing minimal snippets of theory in one or two survey seminars rather than offering semester-long seminars addressing salient research questions. Of course, this approach grossly reduces the comparative importance of individual theories by jamming them into one or two survey courses, which greatly diminishes their individual distinctiveness.

There is less of a consensus about whether students should focus all of their theoretical training on the main questions in entrepreneurship, using the entrepreneurship literature organized in guided seminars, or whether programs should leave room in their curricula for students to select a minor area of study (Katz, 2020). When programs accommodate minor areas, students almost universally take three courses. An unresolved question is whether this option to pursue a minor area of study leads to the creation of more silos of knowledge rather than the cumulation of knowledge about the key questions that puzzle scholars.

THE ESSENTIAL ROLE OF THEORY

I argue that theory is the most essential part of a doctoral program. Because methodological training seldom distinguishes one program from another, what can make a difference is how students are trained theoretically. Why is theory essential?

Theory is essential because someone going before us has attempted to distill the rules according to which events occur. These rules consist of key constructs and their relations to each other, which have been reduced to a formula whose purpose could be to predict the future (Fiet, 2008), explain superior outcomes (Barney, 1991), how best to organize (DiMaggio & Powell, 1983, 1991), how to create value (Barney, 1997), or to explain how entrepreneurs view their world and its opportunities (Davidsson, 2015; Fiet, 2020), together with the motivations to exploit them (Baron, 1991). Theories are simplified views of the world that depend on assumptions to justify their simplification (Fiet, 2020). A theory can be used to make predictions provided it is valid and that researchers abide by their theory's assumptions.

Some assumptions of nearly all theory in the social sciences are the following: What is the unit of analysis? That is, what is the theory intended to explain? Second, because most theories are static, not dynamic, what is the point in time that is being studied? Third, in organizational settings, it is important to specify, what is the level of analysis? Examples of different levels would be functional, business, and corporate. Fourth, what are the relationships among the unit of analysis and other factors and how are these items of interest measured?

WHAT HAPPENS IN THE ABSENCE OF THEORY?

Early in my own masters-level training in entrepreneurship, courses consisted of my professors inviting successful entrepreneurs to tell us how they had become successful and ultimately fabulously wealthy. Their stories were frequently accompanied by anecdotal recommendations about how we could become successful like them. Little did they know that it was impossible to generalize from their own single cases (Kerlinger, 1966); nor did our professors point out the futility of this sort of generalization.

In retrospect, it was what I have since referred to as edutainment (Fiet, 2008). It was enjoyable, entertaining, and motivational. However, once I had graduated, I thought about what I had learned and realized that I would never encounter the same situations as these entrepreneurs.

I did not realize it but what had been missing from my graduate courses in 1973 and 1974 was theory. I had not received training in entrepreneurship theory. At the very least, I think I had the right to expect that I would be exposed to general knowledge about average entrepreneurs. Unfortunately, there was nothing in my education that prepared me to launch my own ventures or to understand why others had been successful. I felt as though I had been induced under false pretenses to pursue a masters degree when I would have been better off entering immediately into the school of hard knocks.

THE IMPROPER USE OF THEORY

My observation is that scholars are often not very different from undergraduate students even though they enjoy a vastly greater knowledge advantage. Undergraduate students tend to combine abstract ideas together if they seem as though they have face validity. For example, students could easily confuse agency theory with transaction cost economics (TCE) because they appear to have similar assumptions. Scholars understand that TCE addresses why markets fail to function efficiently (Williamson, 1979, 1985); whereas agency theory assumes that markets never fail as it tries to explain why a venture's capital structure should not affect its value when in fact it does affect its value (Jensen, 1994; Jensen & Meckling, 1976). It affects it because principals and agents could pursue separate and possibly divergent self-interests (Jensen, 1994). In other words, TCE allows for market failure, whereas agency theory does not. Combining their precepts indiscriminately will lead to a clash of their underlying assumptions, which would negate the combination.

Students combine conflicting assumptions unwittingly; whereas scholars who know the difference sometimes do the same due to critical carelessness. Because scholarly articles often omit discussing the underlying assumptions of their theoretical perspectives, they can be written as if they did not have boundary conditions. Failing to specify theoretical boundary conditions is similar to assuming that they do not exist. I was once told by a senior scholar that he did not specify boundary conditions because it would lessen the generality of his arguments and make his findings less consequential. Such planned ignorance inhibits the implications of our research as well as its theoretical insights.

ENTREPRENEURSHIP THEORY AND CRITICAL THINKING

Students can resolve theoretical conflicts by first identifying the underlying assumptions of the theories that they use. The second step would be to inquire regarding what evidence is there for their assumptions. Third, they could ask what alternative theories they could employ that would have superior empirical support while not violating a theory's assumptions. We can think of these three questions as providing a framework for critical thinking.

Boundary conditions are used to specify the domains within which the assumptions of a theory are valid. When we specify a theory's boundary conditions, we also specify its underlying assumptions. We never want to find ourselves conducting research with a theory that falls outside its boundary conditions. As scholars, we need to specify both assumptions and boundary conditions. Boundary conditions identify empirical domains wherein a researcher conducting research will know that it will not be invalidated theoretically. Specifying assumptions is also important because they help us to understand whether a particular theory may be used to address a research question. Otherwise, a theory may be inappropriate theoretically.

One of the greatest services that doctoral programs provide is to highlight the theoretical assumptions of each perspective as well as the need to emphasize that a scholar's assumptions must conform with his or her project's empirical constraints. If there is no conformity, then researchers must modify a theory's implications, based on differences in underlying assumptions.

Why do we as scholars bother with specifying assumptions? Essentially, it pertains to the phenomena that we are trying to understand, which is often surrounded by a great deal of uncertainty and temporal dependence. In effect we are taking snapshots of possible answers to our research questions, which we must contextualize to be meaningful, which we do by specifying our assumptions, which are really not our assumptions but those that come prepackaged with the theories themselves. Theoretical assumptions limit the scope of our generalizing in order to ground the conclusions that we can draw to the empirical conditions that we find as researchers.

THEORY IN DOCTORAL PROGRAM DESIGN

What is the relationship between theory and doctoral program design? Theory is the glue that connects our conclusions to their underlying assumptions. These assumptions are built into the theories that we select. Is it possible to think critically without using theory? That is, can we ensure that our assumptions are internally consistent and externally valid without using theory? The answer is that we can but it is much more difficult because we would need to analyze every research question as if it were one about which we had no previous knowledge. We would need to start over from the beginning with each new research project. Whereas, theory does most of this hard work for us by allowing us to build on what we have learned from previous research by identifying underlying assumptions and the impact that they have on the conclusions that we draw.

In fact, research anchored in a theoretical context equips students to conduct their own research as well as expand the boundaries of what we understand about a phenomenon. A theoretical foundation enables connections that might otherwise have been overlooked to be made.

It is my view that the most helpful way for a doctoral program to contribute to a student's scholarly development is to ensure that he or she is exposed to as many potentially informative theories as possible while ensuring that their underlying assumptions and boundary conditions are unambiguous. In addition, when we frame our research in this way, we will be obligated to explain what is the theory and what is the theoretical contribution of the research.

FITTING THEORY INTO AN ENTREPRENEURSHIP DOCTORAL PROGRAM

There are three ways that a doctoral-level entrepreneurship program could organize the theories in its seminars. First, organize them around a broad outline of the most general theories. Second, take a more phenomenological approach to theory selection by focusing on the processes or milestones in launching a venture. Third, focus on particular contexts in which entrepreneurship occurs. It is impossible in a short chapter to comprehensively review all the available theories. Nevertheless, I begin by illustrating how to apply six theories from the first approach, which are highlighted below in italics. The others are outside the scope of this chapter.

The following are general theories that could serve as an outline for a series of doctoral seminars and/or the components of them: *institutional theory, transaction cost economics, industrial organization theory, social embeddedness theory, informational economics, resource-based view,* capabilities theory, network theory, social capital theory, population ecology, game theory, resource dependence theory, agency theory, life cycle, behavioral theory, organizational learning theory, upper echelons theory, organizational change theory, and entrepreneurial orientation.

The following topics explore how entrepreneurship could be viewed as either a process or the achievement of milestones: theory about the individual and team, the opportunity or discovery, alertness and intentions, opportunity recognition, creation versus discovery, innovation and concept development, opportunity exploitation, organizing and founding, growth, failure, network influences, and venture finance. Researchers studying processes or milestones assume that they are essential to the creation of new wealth, and thus assume less responsibility for justifying their study.

The third way of organizing a doctoral seminar is to focus on the contexts in which entrepreneurship occurs. For example, focus on family business, female entrepreneurship, in addition to feminist critical theory, franchising, social entrepreneurship, youth entrepreneurship, hybrid entrepreneurship, entrepreneurship in a developing economy, entrepreneurship in a particular country, or international entrepreneurship across countries. Theoretically, these contextual approaches are more challenging because researchers must demonstrate that a particular context makes a theoretical difference, and such a contribution is typically not the intent of selecting a particular context. One could suppose that these types of selections are more autobiographical than theoretical. Regardless of the reasons, students who are exposed to fewer theoretical perspectives have fewer options in their tool kit to address the questions of interest.

GENERAL THEORIES OF ENTREPRENEURSHIP

The following sections review six general theories that are potentially applicable to questions about entrepreneurship. No effort in selecting these theories is made to advocate for them nor to ignore the contribution of other theories not included.

Institutional Theory

Institutional theory focuses on the more resilient or structural aspects of how individuals interact in a social structure (DiMaggio & Powell, 1983). It can be reduced to routines, norms, rules, and schemes, which can become so accepted that they can become guidelines for behavior (Scott, 2004; Meyer & Rowan, 1977). These guidelines consist of legitimacy, myths, and isomorphism that emphasize similar ways of organizing (Suchman, 1995). In fact, these similarities develop through imitation, which is a key mechanism in the institutional view.

It is noteworthy that the market is only one among many of the institutions that can develop. For example, families, government, and religion can be just as important as markets, or even more so in non-market economies (Polanyi, 1968).

The newest view of institutionalism rejects rational actor models in favor of cultural, cognitive, and social explanations about why similar structures develop. In fact, Scott (1995) justifies institutional isomorphism as a means of survival, meaning that conformity is a survival mechanism. Thus, actors tend to make decisions that lead to similar structures and behavior rather than respond to particular external contingencies.

The institutional view is a way of understanding group dynamics within an organization, which is the unit of analysis. What does it assume? It tends to be inappropriate for understanding individual behavior, which would be outside its boundary conditions. It assumes that the behavior of those in a cohort is known by the other actors. It also assumes that conformity is the most effective form of survival. Finally, it assumes that actors possess the resources to be able to conform.

Transaction Cost Economics

TCE attempts to explain why firms exist. It assumes that markets always exist but that firms are optional. Firms fail when they become less efficient than markets. Firms become less efficient than markets and fail when the cost of doing business within the hierarchical structure of a firm is more costly than in a market. Of course, the cost of doing business in a market is determined by the prices set by competitors. Coase (1937) and Williamson (1979, 1985) explain that part of the cost of doing business consists of transaction costs that do not normally appear on a balance sheet. These include uncertainty/complexity, bounded rationality, opportunism, small numbers bargaining, and added later, asset specificity.

Uncertainty and complexity increase the cost of writing exchange contracts; bounded rationality suggests that humans can only process information until a certain point due to neurological limitations, after which their brains become overloaded and they cease to make rational decisions. Opportunism involves the strategic misuse of information with the objective of deception, which is known technically as self-interest seeking with guile, or having a secret plan. Small numbers bargaining increases the risk of collusion that can increase costs (Williamson, 1985). Finally, asset specificity causes market failure when an actor wants to use an asset for a purpose other than that for which it was originally intended. Asset specificity implies that an asset can only be used for its original purpose (Whyte, 1994).

What are TCE's assumptions? The unit of analysis is the transaction on which a firm's organization (vertical integration) depends. It is not individuals. It is not some internal process or some aspect of the environment. It is a transaction, which individual actors can consummate or pass up. Upon their ultimate decision will depend whether markets fail and firms come into existence. In other words, firms can replace or substitute for failed markets. The human assumptions are bounded rationality and opportunism, whereas the environmental assumptions are uncertainty/complexity and small numbers bargaining. If any of these assumptions do not hold, then predictions about how actors will behave with these assumptions are null and void. For example, TCE could not be applied to God because He does not suffer from bounded rationality.

Industrial Organization Theory

Industrial Organization Theory (IOT) builds on the theory of the firm and attempts to answer two questions: the first question is why do firms exist, which is a corollary to why are entrepreneurs successful? Another way to consider this first question is what is the need that firms fulfill in the economy? The second question follows the first and relates to what the scale and scope of their activities are. Together these questions address the comparative advantage of industries, and are typically applied to very large-scale business activity. Thus, the unit of analysis is the industry. A major application of IOT was proposed by Michael Porter in 1980 and became known as the Five Forces Model of Competitive Threats. Porter's model was both powerful and influential and became the most important model in the study of strategic management, even though it has frequently been misapplied, which was particularly unfortunate due to its influence. I will first consider the elements of the model, and its predictions, followed by its assumptions and misapplications.

IOT economists noted that certain features of the environment were slow to change and could be relied on as guideposts for how competitive pressures would unfold. These slow-to-change features were viewed as being structural. They were tasked by policy makers with predicting when firms would develop monopoly power so that the policy makers could formulate preventive policies. To make their predictions, IOT economists, led by Porter, combined industry features that were structural, noted as five forces: buyers, rivals, substitutes, suppliers, and potential entrants.

Which begs the question, what is an industry? An industry is a group of firms that provide close substitutes for each other's products and services. Buyers determine industry structure by determining which close substitutes are to be included in an industry. It is important to note that a potential entrant is not a new entrant. A new entrant would be a rival.

In the model, buyers, suppliers, potential entrants, and substitutes contribute to the level of rivalry and thus the average level of profitability for firms in an industry. There are, however, a number of misapplied assumptions, which are widely violated as to make the model not very useful in practice. This lack of usefulness is more likely the fault of the users, not the theory.

The first misapplied assumption relates to competitive interdependence. Rivals must be competitively interdependent. Competitive interdependence occurs when the competitive actions of one firm affect the profitability of rivals. If there is no effect, then the industry is referred to as being fragmented. An industry with a high degree of competitive interdependence is referred to as being consolidated. If an industry is not consolidated, then it must be more narrowly defined, even if it must focus on a single fragment, which itself is consolidated. Second, the five forces model is a static model, meaning that it cannot be used to predict the level of rivalry at different points in time. It is possible to draw inferences outside of the model by conducting parallel analyses and then hypothesizing about what created the differences. Thus, it is necessary to select a specific point in time for a five forces analysis. Third, so that a five forces model will have analytical power, it is necessary to define an industry as narrowly as possible so that there is no doubt about the rival products being able to act as very close substitutes in the minds of buyers.

Finally, this is a model that relies on market power, not on efficiency. Its competitive prescription is for incumbent rivals to erect barriers to entry to keep out potential entrants so that they will be freer to collude and raise their prices in order to earn greater profits. Thus, the five forces model relies more on power than it does on efficiency, which seems to contradict neoclassical assumptions. Thus, although it is taught as an application of economics, it depends on power rather than on efficiency.

Social Embeddedness Theory

In a sense, social embeddedness theory is an extension of the institutional view, in that it assumes that wealth creation does not depend on economic exchange but on reciprocity and redistribution. Reciprocity is the assumption that exchangers will consummate a transaction when they have an expectation that the other party will do the same in the future. Redistribution can occur in the presence of institutional leadership, which can take possession of economic goods and then redistribute them to others who may not be parties to the original exchange. The more frequently exchanges occur, then the higher the likelihood that future exchanges will be embedded and subject to reciprocity and redistribution. The unit of analysis for embeddedness theory is the relationship of the parties to an exchange.

The economic sociologist, Mark Granovetter, used embeddedness theory to confront neoclassical economics (NE). NE is a theory that assumes efficiency governs economic exchange without regard for the actors themselves. Granovetter argued forcefully that NE was an "undersocialized" explanation and that, in fact, the actors themselves and their feelings toward each other intervene to satisfy the preferences of the exchangers rather than rely on a strict accounting of the money involved in an exchange (Granovetter, 1985). Granovetter seemed to take particular glee in debating Oliver Williamson (1985), the one who popularized TCE, which is a subset of NE, by arguing that accepting its undersocialized interpretation was to assume that human beings were acting like automatons. Granovetter's 1985 article on embeddedness became one of the most cited articles in the history of social science literature, yet there have been no known empirical studies to validate its embeddedness arguments, which few enthusiasts understand. Nevertheless, he argued,

> Actors do not behave or decide as atoms outside a social context, nor do they adhere slavishly to a script written for them by the particular intersection of social categories that they happen to occupy. Their attempts at purposive action are instead embedded in concrete, ongoing systems of social relations. (Granovetter 1985: 487)

Thus, social embeddedness theory is an excellent example of one that relies entirely on assumptions to establish its predictive power.

What are the assumptions of social embeddedness? First, humans reduce exchange uncertainty by allowing themselves to become embedded in systems of exchange with the same actors. The repetition of expected exchange behavior by the parties to an exchange will build trust, which will act as a self-monitoring mechanism against potential malfeasance. Markets are only one type of institution. Institutions provide the context in which exchanges occur. Most exchanges are quite socialized and subject to becoming embedded, which will serve as a monitoring device to prevent malfeasance in economic exchange.

Informational Economics

Informational economics examines how information affects a market as well as economic decisions. Information itself has several unique characteristics. It does not come in natural units that can be cumulated (Arrow, 1989). The fact that it does not have natural units complicates its being a unit of analysis. In order for it to be cumulated, it must first be dimensionalized into specific information, which I will say more about soon. It is relatively inexpensive to acquire but not always simple to trust. It spreads inexpensively but is very costly to control while it is spreading.

Hayek (1945) noted that even though information spreads quite inexpensively, it is nearly impossible for anyone to gain total control of it. Thus, the major informational challenge is to trade off the cost and benefit of acquiring specific information that may be available. Building on Hayek (1945), Fiet (2002, 2008, 2020) noted that there are two types of information: specific and general. Specific information concerns facts with regard to people, places, special circumstances, timing, and technology. It is the type of information that is quite costly to transfer, which could enable someone to invest in its acquisition in order to gain a quasi-monopoly over it. In contrast, general information is typically publicly available because it can be reduced to rules and procedures that can be inexpensively conveyed to others.

A key insight from informational economics is that differences in specificity determine how useful a signal can be in identifying an opportunity, which may be cumulated to evaluate the potential value of an opportunity. Because general information is widely available, it cannot generate above normal economic returns. Nearly everyone possesses the same general information. Thus, the discovery of a valuable opportunity depends on gaining specific information related to it that is not possessed by others.

There is some risk in the acquisition of specific information because it could become a sunk cost if it is not informative or pertinent. This risk of loss is the reason that we do not see entrepreneurs continuously invest in specific information because of the risk of losing their investment. Nevertheless, it is much less costly to invest in uninformative, specific information related to an opportunity than it would be to launch a failed venture without the information. This differential is one key that entrepreneurs can use to unlock opportunities, even when they are not well endowed with resources.

Informational economics depends on the following assumptions. First, discoveries require specific information, which can be both costly and risky to acquire. Second, entrepreneurs can create temporary monopolies by exploiting specific information. Third, market efficiency cannot disclose specific infor-mation. Fourth, differences in informational specificity form the basis for the discovery of value. Fifth, entrepreneurs can search systematically for specific information by consulting information channels, which can be grouped into an entrepreneur's consideration set. Information channels are frequent sources of low-cost signals (Fiet, 2002).

Resource-Based View

This is a perspective that views firms as bundles of resources, from which rents can be exploited. In other words, a rent stream is an attribute of a particular bundle of resources and or capabilities (Penrose, 1959). Different resources could have different rents associated with them or no rents at all. In practice, the resource-based view (RBV) is a framework used to determine which resources and capabilities to exploit in order to maintain and sustain a compet-itive advantage.

RBV was developed in response to an over-reliance on the analysis of exter-nal factors. It emphasizes the contingent nature of the choices that managers must make, which until the advent of this perspective had ignored the strengths and weaknesses possessed by a firm, which are rooted in its internal resources and capabilities. Resources are analogous to functional-level assets, whereas capabilities are derived from how managers combine resources at the business level.

A resource that is valuable has the potential to create new wealth, based on its rent stream (Ricardo, 1817). A resource that is valuable also has the potential to create a competitive advantage; a resource that is not valuable can lead to a competitive disadvantage. A resource that is common (that is, not rare) could only result in parity and normal economic returns. A resource that is valuable and rare but not costly to imitate could generate a temporary competitive advantage. (If it were not valuable, it could lead to a temporary competitive disadvantage.) A resource that is valuable, rare, costly to imitate and exploited by an organization or entrepreneur can generate a sustainable competitive advantage (Barney, 1991).

RBV depends on a few crucial assumptions. First, resources and capabilities are the units of analysis. The second assumption is resource heterogeneity; that is, firms must possess different resources. If they were the same, they could only potentially generate the same stream of rents. Third, the resources must be immobile, meaning that they cannot be moved without cost from one firm to another. Fourth, if all firms possessed the same resources, then it would make sense to refocus on the external environments for clues about improving firm performance.

CHALLENGES IN IMPLEMENTING A THEORY-BASED DOCTORAL PROGRAM IN ENTREPRENEURSHIP

As can be seen from only this partial overview of the theories that could be taught, the first challenge in implementing a theory-based program is that there are a lot of theories. Few programs have sufficient expert faculty to cover all of the theories that students could learn. The remaining options are (1) to limit the coverage of the theories to be taught, (2) to borrow expertise from the faculty at other universities, or (3) to enable the students through the use of independent studies to master the content, largely as a consequence of their own efforts, which loosely follows the British model. This second approach was the one that I was able to implement for the University of Louisville. It enabled us to have the broadest possible theoretical coverage. It also exposed our students to truly inspiring scholars who felt privileged to work with competent and enthusiastic doctoral students.

Limiting Theoretical Coverage

Limiting theoretical coverage is the default approach for most entrepreneurship doctoral programs. These programs are concerned about the possibility of ballooning the required course requirements. They are also concerned about possible resistance from students who wish to focus on conducting their own research. In addition, college administrators are concerned about the additional cost of hiring faculty qualified to teach the required number of seminars. Thus, there are very few programs in the world that have sufficient faculty to cover all of the relevant theories that could be taught. Finally, it is quite possible that most faculty focused on their own silo of paradigms are unaware themselves of the theories not being taught to students.

One of the reasons for this chapter is to draw attention to this problem of limited theoretical coverage. It may exist because some program administrators do not see it as a problem because they think their main task is to provide just enough coverage so that students can complete their dissertations. Completing a dissertation is the gateway to beginning a career as a scholar; however, becoming a scholar is not something that an aspirant achieves all at once with a single accomplishment. It is a journey consisting of continuing achievements and contributions, such as serving as a journal reviewer or editor, leading doctoral consortia, appreciating the contributions of other scholars, leading programs themselves, and being aware that there are many different ways in which to make scholarly contributions that they may not find to be personally interesting, but which are still vital to progress in the field. Also, being aware of the contributions of others creates comradery and respect for their work, both of which contribute to the potential growth of the field of entrepreneurship research. Anyone who has worked in the field for two or three decades will acknowledge it has become much easier to make personal contributions as the level of scholarly development in the field has progressed. Thus, all scholars have a responsibility to contribute to the advancement of the field as a whole. I argue that more broadly trained scholars will be better trained to advance the field as well as pursue their individual research goals.

Using External Faculty Scholars

For the last 15 years at the University of Louisville, we have delivered theoretical seminars through the use of eight external, topical scholars who had the most publications in their fields of expertise, which gave us the broadest possible coverage of the extant theories, as well as a rich learning environment for the doctoral students. Louisville-based faculty also provided seminars and chaired dissertations, as well as served on committees. My experience with these external faculty was that they were honored to be selected; they greatly enjoyed interacting with the excellent doctoral students, and in many cases, they volunteered to serve on dissertation committees. The advantage for the invited faculty members is that they can spread the influence of their ideas, plus earn a lot of money for teaching an intensive seminar. The advantage to the University of Louisville financially is that it was able to hire all of these external faculty for less than the cost of hiring one senior scholar and paying for his or her benefits.

The University of Louisville program was mainly taught using intensive seminars, supplemented by semester-long seminars. What is an intensive seminar? It usually spans five days, which can be spread across one or several weeks. Students receive their reading list in advance together with individual assignments to lead the discussion of sub-topics. Students are required to write a paper on a topic in the seminar. Sometimes the students bring to the seminar a draft of their paper on the first day of class, so that it can be discussed throughout their seminar meetings. More commonly, students write a paper to be submitted within four to six weeks after the seminar.

What about academic credit for an intensive seminar? AACSB requires 42 contact hours for a three-hour seminar. Two hours of work completed outside of a seminar can substitute for one hour of in-seminar instruction. For example, if a seminar meets six hours a day, with a one-hour break for lunch, for a week, that would be 30 of the required 42 contact hours. Then, if students spend 24 hours outside a seminar preparing for it or completing assignments, that would be equivalent to fulfilling the remaining 12 hours of those required for three credit hours. Normally, students spend far more than 24 hours reading the assigned readings and writing their seminar paper. In a typical semester, students would take four seminars and earn 12 credits.

The advantage for the university is that it is a very efficient model for hiring targeted expertise and it does not need to pay benefits for faculty who are not employed full time. A complication of this approach is the Internal Revenue Service (IRS) withholding at the top rate, which greatly reduces the incentive for external faculty to participate. A solution to this problem is to hire the external faculty as independent contractors who are responsible for paying their own taxes. Unfortunately, universities face a lot of pressure from the IRS to treat external faculty as regular employees, rather than outside contractors. We were able to treat our external faculty as independent contractors but it required a lot of consultation among the university attorney, the IRS compliance group, the human resources group, and the payroll office. When faculty are treated as independent contractors, they cannot be listed as the instructor of record for a seminar, which runs the risk of losing accreditation. No doctoral program can afford to be unaccredited, so the external faculty must be listed as the instructors of record, which calls into question again of how to remain compliant with IRS guidelines.

The above list is a fair summary of the internal problems in operating a doctoral program with many external faculty members. However, there is also the question of on-campus faculty acceptance by those who are not teaching in the doctoral program. The successful operation of this sort of a program requires a cultural shift, which does not happen quickly. It also requires the support of the dean's office who also must become acculturated to operating a program differently. Both the college faculty and the dean's office face internal and external pressures, which must be resisted.

My experience is that it is very difficult for those who are not mentoring doctoral students in the program to understand its advantages, especially when there is no consensus among entrepreneurship faculty world-wide about the theoretical topics that should be included in a comprehensive, theoretical curriculum.

Using Independent Studies

The third way to broaden the theoretical coverage of an entrepreneurship doctoral program is to use independent studies. In this case, an independent study would consist of individual students reading assigned readings and then reacting to them by writing an original paper, suitable for submitting to a conference or a journal for publication. There would be no seminar meetings, but there could be periodic meetings during the semester to monitor a student's progress and to provide mentoring. Collaboration among scholars in the field could develop the reading lists for these independent studies. As noted, they must still be supervised by the best-qualified, on-campus scholars to monitor compliance with the terms of the studies, as well as to evaluate the quality of the student papers.

Eventually, the faculty overhead required to supervise independent studies can become burdensome, especially if the supervising faculty are not given teaching credit for this work. In my view, it should be part of a faculty member's teaching load, in the same way as serving on a dissertation committee should also be part of a faculty member's teaching load.

The advantage of independent studies over the other options for developing theoretical coverage is that they are the most flexible, and probably the least expensive options because they can be provided with existing faculty resources. A disadvantage is that because students are not required to work together on them, the students find it more difficult to teach each other and to build the comradery that is normally a byproduct of a seminar experience.

CONCLUSION

I look forward to the day when every doctoral student will be exposed to the theories that are being used, or could be used to study entrepreneurship. For that day to arrive, there must be a consensus among scholars and seminar administrators that broad theoretical coverage is a goal that can improve the training of their students, as well as advance the quality of research that we are able to conduct. In addition to these benefits, students trained in a wide variety of theories will be more effective conveyors of fact-based research, based on the proper application of theory, which will enhance our appreciation and understanding of how entrepreneurs can and do succeed.

In the near future, I predict that there will be a demand for compendiums to facilitate access to the broad array of entrepreneurship theories that both students and scholars will demand. I invite anyone who is interested to join me in developing these materials.

REFERENCES

Arrow, K. J. 1989. "Economics of information." Public lecture reproduced in first report to Indira Gandhi Institute of Development Research, Bombay, March, p. 41.

Barney, J. B. 1991. "Firm resources and sustained competitive advantage." *Journal of Management* 17: 99–120.

Barney, J. B. 1997. *Gaining and Sustaining Competitive Advantage*. Reading, MA: Addison-Wesley.

Baron, R. A. 1991. "Motivation in work settings: Reflections on the core of organizational research." *Motivation and Emotion* 15(1): 1–8. https://doi.org/10.1007/BF00991472

Coase, R. 1937. "The nature of the firm." *Economica* 4(6): 386–405.

Davidsson, P. 2015. "Entrepreneurial opportunities and the entrepreneurship nexus: A re-conceptualization." *Journal of Business Venturing* 30(5): 674–95.

DiMaggio, P. M., & Powell, W. W. 1983. "The iron cage revisited: Institutional isomorphism and collective rationality in organizational fields." *American Sociological Review* 48: 147–60.

DiMaggio, P. J., & Powell, W. W. 1991. "Introduction." In P. J. DiMaggio & W. Powell (eds), *The New Institutionalism and Organizational Analysis*, 1–38. Chicago, IL: University of Chicago Press.

Fiet, J. O. 2002. *The Systematic Search for Entrepreneurial Discoveries*. Westport, CN: Quorum Books.

Fiet, J. O. 2008. *Prescriptive Entrepreneurship*. Cheltenham, UK and Northampton, MA, USA: Edward Elgar Publishing.

Fiet, J. O. 2020. *Time, Space and Entrepreneurship*. New York: Routledge.

Granovetter, M. 1985. "Economic action and social structure: The problem of embeddedness." *American Journal of Sociology* 91(November): 481–510.

Hayek, F. A. 1945. The use of knowledge in society. *American Economic Review*, 35(4): 519–30.

Jensen, M. C. 1994. "Self-interest, altruism, and agency theory." *Journal of Applied Corporate Finance* 78(2): 40–5.

Jensen, M. C., & Meckling, W. H. 1976. "Theory of the firm: Managerial behavior, agency costs and ownership structure." *Journal of Financial Economics* 3: 305–60.

Katz, J. 2020. "Doctoral programs in entrepreneurship." https://sites.google.com/a/slu.edu/eweb/doctoral-programs-in-entrepreneurship

Kerlinger, F. N. 1966. *Foundations of Behavioral Research*. New York: Holt, Rinehart and Winston.

Meyer, J. W., & Rowan, B. 1977. "Institutionalized organizations: Formal structure as myth and ceremony." *American Journal of Sociology* 83: 340–63.

Penrose, E. T. 1959. *The Theory of the Growth of the Firm*. New York: John Wiley.

Polyani, C. 1968. *Primitive, Archaic, and Modern Economics: Essays of Karl Polanyi.* New York: Doubleday & Company.

Ricardo, D. 1817. *On the Principles of Political Economy and Taxation* (1st ed.). London: John Murray, retrieved via Google Books.

Scott, S. M. 1995. *Institutions and Organizations.* Thousand Oaks, CA: Sage.

Scott, W. R. 2004. *Institutional Theory in Encyclopedia of Social Theory,* George Ritzer, ed. Thousand Oaks, CA: Sage.

Suchman, M. C. 1995. "Localism and globalism in institutional analysis: The emergence of contractual norms in venture finance." In W. R. Scott & S. Christensen (eds), *The Institutional Construction of Organizations: International and Longitudinal Studies,* 39–763. Thousand Oaks, CA: Sage.

Whyte, G. 1994. "The role of asset specificity in the vertical integration decision." *Journal of Economic Behavior and Organization* 23(3): 287–302.

Williamson, O. E. 1979. "Transaction cost economics: The governance of contractual relations." *Journal of Law and Economics* 22: 233–61.

Williamson, O. E. 1985. *The Economic Institutions of Capitalism.* New York: Free Press.

3. Spaces for entrepreneurship education: a new campus arms race?

Luke Pittaway

INTRODUCTION

This chapter is an addendum to research recently published on *University Spaces for Entrepreneurship: A Process Model* (Pittaway, Aissaoui, Ferrier, & Mass, 2019). The work reports the results of action research exploring the nature of new entrepreneurship education spaces added to campuses across the United States (US). The prior paper presented characteristics of innovation proposed for physical environments, explored the types of existing spaces that have been created, and proposed a process model for the construction of new spaces (Pittaway et al., 2019). This chapter extends that work and adds to our understanding of the nature of creating entrepreneurship education spaces by providing a deeper review of the literature in entrepreneurship education that both highlights the paucity of study on the subject and demonstrates its increasing need. This chapter also introduces additional illustrative case studies and provides a practical framework for use when educators are considering the construction of new spaces with a focus on innovation and entrepreneurship education.

Across the US, and increasingly around the globe, universities are constructing dedicated physical spaces for entrepreneurship education (Morris, Kuratko, & Cornwall, 2013). The form and type of facilities constructed varies. Examples of new spaces include dorms, student pre-incubators, student incubators, mixed-used facilities, as well as many different forms of prototyping labs (Pittaway et al., 2019). The trend is relatively recent and appears to be accelerating (Neck & Greene, 2011). There are some identifiable roots that explain how this trend started.

One root can be found in the United Kingdom, where the Science Enterprise Challenge program in the late 1990s and early 2000s encouraged research-intensive universities to embed entrepreneurship education in the science and engineering disciplines (NCGE, 2004a). The spread of "embedded entrepreneurship education" across campuses led to coordination difficulties.

Subsequently, the Centers for Excellence in the Teaching and Learning of Enterprise program followed to help address coordination issues, which led to the construction of dedicated facilities at a number of campuses (among others the universities of Leeds, York, Sheffield, and Leeds Beckett).

A second root can be traced to the US from 2003 to 2013, and the Kauffman Campuses Initiative (Menzies, 2004). In this program the Kauffman Foundation awarded up to $5 million to campuses that created university-wide entrepreneurship education. These funds were matched by the university or donors and had a significant impact on the growth of university-wide entrepreneurship education in the US. Again, universities found coordination of activities difficult and resorted to the construction of physical facilities to provide a focal point.

A third root can be found in the expansion of traditional university-based incubation of startups for "student" and "graduate" entrepreneurs (NCGE, 2004b). Here, universities have aimed to create dedicated facilities designed to house and support students who are trying to start businesses. These facilities have sought to emulate MIT's iconic Building 20.

The final root appears to be more recent and linked to a growth in design thinking and some reimagination of how workspace should be designed (Morris et al., 2013). Design thinking in entrepreneurship education has led to the rise of accelerator programs focused on venture launch and open innovation labs focused on assisting prototype development.

This interest amongst universities to develop new spaces for entrepreneurship, innovation, and creativity was captured by a story in the *New York Times*[1] in which it was noted that US universities have begun to invest in high-tech buildings. Having reviewed a number of examples, the article declared the trend to be "a new campus amenities arms race" and highlighted that many of the spaces "closely resemble the high-tech workplace, itself inspired by the minimally partitioned spaces of the garage and the factory." The article highlighted several developments including Cornell's new 12-acre technology campus on Roosevelt Island, NY, the University of Utah's $45 million Lassonde Studies (dorms), York University's $25 million Lassonde School of Engineering, Northwestern University's 11,000 square-foot garage accelerator "Park Here," the University of Iowa's new Art School, and Wichita State University's new Innovation Campus. These developments held a common desire to emulate the high-tech spaces that have led to significant entrepreneurial businesses. Many of these efforts are directly targeted at redesigning learning infrastructure in order to promote more entrepreneurship on campus. This research, therefore, considers several critical questions. First, it explores why this trend is developing. Second, what is being built on university campuses is examined. Finally, it examines how universities can better develop processes and measures, which allow the success of such spaces to be considered.

The chapter begins by providing a detailed chronology of entrepreneurship education research on the topic in order to explore and inform how research considered the role of physical space in entrepreneurship education previously. The chronology focuses on reviews of the subject, at different points in time, that have sought to summarize the field of study.

A CHRONOLOGY OF ENTREPRENEURSHIP EDUCATION RESEARCH

In general, the entrepreneurship education literature seems strangely quiet on the role of educational spaces, despite the trends noted earlier (Pittaway & Cope 2007; Pittaway & Hannon 2008). Over the last four decades there have been a series of reviews of entrepreneurship education that have systematically considered the field (Solomon, 2007). These reviews are explored chronologically to consider how the literature informs the current trend. Dainow (1986) undertook the first review of the subject surveying entrepreneurship education for a ten-year period up to 1984. The study was driven by the context of the 1980s and had a focus on small businesses (Gibb 1993), consequently it explores entrepreneurship and small business training. Dainow's review selected 18 key journals and conference proceedings as its focus for the period 1973–84. The search of relevant databases sourced 58 articles on entrepreneurship education. A coding technique was applied to make sense of the emerging themes. Entrepreneurship education had already begun to focus on the higher education context and 55 percent of the papers focused on programs at universities. These studies focus on needs analysis (of programs) and have a tendency to examine program design, course design, and analysis of training effects, but no articles focus on infrastructure and space.

Garavan and O'Cinneide (1994a, 1994b) published two papers that provide a reflective account of entrepreneurship education research from the 1980s. The first explored issues and difficulties highlighted in the literature, and the second compared six entrepreneurship training programs. Garavan and O'Cinneide (1994a: 4) explained that "while the field is expanding, most research has tended to be fragmented and with an exploratory, descriptive nature." The research they explored focuses on particular programs, although there did appear to be a growth of evaluative studies. They also offered a typology in the research themes and identified four groups: (1) education and training for small business ownership; (2) education focused on new venture creation; (3) continuing small business education, and (4) small business awareness education.

Gorman, Hanlon, and King (1997) followed Dainow's (1986) paper and re-examined the literature ten years later (1985–94). They were interested in descriptive and empirical research and focused on contexts including, "stu-

dents enrolled in the formal education system, out-of-school potential entrepreneurs, existing business owners and others" (Gorman et al., 1997: 56). They
focused on leading academic journals in the subject and selected 92 articles
for review (Hytti & O'Gorman, 2004). Their first theme was "entrepreneurial
propensity," focused on research to understand how educational interventions
could change students' propensity to be entrepreneurial (Ulrich & Cole, 1987;
Chamard, 1989). Papers also focused on "preparation for startup" exploring
how education interventions prepared students to start businesses and explored
"managing small businesses." Like Dainow, Gorman et al. (1997) saw a tendency for research to "address various aspects of educational process and
structure with a primary focus on the post-secondary level" (Gorman et al.,
1997: 61) but again no evidence was presented that researchers had focused, to
any degree, on educational infrastructure.

Henry, Hill, and Leitch (2005a, 2005b) published two reflective essays. The
first focused on "difficulties associated with the design of programs, as well as
their objectives, content and delivery methods" (Henry et al., 2005a), while the
second considered approaches to program evaluation and the measurement of
effectiveness (Henry et al., 2005b). At this point, it is clear that as research on
programs accelerates, increased work on learning methods leads to fragmentation in the subject, and questions occur about whether entrepreneurship can
be taught (Fiet, 2000). In order to manage fragmentation Henry et al. (2005a)
point to the need to categorize forms and agree with Gorman et al.'s (1997)
segmentation. The second paper focused on how program effectiveness is
determined and measured (Henry et al., 2005b). It is evident that studies on
evaluation continue to grow but that the challenge of measuring effectiveness
remains (Westhead, Storey, & Martin, 2001). Debate revolves around what
should be measured, for example, economic benefits versus educational
outcomes (Wyckham, 1989), and focuses on how best to measure outcomes
(Westhead et al., 2001). Again, at this point there remains no evidence of any
research focused on physical space.

Next are a series of more comprehensive reviews following systematic
approaches based on scientific methods and using bibliometrics. Ten years
after Gorman et al. (1997), Pittaway and Cope (2007) conducted a Systematic
Literature Review. Their study reviewed the literature from 1970 to 2004
and sourced 185 academic papers via systematic search protocols applied to
a series of bibliometric databases. The authors coded abstracts, conducted
a thematic analysis, and presented a thematic framework of entrepreneurship
education research (Pittaway & Cope, 2007). Like prior reviews they noted
a wealth of studies on program design, evaluation, and propensity, but also
highlighted a significant lack of studies on other aspects, such as study of
extra-curricular activities, assessment, graduate entrepreneurship, and student
placement. Relevant to this study, they noted that contextual factors in the

university setting, such as enterprise infrastructure or the supply of faculty and the institution's commercialization policies, impact on how entrepreneurship education is implemented at the institutional level. Reviewing studies on educational policy they later argued that, "assessments of policy initiatives... do illustrate the role of institutional strategies, infrastructure, people and relationships, as essential factors in the diversity of implementation and levels of 'success' when introducing entrepreneurship education" (Pittaway & Cope, 2007: 487). Simultaneously, their review reveals a dearth of studies on these subjects. Pittaway and Hannon (2008) later argued that studies on institutional activity do suggest a role for infrastructure in supporting educational activity (see also Grigg, 1994; Poole & Robertson, 2003). The authors further noted that, "having appropriate infrastructure to support the form of enterprise education being developed seems to be accepted as having an impact on sustainability (of programs)" (Pittaway & Hannon, 2008: 207). Despite its importance the systematic literature review does not register it as key subject of concern amongst researchers (Pittaway & Cope, 2007).

From 2010 onwards, there has been a series of more recent reviews (Wang & Chugh, 2014). The first of these was conducted by Mwasalwiba (2010), who sourced 108 papers via a "semi-systematic" review procedure. Martin, McNally, and Kay (2013) undertook a meta-analysis of entrepreneurship educational outcomes; Naia, Baptista, Januário, and Trigo (2014) focused on the period 2000–11; Byrne, Fayolle, and Toutain (2014) reviewed seven mainstream journals over a 25-year period (replicating the Pittaway & Cope 2007 systematic literature review); and most recently Loi, Castriotta, and Chiara Di Guardo (2016) conducted a "co-citation analysis" covering the period 1991–2014. Collectively, these reviews note the significant growth and diversity in entrepreneurship education research and that this trend is being driven by increasing attention to the subject amongst educators and policy makers (Mwasalwiba, 2010; Naia et al., 2014). Subjects that attract attention in the domain continue to focus on the "educational process" and the "acquisition of entrepreneurial skills" (Mwasalwiba, 2010; Naia et al., 2014). For example, Mwasalwiba (2010: 30) reports that, "the review has come across an overwhelming number of articles addressing teaching methods"; and Naia et al. (2014: 92) concluded, "Most articles present specific cases/programmes with best practices that are successful in a specific context, but provide no evidence that these practices could be extended," while studies researching the impact of entrepreneurship education, in contrast, were investigating success indicators and entrepreneurship education's perceived economic role (Mwasalwiba, 2010: 33).

Considering the thematic structure of the field, Byrne et al. (2014) concluded that there are currently five themes. (1) "State of the play" work explores entrepreneurship education's scope, evolution, and institutionalization. (2) "Specific audiences" research focuses on entrepreneurship education for specific groups (e.g. female entrepreneurs). (3) "Entrepreneurial learning" explores how entrepreneurs learn. (4) "Measurement and evaluation" investigates the value-added of training and development. (5) "Methodology" studies focus on methods and strategies for educators in entrepreneurship. Loi et al.'s (2016) co-citation analysis provides another set of themes and concludes that there is a sixth theme, "polycentric structure," to entrepreneurship education research. In their study the themes that emerge appear to focus on "entrepreneurial learning," "entrepreneurial intentions," "evaluation," and "pedagogy" (Loi et al., 2016).

What this four-decade chronology of entrepreneurship education research shows (as highlighted in Table 3.1) is a nearly *complete absence of research on educational infrastructure*. This lack of attention to the role that physical space plays in entrepreneurship education is important because innovative instructional design may be inhibited by poorly designed instructional spaces. Additionally, the current trends in building new spaces suggest that universities are interested in how to design new spaces that encourage entrepreneurial activity on campus. Researchers focus on the following areas of interest:

1. *Pedagogy and andragogy* – a focus on the methods, design, and strategy associated with specific educational interventions.
2. *Propensity, intentionality, and self-efficacy* – aims to understand the extent to which entrepreneurship educational interventions change students' perceptions and behaviors in critical ways.
3. *Entrepreneurial learning* – studies on how entrepreneurs learn in the context of their work and the implications this may have for the design of educational practice.
4. *Measurement and evaluation* – growth in research on the extent to which entrepreneurship education creates outcomes that are sought after by educators and policy makers.
5. *Typologies and taxonomies* – consideration of the different forms and philosophies guiding educational practice and typologies that make sense of these differences.
6. *Context and application* – work that explores the different contexts and practices that might be relevant to entrepreneurship educators.

This chronology, therefore, highlights some notable and continuing absences from the research field that are not addressed. Notable amongst these is an absence of study that focuses on extra or co-curricular activity (for example, clubs or business plan competitions); limited focus on student–entrepreneur relationships (consulting, internships); poor consideration of wider non-programmatic institutional factors (infrastructure, career support);

Table 3.1   *A chronology of entrepreneurship education research reviews*

Authors	Time period	Papers	Study design	Key review themes
Dainow (1986)	1973–83	58	Selected 18 key journals and conference proceedings. Coded papers for themes.	Needs analysis; program design; course design; analysis of training effects.
Garavan and O'Cinneide (1994a, 1994b)	Up to 1992	N/A	Reflective essay reviewing the field.	Program design; evaluation; training for small businesses; education for venture creation; continuing small business education; small business awareness education.
Gorman et al. (1997)	1985–94	92	Census-style sampling procedure, followed by a three-step classification.	Entrepreneurial propensity; preparation for startup; managing small businesses; program design; post-secondary education.
Henry et al. (2005a, 2005b)	Up to 2003	N/A	Reflective essay reviewing the field.	Program design; program objectives; program content; program delivery methods; program evaluation and measurement; typologies of entrepreneurship education.
Pittaway and Cope (2007)	1970–2004	185	Systematic literature review with thematic coding.	Management development pedagogy; student propensity; higher education teaching and learning pedagogy; institutional policies; mapping supply.
Mwasalwiba (2010)	2004–07 + bibliographies	108	Semi-systematic review and data extract sheets.	Objectives; program types; content; teaching methods; community outreach; evaluation and impact.
Martin et al. (2013)	Up to 2011	42	Meta-analysis of entrepreneurship education outcomes.	Impact of entrepreneurship education on human capital assets; impact of entrepreneurship education on startup and entrepreneurial performance; education has more impact on outcomes than training.

Authors	Time period	Papers	Study design	Key review themes
Naia et al. (2014)	2000–11	60	Systematic-like review and classification.	Classified into "how," "what," and "which," as well as, combined typologies (e.g. "how + what").
Byrne et al. (2014)	1984–2011	86	Systematic literature review and classification.	State of the play; specific audiences; entrepreneurial learning; measurement and evaluation; methodology.
Loi et al. (2016)	1991–2014	79	Bibliometrics with co-citation analysis.	Introspection; entrepreneurial intentions; pedagogy; entrepreneurial learning; evaluation.

and limited research on graduate entrepreneurship and placement outcomes (family business succession, employment in small businesses, or career trajectories). These absences continue to exist despite several decades of growth in research on entrepreneurship education. Lack of study in these aspects of entrepreneurship education creates some blind spots in the research domain. Much valuable entrepreneurship education occurs through extra-curricular activities, such as, clubs, events, and competitions. Institutional contexts influence the type of entrepreneurship education that is relevant, as well as enabling and constraining practice. Outcomes from educational practice, such as impacts on venture creation and employment, are important when considering the value of programs developed. For the purposes of this study there is a notable absence of study of physical space in educational practice. The topic is important to research as universities building these spaces need to understand how they enable and/or inhibit educational practice, and promote or restrain innovation, creativity, and entrepreneurship by students.

ILLUSTRATIVE CASE STUDIES

This part of the chapter presents five illustrative case studies that demonstrate examples of entrepreneurship education spaces that have been constructed on US campuses in recent years. The research study, as noted earlier, explored 57 examples of such spaces across the US (Pittaway et al., 2019) as well as presenting an entrepreneurship education infrastructure typology, which is explained following the illustrative case studies.

Case Study 1: Harvard's iLab (and Pagliuca Harvard Life Lab)

The distinctive Hi red logo and exterior design signifies the Harvard Innovation Lab is a space that is designed to be a "unique collaboration and education space." The iLab is at the gateway to Harvard University's Allston campus and is designed to become "a cross-disciplinary research and innovation focused learning and development community." The iLab focuses on venture incubation and feeds into a "launch lab." With red distinctive coloring and nighttime lighting the iLab stands out in the streetscape. Internally it has an industrial open-plan feel, with dedicated but flexible spaces and an underlying mixed-use design. Spaces include many forms of collaborative space (for instance, informal meeting, ideation, incubation, semi-formal meeting, and flexible classroom space) and the space hosts a venture development program that emphasizes ideation, incubation, and mentoring. In 2017, Harvard iLab also opened seven 15,000 square feet "life labs" (Pagliuca Harvard Life Lab) – fully equipped laboratories, office space, and mentorship for biotech companies. Harvard Launch Lab is located in the same building and is described as a "co-working space" for alumni ventures. Utilizing cross-overs between ideation (and students) and launch (including alumni), the space aims to maximize organized serendipity between pre-incubation projects and ventures in launch mode. Building layout is designed to support ventures at different stages of development and open-plan spaces are ringed with offices for visitors, mentors, and other professionals to drop in and provide support/advice to student and graduate entrepreneurs.

Case Study 2: Babson College

With its general focus on entrepreneurship Babson College has a number of physical spaces designed to support entrepreneurial activity. The study reviewed the Arthur M. Blank Center for Entrepreneurship and the Leonard A. Schlesinger First-Year Innovation Center. The Arthur M. Blank Center for Entrepreneurship was completed in 1998, is 18,000 square feet, and is home to Babson's graduate programs in business and entrepreneurship. The center was an addition to the 1920s Luksic Hall and needed to blend in with existing buildings on campus while offering innovative space. It is notable for its circular and semi-circular configurations and its open-plan exhibit and display area. The exhibit area, over time, has featured famous graduates and their ventures. The interior space has a mixture of casual and formal interaction spaces including an atrium, rotunda, informal collaboration, formal collaboration, and teaching spaces. The Leonard A. Schlesinger First-Year Innovation Center is a new entrepreneurial hub built in 2015 on the Babson campus within the Park Manor residence hall and was named after a former president of the university. It is a startup space within a residence hall, and includes an amphitheater, classroom, and collaboration space designed as a "student laboratory." It is also linked to the first-year program "Foundations of Management and Entrepreneurship." The space extensively utilizes natural light, has informal and formal space, and is largely flexible. Quiet and private space is limited, as is sound control. Labs at Babson are designed for different venture forms and stages.

Case Study 3: University of Utah's Lassonde Studios

The University of Utah built a $45 million learning community (dorm) focused on entrepreneurship and it houses programs associated with the Lassonde Entrepreneur Institute. The dorm hosts approximately 400 students including living, sleeping, catering, and spaces for students to focus on startup ideas. Its tagline is "live, learn and launch." The structure was opened in 2016 and has an impressive "flow-like" external structure designed by Yazdani Studio of CannonDesign (with EDA Architecture). Lassonde includes ample "maker-space" facilities including 3-D printers, laser cutters, and power tools, as well as collaboration space. It includes 400 unique student residences and a 20,000 square feet "garage" space for venture ideation, incubation, and launch. Once again interior design is "industrial" with treated concrete floors throughout and open ceilings with visible air conditioning and wiring systems. Lassonde emphasizes "student driven space" and "student driven design," has themed living floors, and 24-hour access to all areas. It focuses on design flexibility in the open spaces and aims to be at the cutting edge in terms of the use of existing technologies (for example, audio-visual tools, video editing, or greenspace).

Case Study 4: Arizona State University

Arizona State University (ASU) has a distributed set of spaces across several campuses that are coordinated by ASU Entrepreneurship + Innovation. Spaces include: the ASU Chandler Innovation Center (and TechShop), student-led Changemaker Central spaces (on each campus), an Entrepreneurship + Innovation HEALab (health innovation), an Innovation Hub (ideation and prototyping), MKR services (maker-space and services), and a New Media Innovation and Entrepreneurship Lab (focused on collaboration between journalism, computer engineering, design, and business students). Each space is focused on student and graduate collaboration, pre-incubation and launch, with different venues offering different types of support based on the venture type and focus.

Case Study 5: University of North Carolina at Chapel Hill

The University of North Carolina at Chapel Hill has two sites which were included in the study noted earlier (Pittaway et al., 2019). The 1789 Venture Lab (located on Franklin Street) provides space and services to support student and graduate entrepreneurs. The facility has open and flexible workspace including features such as a "bar" workspace area, conference rooms, and office space. Key entrepreneurship support programs include mentoring and venture development acceleration. With an open-plan flexible space, an industrial feel, and wooden floors it follows many of the design approaches used by other case study examples. The 1789 Lab welcomes students, alumni, and local entrepreneurs. In contrast, Launch Chapel Hill is a university-led accelerator program with a physical facility. It offers private offices, assigned (co-working) desks, and "come and go" hot-desks. The first floor includes a 2,000 square feet co-working area with four offices, a large conference room, and kitchen. The second floor is 1,500 square feet and has four small offices, two large offices, and a small conference room. As an accelerator it is more focused on venture launch.

These five cases studies elicit a series of observations. First, the spaces range in size considerably and there are likely to be some identifiable types, such as those focused on venture creation and those focused on wider aspects of entrepreneurship. Second, each case study illustrates some key aspects of design, such as open-plan configurations, which are considered to support the innovation and entrepreneurship purpose of the space. Finally, the combination of design aspects appears to be differentiated between spaces based on the space's purpose and the type of innovation it seeks to promote. These observations suggested that further action research and more detailed review of a wider selection of examples was needed and this work is highlighted next (Pittaway et al., 2019). A summary of two key aspects of this work are provided. First, a review of the different types of spaces identified in the study. Second, an explanation of the innovation characteristics that were observed, both from the literature and the field research.

SPACES FOR ENTREPRENEURSHIP: A TYPOLOGY

When reviewing the illustrative case studies, the 57 examples across the US, and the action research conducted the study identified a series of types of entrepreneurship education infrastructure (Pittaway et al., 2019). The prior study developed an entrepreneurship education infrastructure typology and mapped it against different types of innovation practice. Here, these types are explained, and they are highlighted in Figure 3.1. The typology further illustrates that the growth of physical spaces comes in many forms:

- Type 1 – Ideation spaces, which included two types. 1a idea gestation spaces, designed for quiet contemplation and 1b idea-sharing spaces, designed for collaboration and creative ideation. The ideation spaces require two very different architectural designs and innovation characteristics. The focus in 1a was quiet, reflection-thinking spaces emphasizing cognitive elements of innovation, while 1b required collaborative spaces encouraging communication, teamwork, and active creativity, emphasizing the social elements of innovation (Pittaway et al., 2019).
- Type 2 – Incubators and accelerators. These spaces can also come in several forms. 2a typically focuses more on "pre-incubation" while 2b focuses more on incubation, acceleration, and launch. Here the focus is on the venture creation part of the innovation process and spaces have more "closed and dedicated spaces," such as offices, conference rooms, and dedicated mentoring suites. The supporting elements of innovation including flexible configurations and dedicated programming were important components.
- Type 3 – Materialization spaces. Such spaces consist of labs, maker-spaces, and other rapid prototyping facilities. These came in multiple forms, while many focused on product innovations, there were also life science labs dedicated to venture creation and discipline specific spaces (e.g., fine arts). In most cases these were often labs in the traditional sense that provided new "maker"-focused machines and technologies. In terms of innovation these were almost entirely focused on the "active-doing" part of the innovation process and rarely included space for other aspects, such as the social and cognitive aspects of innovation.
- Type 4 – Integrative spaces. These were generally in line with the trend toward "university-wide" entrepreneurship education and sought central spaces to bring together cross-disciplinary entrepreneurship and innovation activity and in multiple forms (e.g., ideation, materialization, and venture creation). Depending on the nature of the entrepreneurship programs these appeared to fall into two forms. 4a sought to integrate all entrepreneurship activities under one roof at a central location on campus, while 4b aimed to provide multiple facilities across the campus, connected together in a network. Design principles in these spaces varied considerably but tended to aim to bring together all aspects of innovation in a coherent way for the campus. 4b spaces were often described as gateways, hubs, or bridges and they sought to provide central connection points to multiple entrepreneurship facilities across a campus, with each facility (outside of the hub) likely having a different focus in the innovation process.

- Type 5 – Dorms and living communities. This type appears to be just emerging and there were only a few examples of practice (e.g., Babson and Lassonde), these were very similar to Type 4a and were integrative. They aimed to bring together all aspects of entrepreneurship and innovation under one roof but also included community, living, and recreational components.

When reviewing the examples of entrepreneurship education spaces in the US it was evident that they followed certain principles of innovation. For example, Type 1a focused almost exclusively on the cognitive innovation process;

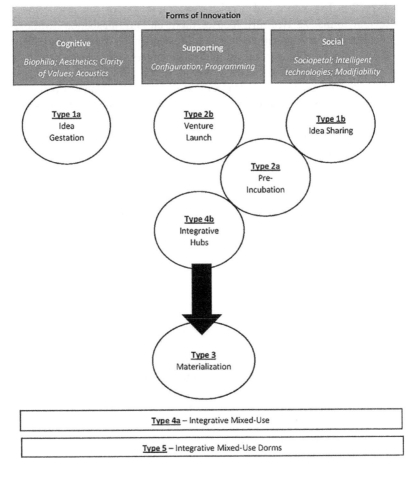

Figure 3.1   Typology of physical spaces in entrepreneurship education

Type 2 and Type 4b focused on the supporting aspects of innovation; Type 1b focused on the social aspects of innovation; and Type 3 focused almost exclusively on the materialization form of innovation (Pittaway et al., 2019). It was also evident that motivations, stakeholder focus, and performance measures for the construction of such spaces were often unclear, with considerable copying behavior occurring through a genuine "campus arms race" as described by the *New York Times*. The Pittaway et al. (2019) study also found some key innovative components that were incorporated into the different types of space in different ways. These are explained next.

Cognitive elements for innovation focused on biophilia, aesthetics, clarity of values, and acoustics. Biophilia argues that human biological affinity for the natural environment is associated with innovation and requires space designs that maximize natural light, views of the natural environment and natural materials (Jackson, Maleganos, & Alamantariotou, 2017; Ulrich, 1993). Aesthetics focuses on the need for innovative space to be "interesting" and "attractive" including complex spatial and ornamental configurations, multiple shapes, visual details, as well as the effective use of art and sculpture (Waters-Lynch, Potts, Butcher, Dodson, & Hurley, 2016). Clarity of values suggests that innovative spaces exhibit values and meaning within the space, including through the use of symbols and interior design that have a psychosocial impact on users, giving them permission to be creative and codifying such behaviors (Oksanen & Ståhle, 2013), while acoustics focuses on making sure noise is managed to ensure quiet and contemplative space for thoughtful ideation (Assenza, 2015).

Social elements of innovation inherent in physical space included sociopetal design, intelligent technologies, and modifiability (Pittaway et al., 2019). Sociopetal design argues that for innovation spaces to be effective they must be designed to encourage cooperation, collaboration, and social support. Innovation increasingly requires collaboration across space and so intelligent technologies implies that innovative space must be both sophisticated in its application of collaborative technologies and "smart" indicating to users that the space is designed for innovative purposes. Modifiability suggests that innovative space needs to provide a platform for users to use, amend, and adapt the space to their needs as they occur (Parrino, 2013).

The supporting elements of innovative space focused on configuration, programming, and materialization. Configuration related to how spatial relations between spaces and their adjacency and permeability worked (Hillier, 1996). Innovative spaces are considered to encourage flow, social collaboration, and serendipitous exchanges that occur due to the design configuration (McCoy & Evans, 2002). Programming focused on the concept of "space as a service" (Pritchard, 2008) where programmatic components, such as mentoring programs and venture creation support, are seen to be essential in the innovation space (i.e., it is not always the space, it is the activity that encourages innovation and so space needs to be designed to encourage the activity intended). Materialization suggests that innovative spaces need additional aspects that encourage users to materialize concepts through prototyping, playing with models, drawing out ideas, and other tactics that allow concepts to be turned into models (Kristensen, 2004).

A summary of these innovation characteristics is provided in Table 3.2, along with implications that might occur for the design and construction of an entrepreneurship education space.

CONCLUSION

This chapter provides an addendum to research work recently published on university spaces for entrepreneurship (Pittaway et al., 2019). It demonstrates that entrepreneurship education research, despite a long history, has barely considered the role of physical space in entrepreneurship education despite the fact it is clearly an important topic in practice. Educational spaces can have impact on the learning process and more research to understand the nature of the relationship may assist developments in learning design and the design of physical space for educational purposes. In addition, the considerable growth of construction on university campuses of such spaces demonstrates a need to undertake more research on the topic. In this sense the chapter is a "call to arms" to fellow researchers: this is a critically important topic and there is insufficient understanding about a range of aspects associated with the subject. For example, the Pittaway et al. (2019) work considers the types of spaces being constructed and reviewed these according to known innovation characteristics. It also demonstrated a lack of clarity regarding the underlying motivations for the construction of spaces, did not delve deeply into the funding models that allowed spaces to be financed, and was unable to investigate or make sense of the performance measures universities were using to judge the success of the spaces constructed. In many cases this means there is a deficit in our knowledge both from a research perspective and practical perspective. Significant resources are being expended at many universities, following the "hope" that such spaces will encourage innovation, entrepreneurship, and multi-disciplinary collaboration. Yet there is little evidence that innovation processes have been thoughtfully considered in the design and construction process and there is limited evidence that universities know how to measure the success of such spaces once constructed. As demonstrated in the review, the literature is almost silent on these issues but there are identified parameters that support innovation in physical spaces and there are processes that can be used to ensure success (Pittaway et al., 2019).

Table 3.2   *Planning principles for entrepreneurship education spaces*

Innovation principle	Possible application in construction project
Natural (biophilia)	Draw on and maximize the natural environment. Use carefully selected and positioned natural materials. Maximize natural light wherever possible. Maximize natural views where possible. Enhance visual and tactile stimuli.
Interesting (aesthetics)	Creativity space needs to be interesting. Need to consider aesthetics, complex spatial and ornamental attraction where appropriate. Interesting shapes and visual details that might catch the eye. Use of art work or sculptures. Interior design, ergonomics, and art are important to symbolize that the space should be used to be innovative.
Values	Innovative space portrays value and meaning of space both outside the building and inside. Symbolism of the values, mission, and purpose of the building. May include origin stories (implicit and explicit), founding stories, symbols of success, symbols of caution – ways to define to the user how the building is intended to be used.
Acoustics	Noise is carefully managed. Social aspects of innovation do not crowd out the individual-centric aspects of innovation. Dedicated space is provided for quiet thinking-reflecting.
Collaboration, people-centric (sociopetal)	Maximize intense collaboration, cooperation, and social support. Make some spaces clear in the purpose of interaction (e.g., team work). Have some spaces where interaction form is unclear. Avoid single-occupancy space as much as possible. Avoid "ownership" of space as much as possible.
Smart space	Building needs to incorporate intelligent collaboration beyond immediate location (e.g., virtual meetings, video conferencing, etc.). Research indicates that the building needs to come across as "smart" for users to be innovative (e.g., careful implementation of technological sophistication). Can include "wireless," user of up-to-date sensors, inclusion of smart visual and audio sensing systems, etc.

Innovation principle	Possible application in construction project
Modifiability	Ensure maximum flexibility in use of the space (in present).
	Have design that encourages users to reconfigure the space and gives permission for the users to do so.
	Use moveable partitions and other methods to maximize modifiability.
	Ensure teaching spaces are truly flexible and modifiable.
	Provide symbols that help users understand that they are expected to modify the space.
	Consider modifiable lighting, walls, seating arrangements, and furniture layouts.
Configuration	Communal space most accessible to entry and exits and building pedestrian traffic (flow).
	Maximize open-plan flat structures, remove walls, reduce corridors, and open the space out.
	Explore circular/radial configuration with most dense collaboration in center, most private space on the periphery (increasingly less communal space radiates out from a central hub).
	Focus on flow between adjacent spaces to maximize serendipitous exchanges.
	Mixed configuration of spaces to encourage formal interactions to flow out into informal space (overflow).
Programming	Needs to follow space as a service model.
	Design should be guided by how the building will be used.
	Being adaptable to new uses over time.
	Provides a platform that allows users to select, utilize, and create usage modes.
Materialization	Space and materials to encourage ideation in collaborative zones (e.g., lots of whiteboard, glass that can be written on, etc.).
	Idea gestation – will require "individual" space for thinking.
	Materialization requires sensory experiences that allow the construction of artefacts (prototypes, models, designs, pictures, and images).

NOTE

1. "The Innovation Campus" Building Better Ideas, *New York Times*, August 7, 2016.

REFERENCES

Assenza, P. (2015). "If You Build It Will They Come? The Influence of Spatial Configuration on Social and Cognitive Functioning and Knowledge Spillover in Entrepreneurial Co-Working and Hacker Spaces," *Journal of Management Policy and Practice* 16(3), 35–48.

Byrne, J., A. Fayolle, & O. Toutain (2014). "Entrepreneurship Education: What We Know and What We Need to Know," in E. Chell & M. Karataş-Özkan (Eds), *The Handbook of Research on Small Business and Entrepreneurship*. Cheltenham, UK and Northampton, MA, USA: Edward Elgar Publishing, 261–88.

Chamard, J. (1989). "Public Education: Its Effect on Entrepreneurial Characteristics," *Journal of Small Business and Entrepreneurship* 6(2), 23–30.

Dainow, R. (1986). "Training and Education for Entrepreneurs: The Current State of the Literature," *Journal of Small Business and Entrepreneurship* 3(4), 10–23.

Fiet, J. O. (2000). "Theoretical Side of Teaching Entrepreneurship Theory," *Journal of Business Venturing* 16(1), 1–24.

Garavan T. N., & B. O'Cinneide (1994a). "Entrepreneurship Education and Training Programmes: A Review and Evaluation – Part 1," *Journal of European Industrial Training* 18(8), 3–12.

Garavan T. N., & B. O'Cinneide (1994b). "Entrepreneurship Education and Training Programmes: A Review and Evaluation – Part 2," *Journal of European Industrial Training* 18(8), 13–21.

Gibb, A. (1993). "The Enterprise Culture and Education: Understanding Enterprise Education and Its Links with Small Business, Entrepreneurship and Wider Educational Goals," *International Small Business Journal* 11(3), 11–34.

Gorman, G., D. Hanlon, & W. King (1997). "Some Research Perspectives on Entrepreneurship Education, Enterprise Education and Education for Small Business Management: A Ten Year Literature Review," *International Small Business Journal* 15(3), 56–76.

Grigg, T. (1994). "Adopting an Entrepreneurial Approach in Universities," *Journal of Engineering and Technology Management* 11(3, 4), 273–98.

Henry, C., F. Hill, & C. Leitch (2005a). "Entrepreneurship Education and Training: Can Entrepreneurship Be Taught? Part I," *Education and Training* 47(2), 98–111.

Henry, C., F. Hill, & C. Leitch (2005b). "Entrepreneurship Education and Training: Can Entrepreneurship Be Taught? Part II," *Education and Training* 47(2), 158–69.

Hillier, B. (1996). *Space is the Machine*, Cambridge: Cambridge University Press.

Hytti, U., & C. O'Gorman (2004). "What Is Enterprise Education? An Analysis of the Objectives and Methods of Enterprise Education Programmes in Four European Countries," *Education and Training* 46(1), 11–23.

Jackson, S., Maleganos, J., & Alamantariotou, K. (2017). "Lessons from Sustainable Entrepreneurship towards Social Innovation in Healthcare: How Green Buildings Can Promote Health and Wellbeing," in K. Nicolopoulou, M. Karatas-Ozkan, F. Janssen, & J. Jermier (Eds), *Sustainable Entrepreneurship and Social Innovation*, London: Routledge, 143–69.

Kristensen, T. (2004). "The Physical Context of Creativity," *Creativity and Innovation Management* 13(2), 89–96.

Loi, M., M. Castriotta, & M. Chiara Di Guardo (2016). "The Theoretical Foundations of Entrepreneurship Education: How Co-Citations Are Shaping the Field," *International Small Business Journal* 34(7), 948–73.

Martin, B., J. McNally, & M. Kay (2013). "Examining the Formation of Human Capital in Entrepreneurship: A Meta-Analysis of Entrepreneurship Education Outcomes," *Journal of Business Venturing* 28(2), 211–24.

McCoy, J. M., & G. W. Evans (2002). "The Potential Role of the Physical Environment in Fostering Creativity," *Creativity Research Journal* 14(3–4), 409–26.

Menzies, T. (2004). "Are Universities Playing a Role in Nurturing and Developing High-Technology Entrepreneurs? The Administrators' Perspective," *International Journal of Entrepreneurship and Innovation* 5(3), 149–55.

Morris, M. H., D. Kuratko, & J. R. Cornwall (2013). *Entrepreneurship Programs and the Modern University*, Cheltenham, UK and Northampton, MA, USA: Edward Elgar Publishing.

Mwasalwiba, E. S. (2010). "Entrepreneurship Education: A Review of Its Objectives, Teaching Methods, and Impact Indicators," *Education and Training* 52(1), 20–47.

Naia, A., R. Baptista, C. Januário, & V. Trigo (2014). "A Systematization of the Literature on Entrepreneurship Education," *Industry and Higher Education* 28(2), 79–96.

NCGE (2004a). "Mapping of Existing Activity to Support Graduate Entrepreneurs," National Council for Graduate Entrepreneurship Report.

NCGE (2004b). "Making the Journey from Student to Entrepreneur: A Review of the Existing Research into Graduate Entrepreneurship," National Council for Graduate Entrepreneurship Report.

Neck, H. M., & P. G. Greene (2011). "Entrepreneurship Education: Known Worlds and New Frontiers," *Journal of Small Business Management* 49(1), 55–70.

Oksanen, K., & P. Ståhle (2013). Physical Environment as a Source for Innovation: Investigating the Attributes of Innovative Space," *Journal of Knowledge Management* 17(6), 815–27.

Parrino, L. (2013). "Coworking: Assessing the Role of Proximity in Knowledge Exchange," *Knowledge Management Research and Practice*, 13(3), 261–71.

Pittaway, L., & J. Cope (2007). "Entrepreneurship Education: A Systematic Review of the Evidence," *International Small Business Journal* 25(5), 477–506.

Pittaway, L., & P. Hannon (2008). "Institutional Strategies for Developing Enterprise Education: A Conceptual Analysis," *Journal of Small Business and Enterprise Development* 15(1), 202–26.

Pittaway, L., R. Aissaoui, M. Ferrier, & P. Mass (2019). "University Spaces for Entrepreneurship: A Process Model," *International Journal of Entrepreneurial Behavior and Research*. DOI: IJEBR-09-2018-0584.

Poole, D., & B. Robertson (2003). "Hunting the Snark or Leading with Purpose? Managing the Enterprise University," *Journal of the Australian and New Zealand Academy of Management* 9(3), 8–24.

Pritchard, S. M. (2008). "Deconstructing the Library: Reconceptualising Collections, Spaces and Services," *Journal of Library Administration* 48(2), 219–33.

Solomon, G. (2007). "An Examination of Entrepreneurship Education in the United States," *Journal of Small Business and Enterprise Development* 14(2), 168-182.

Ulrich, R. S. (1993). "Biophilia, Biophobia, and Natural Landscapes," *The Biophilia Hypothesis*, 7, 73–137.

Ulrich, T. A., & G. S. Cole (1987). "Toward More Effective Training of Future Entrepreneurs," *Journal of Small Business Management* 25(4), 32–9.

Wang, C. L., & H. Chugh (2014). "Entrepreneurial Learning: Past Research and Future Challenges," *International Journal of Management Review* 16(1), 24–61.

Waters-Lynch, J., Potts, J., Butcher, T., Dodson, J., & Hurley, J. (2016). "Coworking: A Transdisciplinary Overview." Working paper.

Westhead, P., D. J. Storey, & F. Martin (2001). "Outcomes Reported by Students Who Participated in the 1994 Shell Technology Enterprise Programme," *Entrepreneurship and Regional Development* 13(2), 163–85.

Wyckham, R. G. (1989). "Ventures Launched by Participants of an Entrepreneurial Education Program," *Journal of Small Business Management* 27(2), 54–61.

4. Ideation techniques and applications to entrepreneurship

Lee Zane and Andrew Zimbroff

INTRODUCTION

While the benefits of brainstorming are well documented, it can be difficult to employ it effectively. It is important to teach this skill to students in an effective manner so that they can use it both in school and in their careers. One particular challenge of teaching brainstorming effectively in formal educational settings is creating the unstructured setting that produces the best brainstorming outcomes. In this chapter, we will introduce various ways to apply brainstorming and other ideation techniques to entrepreneurship applications. We will introduce applications for creating or enhancing products and services that businesses offer, as well as the business frameworks that allow a business to become profitable and grow. We will also provide examples of how it can be introduced in classroom settings that will optimize the efficacy of creative output as well as student learning outcomes.

In teaching and employing the *knowledge* and *skills* necessary to successfully start and lead ventures, we are frequently teaching our students to attempt to solve problems creatively, often in the domain of generating or improving business concepts (products or services), business models, and for other business situations. Ideation is defined as "the capacity for or the act of forming or entertaining ideas" (Merriam-Webster, 2003: p. 616). It is an umbrella term with multiple means of accomplishing its goal. Ideation has been incorporated into Human Centered Design (HCD), a framework developed by the Hasso Plattner Institute of Design at Stanford University. HCD is a feedback-based, iterative framework with the objective of creating products suited for an end user. The HCD process consists of five stages or modes: Empathize, Define, Ideate, Prototype, and Test, which are employed iteratively as the design is developed, tested, and refined. With ideation, the focus is primarily on idea generation with an emphasis on quantity over quality, and so ideation techniques can be used within HCD or as a stand-alone method of solving problems. A commonly used technique for ideation is brainstorming, of which several formats will be discussed below.

What is brainstorming? While some define brainstorming as a group discussion to produce ideas or solve problems, a better definition can be found in the Merriam-Webster's Collegiate Dictionary where it is defined as a "group problem-solving technique that involves the spontaneous contribution of ideas from all members of the group" (2003: p. 150). Alex Osborn (1963) was one of the first to popularize the term brainstorming for use in business applications. His work is also widely referenced when applying ideation techniques in various entrepreneurship settings. He identified four rules for effective brainstorming, summarized here:

- aim for a high quantity of ideas;
- withhold criticism of generated ideas;
- welcome wild ideas; and
- combine and improve ideas.

While brainstorming can be an individual activity, it is most powerful when practiced in small groups to encourage diverse and cumulative thoughts. Furthermore, there is no single "best case" for applying ideation principles. For example, there are many ways to apply Osborn's "Combine and improve ideas" rule – ideas can be shared by a group via email or text message or simply have everyone in the group share their idea. Nevertheless, there are additional ways to build upon shared ideas and the creativity the group process inspires. As an example: imagine a group of five people gets together. Persons A and B share their ideas. Persons C and D take these ideas and offer modifications to make them better. Then E, listening to these original and improved ideas being shared, takes it all in and proposes an idea that synthesizes what was heard from the others, but filtered through the perceptions and cognition of E. Following E's pronouncement, A and B see the idea or solution in a different light, build on that idea, and improve it still further. Therefore, brainstorming is a technique or procedure used by a group of people to encourage creativity, the sharing of ideas, and building upon each other's ideas to problem solve.

APPLICATIONS OF BRAINSTORMING WITHIN ENTREPRENEURSHIP

There are various applications of brainstorming within entrepreneurship practice and teaching. Below we detail several that are commonly used.

Generating Ideas for Products/Services that a Startup will Offer to Customers

Customer research is a crucial part of new business creation and is employed by almost all successful entrepreneurs. Sometimes this customer research will identify a problem or pain point that potential customers are willing to pay a business to solve for them. Ideation methods such as brainstorming can serve as a great complement to these customer research techniques as they can be used to help generate a product or service that fits the desired criteria. Participants can then develop a prototype of a potential product or service, the *solution*, and test it during later stage customer interviews. Hence, it is fruitful to integrate ideation methodology with customer research and other entrepreneurship actions.

Generating Business/Revenue Frameworks

In addition to the creation of products and services that a startup can offer, ideation can be used to develop or enhance business frameworks to make the venture financially sustainable. There are many different business frameworks a new venture can employ, even for the same type of product or service offered. Brainstorming can be employed to generate various business model/revenue frameworks as well as ancillary business concepts which can be later incorporated into the revenue model. It also fits well with methods like the lean or business model canvas, which were designed with the intent of rapidly creating and modifying business frameworks for evolving startups.

Encouraging an Entrepreneurship Mindset in Students

Further, teaching students ideation techniques can have an indirect positive influence on aspiring entrepreneurs; its methodology can help individuals enhance an *entrepreneurial mindset*, which is encouraged for successful entrepreneurship. Design, which entails concepts like ideation and prototyping, is highly iterative and encourages the use of fast, "cheap" trials and exercises. This fits well with lean methodology, which is increasingly used within business creation. There are many similarities between this approach and the Osborn rule, "combine and improve ideas" (Osborn, 1963).

In addition, fear of failure is widely recognized as a deterrent to aspiring entrepreneurs. The Global Entrepreneurship Monitor, as well as others, use it as a metric that is an indicator of future entrepreneurship activity (Harding, Hart, Jones-Evans, & Levie, 2002). Ideation and other design principles can help address this negative mindset. Lean and design thinking are methodologies that encourage the collection of all feedback, including that which is negative, to improve the final concept. Therefore, failure or non-viable concepts are not seen as a bad thing, but as an opportunity for learning and future improvement.

GUIDELINES FOR SUCCESSFUL BRAINSTORMING

Whether in the classroom or business, there are several ways to successfully complete a brainstorming session. Below are some guidelines that can be applied to help ensure successful concept generation.

Initial Stages of Brainstorming

First, it is vital to remember that the ideation process should initially focus purposefully on a *divergent* set of thoughts. Further, it is beneficial to gather as many wild ideas as possible during the initial stages. While later-stage ideation will focus on the *convergent* phase to evaluate the ideas, early on, it is essential to allow all ideas, including those that are close to ridiculous, to have the best possible chance of deriving something brilliant.

Second, building on the work of Osborn (1963) and others, elaborated below are several best practices that the group should do, or encourage, and those they should try not to do. In the "*Do*" category, capture everything, encourage participation, permit clarifying questions, encourage wild ideas, build on the ideas of others, go for volume, be visual, and stay on topic. By this, we mean the following:

Capture everything – Use a whiteboard or flip chart and capture everything, no matter how outlandish it may sound. Every suggestion is written on the board, or Post-it notes and placed on the board, for others to see and build upon.

Encourage participation – To obtain a large quantity of divergent ideas, all group members must be active in ideation functions. Further, it is okay to ask gently those who are not contributing what they think, or whether they would like to add something to the conversation. However, there is no exact procedure for encouraging participation, other than to aim for all team members contributing to the ideation process.

Permit clarifying questions – If a suggestion or idea put forth is ambiguous to one or more members of the group, it is acceptable to ask whether the suggestion applies to say situation A versus situation B, or whether you misunderstood the idea. This type of non-threatening clarifying question permits greater understanding or insight regarding the suggestion without stopping the creative flow.

Encourage wild ideas – When the creative juices flow, sometimes group members will come up with what may seem to be a wild or crazy idea. Encourage the sharing of these wild ideas just as much, if not more than the regular ideas. While the wild or crazy ideas may seem outlandish or not workable, they have the power to ignite additional creativity. It is these types of ideas that get people thinking – "hey, if we tweak this idea, or combine it with another idea, or pull it back just a bit, we may have a workable solution."

Build on the ideas of others – As ideas flow, encourage the building of ideas on other ideas using the "yes and" method where members add features or details to an idea proposed by another. Alternatively, combine details from multiple ideas that have been put forth. Either it is in this space where those wild or crazy ideas start to find a home as others evolve them, or slivers of the wild or crazy ideas are combined with previous or new ideas to generate genuinely great ideas.

Go for volume – Group members can often easily come up with a few ideas, which is a good start. However, these first few ideas are typically generic or safe. Evidence supports the notion that when we stretch ourselves for that fifth, sixth, or tenth idea, we must go outside our comfort zone. We need to think of the wild and crazy ideas mentioned above. This is where the seeds for great ideas come from. So, push the group to go for volume. If the group has identified 40 ideas and is slowing down, consider saying something like, "Let's go for 100 ideas."

Be visual – Whenever possible, draw or sketch the idea to quickly communicate the idea to the group. Visual clues permit others to assess the idea rapidly and perhaps to make additions instantly.

Stay on topic – The brainstorming session was called to solve some problem or issue, and the group needs to keep this topic in mind as they come up with ideas for possible solutions. However, some members of the group may wander from time to time into other areas and so the group leader may need to gently bring the group back to the topic if the brainstorming session is to be a success.

In the "*Should Not Do*" category, try not to evaluate or judge, force participation, allow side conversations, or use a strict round-robin method of suggestions. By this, we mean the following:

Evaluate or judge – This is not the time to evaluate ideas. The first reason is that stopping to evaluate or judge an idea tends to stop the creative process and focuses attention on this particular idea. The second reason is that while a particular idea may not appear to be a viable concept, it may inspire a later idea, or be combined with other ideas to move the needle forward.

Force participation – Encourage, but do not force members to contribute on command. Some team members may be thinking through their idea and may not be ready to contribute at this point. Others are shy about sharing ideas for fear of ridicule – they may need time to watch the process unfold before they are ready to contribute. Still, others observe, contemplate, and contribute when they feel they have something worthy of the discussion.

Side conversations – In the same vein as stay on topic, we cannot allow group members to have side conversations while others are suggesting ideas on the topic. If group members A and B are discussing a topic by themselves, they are not listening or participating in the group session. Likewise, other team members do not benefit from anything said by A and B. In this situation, the team leader needs to bring wayward group members back into the group conversation.

Round robin participation – On the one hand, you do not want to force people to contribute "on demand," but on the other hand, you do not want to force people to wait their turn. An organic process is best, so let everyone shout out their idea (without interrupting others), or add to each other's ideas as concepts pop into their minds.

Building on Initial Ideation

After the initial stage, where the focus is generating a high quantity of ideas, it is time to move to the next phase of brainstorming, which will build on these initial concepts. In this next stage, participants will categorize, eliminate, and analyze generated concepts.

Categorize the ideas – Review and categorize all of the ideas. The group may have produced numerous individual ideas, with many being variations on a theme. To simplify the process of evaluation, start by grouping ideas that are similar in nature.

Eliminate – The ideas that are clearly off topic or will not be approved (for various reasons) are eliminated to permit time and attention to be focused on the remaining ideas.

Analyze – The remaining ideas are analyzed (quickly) to determine which ones should be brought forward for the next steps.

CLASSROOM EXERCISES FOR IDEATION AND BRAINSTORMING

Exercise 1: Ideation Workshop

The following is a systematic one-hour classroom exercise to introduce brainstorming as the ideation portion of a design thinking methodology. At Rowan University, this session is currently led by Andrew Bunoza, a graduate assistant in the entrepreneurship center who helped shape this exercise. At Rowan, teachers schedule a time to bring their class to the entrepreneurship center for this experience.

The moderator's comments are in quotes, possible comments from the students are in italics.

Introduction (five minutes)
"Someone please shout out something random..."

- *Elephant*
- *Crayon*
- *Apple juice*

"So, everyone in this room knows how to have an idea. But – this is surface level. It is much harder to generate ideas with value."

"Ok, what makes an idea valuable?"

[*Note*: Permit students to give suggestions. The moderator can either pick up and add to their suggestions or propose some of the items below.

- Unique or different products and services
- Ten times better than anything before
- Easy to execute
- Multiple positive outcomes.]

"To produce ideas with significant value, we have to understand and consider both the *environment and purpose or goals of the session*. In other words, what is the topic and goal of the brainstorming session? For example, a toy company may be attempting to develop toys for 8–10-year-old musically inclined children, or an auto manufacturer may be seeking to reduce the cost of delivering automobiles from the factory to the dealer, or a hospital may be seeking to increase the quality of life for parents of children in cancer treatment centers.

To have value, the ideas put forth need to be on-topic, and with keeping the goals in mind."

"Why is having lots of valuable ideas available while designing new or improved products and services important to our success?"

[*Note*: Permit students to give suggestions. The moderator can either pick up and add to their suggestions or propose some of the items below.

- Save time and money
- Create better end products
- We can be more productive as a group.]

First activity (ten minutes)
[*Note*: This activity has several objectives: (1) help students understand that not everyone thinks the way they do, (2) that it is ok to disagree or think differently from those around them, (3) get students comfortable with making decisions or choices that visibly differ from those around them, and (4) get students warmed up for the activities to follow.]

"We are going to play a game called *this or that*. I am going to ask a question of the group and direct you to one side of the room, or the other, depending on your answer."

1. "Would you rather be very poor with lots of good friends, or very rich with no friends?"
   Poor with lots of good friends to the right, rich with no friends to the left.
2. "Would you rather control space or time?"
   Ability to control space to the right, control time to the left.
3. "Would you rather be deaf or blind?"
   Deaf to the right, blind to the left.
4. "Would you rather be completely alone for five years, or constantly be surrounded by people and never be alone for five years?"
   Always alone to the right, never alone to the left.

[*Note*: Other question sets may be used in addition to or as substitutes for the above questions (For example: "Would you rather have no hands or no feet?") The point is to provide clear choices, not necessarily easy ones. As the moderator, you may choose to ask the group questions about their choices such as which majors choose right versus left. In addition, you may point out to the group that certain majors chose right versus left on a particular question (i.e., engineers mostly chose one option while arts students chose the other), or that males tended to select one choice while females chose the other.]

Debrief: Inform the group as to the intentions and goals of the exercise. Students need to understand that not everyone thinks the same way they do and that it is ok to disagree or think differently from those around them. We should all feel safe in making decisions or choices that are different from what others decide to say or do. In fact, divergent thinking will make the session much more productive. Hopefully, when we have what we think might be a wild or crazy idea, we will not be afraid to say it out loud.

There is an interesting concept called Psychological Safety. Psychological safety is a shared belief that the team is safe for interpersonal risk-taking (Edmondson, 1999). It can be defined as "being able to show and employ one's self without fear of negative consequences of self-image, status or career" (Kahn, 1990: p. 708). In psychologically safe teams, team members feel accepted and respected.

When going through these exercises, you may be thinking, is what I am about to say going to embarrass me or make me seem unintelligent in this group? As a group, we cannot let this happen. When people feel comfortable in a group, they are more creative, more productive, they grow. And we all benefit.

In order to foster this concept of safety, → we can try these affirmations:

- This person has beliefs, perspectives, and opinions, just like me.
- This person has hopes, anxieties, and vulnerabilities, just like me.
- This person has friends, family, and perhaps children who love them, just like me.
- This person wants to feel respected, appreciated, and competent, just like me.
- This person wishes for peace, joy, and happiness, just like me. (Delizonna, 2017)

Debrief: "Why are we asking/saying these things? → Start With Empathy"

"So now come back to brainstorming. Why is it good to work in groups?"
[*Note*: Permit students to give suggestions. The moderator can either pick up and add to their suggestions or propose a form of the text below.]

It is scientifically proven that in groups, the end result is typically greater than the sum of the individual contributions. What does this mean? Humans have the potential to achieve more in groups than they do working alone! Brainstorming is an important skill to master → it is universally transferable.

Second activity (ten minutes): rapid-fire idea exercise (each round should take three minutes, try two rounds)

Ideation/brainstorming: instructions to the group
"Some rules of effective brainstorming?

1. Stay on topic – I will give each group a topic on which to focus
2. Capture everything on the board
3. Encourage wild ideas – practice yes and, yes and, yes and
4. Defer judgment of ideas
5. Build on the ideas of others
6. One conversation at a time – try not to veer off into multiple simultaneous conversations.
7. Be visual – draw pictures if possible
8. And most of all, go for volume."
   - "Everyone gets a marker and stack of Post-it notes."
   - "Divide into groups of four."
   - "Every group gets a prompt on a piece of paper face down."
   - "The goal is to get as many ideas as possible."
     (a) "Each idea must be unique ("Banana" and "bananas" do not count as two)."
     (b) "Each idea must relate in some defendable way to the prompt."

Sample prompts for groups

1. How to give the best interview of your life
2. How to cook the world's best pizza
3. The perfect cold call sales pitch for pet rocks
4. Construct a lesson plan around group work for kindergarteners
5. Things that do not exist, but they should (please keep this appropriate)
6. Things that exist, but they should not (please keep this appropriate)

Debrief: "Did someone take charge?" "What worked? What did not?" "What questions did you ask yourself?" "What surprised you?" "How many ideas did you identify?"

Round 2: "Now, we will try this again, but let's remove all limits and barriers!"

"What if money was no object?"
"What if you had 1,000 volunteers to help?"
"What if instead of an incremental improvement, we aimed for 10X improvement?"

Debrief: What questions did you ask? Did you notice any difference between the second set of ideas and the first? Why do you think this happened?

"Think about the second set where I told you to remove all limitations – did you come up with more wild and crazy ideas?"

"The interesting fact is that no one actually put any limits on the first time – we do that to ourselves – we need to let ourselves think big and bold."

[*Note*: Depending on what is seen/heard, the moderator may choose to say, "So this is great. Right? We are now all expert idea generators. Let me highlight some of the good things I noticed..."

"We have a responsibility in teams, not only to think and contribute – but also to kindle that fire, that energy that comes from passion. Both in ourselves and our teammates."]

"So, what is moonshot thinking?"

[*Note*: Permit students to give suggestions. The moderator can either pick up and add to their suggestions or propose some of the items below.]

- "Brainstorming UNLEASHED".
- "Being bold – saying the ideas that might make others think you are crazy."
- "Most companies would be happy to improve their core offering/product by 10 percent, but, if you are focused on 10 percent improvements, chances are, you are doing the same thing as the competition, but just a little faster, a little cheaper."
    (a) "So, if you are smart, you're probably not going to fail spectacularly."
    (b) "However, you are also guaranteed not to succeed wildly."

"How can it be easier to make something 10X better than it is to make it 10 percent better?"

[*Note*: Permit students to give suggestions. The moderator can pick up and add to their suggestions, then say, "How? By not playing within the same FRAMEWORK."]

"Oftentimes, by reframing our reality, we can begin to see things differently, creating new things and ideas so new, they do not have the stigmas and imaginary boundaries that people like to place around things." (Studio, 2016)

"Today, we are going to use frameworks to allow our minds to work outside the boundaries of incremental improvements. Today, we are going to think about 10X better."

Third activity (ten minutes) → design sprint
Prompts:

1. Invent a never before futuristic technology
2. How to go from 0 to 1,000 subscribers on YouTube in a day
3. Things cell phones cannot do, but they totally should
4. Design the world's best first date
5. Create the world's best college advice book applicable to anyone
6. Redesign the freshman dorm experience, from roommates to floorplan.

Meta Debrief (five minutes): "Why is brainstorming so powerful?"

[*Note*: Permit students to give suggestions. The moderator can either pick up and add to their suggestions or propose some of the items below.

"It releases us from imaginary boundaries that limit creativity/originality."
"It is more fun!"
"Allows us to DREAM."
"Some things are not as hard as they seem once we work together."]

"How might we create a culture of psychological safety in our own lives/on our teams?"

[*Note*: Permit students to give suggestions. The moderator can either pick up and add to their suggestions or propose some of the items below.

"Be inclusive. (Remember our affirmations)"
"Encourage failure. (BUT debrief, learn from it)"
"Ask lots of questions. (Be curious! NOT judgmental)"
"Have "anxiety parties" (It is okay to be anxious/nervous)"
"Remove the fear. (Call it out – it is okay)"
"Establish accountability. (Empower people to take charge of tasks)"
"Admit to your own mistakes. (Keep yourself accountable)"
"Be available. (The best ability is availability)"]

Please have class submit feedback (five minutes).
Total planned time: 55 minutes.

Teaching notes/observations from the workshop
It is enjoyable to watch the workshop unfold. Without interfering with or usurping the authority of the moderator, walk around the room to ask questions of teams as to how they came up with certain ideas, or offer encouragement,

or cheer them on. Time permitting; groups should announce to the class what concepts or items they came up with. This is always interesting.

The depth and originality of the items each group develops vary, but you will be impressed by students, teams, and what they come up with. This experience not only teaches the concepts of brainstorming but permits students to become comfortable with expressing themselves and working well with those in their group.

Students come out of this session smiling. They had fun, and are pleased with what they accomplished. In addition, they understand the potential for use of these techniques going forward. Interestingly enough, you may notice students leading a brainstorming session with other groups later in their academic life.

Pedagogical use – assuming teams develop an innovative business concept

A suggestion would be to utilize the above workshop in your introductory entrepreneurship class. Consider inserting the workshop after forming multi-functional teams, but before the team chooses their semester project. Also, just prior to the workshop, consider asking each student to develop a "bug" list – students list 25 items that bug them or others and write down several possible solutions for each. Students are instructed to bring their bug list to the brainstorming session.

Rather than random groups, have the assigned teams work together during the workshop. Use the brainstorming workshop to not only teach students how to brainstorm but help them learn about each other and bond as a team. Following this session, the students are now comfortable with sharing ideas and even disagreeing. Depending on the time available for the class, allocate 25–30 minutes at the end of class for the teams to work on choosing their semester project. Instruct students to pull out their bug lists and start collaborating on a problem to solve and/or a business concept for their semester project.

Another benefit of this team-bonding experience is that team leaders start to emerge. Someone or a small group tends to take the lead in writing on the board, leading the group discussion, speaking to the class, and so forth.

Following this class, consider having teams develop a set of rules regarding where and when they will meet to work on the project, how they will communicate with the team, the procedures for making decisions, and name team leader(s).

Exercise 2: Hybrid Brainstorming as an Alternative to Traditional Brainstorming

Teachers will want to introduce brainstorming into the classroom to familiarize students with the methodology and permit its use by students to solve problems. While it is quite easy to explain to students what brainstorming is, and how it works, it is more challenging to get every student to contribute and benefit from the experience. Some students may, for a variety of reasons, be quiet in class. Others may feel insecure about their classroom status or ideas. One method to help with this situation is to modify the brainstorming process to provide students ample warning and time to prepare.

In hybrid brainstorming, group members are given advanced notice of the brainstorming session along with the topic and asked to bring their ideas to the meeting. This procedure permits everyone time to ponder their ideas and develop them. While it does not appear to generate as many wild or crazy ideas, it does permit everyone to participate, a key to classroom exercises. For example, a Monday–Wednesday class may go as follows.

> Monday – The teacher explains the purpose and method of brainstorming, followed by an announcement such as: "Class, on Wednesday we are going to have a brainstorming session. The topic is *The next big non-alcoholic drink*. Everyone should come to class with three to five ideas. After you think of some regular ideas, stretch yourself to come up with some wild or crazy ideas. This is where breakthroughs are made – often when we combine these wild ideas with later iterations. Most of all, have fun with it. I promise you will be surprised by what we will come up with."

> Wednesday – Announce that the brainstorming session will start in a few minutes to give students time to pull out and review their ideas, or for some students actually to write something down. Now you have a choice, you can either let students raise their hand and volunteer ideas for writing on the board, or go round-robin (breaking an earlier rule) to make sure everyone gets an opportunity to contribute. In the classroom setting, we recommend the round-robin method (initially) as this allows every student the opportunity to participate. However, consider starting with a section of the room having students who are relatively vocal in class, thus permitting the quieter students time to see the process unfold and hopefully feel they can contribute. Every suggested idea should be written on the board. Once everyone has had an opportunity to suggest a few ideas, open the floor to additional ideas and combinations of ideas.

By the time the exercise is finished, the board will be filled with ideas. At this point, the teacher can choose to go through the categorization step to show linkages of ideas, but to conserve class time we recommend explaining, rather than performing, the elimination and analysis steps in the classroom.

At this point, it can be instructive to let students know that hybrid brainstorming is very good for business. See below for examples.

Pedagogical use

If you do not have the option to conduct the full brainstorming workshop (described above), please consider using a hybrid brainstorming session in your class. Not only will students gain much of the benefits of learning about brainstorming, but also this method permits every student to prepare for the session and participate. After going through this session in the classroom, students are typically quite pleased both with the plethora of ideas offered and at how many of the ideas are quite good.

Using hybrid brainstorming in business

Many managers and other group leaders have used this method successfully in business. Essentially, the manager or group leader informs a group of employees that we have a task. A meeting is scheduled, the topic or issue is provided, and each member of the group is asked to come armed with three–five ideas as possible solutions for the brainstorming session. The meeting is run as outlined above with the leader or another individual taking notes on a flipchart or board. At the end of the meeting, the ideas are grouped and initial evaluation takes place. The leader should thank all attendees for their contribution.

This method has been used extensively in business – we found it quite useful for developing creative solutions to problems and other issues. These issues are not limited to new products and services – we enlisted various multi-functional teams to brainstorm customer service issues, office procedures, sales presentations, and so much more.

Exercise 3: 6-3-5 Brainwriting

This exercise develops concepts in more depth and takes advantage of iterative group collaboration to generate refined ideas. It is typically done at later stages of the ideation process and builds off initial high-volume concept generation.

The name of the exercise comes from the following:

- 6 participants
- 3 concepts developed per group member per round
- 5 minutes per round.

The exercise is ideally done in a group of six (though this is not required, and groups slightly larger or smaller can be used effectively as well). At the start of the exercise, there is a single prompt or design charge that everyone uses as a reference, and all concepts should focus on this prompt.

For the first round, each group member has a large sheet of paper (11 x 17 works great, though any size greater than 8.5 x 11 will work) divided into thirds. A timer is set for five minutes, and each group member sketches three concepts for the solution on their sheet of paper. This first step provides 18 concepts or variations that will be developed through the exercise.

After the initial five minutes is completed, each member of the group passes their sheet of paper (this works best if all participants are in a circle, and everyone passes their sheet to the left/right). Once everyone has passed their paper, the timer is once again set for five minutes. Now, each participant spends five minutes refining the ideas on the paper in front of them. They can make additions that add details to the initial concept. This step brings a fresh perspective to each concept or variation and allows the group to build off and improve ideas from the first round. After five minutes, the papers are passed and the next round can begin.

This process is then repeated as long as it is beneficial to provide more iterations. While there is no defined number of rounds, typically three–five rounds are optimal for providing the best level of refined concepts. Once all rounds are completed, the groups should spend some time reviewing all concepts. The exercise can conclude with a discussion about what concepts the group likes best and would want to develop or test further.

Teaching notes/observations from the workshop

This exercise receives an overwhelmingly positive response from students when applied in classroom settings. Many participants in this activity find it valuable and effective at generating new concepts. Many also state that they enjoy this process, as it allows them to build off their simple ideas from earlier high-volume, low-detail actions, and go into more depth than with previous design actions. Further, many students enjoy the process – even though they work individually, they still receive feedback on ideas from others in their group, who also propose incremental improvements to the ideas they developed.

Using 6-3-5 Brainwriting in business

This exercise is also widely used in industry for design actions. Small teams will use this technique during the ideate phase of design to come up with potential solution concepts (the exercise is often facilitated by a team leader or manager). Final concepts often contain enough detail to be converted into a prototype for initial testing. Further, it is an effective way to collect input from an entire team in a short period of time. As a result, it remains popular with design teams in industry for creating innovative new products.

CONCLUSION

Ideation and brainstorming can be used to generate a broad range of concepts for a designated design prompt. This can be an effective tool for entrepreneurs who aim to create businesses that solve problems for their customers as well as solving the types of problems that arise in business every day. Subsequently, entrepreneurship programs should consider the incorporation of these concepts as part of a comprehensive entrepreneurship curriculum. This can take the form of the exercises outlined in this chapter, or other embodiments that will effectively combine with other programming and workshops. Educators aiming to introduce ideation to their students should be mindful of Osborn's rules for brainstorming, as well as the best practices mentioned in this chapter when selecting or creating brainstorming exercises for their students.

REFERENCES

Delizonna, L. 2017. High-performing teams need psychological safety. Here's how to create it. *Harvard Business Review*. https://hbr.org/2017/08/high-performing-teams-need-psychological-safety-heres-how-to-create-it

Edmondson, A. 1999. Psychological safety and learning behavior in work teams. *Administrative Science Quarterly*: 350–83.

Harding, R., Hart, M., Jones-Evans, D., & Levie, J. 2002. *Global Entrepreneurship Monitor*. London: London Business School.

Kahn, W. 1990. Psychological conditions of personal engagement and disengagement at work. *Academy of Management Journal*, 33(4): 692–724.

Merriam-Webster, I. 2003. *Merriam-Webster's Collegiate Dictionary*, 11th ed. Springfield, MA: Merriam-Webster.

Osborn, A. F. 1963. *Applied Imagination: Principles and Procedures of Creative Problem Solving*, 3rd ed. New York: Charles Scribner's Sons.

Studio, A. 2016. THINK 10X innovation mindset from Google. *Leadership and Management*. www.slideshare.net/romankotyk/10x-thinking-innovation-mindset-from-google

5. Effectively introducing effectuation into the MBA curriculum

Birton Cowden, Mark Hiatt, James Swaim and Gregory Quinet

INTRODUCTION

The phenomenon of established companies not being equipped to be disruptors is well documented in the literature (Christensen, 1997; Schmidt & Druehl, 2008; Tushman & Anderson, 1986). While scholars debate definitions, measurements, and outcomes of corporate entrepreneurship, firms are on a quest to integrate aspects of this concept into their business strategy and operations. We follow the definition of entrepreneurship as "the process of creating venture and value for multiple constituencies, including, but not limited to customers, employees, communities, and countries" (Matthews, 2018, p. xviii). This intention to create more constituent value within various affected stakeholder groups is derived from either a fear of becoming the next Circuit City or the fear that one of the 400 unicorn startups will make them irrelevant in the future. While they would never use hope as a strategy in their core business, it often appears that these companies are not well equipped in terms of knowledge and capabilities to take necessary actions to launch or acquire something completely new and valuable.

It is from this basis that we wanted to evaluate if we as educators may have the ability to influence future leaders to, at the very least, entertain and evaluate disruptive ideas in a serious manner. More specifically, we wanted to evaluate this from the Masters of Business Administration (MBA) level, as this degree is perceived as the necessary degree for future managers and leaders. It is at the MBA level where we train individuals how to think and make decisions for a company. However, are we training them with updated skills and processes to survive and thrive in the growing uncertainty of today's market? We argue that we as educators can do better. More specifically, we argue that all of the core MBA classes need to incorporate new concepts around how to handle more disruptive ideas and projects within the company.

THE BACKDROP

There is little doubt that markets have become increasingly more complex and uncertain (Hitt & He, 2008; Hitt, Li, & Xu, 2016). Product variety has increased and product lifecycles have decreased (Sabadka, 2013). Entire platforms, that remove many traditional barriers of entry, have been created so that nearly anyone can find necessary inputs, contract manufacturers, and communicate directly with thousands of potential customers. With these lowered barriers of entry (Porter, 1980), there has been a rise of new ventures creating and employing disruptive technology that can provide a serious threat to larger, more established corporations. Rare, extreme examples of this include Airbnb taking on the traditional hospitality chains, Uber and Lyft taking on taxis and now other transportation companies, and Impossible Foods taking on the beef industry. However, this environment produces a lot of uncertainty that is hard to navigate for any decision maker, but is especially difficult for corporations that try to avoid uncertainty. Uncertainty occurs when one is unable to know what are the stakes and what are the possible outcomes (Knight, 1921). With the predominant logic of most firms to remove uncertainty and manage risk, the inability to process and work on uncertain projects further impair existing companies on surviving potential disruptors in their markets.

In conjunction with this, MBA programs have witnessed a recent reduction in applications (Graduate Management Admission Council, 2018). Common complaints about MBA programs surround the idea that traditional methods and frameworks are difficult to enact inside the business with the confluence of macro and micro pressures (Bennis & O'Toole, 2005; Ghoshal, 2005; Podolny, 2009; Trkman, 2019). As stated by Waddock and Lozano (2013) business education is "too narrowly and analytically orienting future managers who will need to lead in a complex, socially and ecologically fraught world, where simple answers just don't work" (p. 265). For some, this has led to a call to transfer from teaching administrators to transformational leaders (e.g., Kuechler & Stedham, 2018). For other programs, the answer to this problem is to get MBAs to adopt an entrepreneurial mindset (McGrath & MacMillan, 2000). However, this concept is defined and taught in many different ways among MBA programs. In a general sense, it is described as the ability to sense, act, and mobilize under uncertain situations and conditions (Bhatia, 2019; Boisot & MacMillan, 2004; Haynie, Shepherd, Mosakowski, & Early, 2010). The logic would follow that if we teach everyone to have an entrepreneurial mindset then future managers will act with a more creative and innovative foundation, enabling the whole company to pursue entrepreneurship goals more successfully. However, is that realistic or even desirable? We argue that it is not, and still does not provide sustainable processes for a company to incorporate disruptive ideas into its current processes.

MORE ENTREPRENEURSHIP COURSES ARE NOT THE ANSWER

Again, with the notion of the desire to teach the entrepreneurial mindset to all, entrepreneurship courses have increasingly been added into the core curriculum for MBA programs, or have been added as electives. Depending on how much entrepreneurship expertise the program has will dictate how much entrepreneurship the degree will offer. Because of this, a student in one program may get one course, while another program may offer several. Drilling even deeper, a focus on corporate entrepreneurship and innovation may be completely absent (in favor of the popularity of the Lean Launchpad), may get a module of one course, or might get a standalone course.

Noticing this gap, a new trend for entrepreneurship education has been to offer a separate masters in entrepreneurship and/or innovation. Such programs are offered at Babson College, Harvard University, University of Florida, University of Southern California, and Indiana University to name a few. While beneficial, these programs vary in the amount of discussion of corporate entrepreneurship and innovation. Additionally, while the number of students has increased in these new programs, traditional MBAs overwhelmingly outnumber them, and are most likely to be the ones making decisions within a firm. Discussions on how to create your own new venture is very different than starting a new, novel project within an existing business and all of the constraints of being inside that business. Thus, having more entrepreneurship courses is not the cure-all for the problem.

We believe the problem can be addressed by focusing on the decision-making models that we teach MBAs. We propose that if we train MBAs on traditional and new decision-making models, we can provide them with tangible tools to evaluate different types of ideas in different environments. We maintain that all the core MBA classes need to add effectual decision-making models along with their existing causal models. We describe below what this means and how a program can go about doing it. First, we need to outline the traditional MBA model and understand how it utilizes causal decision-making models.

THE CURRENT MBA COURSE PARADIGM

In the US alone, nearly 200,000 MBAs graduate each year (Byrne, 2018). Depending on the program, each student takes 36–60 credit hours to graduate.

While there is some variability of courses offered among programs, the core curriculum typically involves the following courses:

- Finance
- Accounting
- Marketing
- Operations/decision management
- Human resources/organizational behavior
- Management/leadership
- Strategic management as the capstone.

In these core courses, students are taught frameworks, philosophies, and equations on how to make solid business decisions. Readings, cases, and expert speakers are all utilized to solidify that these tried-and-true methods have historically worked. In the process, students derive a path forward based on a financial outcome, historical data and knowledge, and the ability to calculate some estimate of a cost/benefit ratio.

This may be a highly appropriate decision-making process a majority of the time, but what if the idea is so new that one cannot calculate potential outcomes? What if there is not proper historical data? When this occurs, it breaks the model for how business decisions are typically made. So, what do rational business decision makers do? Historically speaking, they do not consider those ideas. Why did Blockbuster not acquire Netflix when Netflix made the ask? Why are many novel ideas squashed internally? Why do corporations acquire startups, but find it hard to gain the benefits from what that startup created? In essence, the traditional methods break down under conditions of uncertainty, which is increasingly the conditions most firms have to operate in in today's market.

MBA COURSE DECISION MODEL INSTRUCTION

The decision model that we have taught our MBAs is known as causation or a causal model of decision making. Derived from classic management literature (Drucker, 1985; Fagerberg, 2004; Johne, 1984; Pierce & Delbecq, 1977), it focuses on decision making to achieve a desired outcome. Using causal reasoning, firms engage in new projects only after profitability goals are set and risks are calculated. If this meets the firm's comfort level, it then invests in the means to exploit the perceived opportunity. This model is commonplace within organizations and is imbedded in traditional resource allocation and strategy processes (Burgelman, 1983; Elbanna, 2006; Miles & Snow, 1978). A causal model is based on removing uncertainty and, thus, assumes a fairly predictable future (Welter & Kim, 2018). However, as noted above, many factors in competitive markets have changed over the decades, and the change continues to accelerate. Thus, we may be teaching on a paradigm that needs uncertainty to be as low as possible, but sending our graduates into a world where they are not afforded that luxury. Luckily, there are other ways.

An alternative to causation is effectuation (Sarasvathy, 2001). Managers using effectuation logic assess the means and resources at their disposal and experiment to find positive outcomes that can be created from them. In other words, rather than starting with desired financial outcomes, managers using an effectuation logic determine how existing means and resources can be reconfigured to create new solutions. Unlike causation, effectuation assumes uncertain, dynamic environments, where future states are not predetermined (Sarasvathy, 2008). Using this approach, decision makers start with accesible resources rather than established market goals (i.e., 10 percent market share increase). The effectuation process begins with the firm asking, "Who are we? What do we know? Who do we know?" (Sarasvathy, 2001). If decisions start with the end goal, then the traditional strategic planning processes take hold (Brinkmann, Grichnik, & Kapsa, 2010), which lead to predictable outcomes. Starting with the means, however, requires those going through the process to alleviate themselves of path and resource dependency (Langlois, 2007), and evaluate their means and resources in a new light to move towards a new future state (Sarasvathy, 2008). Effecutation provides potential solutions in new markets not within the the firm's current core, or potentially disruptive solutions within its core (Fisher, 2012). However, if we are not teaching our MBAs effectual decision making, along with the causal decison making, and when it might be appropriate to use each, there is little hope that effectuation will be adopted inside companies.

THE FOUR ELEMENTS OF EFFECTUATION

While some pedagogical artifacts are beginning to emerge (see effectuation. org), we wanted to take this a step further to show how effectuation can be added to the core curriculum. This can be demonstrated by diving deeper into the elements of effectuation. Effectuation includes four elements: flexibility, short-term experimentation, affordable loss, and pre-commitments and alliances (Chandler, DeTienne, McKelvie, & Mumford, 2011; Dew, Sarasvathy, Read, & Wiltbank, 2009; Sarasvathy & Dew, 2005).

Flexibility

With effectuation, firms remain flexible in that market contingencies and surprises are outlets for opportunities to turn "lemons into lemonade" (Sarasvathy, Kumar, York, & Bhagavatula, 2014). This flexibility gives the firm the capability to not be beholden to a plan, and makes it acceptable for the project to pivot as the opportunity arises (Brush, Edelman, & Manolova, 2015).

Experimentation

Another aspect of effectuation, short-term experimentation, allows firms to test different combinations of means in new ways to gain information about what outcomes might happen. In contrast, full product launch procedures would most typically require a firm to do full due diligence on the calculable potential market, establish a full project plan with corresponding team, budget, and production schedule, and go to market with a sizable marketing push. However, with short-term experiments, the firm can reduce its uncertainty by testing certain elements in small batches to see how the market may respond before putting time and money into the project.

Affordable Loss

In conjunction with these experiments, another element of effectuation involves the use of affordable loss instead of determining calculated gains in known markets. Affordable loss allows the firm to decide how much it is willing to spend in time and money on the short-term experiments or the entire endeavor (Dew et al., 2009). By establishing affordable loss, the firm can gain information about the value of a new initiative without fear of affecting other aspects of the business. Should all of these experiements fail, the firm should not be in a dire financial position, and may even be in a better position moving forward due to the knowledge it gained from those experiments. Once the budget allows for more experimentation, this prior knowledge might lead to a fruitful opportunity (Shane, 2000).

Alliances

Lastly, effectuation calls for pre-commitments from customers and alliances with key stakeholders to further control the future state (Sarasvathy, 2008). This forces more to have "skin in the game" of the emerging opportunity, and increases the spread of means needed to force a potential paradigm shift. Through these partnerships, a firm will be better positioned to capitalize on environmental contigencies when they occur rather than being focused on competitive dynamics and insular means, as its network may provide the necessary resources to exploit a newly defined opportunity (Read, Song, & Smit, 2009).

PRACTICAL CONSIDERATIONS WHEN INTRODUCING EFFECTUATION INTO A TRADITIONAL MBA PROGRAM

In concept, a wide range of effectuation instruction can be adopted within an existing or future MBA curriculum. As the university sub-unit generally responsible for managing an MBA program, and from a strategic decision-making process, a business college can: (1) support a more traditional master's level business program, (2) opt to develop one that is completely oriented towards effectuation skill development, or (3) pursue the development of a program that intermixes both models, which is believed to be how most decisions are made (Fisher, 2012). Practically, with the large number of existing MBA programs, some initial level of introduction of effectuation into the base curriculum probably makes the most sense. The primary question is: How best to acccomplish a somewhat gradual introduction of effectuation into the more standard MBA core curriculum?

Change to established educational curricula is best accomplished in a step-wise and careful manner (Richards-Wilson, 2002). Many reasons exist for a carefully thought-out change management process in academic programs, which include: accreditation requirements, attractiveness to potential student customers, and acceptance by faculty (Richards-Wilson, 2002). A business college contemplating some level of indoctrination of effectuation principles can start with the four basic principles of effectuation and carefully modify existing learning objectives with core and elective courses to expose MBA students to a new decision-making paradigm. Based on an incremental approach to introduce effectuation alongside causation in MBA courses, we provide suggestions on how programs could introduce or add effectuation into existing core courses.

Managing and Leading

One example could involve the introduction to management course within many MBA programs. Typically, the differences between managing and leading organizations is investigated. The practice of management is generally demonstrated to be the maintenance of the status quo, in that current systems, processes, and procedures that are useful to the overall mission and vision of the organization are retained. Leading, or the practice of leadership can involve creating positive changes within the organization (Kent, 2005). Many managers overemphasize the administrative aspects of their position by focusing extensively on planning, organizing, leading, and control. Their relationships with others are characterized by a series of transactions, often not producing desired results in terms of expected outcomes and employee well-being. Bass (1990) argues for an adoption of transformation leadership as a replacement for transactional. Transformational leadership can be operationalized horizontally (working with peers) and vertically (working with superiors and subordinates). It is through non-transactional leadership where effectual decision making becomes a more viable process that is acceptable within the company. A more effectuation-oriented approach in this type of coursework would demonstrate the flexibility and experimentation of a more non-transactional approach to leading an organization.

Operations/Decision Management

Paralysis by analysis is frequently a result of over-rationalized planning. It occurs when individuals are overwhelmed by a barrage of information and options that are difficult to process and rely on to make decisions. Organizational and technical forces contribute to paralysis, including over-professionalizing a planner's job, unqualified acceptance and misapplication of premises, the drive for administrative efficiency, and excessive emphasis on decisions based on quantification (Lenz & Lyles, 1985). However, many fear the opposite of analysis, which is making decisions based on instinct (Langley, 1995). By teaching MBA students the effectual process, one can see an alternative path from too much analysis that at best leads to incremental innovation, with more discipline and rigor than intuition. Operations classes should study experimentation within companies, how to operationalize alliances with these experimentations, and how to operationalize an affordable loss-type budget. Of course, decision-making models should incorporate the elements of effectuation.

Accounting and Risk Management

The effectuation component of experimentation and affordable loss can directly apply to graduate-level business courses in accounting. MBA students could learn that the periodic budgeting process can be recast to include considerations for the allocation of resources towards various "projects" that can be pursued with the initial intent of open investigation into perceived business opportunities for the organization. Additionally, too often, risk is viewed as something negative to be avoided. There is frequently a focus on expected outcomes and appropriate controls to achieve these outcomes. However, in the process, potential upsides (positive risks/opportunity management) are ignored or not even identified. Research finds that many practitioners use a reactive versus proactive approach to risk management (Lehtiranta, 2014). While awareness of risk as a threat is important, so too is the recognition that risks can provide opportunities leading to a competitive advantage (Hillson,

2016). As it relates to effectuation, risk management courses should increase their emphasis on positive risk, which provides a pathway for the company to be more flexible and take advantage of market contingencies, instead of being paralyzed by them in the fear of what might go wrong.

Marketing

Graduate-level marketing courses can be an excellent subject area to extend effectuation principles, especially with respect to flexibility, experimentation, and alliances. Consider the major components of the customer interaction process, that being marketing (or more directly market segmentation), advertising, and sales. A higher focus on teaching an experimentation methodology during the customer discovery process (Blank, 2013) can expose students to a means by which the potential list of target market customers can expand. In this manner, a firm is better posititioned to explore opportunities that add new markets or businesses to its portfolio, as the effectuation process allows for uncertainty and the unknown. The use of short-term experimentation particularly in firms that conduct business activities in constantly changing markets, like the digital media industry, can provide more opportunities for effective advertising to formerly unknown potential customers (Rohrbeck, Günzel, & Uliyanova, 2012).

Human Resources/Organizational Behavior

Two direct areas in which effectuation can be introduced to MBA students involve organizational design and the talent attraction, hiring, and retention process. Designing organizations or parts thereof that can take advantage of effectuation principles, particularly in terms of flexibility of the organizational sub-structure, can significantly support an effectuation mindset. Establishing a self-managed division or department with a mission to experiment with various undefined products and/or services owned by the larger corporate organization can have a significant impact on the overall firm's bottom line. These "effectuated" teams would have direct relationships with virtually all of the organization's functional areas (read alliances), in that they could almost exist as a highly reactive or responsive matrix unit, moving in and out of various types of relationships with the more typical organizational functions. Showing MBA students how this type of organizational structure can first be designed within a more traditional form, then second, demonstrating how such an effectuated unit can co-exist with this same form, can provide the students with a viable organizational structure option. Further, hiring the correct employees to staff such a unit or division would be quite important and would determine its long-term success and viability (da Costa & Brettel, 2011). MBA students could discover the types of skills and abilities that would generally allow a new employee to materially contribute to the mission and vision of the effectuated team. Additionally, showing the student cohort how to retain these different types of employees, that is, determining what motivates them and might further encourage them to remain with the organization for a period of time. While a significant task or undertaking, staffing the new team with the proper personnel that are aware of and support the process of effectuation will be key to the success of this unit.

Project Management

While traditional methods of project management tend to be causation-oriented and -derived, other methods are moving away from this method and process. The Agile project management process allows anyone responsible for time-dependent actions to adapt and change their orientation depending on the circumstances presented at the time. Agile rejects rigid, more formal linear, or sequential development methods in favor of a more adaptive approach (Augustine, Payne, Sencindiver, & Woodcock, 2005). In corporate business models that have become increasingly collaborative, globally oriented, and subject to constant change, project management methods that embrace this type of perspective are becoming more predominate (Fernandez & Fernandez, 2008). Exposing MBA students to the altered process of more effectuation-oriented project management techniques can greatly prepare them for business environments that exist within markets that are in constant flux (Venkatagiri, 2011).

Strategy

Traditional MBA course content typically teaches that the strategic process begins at the upper levels in most organizations, with mid- and lower-level managers participating in this process to one degree or another (Wooldridge, Schmid, & Floyd, 2008). With strategic management, students are typically taught about strategies at different levels of the company, and how to enact them given an assumed goal of growth. Effectuation is another pathway for this growth, but is hard to capture in a simulation or certain case studies, especially if the student is not trained to approach the problem in that manner. Through the effectuation lens, strategy can become a dynamic capability and result in sustainable competitive advantages. Thus, it is in the capstone course where the ideas of effectuation taught in the other courses should come together and be taught in full to show how these elements are practical and appropriate in certain circumstances when enacting the company's strategy. To further this point as well as the outcomes derived from the differences in causation and effectuation, instructors could provide a case study and have half the class analyze with a causal model, and the other half with an effectual model.

By adding effectuation to the core curriculum, this will elevate effectuation to be on equal footing with causal models. If we can teach our students that effectuation is part of the norm and a legitimate model to use when dealing with uncertain variables, then we have a chance to make effectuation part of various companies' dominant logic (Prahalad & Bettis, 1986). Once it becomes part of the dominant logic, a company can translate that into real actions, such as structuring decision making and approvals for new ideas and how to budget for such projects. This helps the company become more comfortable with the process and allows its entrepreneurship efforts to have boundaries and processes like every other aspect of the company. This may open the "black box" of corporate entrepreneurship (Sirmon, Hitt, & Ireland, 2007), all while not holding to the idea that everyone in the company should be creative, innovative, and pursue entrepreneurship activities. If we do our part and are successful at it, then we believe that we may be able to influence future leaders of corporations to have the tools to be disruptive.

CONCLUSION

Given the aforementioned information, it is clear that traditional MBA programs can benefit from increased levels of relevance to conditions that future managers face in the business world. In addition to existing causal models, students need to adopt new tools to survive and thrive in conditions of uncertainty. We propose that one path forward for this is to incorporate effectuation into the core MBA courses. Instructors can facilitate effectuation by introducing scenario building grounded in uncertainty and difficult-to-predict outcomes.

Our conceptual treatment and recommendations for including effectuation in an MBA program can benefit from empirical investigation. Future research should empirically explore our proposal and add to it to understand the contextual elements that matter most in this relationship. This approach can be piloted first in a single MBA program on an exploratory basis and later expanded to several MBA programs to determine similarities and differences. Based on the temporal elements of these relationships, the ideal data would derive from a panel study over several years to not only note the pedagogical variables of the student's learning, but also how this knowledge got transferred to his/her organization, and the impact that had for the organization. Thus, the ultimate outcome would be to demonstrate that changes to our courses positively impacted organizational behavior to thrive under uncertainty.

REFERENCES

Augustine, S., Payne, B., Sencindiver, F., & Woodcock, S. (2005). Agile project management: Steering from the edges. *Communications of the ACM, 48*(12), 85–9.

Bass, B. M. (1990). From transactional to transformational leadership: Learning to share the vision. *Organizational Dynamics, 18*(3), 19–31.

Bennis, W., & O'Toole, J. (2005). How business schools have lost their way. *Harvard Business Review, 83*(5), 96–104.

Bhatia, A. K. (2019). Fostering an entrepreneurial mindset in selective MBA programs. Dissertation, University of Pennsylvania.

Blank, S. (2013). Why the lean startup changes everything. *Harvard Business Review, 91*(5), 63–72.

Boisot, M., & MacMillan, I. C. (2004). Crossing epistemological boundaries: Managerial and entrepreneurial approaches to knowledge management. *Long Range Planning, 37*(6), 505–24.

Brinkmann, J., Grichnik, D., & Kapsa, D. (2010). Should entrepreneurs plan or just storm the castle? A meta-analysis on contextual factors impacting the business planning–performance relationship in small firms. *Journal of Business Venturing, 25*, 24–40.

Brush, C. G., Edelman, L. F., & Manolova, T. S. (2015). To pivot or not to pivot: Why do nascent ventures change their business models? *Frontiers of Entrepreneurship Research, 35*(1), 3.

Burgelman, R. A. (1983). A process model of internal corporate venturing in the diversified major firm. *Administrative Science Quarterly, 28*(2), 223–44.

Byrne, J. A. (2018). The alarming decline of the MBA's "value added ratio." Retrieved November 13, 2019, from https://poetsandquants.com/2018/03/21/the-alarming -decline-of-the-mbas-value-added-ratio/

Chandler, G. N., DeTienne, D., McKelvie, A., & Mumford, A. (2011). Causation and effectuation processes: A validation study. *Journal of Business Venturing, 26*, 375–90.

Christensen, C. M. (1997). *The Innovator's Dilemma.* New York: HarperCollins Publishing.

da Costa, A. F., & Brettel, M. (2011). Employee effectuation: What makes corporate employees act like entrepreneurs? *Frontiers of Entrepreneurship Research, 31*(17), 2.

Dew, N., Sarasvathy, S. D., Read, S., & Wiltbank, R. (2009). Affordable loss: Behavioral economic aspects of the plunge decision. *Strategic Entrepreneurship Journal, 3*, 105–26.

Drucker, P. (1985). *Innovation and Entrepreneurship: Practice and Principles.* New York: Harper and Row.

Elbanna, S. (2006). Strategic decision-making: Process perspectives. *International Journal of Management Reviews, 8*(1), 1–20.

Fagerberg, J. (2004). Innovation: A guide to the literature. In J. Fagerberg, D. Mowery, & R. R. Nelson (eds), *The Oxford Handbook of Innovation* (pp. 1–26). Oxford: Oxford University Press.

Fernandez, D. J., & Fernandez, J. D. (2008). Agile project management: Agilism versus traditional approaches. *Journal of Computer Information Systems, 49*(2), 10–17.

Fisher, G. (2012). Effectuation, causation, and bricolage: A behavioral comparison of emerging theories in entrepreneurship research. *Entrepreneurship Theory and Practice, 36*(5), 1019–51.

Ghoshal, S. (2005). Bad management theories are destroying good management practices. *Academy of Management Learning and Education, 4*(1), 75–91.

Graduate Management Admission Council (2018). Application trends survey report 2018. Retrieved November 13, 2019, from www.gmac.com/-/media/files/gmac/research/admissions-and-application-trends/gmac-application-trends-survey-report-2018.pdf

Haynie, J. M., Shepherd, D., Mosakowski, E., & Early, P. C. (2010). A situated metacognitve model of the entrepreneurial mindset. *Journal of Business Venturing, 25*(2), 217–29.

Hillson, D. (2016). *The Risk Management Handbook: A Practical Guide to Managing the Multiple Dimensions of Risk.* London: Kogan Page.

Hitt, M. A., & He, X. (2008). Firm strategies in a changing global competitive landscape. *Business Horizons, 51*, 363–9.

Hitt, M. A., Li, D. D., & Xu, K. (2016). International strategy: From local to global and beyond. *Journal of World Business, 51*, 58–73.

Johne, F. A. (1984). How experienced product innovators organize. *Journal of Product Innovation Management, 4*(12), 210–23.

Kent, T. W. (2005). Leading and managing: It takes two to tango. *Management Decision, 43*(7/8), 1010–17.

Knight, F. (1921). *Risk, Uncertainty and Profit.* Boston, MA: Houghton Mifflin.

Kuechler, W., & Stedham, Y. (2018). Management education and transformational learning: The integration of mindfulness in an MBA course. *Journal of Management Education, 42*(1), 8–33.

Langley, A. (1995). Between "paralysis by analysis" and "extinction by instinct." *Sloan Management Review, 36*, 63.

Langlois, R. N. (2007). The entrepreneurial theory of the firm and the theory of the entrepreneurial firm. *Journal of Management Studies, 44*(7), 1107–24.

Lehtiranta, L. (2014). Risk perceptions and approaches in multi-organizations: A research review 2000–2012. *International Journal of Project Management, 32*(4), 640–53.

Lenz, R., & Lyles, M. A. (1985). Paralysis by analysis: Is your planning system becoming too rational? *Long Range Planning, 18*(4), 64–72.

Matthews, C. H. (2018). Preface: Three key challenges to advancing entrepreneurship education and pedagogy. In C. H. Matthews & E. W. Liguori (eds), *Annals of Entrepreneurship Education and Pedagogy* (Vol. 3). Cheltenham, UK and Northampton, MA, USA: Edward Elgar Publishing.

McGrath, R. G., & MacMillan, I. C. (2000). *The Entrepreneurial Mindset: Strategies for Continuously Creating Opportunity in an Age of Uncertainty.* Cambridge, MA: Harvard Business School Press.

Miles, R. E., & Snow, C. C. (1978). *Organizational Strategy, Structure, and Process.* Stanford, CA: Stanford Univerity Press.

Pierce, J. L., & Delbecq, A. L. (1977). Organization structure, individual attitudes and innovation. *Academy of Management Review, 2*(1), 27–37.

Podolny, J. M. (2009). The buck stops (and starts) at business school. *Harvard Business Review, 87*(6), 62–7.

Porter, M. E. (1980). *Competitive Strategy: Techniques for Analyzing Industries and Competitors.* New York: Free Press.

Prahalad, C. K., & Bettis, R. A. (1986). The dominant logic: A new linkage between diversity and performance. *Strategic Management Journal, 7*(6), 485–501.

Read, S., Song, M., & Smit, W. (2009). A meta-analytic review of effectuation and venture performance. *Journal of Business Venturing, 24*(6), 573–87.

Richards-Wilson, S. (2002). Changing the way MBA programs do business: Lead or languish. *Journal of Education for Business, 77*(5), 296–300.

Rohrbeck, R., Günzel, F., & Uliyanova, A. (2012). Business model innovation: The role of experimentation. Paper presented at the R&D Management Conference.

Sabadka, I. D. (2013). Impacts of shortening product life cycle in the automotive industry. *Transfer Inovacil, 29*, 251–3.

Sarasvathy, S. D. (2001). Causation and effectuation: Towards a theoretical shift from economic inevitability to entrepreneurial contingency. *Academy of Management Review, 26*(2), 243–88.

Sarasvathy, S. D. (2008). *Effectuation: Elements of Entrepreneurial Expertise. New Horizons in Entrepreneurship Research.* Cheltenham, UK and Northampton, MA, USA: Edward Elgar Publishing.

Sarasvathy, S. D., & Dew, N. (2005). New market creation as transformation. *Journal of Evolutionary Economics, 15*(5), 533–65.

Sarasvathy, S. D., Kumar, K., York, J. G., & Bhagavatula, S. (2014). An effectual approach to international entrepreneurship: Overlaps, challenges, and provocative possibilities. *Entrepreneurship Theory and Practice, 38*(1), 71–93.

Schmidt, G. M., & Druehl, C. T. (2008). When is a disruptive innovation disruptive? *Journal of Product Innovation Management, 25*(4), 347–69.

Shane, S. (2000). Prior knowledge and the discovery of entrepreneurial opportunities. *Organization Science, 11*(4), 448–69.

Sirmon, D. G., Hitt, M. A., & Ireland, R. D. (2007). Managing firm resources in dynamic environments to create value: Looking inside the black box. *Academy of Management Review, 32*(1), 273–92.

Trkman, P. (2019). Value proposition of business schools: More than meets the eye. *International Journal of Management Education, 17*(3), 100310.

Tushman, M. L., & Anderson, P. (1986). Technological discontinuities and organizational environments. *Administrative Science Quarterly, 31*(3), 439–65.

Venkatagiri, S. (2011). Teach project management, pack an agile punch. Paper presented at the 2011 24th IEEE-CS Conference on Software Engineering Education and Training.

Waddock, S., & Lozano, J. M. (2013). Developing more holistic management education: Lessons learned from two programs. *Academy of Management Learning and Education, 12*(2), 265–84.

Welter, C., & Kim, S. (2018). Effectuation under risk and uncertainty: A simulation model. *Journal of Business Venturing, 33*, 100–16.

Wooldridge, B., Schmid, T., & Floyd, S. W. (2008). The middle management perspective on strategy process: Contributions, synthesis, and future research. *Journal of Management, 34*(6), 1190–221.

6. "Aha, so that's how you see it!" Educators' experiences of using a visual exercise as a student-centered educational approach

Katarina Ellborg

INTRODUCTION

The last few decades have seen a comprehensive increase in entrepreneurship education in higher education, especially in Europe and the United States. Entrepreneurship has become more and more commonplace as a learning content in various educations, both inside as well as outside business schools (Béchard & Grégoire, 2005; Blenker, Korsgaard, Neergaard, & Thrane, 2011; Fayolle, 2018; Kuratko, 2005; Matlay & Carey, 2007; Matthews & Liguori, 2019; Neck & Corbett, 2018; Solomon, 2007). The development has in turn led to challenges with regard to content and target groups. This chapter sheds light on how visual artifacts play a role in didactic analysis in order to approach students' contemporary meaning of entrepreneurship in the beginning of the learning process.

Entrepreneurship Education with Various Objectives and Target Groups

Parallel to the spread of entrepreneurship courses beyond business schools, the subject has progressed from a relatively narrow focus on business matters to encompassing general development processes in a number of sectors (Gibb, 2002). Entrepreneurship education has also come to include both theoretical knowledge about entrepreneurship as well as the aim to reinforce students' entrepreneurship skills and attitudes (Kyrö, 2015; Samwel Mwasalwiba, 2010). Current entrepreneurship education is therefore partially supposed to encourage more students to start their own businesses, but also to fill the students with skills such as creativity, innovation, and the ability to handle risks

(Blenker, Trolle Elmholdt, Hedeboe Frederiksen, Korsgaard, & Wagner, 2014; European Commission, 2006; Fayolle & Gailly, 2008; Tapio, 2004).

The increased complexity in entrepreneurship education in terms of objectives and target groups has contributed to the entrepreneurship field showing a growing interest in educational science (Fayolle, 2018; Gabrielsson, Landström, Politis, & Hägg, 2018). An increase in research conducted at the intersection between entrepreneurship and educational science can also be noticed (Blenker, Dreisler, Færgemann, & Kjeldsen, 2008; Matthews & Liguori, 2019). However, as entrepreneurship education is continuously becoming more widespread throughout different disciplinary domains, the value of retrieving additional knowledge from educational science is advocated in the field (Byrne, Fayolle, & Toutain, 2014; Fayolle, 2018; Gabrielsson et al., 2018). Recent studies are especially highlighting the need for deeper knowledge about students' pre-understandings, and the involvement of students as co-creators in the learning process (Liguori et al., 2018; Robinson, Neergaard, Tanggaard, & Krueger, 2016).

Neck and Corbett (2018) are among the entrepreneurship education researchers who stress these arguments. They request teachers that are able to "meet learners where they are" (p. 26) by connecting the subject matter with students' points of departure. In the same vein, Fayolle, Verzat, and Wapshott (2016, p. 898) advocate awareness about the relationship between students' pre-understandings and learning content, to detect "the misrepresentations and erroneous beliefs that must be dispelled to enable entrepreneurial reasoning." Likewise, Nabi, Liñán, Fayolle, Krueger, and Walmsley (2017) show how such a student-centered perspective supports and facilitates the learning process. Considering students' preconceptions has also been suggested in several previous studies as a feasible way for teachers to introduce entrepreneurship to students with diverse experiences of the phenomenon (for example, Hynes, 1996; Jones, 2013; Kyrö, 2015; Lepistö & Ronkko, 2013; Williams Middleton & Donnellon, 2014).

Students' Contemporary Meanings of Entrepreneurship

The interest in students' pre-understandings that characterizes the entrepreneurship education field follows general developments in modern adult-learning research. Here, experiences and pre-understandings brought into the classroom by the learners are termed *students' contemporary meaning* (Gudmundsdottir, Reinertsen, & Nordtømme, 1999). Already in 1973, Knowles – recognized as the father of adult learning theory – advocated an educational approach that "relates to and makes use of the experience of the learners" (p. 71). In 1988, Marton and Ramsden (1988, p. 272) describe educators' "emphasis on students' conceptions and preconceptions, and learning about students thinking" as "the key that will unlock the door to better teaching and course design." Contemporary voices also claim that the most central thing in adult learning is that the teachers take advantage of students' pre-understandings (Samson, 2015). Students' contemporary meaning is thus underscored within educational science in general (Ramsden, 1988) and in entrepreneurship education in particular.

It is, however, not always obvious *how* teachers should visualize or give space to students' contemporary meanings. This is especially true for university educators, who might have more experiences of their specific subject matter than of applying student-centered education in their classrooms (Prosser & Trigwell, 1999). Such circumstances are for example described in a study of new academics (Sadler, 2012, p. 738), where they declared that they lack knowledge about "how to ask questions to check the students' understanding; how to monitor and manage student interactions and behaviour; and how to design tasks that achieve the aim of a specific session."

Exploring the How with a Didactical Perspective and a Visual Exercise

This study elaborates on these *how*-questions by applying a didactical perspective to examine the potential of a visual exercise as a way for educators to generate insight into students' contemporary meaning of entrepreneurship. This has been done by exploring teachers' experiences (Prosser & Trigwell, 1999) of the visual exercise *Images of entrepreneurship*, developed for introductory sessions in entrepreneurship education (Ellborg, 2018). *Images of entrepreneurship* is further described in the method section below. The study is hence methodologically based in the visual field, because it reviews a visual method intended to capture students' pre-understandings (Holm, 2008).

The work is theoretically based in educational science, more specifically in *didactics*, since it suggests Klafki's didactic analysis as a theoretical framework. Didactics (from the German *Didaktik*) is a sub-discipline in pedagogy that "provides teachers with ways of considering the essential what, how, and why questions around their teaching of their students in their classrooms" (Westbury, 2000, p. 36). In addition, the study applies an extended didactic triangle, as an analytical tool to discuss visual artifacts' interaction with the relations between students, the subject, and the teacher.

Altogether, this study follows research streams where theories from the educational field meet entrepreneurship in educational settings, with an emphasis on students' perspectives (Brush, Neck, & Greene, 2015; Fox, Pittaway, & Uzuegbunam, 2018; Neck, Greene, & Brush, 2014), reflections (Hägg & Kurczewska, 2016), and emotions (Lackéus, 2016). The study contributes to this area in a theoretical sense by discussing didactical constructs in entrepreneurship education, and in a practical sense by exploring teachers' different ways of understanding a specific didactic situation (Marton & Booth, 1997; Sadler, 2012; Teerijoki & Murdock, 2014).

The question dealt with is

> How do entrepreneurship educators experience the use of a visual exercise as a student-centered educational approach?

The study is based on interviews with entrepreneurship educators and the unit of analysis is the educators' experiences. Since the study concerns students' pre-understanding of entrepreneurship in the beginning of a learning process, it thus differs from earlier studies on entrepreneurship educators' experiences that focus on assessments and learning outcomes, rather than students' contemporary meaning (for example, Deacon & Harris, 2011; Fayolle, Gailly, & Lassas-Clerc, 2006; Honig, 2004; Pittaway & Edwards, 2012).

The text is structured as follows. First, didactics is described with a focus on student-centered learning. The didactic analysis is presented as a theoretical framework followed by a presentation of an extended didactic triangle, whereafter the potential of visual material in education and research is discussed. Then, the visual exercise is outlined, together with a description of the methodology. Finally, the interviews with teachers are presented and discussed in relation to the extended didactic triangle, and conclusions are made about the visual exercise's potential as part of a didactic analysis.

THEORETICAL FRAMEWORK

Didactics and Student-Centered Education

Didactics is a general theory for education and learning, with roots in German pedagogical research. Didactics comprises dimensions of objective, content, and method as well as discussions on how education can address a diversity of students in order to promote learning (Hopmann, 1997; Klafki, 1995). Hudson and Schneuwly describe teachers' didactic work as "systematic reflection about how to organize teaching in a way that brings about the individual growth of the student." The authors further highlight that "this means that subject matters can open up different educative meanings for learners" (2007, pp. 106–7). Learning in such a student-centered approach is in Jarvis' (2012, p. 87) words: "the transformative outcome from our experience...starting from what we already know." Jarvis' point of view in turn goes back to the knowledge theorist Piaget, whose interpretation of a learning process was that students acquire new knowledge by relating it to already conquered knowledge and to their own pre-understanding (Piaget, 1964).

A student-centered learning process thus requires "an act of imagination through which the teacher first envisages the subject from the students' perspective, and then devises ways of helping the students across the initial gulf of incomprehension which separates them from the discourse of the discipline or profession" (Entwistle & Walker, 2002, p. 22). Gaining insight into students' pre-understanding is also described as especially important in higher education because "the adult is a rich resource for learning because of the widely varying uniqueness of his experiences" (Newton, 1977, p. 362). Knowles (1973, p. 46) advises teachers to use "experiential techniques which tap the experience of the learners and involve them in analyzing their experience." Likewise, Klafki recommends teachers to always organize learning so that the students' pre-understandings become visible and thus contribute to the design of the educational setting (Gudmundsdottir et al., 1999; Klafki, 1995, 1997). In order to set the learning content in relation to students' everyday lives Klafki developed a didactic analysis (Klafki, 1958, 1995).

The Didactic Analysis

Klafki's didactic analysis is a way to guide teachers in a more student-centered direction, focusing on the learners' interests, questions, and attitudes in relation to the learning content (Gudmundsdottir et al., 1999; Klafki, 1995, 1997). The analysis is intended to be a model for the teachers to plan their education (Uljens, 2004). Together the questions in the analysis cover the contemporary and future meanings of the content from a student perspective, but also what wider reality the content exemplifies, how the content can be structured, and what pedagogical representations are suitable to use. When introducing new content, Klafki suggests that the teacher begins by asking whether the subject is familiar to the learner and what experiences the students already have (or do not have) of the subject matter being covered in the syllabus. In the didactic analysis, Klafki (1995, p. 24) formulates this initial question as: "From which angles do the students already have access to the topic?"

As this particular study evaluates and discusses an introductory exercise exploring students' contemporary meaning of entrepreneurship, it lends itself well for using the initial question in Klafki's analysis. According to Klafki, detected contemporary meaning can later form the basis for the analyses of future meaning, content structure, examples, and pedagogical representation – although such analyses are beyond the scope of this study.

In addition to serving as a planning model, the didactic analysis is also a suitable theoretical construct when examining teaching practices. Gudmundsdottir et al. (1999, p. 560) write, "when Didactic analysis is used as a research instrument, teachers are invited to systematically tell about what they have done, and why." This study follows both the original intent with the analysis as well as the suggestion made by Gudmundsdottir et al., since it considers the learners' preconception about the learning content by examining the teachers' experiences of a specific didactic situation.

The Didactic Triangle

In didactics, the interdependent relations between the teacher and the subject matter, between the teacher and the students, and between the students and the subject matter, are usually illustrated as a triangle (Herbert, 2018; Hudson, 2007; Kansanen & Meri, 1999; Künzli, 2000; see Figure 6.1). In the triangular model the *teacher–subject* relation involves educators' decisions on learning content and reflects a research-based understanding of the subject. The *teacher–student* relation refers to pedagogical relations and how predefined contents are to be taught. Finally, the *student–subject* relation concerns students' understandings of the content, based on their mundane experiences and their life-world – that is, their contemporary meaning – as well as the development of their understandings during the educational process.

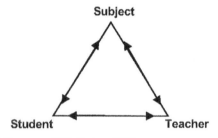

Source: Herbert, 2018; Hopmann, 1997; Hudson, 2007.

Figure 6.1   The didactic triangle

Artifacts in Education Providing a Didactic Tetrahedron

In the search for an educational setting that makes room for students' contemporary meanings of entrepreneurship, this study has turned to the potential of artifacts as a basis for reflexive learning (Hattwig, Bussert, Medaille, & Burgess, 2013; Säljö, 2010). The role of artifacts in education has been observed by, for example, Säljö (2005, p. 181), who writes, "We learn to see and understand, with the support of artifacts and the meaning they offer." When artifacts are brought into the classroom as educational tools, they have "structuring effects on teaching and learning activities" (Rezat & Sträßer, 2012, p. 644). That is, artifacts used in educational settings interfere with the original didactic triangle, transforming it into a tetrahedron (Prediger, Roesken-Winter, & Leuders, 2019; Rezat & Sträßer, 2012). Figure 6.2 illustrates how "each of the triangular faces of the tetrahedron stands for a particular perspective on the role of artifacts" within education (Rezat & Sträßer, 2012, p. 645). Artifacts in education are all kinds of tools provided for teaching. In this work, photographs are used as educational artifacts. Visual materials have previously shown to be meaningful as reflexive educational tools because images mirror individual interpretations, and "we 'read' the images in front of our eyes through the pictures we have in our heads" (Spencer, 2010, p. 19). Interpretation is not necessarily generalizable, but is rather context-specific, making it a relevant method also in student-centered education where individual understandings are in focus (Säljö, 2010).

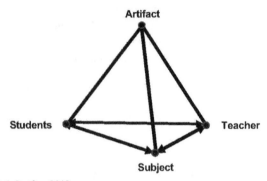

Source: Rezat & Sträßer, 2012.

Figure 6.2   The didactic triangle turned in to a tetrahedron

Visual material is used here as a medium aiming to express thoughts (Hattwig et al., 2013), to enable student–teacher interactions, and to make students' contemporary meanings about entrepreneurship visible and able to be reflected upon (Clarke, 2007; Clarke & Holt, 2017).

METHOD

The visual exercise *Images of entrepreneurship*, examined in this study, was developed at a Swedish university. The exercise has been conducted during mandatory introductory entrepreneurship classes in different educational disciplines since 2012 (Ellborg, 2018). The exercise is based on 31 black and white photographs (see Figure 6.3). The intention is not that these pictures should explain or illustrate entrepreneurship per se, but that they should offer a rich and varied set of general visual rhetorical signs (Foss, 2004) onto which the viewers can read their own interpretations. Photos are thus, in the exercise, used to constitute the point of departure for students' reflections on entrepreneurship. In order to assemble a diverse set of photos that for example does not just portray canonical images of entrepreneurship, a professional photographer with long experience of working with group development and dialogic processes was asked to compile a mixed set of photos from her rich collection of images.

Source: Photographer Cecilia Ekroth; first published in Ellborg (2018).

Figure 6.3   The 31 pictures used in Images of entrepreneurship

In the exercise, the pictures are presented to the students as a collage of printed A5 cards (148 x 210 mm or 5.8 x 8.3") attached with magnets to a whiteboard. The students are asked to review the pictures and then choose one of them as a representation for their own understanding of entrepreneurship. They make some short notes individually, and then each student expresses their choice of photo based on their understanding of entrepreneurship. Their descriptions are documented by the teacher on the whiteboard and constitute the basis for the following joint reflections.

To explore the possible contribution of the exercise to student-centered education, interviews were conducted with five entrepreneurship teachers in higher education. They had all conducted the exercise as part of introductory classes. The interviews were held within three weeks after the exercise had been conducted, depending on when the teachers had time to do the interview. The teachers were interviewed individually through semi-structured interviews (Bell, Bryman, & Harley, 2018) that lasted for about 45 minutes each and were documented with notes. The interviews covered how the teachers experienced the exercise as such (Collier & Collier, 1986; Rose, 2001; Spencer, 2010) and how they understood its structuring effects on the relationships in the didactic triangle (Rezat & Sträßer, 2012). The main themes of the questions and discussions were:

1. The teacher's overall impression of the exercise.
2. How the teachers experienced using visual artifacts in relation to verbal and written expressions.
3. The teacher's understanding of the exercise from a didactic point of view.
4. The teacher's impression of the exercise from a learning perspective.
5. Whether the teacher saw deficiencies in the method or proposed changes.
6. The teacher's opinions about the pictures used.

The teachers represented two universities in Sweden, both with stated strategic goals of offering entrepreneurship as content within the majority of their educational programs. The interviewees were all affiliated to business and entrepreneurship departments, but at the same time active as teachers in courses that were offered within educational programs that not only addressed business students. The teachers interviewed in this study all had several years of teaching experience but performed this specific exercise for the first time, and they had all received the same instructions and the same set of photos. The students were all in their second or third year of education, representing five different compulsory entrepreneurship courses in various bachelor programs at different faculties (see Table 6.1). The student groups consisted of 11, 11, 13, 21, and 16 persons respectively.

Table 6.1   *The interviews*

Interviewee	Educational program, course, and date for course introduction (i.e., when the visual exercise was held)	Date for the interview
Teacher A, Lecturer, School of Business and Economics, University X	Media and Entrepreneurship Program, 180 credits, Faculty of Arts and Humanities *Entrepreneurship – Specialization Media, 15 credits* September 3, 2018	September 12, 2018 (nine days after the exercise)
Teacher B, Senior Lecturer, School of Business and Economics, University X	Tourism Program, 180 credits, School of Business and Economics *Business Development and Entrepreneurship, 7.5 credits* November 6, 2018	November 8, 2018 (two days after the exercise)
Teacher C, Lecturer, School of Business and Economics, University X	Sports Science Program, 180 credits, Faculty of Social Science *Entrepreneurship for Health, 15 credits* January 21, 2019	January 21, 2019 (the same day as the exercise)
Teacher D, Associate Professor, Entrepreneurship and Strategy/Technology Management and Economics, University Y	Electrical Engineering, 180 credits, Department of Electrical Engineering *Complementary Engineering Skills, 4.5 credits* March 29, 2019	April 23, 2019 (three weeks after the exercise)
Teacher E, University Lecturer, Entrepreneurship and Strategy/Technology Management and Economics, University Y	Business Development and Entrepreneurship, 180 credits, Architecture and Civil Engineering *Business Development and Entrepreneurship, 7.5 credits* September 6, 2019	September 18, 2019 (twelve days after the exercise)

Since this study was interested in the spread of entrepreneurship education also outside business schools, the context described above constructs the foundation for the selection criteria. The empirical data in this study originate, in that sense, from purposive sampling (Denscombe, 2014; Etikan, 2016; Jupp, 2006), as all five cases have a common setting which represents the study's purposes. The interviewees could be expected to have relevant experience in the educational situations sought after, and were selected as they volunteered to try, and then talk about, the visual exercise.

The sample can also be denoted as convenient (Denscombe, 2014; Etikan, 2016; Jupp, 2006), since three of the teachers were working at the same university where the exercise was developed and the other two were from a university well known to the author.

The applied non-probability sample strategies indicate that the results are not generalizable in the same way as a more comprehensive study with, for example, a larger group of randomly selected teachers. At the same time, visual methods are well recognized to be effective in other education-related contexts, so generalizability of image significance as such was not intended in this particular study. Rather, the study aims at discussing how teachers experience the use of visual methods in entrepreneurship education, which can be done in a small-scale study.

RESULTS

In the following, the teachers' answers are presented. First according to how the teachers experienced the visual exercise as such, illustrated as the *artifact* in Figure 6.4, then how they experience the exercise in relation to the different sides in the didactic tetrahedron, illustrated as the *artifact–students–subject* face in Figure 6.5, the *artifact–teacher–subject* face in Figure 6.6, and the *artifact–students–teacher* face in Figure 6.7. As previously described, each new triangular face that arises in the tetrahedron has structuring effects on the relationships in the didactic triangle.

Teachers' Experiences of the Visual Exercise

Teacher A described the exercise as "an educational tool that made sense, both for me and them [the students]." She noticed that the same picture could

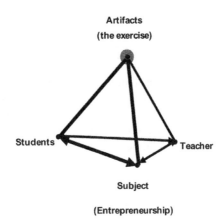

Figure 6.4   *The exercise as the artifact in the didactic tetrahedron*

provide different associations for the students, but added: "It is not the images themselves, but what they evoke that is important. We could have talked about anything from these pictures."

Teacher B experienced the exercise as "more dynamic than I had expected" and as a good introduction because it "turned out to be so associative." She did note that the students were at first a little hesitant, but that that changed when they began to describe what picture they had chosen. The photos "create an arena where all the options make things more open-minded – there are no wrong answers." Teacher B asked herself: "Does the set of pictures limit the students? Might there have been other reasonings with other pictures?" On the other hand, she continued, "one can interpret a lot in every single picture," and she considered the pictures "allowing" and as portraying "relatively universal environments."

Teacher C experienced the students as full of expectations and as amused in relation to the exercise: "They said: 'What? Are we supposed to do this?', but the exercise made them drop their guard and they took it seriously." Teacher C found the photos "neutral positive," and mentioned that there was for example no image representing death or something illegal. On the other hand, he said: "the students did see something as something else…and different students said different things about the same picture."

Teacher D noted that the pictures primarily were depicting scenes from the Western world, and therefore might be limiting, but at the same time he stated, "Our students are used to interpreting pictures from the Western world."

Teacher E considered the exercise to be "a nice way to start" because it had a consolidating effect on the group and constituted a good introduction to the seminars that would follow during the course. The pictures, he explained, "became a tool" that triggered the students to talk to each other. Further, he thought that the "informal" nature of the pictures led to less focus on "the right answer." He experienced the students as "keen on choosing" a photograph, and even commented that they thought it was a fun exercise.

Teachers' Experiences of the Artifact–Students–Subject Face

Teacher A experienced that the students genuinely expressed their own perspectives on entrepreneurship during the exercise. The discussions based on the pictures, she explained, were able to "awaken thoughts in relation to the course." She continued: "The exercise added something pedagogical – it revealed preferences and attitudes. It got them to start thinking, and to put things into words."

"To see is a result of knowing – so what you see in the pictures is a direct result of your knowledge and experience," said Teacher B when reflecting on the exercise in relation to students' pre-understandings of entrepreneurship.

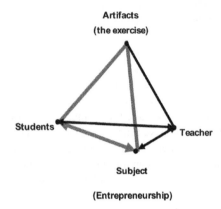

Figure 6.5   The artifact–students–subject face in the didactic tetrahedron

Teacher C stated, "The transformation between different media becomes sense-making as the students get to discuss the subject in relation to themselves and their own relationship to the subject." Teacher C also described how the students interacted and said to each other during the exercise, "Aha, so that's how you see it!" He experienced that the exercise was able to "unveil students' images of entrepreneurship – individually and together." He concluded, "Individual students' perceptions of entrepreneurship might be narrow, but when writing everyone's interpretations on the whiteboard and discussing them, they together show a repertoire of understandings."

Teacher D experienced that the exercise in an essential way constituted a learning occasion where the students "had to think about entrepreneurship."

Teacher E experienced that the students expressed their own thoughts and that they "take a 'from within' perspective and focus on individuals," but also that they raise social perspectives with phrasings such as "consideration," "community," and "support for each other."

Teachers' Experiences of the Artifact–Teacher–Subject Face

In relation to her own research-based understanding of the subject, the variety and depth of the students' interpretations surprised Teacher A a bit: "These students have not studied entrepreneurship previously, but were able to express several concepts and postures."

Teacher B admitted that she had preconceptions about how students might understand the entrepreneurship phenomenon, but these assumptions were partly refuted during the exercise: "I expected the students to focus a lot on business in their descriptions, but I experienced rather the opposite."

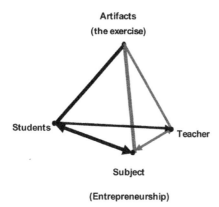

Figure 6.6   The artifact–teacher–subject face in the didactic tetrahedron

Altogether she explains that the students presented "interpretations which I was not prepared for at all," for example, social entrepreneurship.

Teacher C also experienced how students connoted entrepreneurship to "more than just business." During the exercise, he felt no need to validate students' statements in relation to the syllabus, but he described how he as a teacher could "get a sense of what can be fine-tuned" and "enhanced" during the learning process.

To Teacher D, the exercise became "an introduction to the heterogenic field [of entrepreneurship], an opportunity to discuss different interpretations as well as to put students' own interpretations in relation to theoretical perspectives." He was surprised that there were no negative interpretations of entrepreneurship from the students, but he said, "maybe that is because these students are engineers."

Teacher E experienced that the students expressed their own thoughts and that their understandings were "far from the 'dry', more objective, definitions we give them." He explained how they talked about "practices – that is, what it is to make entrepreneurship."

Teachers' Experiences of the Artifact–Students–Teacher Face

According to Teacher A, the pictures "became something concrete to hold on to," and they "do something different than speech and text." She referred to the exercise's interactive setting, and stated that it did show the students that "this is the way we do things here."

Teacher B assumed that the students would have given more conforming and stereotypical answers if the discussion had not started from the photos: "If

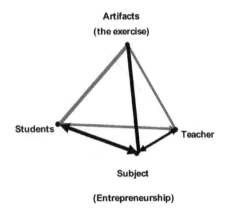

Figure 6.7   The artifact–students–teacher face in the didactic tetrahedron

we had used only words, I think they would have sought to answer correctly, rather than to submit their respective interpretations." She described how she could reconnect to the students' understanding of entrepreneurship during her subsequent lectures and thus was able to present her "image in relation to theirs."

Likewise, Teacher C described how he could relate the subject to statements made by the students during the exercise when he later held his first lecture, "I could turn to a student and say; just as you said…" Altogether, he experienced that the exercise turned the course into "a work of co-creation" where "the students are no longer anonymous." The exercise hence gave him an overview of the specific student group's understanding: "What is written on the whiteboard is unique for this group."

Techer D described how the students became engaged in the exercise by the fact that they were expected to make interpretations and that "they needed to motivate how they were thinking." Teacher D also talked about the pedagogical advantages with the exercise, and he thought it offered "interaction," "activity," and "variation in the classroom."

Teacher E usually introduced the topic with the question "What is entrepreneurship?" and then he let the students discuss this in smaller groups. With the visual exercise, Teacher E felt that the introduction became "more alive." He explained how everyone came to speak. Teacher E said, "It shows that in this course we have room for discussions." He concluded that the exercise started "a reflection process where we will jointly review our images of entrepreneurship, and no one needs to feel that they don't have anything to say."

DISCUSSION

In this study, teachers were invited to systematically tell about their experiences of a specific educational situation (Gudmundsdottir et al., 1999). In the following, their answers are discussed in relation to the visual exercise as such and its structuring effect on the didactic triangle. Conclusions are made on how the teachers experience the exercise's potential to constitute the starting point for a didactic analysis regarding the students' contemporary meaning of entrepreneurship.

The Exercise

When the interviewees described their experiences of using visual material as didactic artifacts, they used overall positively embossed phrasings like "active," "associative," "allowing," "dynamic," and "fun." Despite examples of how students, at first, did not appear to be accustomed to participate in the exercise, they then engaged fully when they understood the purpose. The photos were by the respondents interpreted as concrete educational utensils (Säljö, 2005) that encouraged the students to express their various contemporary meaning of entrepreneurship (Gudmundsdottir et al., 1999). In the teachers' opinion, the exercise contributed to pedagogical variation (Brush et al., 2015; Neck et al., 2014) by promoting emotions (Lackéus, 2016) as well as reflections (Hägg & Kurczewska, 2016).

An overly homogeneous set of images would, as the respondents indicated, risk signaling a narrow view of entrepreneurship, or might influence or limit the students' reflections. This photo compilation proved, although characterized by a Scandinavian context, to be relevant for the domestic students in this study. Teacher A's comment, "It is not the images themselves but what they evoke that is important," also indicates an awareness that the focus is thus not the images, but the spectator's interpretations (Holm, 2008; Spencer, 2010), which from the interviews can be described as varied, even when based on the same picture.

The Exercise's Structuring Effects on the Didactic Triangle

According to the interviewees, the actual transformation between images and words (Hattwig et al., 2013; Spencer, 2010) did contribute to sense-making in the relation between students and subject (Marton & Ramsden, 1988; Ramsden, 1988). The teachers experience the exercise as interactive, and as the basis for more nuanced and analytical conversations than do words alone (Clarke, 2007; Clarke & Holt, 2017). They explain how the exercise creates expectations on the students to make independent interpretations in a context where they "can't be wrong." In this way, the students' pre-understandings become connected to the learning content in a student-centered manner (Jarvis, 2012; Klafki, 1997; Knowles, 1973). The teachers also describe how the students referred to each other's understandings during the exercise. The teachers emphasized that the students, in that sense, became co-creators (Jones, 2013; Lepistö & Ronkko, 2013; Robinson et al., 2016), not just in the actual introductory session, but in the subsequent lectures. During the interviews, the teachers became aware of how they had reflected back to the students' understanding later on in the course. For the learning process, this means that they helped the students to develop their different contemporary meanings in relation to entrepreneurship (Entwistle & Walker, 2002).

The students' statements were described by the teachers as advanced, multifaceted, and a bit uncritical, but also unexpected. This indicated that the students did not merely strive to satisfy the teachers' expectations and give "correct" answers. The teachers' apparent surprise over what the students expressed also indicated a distance between the students' pre-understanding and the teachers' understanding of the established subject matter. The exercise seemed to make this distance visible, and therefore contributed to the teachers' understanding of the group and the insight that every group is unique. In that sense, the exercise emphasizes the relationship between the teacher and the range of experiences of the subject that the students bring to the classroom (Jones, 2013; Klafki, 1997; Neck & Corbett, 2018). The teachers also described that they, by starting from the students' perspective, get a view of what can be "fine-tuned" and "enhanced" during the course. They thus see the potential to base their didactic analysis in the exercise.

CONCLUSIONS

The teachers' experiences showed that they saw the visual exercise as a potential way to visualize and give space to students' perspectives. The exercise thus helps the teachers to see from which angles the students already have access to the topic (Klafki, 1995) and therefore shape their teaching in a more student-centered manner. The teachers' surprise over the students' contemporary meaning of entrepreneurship shows that their agenda and the students' agenda are not always the same, risking the education being teacher-centered if the students' perspectives are not explored.

By describing and analyzing teachers' experiences of an interactive pedagogical method, this study contributes to the understanding of how visual material can be used to explore students' contemporary meaning of entrepreneurship. The visual exercise is, through this study, established as an experimental educational setting for entrepreneurship education that contributes to a permissive climate, opening up for students to interpret the prescribed learning content from their own points of view. The teachers' experiences also confirm that students' pre-understandings might constitute a baseline in the learning process, inviting the students to become co-creators and a substantial part of the entrepreneurship education practice. When teachers become aware of how students with widely different approaches and experiences relate to the learning content, they simultaneously become better equipped to support the learning processes. Employing Klafki's didactic analysis from the educational field in entrepreneurship education research and teaching thus helps to amplify a requested student-centered approach. Moreover, the visual exercise stages this interactive approach in a relevant way.

REFERENCES

Béchard, J.-P., & Grégoire, D. (2005). Entrepreneurship education research revisited: The case of higher education. *Academy of Management Learning and Education,* *4*(1), 22–43.

Bell, E., Bryman, A., & Harley, B. (2018). *Business research methods.* Oxford: Oxford University Pess.

Blenker, P., Dreisler, P., Færgemann, H. M., & Kjeldsen, J. (2008). A framework for developing entrepreneurship education in a university context. *International Journal of Entrepreneurship and Small Business, 5*(1), 45–63.

Blenker, P., Korsgaard, S., Neergaard, H., & Thrane, C. (2011). The questions we care about: paradigms and progression in entrepreneurship education. *Industry and Higher Education, 25*(6), 417–27.

Blenker, P., Trolle Elmholdt, S., Hedeboe Frederiksen, S., Korsgaard, S., & Wagner, K. (2014). Methods in entrepreneurship education research: a review and integrative framework. *Education + Training, 56*(8/9), 697–715.

Brush, C., Neck, H., & Greene, P. (2015). A practice-based approach to entrepreneurship education. In V. L. Crittenden, K. Esper, N. Karst, & R. Slegers (Eds), *Evolving entrepreneurial education: innovation in the Babson classroom* (pp. 35–54). London: Emerald Group Publishing.

Byrne, J., Fayolle, A., & Toutain, O. (2014). Entrepreneurship education: what we know and what we need to know. In E. Chell & M. Karatas-Özkan (Eds), *Handbook of research on small business and entrepreneurship* (pp. 261–88). Cheltenham, UK and Northampton, MA, USA: Edward Elgar Publishing.

Clarke, J. (2007). *Seeing entrepreneurship: visual ethnographies of embodied entrepreneurs.* Leeds: University of Leeds.

Clarke, J., & Holt, R. (2017). Imagery of ad-venture: understanding entrepreneurial identity through metaphor and drawing. *Journal of Business Venturing, 32*(5), 476–97.

Collier, J., & Collier, M. (1986). *Visual anthropology: photography as a research method.* Albuquerque: University of New Mexico Press.

Deacon, J., & Harris, J. (2011). A longitudinal reflection of blended/reflexive enterprise and entrepreneurial education. *Reflective Practice, 12*(5), 599–613. doi:10.1080/14623943.2011.601560

Denscombe, M. (2014). *The good research guide: for small-scale social research projects*. London: McGraw-Hill Education.

Ellborg, K. (2018). Visualizing entrepreneurship: using pictures as ways to see and talk about entrepreneurship in educational settings. In C. H. Matthews & E. Liguori (Eds), *Annals of entrepreneurship education and pedagogy*, Vol. 3 (pp. 79–98). Cheltenham, UK and Northampton, MA, USA: Edward Elgar Publishing.

Entwistle, N., & Walker, P. (2002). Strategic alertness and expanded awareness within sophisticated conceptions of teaching. In H. N. & G. P. (Eds), *Teacher thinking, beliefs and knowledge in higher education* (pp. 15–39). Dordrecht: Kluwer Academic Publishers.

Etikan, I. (2016). Comparison of convenience sampling and purposive sampling. *American Journal of Theoretical and Applied Statistics, 5*(1), 1–4.

European Commission (2006). Entrepreneurship education in Europe: fostering entrepreneurial mindsets through education and learning. Final proceedings of conference held in Oslo, October 26–27.

European Commission (2007). Key competences for lifelong learning: European reference framework. Luxembourg: Office for Official Publications of the European Communities, file:///Users/kaelaa/Downloads/youth-in-action-keycomp-en.pdf

Fayolle, A. (2018). Personal views on the future of entrepreneurship education. In A. Fayolle (Ed.), *A research agenda for entrepreneurship education* (pp. 127–38). Cheltenham, UK and Northampton, MA, USA: Edward Elgar Publishing.

Fayolle, A., & Gailly, B. (2008). From craft to science: teaching models and learning processes in entrepreneurship education. *Journal of European Industrial Training, 32*(7), 569–93.

Fayolle, A., Gailly, B., & Lassas-Clerc, N. (2006). Assessing the impact of entrepreneurship education programmes: a new methodology. *Journal of European Industrial Training, 30*(9), 701–20.

Fayolle, A., Verzat, C., & Wapshott, R. (2016). In quest of legitimacy: the theoretical and methodological foundations of entrepreneurship education research. *International Small Business Journal, 34*(7), 895–904.

Foss, S. K. (2004). Theory of visual rhetoric. In K. L. Smith, S. Moriarty, K. Kenney, & G. Barbatsis (Eds), *Handbook of visual communication: theory, methods, and media* (pp. 141–52). London: Routledge.

Fox, J., Pittaway, L., & Uzuegbunam, I. (2018). Simulations in entrepreneurship education: serious games and learning through play. *Entrepreneurship Education and Pedagogy, 1*(1), 61–89.

Gabrielsson, J., Landström, H., Politis, D., & Hägg, G. (2018). Exemplary contributions from Europe to entrepreneurship education research and practice. In A. Fayolle (Ed.), *A research agenda for entrepreneurship education* (pp. 105–26). Cheltenham, UK and Northampton, MA, USA: Edward Elgar Publishing.

Gibb, A. (2002). In pursuit of a new "enterprise" and "entrepreneurship" paradigm for learning: creative destruction, new values, new ways of doing things and new combinations of knowledge. *International Journal of Management Reviews, 4*(3), 233–69.

Gudmundsdottir, S., Reinertsen, A., & Nordtømme, N. (1999). Klafki's didaktik analysis as a conceptual framework for research on teaching. In I. Westbury, S. Hopmann, & K. Riquarts (Eds), *Teaching as a reflective practice: the German didaktik tradition* (pp. 555–83). Mahwah, NJ: Routledge.

Hägg, G., & Kurczewska, A. (2016). Connecting the dots: a discussion on key concepts in contemporary entrepreneurship education. *Education + Training, 58*(7/8), 700–14.

Hattwig, D., Bussert, K., Medaille, A., & Burgess, J. (2013). Visual literacy standards in higher education: new opportunities for libraries and student learning. *Portal: Libraries and the Academy, 13*(1), 61–89.

Herbert, A. (2018). *Didactics, learning and leadership in higher education: understanding strategy development.* Abingdon: Routledge.

Holm, G. (2008). Photography as a performance. *Forum: Qualitative Social Research, 9*(2), 106–8.

Honig, B. (2004). Entrepreneurship education: toward a model of contingency-based business planning. *Academy of Management Learning and Education, 3*(3), 258–73.

Hopmann, S. (1997). Wolfgang Klafki och den tyska didaktiken. In M. Uljens (Ed.), *Didaktik – teori, refektion och praktik* (pp. 198–214). Lund: Studentlitteratur.

Hudson, B. (2007). Comparing different traditions of teaching and learning: what can we learn about teaching and learning? *European Educational Research Journal, 6*(2), 135–46.

Hudson, B., & Schneuwly, B. (2007). Didactics: learning and teaching in Europe. *European Educational Research Journal, 6*(2), 107–16.

Hynes, B. (1996). Entrepreneurship education and training: introducing entrepreneurship into non-business disciplines. *Journal of European Industrial Training, 20*(8), 10–17.

Jarvis, P. (2012). *Towards a comprehensive theory of human learning.* London: Routledge.

Jones, C. (2013). *Teaching entrepreneurship to postgraduates.* Cheltenham, UK and Northampton, MA, USA: Edward Elgar Publishing.

Jupp, V. (2006). *The Sage dictionary of social research methods.* London: Sage.

Kansanen, P., & Meri, M. (1999). The didactic relation in the teaching-studying-learning process. In B. Hudson, F. Buchberger, P. Kansanen, & H. Seel (Eds), *Didaktik/fachdidaktik as science(-s) of the teaching profession?* (pp. 107–16). Umeå, Sweden: TNTEE Publications.

Klafki, W. (1958). Didaktische analyse als kern der unterrichtsvorbereitung. *Die Deutsche Schule, 50*(10), 450–71.

Klafki, W. (1995). Didaktik analysis as the core of preparation of instruction. *Journal of Curriculum Studies, 27*(1), 13–30.

Klafki, W. (1997). Kritisk-konstruktiv didaktik. In M. Uljens (Ed.), *Didaktik – teori, refektion och praktik Didaktik* (pp. 215–28). Lund: Studentlitteratur.

Knowles, M. (1973). *The adult learner: a neglected species.* Houston, TX: Gulf.

Künzli, R. (2000). German didaktik: models of re-presentation, of intercourse, and of experience (G. Horton-Krüger, trans.). In I. Westbury, S. Hopmann, & K. Riquarts (Eds), *Teaching as a reflective practice: the German didaktik tradition* (pp. 78–105). London: Routledge.

Kuratko, D. F. (2005). The emergence of entrepreneurship education: development, trends, and challenges. *Entrepreneurship Theory and Practice, 29*(5), 577–98.

Kyrö, P. (2015). The conceptual contribution of education to research on entrepreneurship education. *Entrepreneurship and Regional Development, 27*(9–10), 599–618.

Lackéus, M. (2016). *Value creation as educational practice: towards a new educational philosophy grounded in entrepreneurship?* Gothenburg: Chalmers.

Lepistö, J., & Ronkko, M.-L. (2013). Teacher students as future entrepreneurship educators and learning facilitators. *Education + Training, 55*(7), 641–53.

Liguori, E., Winkler, C., Winkel, D., Marvel, M. R., Keels, J. K., van Gelderen, M., & Noyes, E. (2018). *The entrepreneurship education imperative: introducing EE&P.* Los Angeles, CA: Sage.

Marton, F., & Booth, S. (1997). *Learning and awareness*. London: Routledge.

Marton, F., & Ramsden, P. (1988). What does it take to improve learning. In P. Ramsden (Ed.), *Improving learning: new perspectives* (pp. 268–86). London: Kogan Page.

Matlay, H., & Carey, C. (2007). Entrepreneurship education in the UK: a longitudinal perspective. *Journal of Small Business and Enterprise Development*, *14*(2), 252–63.

Matthews, C. H., & Liguori, E. W. (2019). *Annals of entrepreneurship education and pedagogy*, Vol. 3. Cheltenham, UK and Northampton, MA, USA: Edward Elgar Publishing.

Nabi, G., Liñán, F., Fayolle, A., Krueger, N., & Walmsley, A. (2017). The impact of entrepreneurship education in higher education: A systematic review and research agenda. *Academy of Management Learning and Education*, *16*(2), 277–99.

Neck, H. M., & Corbett, A. C. (2018). The scholarship of teaching and learning entrepreneurship. *Entrepreneurship Education and Pedagogy*, *1*(1), 8–41.

Neck, H. M., Greene, P. G., & Brush, C. G. (2014). *Teaching entrepreneurship: a practice-based approach*. Cheltenham, UK and Northamton, MA, USA: Edward Elgar Publishing.

Newton, E. S. (1977). Andragogy: understanding the adult as a learner. *Journal of Reading*, *20*(5), 361–63.

Piaget, J. (1964). Part I: cognitive development in children: Piaget development and learning. *Journal of Research in Science Teaching*, *2*(3), 176–86.

Pittaway, L., & Edwards, C. (2012). Assessment: examining practice in entrepreneurship education. *Education and Training*, *54*, 778–800.

Prediger, S., Roesken-Winter, B., & Leuders, T. (2019). Which research can support PD facilitators? Strategies for content-related PD research in the Three-Tetrahedron Model. *Journal of Mathematics Teacher Education*, 1–19.

Prosser, M., & Trigwell, K. (1999). *Understanding learning and teaching: the experience in higher education*. London: McGraw-Hill Education.

Ramsden, P. (1988). Studying learning: Improving teaching. In P. Ramsden (Ed.), *Improving learning: new perspectives* (pp. 13–31). London: Kogan Page.

Rezat, S., & Sträßer, R. (2012). From the didactical triangle to the socio-didactical tetrahedron: artifacts as fundamental constituents of the didactical situation. *ZDM*, *44*(5), 641–51.

Robinson, S., Neergaard, H., Tanggaard, L., & Krueger, N. F. (2016). New horizons in entrepreneurship education: from teacher-led to student-centered learning. *Education + Training*, *58*(7/8), 661–83.

Sadler, I. (2012). The challenges for new academics in adopting student-centred approaches to teaching. *Studies in Higher Education*, *37*(6), 731–45.

Säljö, R. (2005). *Lärande & kulturella redskap. Om lärprocesser och det kollektiva minnet*. Stockholm: Norstedts Akademiska Förlag.

Säljö, R. (2010). Den lärande människan- teoretiska traditioner. In C. Lindberg, R. Säljö, & U. P. Lundgren (Eds), *Lärande, skola, bildning: grundbok för lärare* (pp. 225–86). Stockholm: Natur & Kultur.

Samson, P. L. (2015). Fostering student engagement: creative problem-solving in small group facilitations. *Collected Essays on Learning and Teaching*, *8*, 153–64.

Samwel Mwasalwiba, E. (2010). Entrepreneurship education: a review of its objectives, teaching methods, and impact indicators. *Education + Training*, *52*(1), 20–47.

Solomon, G. (2007). An examination of entrepreneurship education in the United States. *Journal of Small Business and Enterprise Development*, *14*(2), 168–82.

Spencer, S. (2010). *Visual research methods in the social sciences: awakening visions.* London: Routledge.

Teerijoki, H., & Murdock, K. A. (2014). Assessing the role of the teacher in introducing entrepreneurial education in engineering and science courses. *International Journal of Management Education, 12*(3), 479–89.

Uljens, M. (2004). *School didactics and learning: a school didactic model framing an analysis of pedagogical implications of learning theory.* Hove: Psychology Press.

Westbury, I. (2000). Teaching as a reflective practice: what might didaktik teach curriculum. In I. Westbury, S. Hopmann, & K. Riquarts (Eds), *Teaching as a reflective practice: the German didaktik tradition* (pp. 32–77). London Routledge.

Williams Middleton, K., & Donnellon, A. (2014). Personalizing entrepreneurial learning: a pedagogy for facilitating the know why. *Entrepreneurship Research Journal, 4*(2), 167–204.

7. A model to increase the impact of student consulting projects in rural communities

Dennis Barber III, Michael Harris and Sharon Paynter

INTRODUCTION

Experiential learning and service-learning opportunities are now common in business school curricula. Projects which use student teams as consultants for small businesses are one type of service learning. Students in client-based, service-learning courses are entrepreneurial (Harris & Gibson, 2008), are able to gain professional experience and offer an opinion in dealing with a real business problem (Heriot, Cook, Matthews, & Simpson, 2007), and are more emotionally connected to course experiences which may lead to better knowledge retention (Hoffman & Bechtold, 2018). The Association to Advance Collegiate Schools of Business (AACSB), a global business school accrediting body, announced a new set of values in 2013 which included engagement, innovation, and impact (AACSB, 2013). These values align tightly with student consulting projects and provide standards for the continuance of this pedagogical approach (Bechtold, Hoffman, & Murphy, 2019).

Service learning emerged in the 1980s as a model for experiential learning involving cycles of service and reflection. David Kolb (1984) developed a six-step, four-stage learning process. Kolb presented the process as a cycle moving from concrete experience to reflective observation to abstract conceptualization and finally active experimentation. In this framework, faculty guide students through the experience to ensure reflection and application are well aligned. The student consulting model has been well studied and refined in the almost 40 years since its inception and continues to guide pedagogical practice today.

While the student experience is a critical component in these projects, service-learning initiatives must also benefit the client. In business curricula, the client is usually a small, local business. Small business clients come with a myriad of experiences, technical skills, states of readiness, and complicated contextual factors to consider as projects are proposed, accepted, and formalized. To ensure mutual benefit for all involved, faculty advisors must vet clients properly and guide students to develop actionable recommendations for the organization. The best results are achieved when faculty can invest in finding clients that are ready to engage with students – which can be a time-consuming, complex process. The impact for clients also depends on their ability or capacity to implement the recommendations provided by the student consultants. This chapter presents a model to extend the relationship with small business clients, involve community stakeholders in the selection of clients, and provide additional support for the implementation of recommendations through a grant-funded internship program.

LITERATURE REVIEW

Experiential Learning

Dewey described experiential learning as a process where students learn by doing and which tests hypotheses in the laboratory of real life (1971). This definition was expanded to better determine an experiential learning theory (Kolb & Kolb, 2005). This theory presents more specific propositions including (1) learning is best conceived as a process, not in terms of outcomes, (2) all learning is relearning, (3) learning requires the resolution of conflicts between dialectically opposed modes of adaptation to the world, (4) learning is a holistic process of adaptation to the world, (5) learning results from synergetic transactions between the person and the environment, and (6) learning is a process of creating knowledge (Kolb & Kolb, 2005). Kolb and Kolb relied on extant scholarship, especially that of Dewey (1971), to build their theory and, in doing so, their work was based on Dewey's earlier work and emphasized the importance of critical reflection in experiential learning.

High-impact, experiential learning practices increase student engagement and retention (Kuh, 2008) and are some of the most powerful tools for teaching efficacy (McCarthy & McCarthy, 2006; Winsett, Foster, Dearing, & Bursch, 2016). Experiential learning, internships, and cooperative learning environments are quite common in colleges and universities today (Austin & Rust, 2015). Student learning during internships extends outside of the content of traditionally delivered courses and helps students discover what type of career for which they are suited, which is connected to greater job satisfaction later in life (Steffes, 2004). Not surprisingly, students in work-learning environments and internship programs report significantly greater confidence in goal setting and attainment (Purdie, Ward, McAdie, King, & Drysdale, 2013). Entrepreneurship education should focus on facilitating learning through real-world experience, action, and reflection to lead to enhanced entrepreneurial performance (Kassean, Vanevenhoven, Liguori, & Winkel, 2015).

Service Learning

One form of experiential learning, focused on driving community change through interaction with local agencies and businesses, is service learning (Levesque-Bristol, Knapp, & Fisher, 2011). Service learning couples the reflection component of experiential learning in a structured environment with community service (Cashman & Seifer, 2008). A distinguishing component of service learning, as compared to education from general experiential learning, is the intention of the experience to mutually benefit the provider and the recipient of the service. This places equal focus on the service being provided and the learning which occurs during the process (Furco, 1996). Traditional internships are predominantly focused on the benefit to the student while service learning courses and programs incentivize students to service their community and allow the service to co-occur with the students' learning (Cashman & Seifer, 2008). Seifer (1998) describes several specific elements of service learning by noting it has its theoretical roots in experiential learning theory; is developed, implemented, and evaluated in collaboration with the community; responds to community-identified concerns; attempts to balance the service that is provided and the learning that takes place; enhances the curriculum by extending learning beyond the lecture hall and allowing students to apply what they are learning to real-world situations; and provides opportunities for critical reflection.

Much like internships in general, service-learning programs have been shown to positively influence students' personal development, leadership, and communication skills, racial and cultural understanding, sense of social and civic responsibility, course content learning, and ability to apply classroom learning in real-world situations (Eyler, Giles, Stenson, & Gray, 2001). The longitudinal effects of participating in service-learning projects for undergraduates include better academic performance, stronger values, higher self-efficacy, better leadership skills, higher likelihood to choose service-based careers, and plans to participate in service after college (Astin, Vogelgesang, Ikeda, & Yee, 2000).

Experiential Learning in Business Education

Experiential curricula are commonly used in university-level business education programs (Elam & Spotts, 2004; Marom & Lussier, 2017) and entrepreneurship programs (Neck & Greene, 2010). The AACSB provides accreditation to business schools globally. The AACSB began to emphasize the importance of engaged and experiential learning experiences for students less than ten years ago. The 2013 AACSB accreditation standards identified several attributes expected of accredited business programs, namely that their curricula "facilitate and encourage active student engagement in learning. In addition to time on task related to readings, course participation, knowledge development, projects, and assignments, students engage in experiential and active learning designed to be inclusive for diverse students, and to improve skills and the application of knowledge in practice" (AACSB, 2013, p. 32).

AACSB stated that their values for business education and assessment include innovation, impact, and engagement. Experiential learning projects embody all these values and can better represent a college or department's alignment with AACSB standards (Kosnik, Tingle, & Blanton, 2013). Internships are only one way to have students engage with businesses and they often focus on the day-to-day operations of an employer. Experiential learning projects can create an opportunity for students to work in a team environment and better apply their educational experiences and learnings. Successful experiential learning experiences rely heavily on faculty guidance and sometimes limit the amount of exposure students have with organizations (Kosnik et al., 2013).

PROGRAM AND PROCESS

Program

With the notion that service learning is a high-impact educational practice, universities should create many opportunities for students to enroll in service-learning courses. The added benefit for doing this in rural-serving university communities is that such opportunities can serve the dual role of educational experience and increase the organizational capacity of host sites.

Slightly more than 20 percent of the United States population lives in rural areas (Ratcliffe, Burd, Holder, & Fields, 2016). Defining rural areas is complex and often controversial. Concepts like population thresholds, density, land use, and distance are typical components of the classification (Ratcliffe et al., 2016). Brain drain and population decline create workforce talent deficits in rural communities. Losing population matters because it erodes the local tax base which funds schools and community amenities and is also a proxy for market share and customer base.

However defined, some rural communities are succeeding despite dim predictions. These places have strong cultural connections, shared histories, and even some of the highest rates of upward mobility nationwide (Lettieri, 2017). But to boost competitiveness, rural communities must find ways to level the playing field regarding available public infrastructure, access to broadband connectivity, and lessening the educational attainment gap as compared to more urban regions. One strategy to accomplish these things is to attract emerging entrepreneurs to rural communities.

In doing so, young adults can take advantage of the social connections, sense of community, and even desperation for success that define rural places. With the right combination of community vision, social and investment capital, and innovative ideas, rural entrepreneurship can be a game changer for small towns across America. Arguably, one of the most critical steps in this proposed model is providing opportunities for emerging entrepreneurs to see, experience, and learn about rural places. Universities can assist by offering service-learning courses focused on connections between campus and community that allow students to begin to flex new technical skills and ideas.

Spurred by population loss and declining employment opportunities in rural communities, our university developed a comprehensive strategy for rural economic development that relies on community engagement, innovation, and entrepreneurship. The university's primary service region includes 29 rural counties and a limited infrastructure for business development.

This new strategy is focused on creating an entrepreneurship culture on campus and developing small business capacity in rural communities. Senior campus leaders have convened a "Regional Transformation Council" that meets monthly to provide strategic guidance and resource allocation to initiatives focused on innovation, entrepreneurship, and community engagement. Over the past five years, the group has provided support for curricular and co-curricular programs and resource needs, developed innovation spaces on campus, created an innovation living and learning community, launched a school of entrepreneurship and entrepreneurship baccalaureate degree program, and built partnerships with communities and industries in our region to empower rural prosperity.

These activities set the stage for student entrepreneurs to have programming which supports connections outside the classroom. Thus, the school of entrepreneurship and the university's research and economic development division sought and received a $1 million foundation award to support rural economic prosperity through innovation and entrepreneurship. The grant supports and strengthens strategic partnerships between the university and the region and creates a pipeline of new emerging entrepreneurs for deployment across the service area.

With the award, a university-wide program was launched, targeted toward transforming students into emerging entrepreneurs who represent a new generation of business owners in the region. The grant supports and strengthens strategic partnerships between the university and the region and creates a pipeline of new emerging entrepreneurs for deployment across the service area.

A primary mechanism in the program is the internship. This is a paid internship with an option for course credit. Students are placed into small groups of two–three and matched with a local small business that is looking to expand, transition, or start up. This is not the typical internship course. Students meet with faculty mentors and program directors weekly to debrief and participate in professional development activities. The program directors schedule guest speakers and subject matter experts to deliver specific guidance to students as they work with their clients. The student projects look more like student consulting reports than standard internship deliverables. The students deliver this final consulting report with recommendations and a presentation detailing steps for the business clients to grow, adapt, and/or transition. Student consulting as a service-learning delivery system provides enhanced business experiences and better student knowledge acquisition and retention (Hoffman, Bechtold, Murphy, & Snyman, 2016).

Process

Grant-funded internships are integrated with the existing student consulting process. In the program, two consulting-based courses provide the baseline for our experiential curriculum. These courses carry the service-learning designation from the university and each student in the course normally completes an average of 90 hours of work on the project each semester. In the 45 years since the college began offering consulting courses, over 600 clients have been served. A new internship course was developed to complement existing experiential learning courses and provide even more flexibility for client-based projects. Figure 7.1 provides an illustration of how this program is incorporated into the overall menu of consulting course options, particularly regarding client referrals and follow-up on recommendations and implementation plans.

The beginning of the process includes utilizing county-specific, advisory councils formed through the grant-funded program. These councils are made up of economic developers, business leaders and entrepreneurs, chamber of commerce directors, and/or local policymakers. The goal is for the councils to identify clients which are expanding, going through a transition, or just getting started. The hope is that getting community members involved in the selection process will improve the efficiency in the client-vetting process as projects identified are more likely to be impactful and sustainable in the eyes of the business and community. Projects then undergo further screening by university faculty and staff who determine client eligibility to participate in the program based on a client's ability to provide a positive learning experience, need for consulting, scope of work, and ability to meet the grant outcomes of creating or sustaining jobs in rural communities.

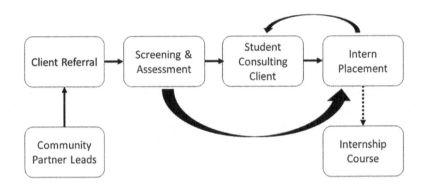

Figure 7.1   Client selection and service process

Clients with a less clear scope of work are likely a better fit for the student consulting projects. Since students in these courses are working with clients for credit and not for pay, the focus is more on the learning outcomes for the students and the viability of the recommendations for the clients. It often takes a few weeks for a clear scope of work to emerge and this is part of the learning process for the students. Also, clients often lack a clear understanding of expectations if they have not previously worked with student consulting teams.

Businesses may participate in projects in the fall, spring, or summer semesters and can have a group of interns for multiple terms. This allows for a much richer interaction between the university and the business community as it extends the relationship from one semester to a year or more. An ideal scenario is to have a client work with a consulting team in one of the courses before connecting with the internship program. The recommendations made by this student team can provide a basis for the scope of work for the internship. The extension of this student engagement allows for the university to provide a service to its community that culminates in the implementation of well-researched suggestions given the timeline and budget. In rural communities, this extension and co-curricular innovation has the potential to build small business resilience and lead to a more sustainable business environment. This program brings together government, university, and business representatives to support students, firms, and communities. A true triple-helix partnership creates local knowledge-rich environments and helps entrepreneurs become aware of their contribution to local economic development (Sá, Casais, & Silva, 2019).

DISCUSSION AND PRACTICAL IMPLICATIONS

Experiential, client-based courses are not new to the academic world, particularly in professional schools such as business and engineering. But often these programs are more outreach-focused and do not involve true engagement opportunities with the regional business community. Additionally, the time period tends to be limited to one semester with no authentic connection before or after the one-semester consulting experience. While creative, cost-effective recommendations are certainly an important part of this process, sustainable impact is limited without additional programming to assist with implementation and evaluation.

This model allows participating students to observe, learn, and engage with the regional small business community at a higher level of engagement to ensure an in-depth connection between the human capital on campus and regional small business owners. These internships serve as the gateway to build partnerships and develop deep understandings of community dynamics that play into the success or failure of entrepreneurship activities across the region.

There are four strategic benefits to this engaged process. First, the process to vet clients is more thorough and has better efficacy for all consulting courses. Identifying clients at the "teachable moment" and connecting them in the experiential learning process at the most appropriate time is critical to ensure implementing and sustainable benefits. This improves the learning experience for students and assists with rural workforce development and organizational capacity through the interns' technical skills and knowledge. Second, an extended relationship allows for more developed recommendations and actual implementation, thereby having a more substantive client impact.

Third, satisfied clients can lead to other engagement opportunities within the region. As more programs, particularly AACSB business schools, grow the number of experiential learning courses it is critical to develop a robust client pipeline. Finally, these added benefits can improve the likelihood of developing philanthropic relationships in the business community. These types of investments can be critical as programs face budget cuts and a greater call for financial independence. Below we delve deeper into these key benefits and practical implications gained from a highly integrated internship program.

Client Selection

The best clients are organizations that have some difficulties but are not in crisis mode. Instability does not allow for students to develop their findings (Robinson, Sherwood, & DePaolo, 2010). For the student experience to be meaningful, clients must be appropriate for the active, service-learning environment of the program (Heriot et al., 2007). Clients must be ready, willing, and able to make themselves and information about their companies available to the students (Cook, 2000), and setting these expectations is a critical component of the process to manage client expectations (Friedman, 1989). The way for these projects to be impactful is through the clients' engagement in the entire process from problem diagnosis to solution formulation (Martinez, Ferreira, & Can, 2016). The role of the business owners in student consulting projects is critical to the potential success, and the business owners must fully understand the nature of the program (i.e. how long it will last, number of students, time and effort, etc.) (Sonfield, 1981). The aim is not to create client "stars" but to focus on client long-run survival and performance that meets realistic expectations and objectives (Sonfield, 2008).

Having the community stakeholders involved in the process of client selection increases the dedication and education of the clients as there are multiple accountability and informative points. The chamber directors and economic developers normally have a better idea of the needs of the business community and where the most impact can be made through a program like this. The community partners can coach the host organizations as this is necessary to make sure the projects are challenging to the students but within the time and resource constraints of the program (Friedman, 1989).

Impactful Recommendations and Implementation

Clients report valuable input, high impact, and relatively high likelihood of the implementation of recommendations made by student consulting teams (Portney, Standiford, Carey, Vu, Kirst, & Zink, 2019), and do not value this type of service any less than Small Business Development Center consulting services (Borstadt & Byron, 1993), but this type of reporting normally happens just after project completion and may have recency bias in the responses. Clients' satisfaction and evaluations of student consulting projects are affected by the perceived economic impact of the recommendations (Madison & Chawla, 1998). The implementation of recommendations and the impact of student consulting projects are a part of the process that is often overlooked, and faculty rely on stories about anecdotal success cases to validate the quality of the report and service provided by student teams.

Even though managers and small business owners are highly satisfied with the consulting services they receive, many report a lack of consultant expertise as a primary reason for not implementing recommendations (Nahavandi & Chesteen, 1988). It is possible that there is a selection bias in the pool of clients. Small business owners which self-select to receive free consulting advice may be more likely to survive, prosper, and grow regardless of the quality of the service than those who do not seek assistance (Chrisman, Nelson, Hoy, & Robinson, Jr., 1985). Even so, small businesses that receive free consulting services have seen a growth in sales, employment, and profits (Chrisman et al., 1985).

The potential impact of these types of consulting services has been shown to be valuable to the students, community, business, and institutions that sponsor the programs. Our program increases the likelihood and magnitude of impact by extending the relationship with the clients. Instead of a semester-long project with a survey to measure impact, clients can have interns, student consultants, and other support (National Science Foundation I-Corp programs, Small Business Technology Development Centers, etc.) to help refine the recommendations. After each semester, the next group of consultants (sometimes the same students) can better identify and define problems and test the feasibility of recommendations. This creates a more tailored client–consultant relationship that is based on experience, data, and trust. Clients can get closer to implementation with a better-defined timeline and budget for recommendations with the extended process with multiple student consultants and interns providing a variety of perspectives. Many of the student-consulting courses live in business and students not in those majors may not have the curricular flexibility to participate in those courses. The program allows for any major to be an intern. Students can be strategically recruited with specific skillsets and backgrounds to match client needs.

Additional Experiential Learning Opportunities

Business education is criticized for failing to keep up with the dynamics of the business environment (O'Mally & Ryan, 2006) and educators have made an intentional effort to include more experiential learning approaches in their content delivery (Karns, 2005). Student self-efficacy (Bandura, 1993), the confidence to tackle a given situation, is asserted to be best attained through experience (Oh & Polidan, 2018). Student consulting projects require students to develop critical thinking skills, which is not a common student improvement during college (Lattuca, Knight, Seifert, Reason, & Liu, 2017), in ways other education experiences cannot (Canziani & Tullar, 2017), and project-based learning helps students gain leadership and professional skills (Portney et al., 2019). Small business and entrepreneurship consulting provides students with insights into the changing dynamics of workplaces including the use of freelancers, contractors, and consultants (Duval-Couetil & Taylor, 2016). Of all the types of experiential learning approaches, including role plays (Deeter-Schmelz, 2015), simulations (Gremler, Hoffman, Keaveney, & Wright, 2000), and workshops (Piercy, 2013), community service-learning client-based projects are recognized as the most effective experiential learning platform (Oh & Polidan, 2018).

The students in the internship course and in the other consulting-based courses are arguably having one of the most impactful learning experiences of their college careers. The team dynamics, real-world environment, and meaningful contribution to their business community have lasting effects on the students participating in this program. The student teams may include students from various majors across the campus. Interdisciplinary courses, such as the internship component of this program, are perceived positively by students (Davis, 1995) regardless of their gender, major, or grade level (Smith Ducoffe, Tromley, & Tucker, 2006). The integration of knowledge and ways of thinking developed through interdisciplinary educational experiences advances learning in a way that single-discipline education cannot (Hannon, Hocking, Legge, & Lugg, 2018). Interdisciplinary learning not only requires the interaction of knowledge from different disciplines, but it also must center around an overarching them, topic, or problem that shapes the learning experience (Holley, 2017).

Students that have participated in service-learning, client-based experiential learning courses report enhancement of problem-solving and communication skills, while using this experience as a highlight on their resume and a talking point during job interviews (Schindler & Stockstill, 1995). Students not only serve the community, gain course credit, and sometimes get paid, they also learn more about the service component and are more likely to serve their communities in the future. In a rural environment where close-knit groups do not often provide a clear opportunity for student involvement, trust is built between the students, university, and business community that can lead to stronger partnerships and a strong, connected cohort of new business owners and managers filtering into the region.

Charitable Giving

Research demonstrates that demographics play a role in financial giving to your alma mater such that age is positively related to giving (Clotfelter, 2001), peaks in a person's 50s (Okunade, Wunnava, & Walsh, Jr., 1994), and rebounds again later in life (Bristol, Jr., 1990). This relationship could be due to an increase in wealth over a person's life and these effects are difficult to separate. Others have suggested that income is not a good predictor of the decision to give but is a good predictor of the size of the gift (Schervish, 1997). These are factors that are not in the control of the institution, but there is a role that these types of engagement may play in the alumni giving decision. The relationship and involvement alumni have after graduation are predictors of giving (Tsao & Coll, 2004). Donors, as opposed to non-donors, have positive feelings towards their alma mater, had good college experiences, and remained engaged after graduation (Wastyn, 2009). Significant correlates with the magnitude of a gift are the number of recent campus visits and contact with a person from the university (Shim, 2001). Another prompt that triggers a financial gift is the willingness of an alumni to volunteer (Van Slyke & Brooks, 2004).

The extended relationship opportunities provided by the program described in this chapter demonstrate the ability to increase the likelihood of a gift in various ways. Clients, often alumni, remain in contact with faculty and program directors and they have the opportunity to visit the campus on multiple occasions. Additionally, this program provides a mechanism to interact with potential donors without having the gift be a topic of conversation. At first, business professionals feel like they are volunteering to help the students. By the end of a three-semester intensive student consulting experience, they realize that they have benefited just as much as the students during the process. This affords the university administrators an appropriate context for the discussion of a gift.

Another potential donor often overlooked in these situations is the student. An experiential and impactful education experience leads to a higher likelihood of a financial gift once the student graduates. Better-engaged students can help overcome the narrative that they are consumers only and faculty can help reinforce this by helping students frame their college experiences differently (Wastyn, 2009).

CONCLUSION

The purpose of this chapter is to offer a framework to better connect universities and the regional business community in rural areas. These relationships are critical to ensure experiential learning courses and internship programs are sustainable for both the students involved and the clients served. The proposed model is rooted in authentic community engagement.

Additionally, relationship and context matter. Our institution is situated in a rural region where entrepreneurship and small business development has been embraced as a viable component of strategic economic development. The challenges presented in a rural setting call for the type of regional partnership embedded in our program, particularly for ones aimed at stimulating small business development and growth. Impactful experiential learning requires a process that allows for the necessary time to develop creative recommendations and follow-up to ensure implementation and subsequent evaluation. If done properly, this type of relationship can lead to more additional partnerships between universities and regional organizations.

In addition to our model, the authors propose a call to action for other academic institutions interested in intersecting experiential learning programs and community engagement. This type of work requires real connections on campus and throughout the community, but it is the most rewarding and beneficial. As a campus with the elective Carnegie Engagement designation, regional transformation is a critical part of our mission. Many other institutions share this same goal, particularly universities in rural areas supported by state funding, so it can be used by faculty interested in developing rich experiential learning experiences with sustainable community impact.

REFERENCES

AACSB (2013). *Eligibility Procedures and Accredidation Standards for Business Accreditation.* Tampa, FL: Association to Advance Collegiate Schools of Business. www.aacsb.edu/-/media/aacsb/docs/accreditation/business/standards-and-tables/2018-business-standards.ashx?la=en&hash=B9AF18F3FA0DF19B352B605CBCE17959E32445D9

Astin, A., Vogelgesang, L., Ikeda, E., & Yee, J. (2000). How Service Learning Affects Students. *Higher Education, 144.* https://digitalcommons.unomaha.edu/slcehighered/144

Austin, M., & Rust, D. (2015). Developing an Experiential Learning Program: Milestones and Challenges. *International Journal of Teaching and Learning in Higher Education,* 143–53.

Bandura, A. (1993). Perceived Self-Efficacy in Cognitive Development and Functioning. *Educational Psychologist, 28,* 117–48. https://doi.org/10.1207/s15326985ep2802_3

Bechtold, D., Hoffman, D. L., & Murphy, A. (2019). Can the SBI Program Survive? An Examination of the Relationship of AACSB and the SBI. *Small Business Institute® Journal, 15*(1), 39–48.

Borstadt, L. F., & Byron, A. (1993). The Impact of Student-Consulting Programs on Decision-Making, Operations and Financial Performance of Small Businesses. *Proceedings of the 1993 Small Business Institute Director's Association* (pp. 79–87). www.sbida.org/Resources/Documents/Proceedings/1993%20Proceedings.pdf#page=79

Bristol, Jr., R. B. (1990). The Life Cycle of Alumni Donations. *Review of Higher Education, 13*(4), 503–17. https://doi.org/10.1353/rhe.1990.0011

Canziani, B., & Tullar, W. L. (2017). Developing Critical Thinking through Student Consultings Projects. *Journal of Education for Business, 92*(6), 271–9. https://doi.org/10.1080/08832323.2017.1345849

Cashman, S., & Seifer, S. D. (2008). Service-Learning: An Integral Part of Undergraduate Public Health. *American Journal of Preventative Medicine,* 273–78. https://doi.org/10.1016/j.amepre.2008.06.012

Chrisman, J. J., Nelson, R. R., Hoy, F., & Robinson, Jr., R. B. (1985). The Impact of SBDC Consulting Activities. *Journal of Small Business Management, 23*(3), 1–11.

Clotfelter, C. T. (2001). Who Are the Alumni Donors? Giving by Two Generations of Alumni from Selective Colleges. *Nonprofit Management and Leadership, 12*(2), 119–38. https://doi.org/10.1002/nml.12201

Cook, R. G. (2000). Quality Field Case Consulting: New Program Possibilities. *Journal of Small Business Strategy, 11*(2), 105–7.

Davis, J. R. (1995). *Interdisciplinary Courses and Team Teaching: New Arrangements for Learning.* Westport, CT: Oryx Press.

Deeter-Schmelz, D. R. (2015). Corporate-Academic Partnerships: Creating a Win–Win in the Classroom. *Journal of Education for Business*, *90*(4), 192–8. https://doi.org/10.1080/08832323.2015.1014457

Dewey, R. (1971). Accredited Experiential Education: Some Definitions. *Urban and Social Change Review*, 10–15.

Duval-Couetil, N., & Taylor, K. (2016). Entrepreneurial Consulting Courses: Increasing Benefits to Students in the New Economy. In M. H. Morris & E. Liguori (Eds), *Annals of Entrepreneurship Education and Pedagogy* (pp. 393–7). Cheltenham, UK and Northampton, MA, USA: Edward Elgar Publishing.

Elam, E., & Spotts, H. (2004). Achieving Markting Curriculum Integration: A Live Case Study Approach. *Journal of Marketing Education*, 50–65. https://doi.org/10.1177/0273475303262351

Eyler, J., Giles, D. E. Jr, Stenson, C. M., & Gray, C. J. (2001). At a Glance: What We Know about the Effects of Service-Learning on College Students, Faculty, Institutions and Communities, 1993–2000, 3rd edition. *Higher Education*, Paper 139. http://digitalcommons.unomaha.edu/slcehighered/139

Friedman, S. D. (1989). Education or Service? Coping with Conflicts in Student Consulting Project Goals. *Organizational Behavior Teaching Review*, *14*(4), 63–77. https://doi.org/10.1177/105256298901400408

Furco, A. (1996). Service-Learning: A Balance Approach to Experiential Education. *Expanding Boundaries: Serving and Learning* (B. Taylor, Ed.) (pp. 23–50). Washington, DC: Corporation for National Service.

Gremler, D. D., Hoffman, K. D., Keaveney, S. M., & Wright, L. K. (2000). Experiential Learning Exercises in Services Marketing Courses. *Journal of Marketing Education*, *22*(1), 35–44. https://doi.org/10.1177/0273475300221005

Hannon, J., Hocking, C., Legge, K., & Lugg, A. (2018). Sustaining Interdisciplinary Education: Developing Boundary Crossing Governance. *Higher Education Research and Development*, *37*(7), 1424–38. https://doi.org/10.1080/07294360.2018.1484706

Harris, M. L., & Gibson, S. G. (2008). Examining the Entrepreneurial Attitudes of US Business Students. *Education + Training*, *50*(7), 568–81. https://doi.org/10.1108/00400910810909036

Heriot, K. C., Cook, R. G., Matthews, C. H., & Simpson, L. (2007). Creating Active and High-Impact Learning: Moving out of the Classroom with Field-Based Student Consulting Projects. *Industry and Higher Education*, *21*(6), 427–34. https://doi.org/10.5367/000000007783099827

Hoffman, D. L., & Bechtold, D. (2018). Can the Small Business Institute's Field-Based Consulting Enhance Knowledge Retention and Acquisition. *Small Business Institute® Journal*, *14*(2), 61–70.

Hoffman, D. L., Bechtold, D., Murphy, A., & Snyman, J. (2016). Strategic Planning and Field Based Consulting. *Small Business Institute® Journal*, *12*(1), 1–9.

Holley, K. (2017). Interdisciplinary Curriculum and Learning in Higher Education. In *Oxford Research Encyclopedia of Education* (pp. 1–23). New York: Oxford University Press. https://doi.org/10.1093/acrefore/9780190264093.013.138

Karns, G. L. (2005). An Update of Marketing Student Perceptions of Learning Activities: Structure, Preferences, and Effectiveness. *Journal of Marketing Education*, *27*(2), 163–71. https://doi.org/10.1177/0273475305276641

Kassean, H., Vanevenhoven, J., Liguori, E., & Winkel, D. E. (2015). Entrepreneurship Education: A Need for Reflection, Real-World Experience and Action. *International Journal of Entrepreneurial Behavior and Research*, *21*(5), 690–708.

Kolb, A., & Kolb, D. A. (2005). Learning Styles and Learning Spaces: Enhancing Experiential Learning in Higher Education. *Academy of Management Learning and Education*, 193–212. https://doi.org/10.5465/amle.2005.17268566

Kolb, D. A. (1984). Experiential Learning: Experience as the Source of Learning and Development. *Journal of Business Ethics*, *15*(1), 45–57.

Kosnik, R., Tingle, J., & Blanton, E. (2013). Transformational Learning in Business Education: The Pivotal Role of Experiential Learning Projects. *American Journal of Business Education*, 613–30. https://doi.org/10.19030/ajbe.v6i6.8166

Kuh, G. (2008). *High Educational Impact Practices: What They Are, Who Has Access to Them and Why They Matter*. Washington, DC: AAC&U.

Lattuca, L. R., Knight, D., Seifert, T. A., Reason, R. D., & Liu, Q. (2017). Examining the Impact of Interdisciplinary Programs on Student Learning. *Innovative Higher Education*, *42*, 337–53. https://doi.org/10.1007/s10755-017-9393-z

Lettieri, J. (2017). *The Challenges and Opportunities of Running a Small Business in Rural America*. Senate Small Business and Entrepreneurship Committee. United States Senate. www.sbc.senate.gov/public/_cache/files/9/1/913100dd-59df-4dd0-a671 -5862740a5411/C2CA9A3BFAC65A5EB0FE24DD2077AA32.lettieri-testimony.pdf

Levesque-Bristol, C., Knapp, T., & Fisher, B. (2011). The Effectiveness of Service-Learning: It's Not Always What You Think. *Journal of Experiential Education*, 208–24. https://doi.org/10.1177/105382590113300302

Madison, T. F., & Chawla, S. K. (1998). SBI Clients' Perceptions of Student Consulting Projects: An Empirical Model. *Journal of Business and Entrepreneurship*, *10*(1), 94–102.

Marom, S., & Lussier, R. (2017). Developing a Small Business Management Concentration within a Business Degree. *Small Business Institute® Journal*, 15–30.

Martinez, L. F., Ferreira, A. I., & Can, A. B. (2016). Consultant–Client Relationship and Knowledge Transfer in Small- and Medium-Sized Enterprises' Change Process. *Psychological Reports*, *118*(2), 608–25. https://doi.org/10.1177/0033294116639429

McCarthy, P., & McCarthy, H. (2006). When Case Studies Are Not Enough: Integrating Experiential Learning into Business Curricula. *Journal of Education for Business*, 201–4. https://doi.org/10.3200/JOEB.81.4.201-204

Nahavandi, A., & Chesteen, S. (1988). The Impact of Consulting on Small Business: A Further Examination. *Entrepreneurship Theory and Practice*, *13*(1), 29–40. https://doi.org/10.1177/104225878801300104

Neck, H., & Greene, P. (2010). Entrepreneurship Education: Known Worlds and New Frontiers. *Journal of Small Business Management*, 55–70. https://doi.org/10.1111/j .1540-627X.2010.00314.x

O'Mally, L., & Ryan, A. (2006). Pedagogy and Relationship Marketing: Opportunities for Frame Restructuring Using African Drumming. *Journal of Marketing Management*, *22*(1–2), 195–214. https://doi.org/10.1362/026725706776022317

Oh, H., & Polidan, M. (2018). Retail Consulting Class: Experiential Learning Platform to Develop Future Retail Talents. *Journal of Marketing Education*, *40*(1), 31–46. https://doi.org/10.1177/0273475317743015

Okunade, A. A., Wunnava, P. V., & Walsh, Jr., R. (1994). Charitable Giving of Alumni: Micro-Data Evidence from a Large Public University. *American Journal of Economics and Sociology*, *53*(1), 73–84. https://doi.org/10.1111/j.1536-7150.1994 .tb02674.x

Piercy, N. (2013). Evaluating Experiential Learning in the Business Context: Contributions to Group-Based and Cross-Functional Working. *Innovations in*

Education and Teaching International, 50(2), 202–13. https://doi.org/10.1080/14703297.2012.760870

Portney, D. S., VonAchen, P., Standiford, T., Carey, M. R., Vu, J., Kirst, N., & Zink, B. (2019). Medical Student Consulting: Providing Students Leadership and Business Opportunities While Positively Impacting the Community. *MedEdPORTAL: Journal of Teaching and Learning Resources, 15.* https://doi.org/10.15766/mep_2374-8265.10838

Purdie, F., Ward, L., McAdie, T., King, N., & Drysdale, M. (2013). Are Work-Integrated Learning (WIL) Students Better Equipped Psychologically for Work Post-Graduation Than Their Non Work-Integrated Learning Peers? Some Initial Findings from a UK University. *Asia Pacific Journal of Cooperative Education*, 117–25. https://doi.org/10.1016/j.sbspro.2011.11.297

Ratcliffe, M., Burd, C., Holder, K., & Fields, A. (2016). *Defining Rural at the US Census Bureau.* Economics and Statistics Administration, US Department of Commerce. United States Census Bureau. www.census.gov/content/dam/Census/library/publications/2016/acs/acsgeo-1.pdf

Robinson, D. F., Sherwood, A. L., & DePaolo, C. A. (2010). Service-Learning by Doing: How a Student-Run Consulting Company Finds Relevance and Purpose in a Business Strategy Capstone Course. *Journal of Management Education, 34*(1), 88–112. https://doi.org/10.1177/1052562909339025

Sá, E., Casais, B., & Silva, J. (2019). Local Development through Rural Entrepreneurship, from the Triple Helix Perspective: The Case of a Peripheral Region in Northern Portugal. *International Journal of Entrepreneurial Behavior and Research, 25*(4), 698–716. https://doi.org/10.1108/IJEBR-03-2018-0172

Schervish, P. G. (1997). Inclination, Obligation, and Association: What We Know and What We Need to Learn about Donor Motivation. In D. F. Burlingame (Ed.), *Critical Issues in Fundraising* (pp. 110–38). New York: Wiley.

Schindler, P. S., & Stockstill, L. E. (1995). Two Decades of Thinking Small: Educational Impacts of the Small Business Institute. *Journal of Business and Entrepreneurship, 7*(2), 29–37.

Seifer, S. (1998). Service-Learning: Community-Campus Partnerships for Health Professions Education. *Academic Medicine*, 273–7. https://doi.org/10.1097/00001888-199803000-00015

Shim, J. M. (2001). *Relationship of Selected Alumnae Characteristics to Alumnae Financial Support at a Women's College.* Unpublished doctoral dissertation, University of Florida, Gainesville.

Smith Ducoffe, S. J., Tromley, C. L., & Tucker, M. (2006). Interdiscplinary, Team-Taught, Undergraduate Business Courses: The Impact of Integration. *Journal of Management Education, 30*(2), 276–94. https://doi.org/10.1177/1052562905284663

Sonfield, M. C. (1981). Can Student Consultants Really Help a Small Business. *Journal of Small Business Management, 19*(4), 3–9.

Sonfield, M. C. (2008). SBI Consulting: "Small Business" Versus "Entrepreneurial" Performance Outcomes. *Small Business Institute® Journal, 1*(1), 62–75.

Steffes, J. (2004). Creating Powerful Learning Environments beyond the Classroom. *Change*, 46–50. https://doi.org/10.1080/00091380409605580

Tsao, J. C., & Coll, G. (2004). To Give or Not to Give: Factors Determining Alumni Intent to Make Donations as a PR Outcome. *Journalism and Mass Communication Educator, 59*(4), 381–92. https://doi.org/10.1177/107769580405900407

Van Slyke, D. M., & Brooks, A. C. (2004). Why Do People Give? New Evidence and Strategies for Nonprofit Managers. *American Review of Public Administration, 35*(3), 199–222. https://doi.org/10.1177/0275074005275308

Wastyn, M. L. (2009). Why Alumni Don't Give: A Qualitative Study of What Motivates Non-Donors to Higher Education. *International Journal of Educational Advancement, 9*, 96–108. https://doi.org/10.1057/ijea.2009.31

Winsett, C., Foster, C., Dearing, J., & Bursch, G. (2016). The Impact of Group Experiential Learning on Student Engagement. *Academy of Business Research Journal*, 20–21.

8. Experience, knowledge, and performance in entrepreneurship education: proposing a dynamic learning model

Sílvia Costa and Arjan Frederiks

INTRODUCTION

This study integrates the theory of entrepreneurship education with learning. We do this by presenting a conceptual model for learning concerned with the ideation, conceptualization, formulation, and implementation of the startup process, or what could be termed "entrepreneurial learning," based on the different configurations that entrepreneurship education can adopt. Specifically, we focus on the analysis of different formats of entrepreneurship education and the dimensions of learning associated with these formats, as well as the expected outcomes, i.e., the dimensions of startup knowledge. Because learning is a dynamic process, we suggest a theoretical model to study learning from a multilevel and longitudinal perspective, across the spectrum of the entrepreneurship process.

The stream of literature focusing on entrepreneurship education is often presented separately from the literature stream on learning (Fayolle, 2013). Instead, we view education methods, knowledge acquisition, and venture outcomes as part of a single learning continuum. As part of that continuum, entrepreneurship learning outside the traditional classroom is posited as equally important as classroom education, and that both, in parallel, lead to the most effective form of knowledge acquisition. In fact, it is important to state that knowledge and learning are fundamentally different. Knowledge refers to what is known, while learning refers to the process through which that knowledge is gathered (Harrison & Leitch, 2005). Because knowledge is an output of the learning process, an integrative view of both processes is necessary in the literature. Nevertheless, scholars studying entrepreneurship education tend to focus on the contents and methods of how entrepreneurship should be taught (i.e., how knowledge should be conveyed and through which practices), while scholars focusing on entrepreneurship learning focus on the outcomes and factors influencing the acquisition of knowledge. The role of experience and application in the entrepreneurship context has been used to explain how learning transforms into knowledge (e.g., Corbett, 2005, 2007; Politis, 2005), which can inform entrepreneurship education about the more adequate practices to adopt to develop knowledge.

On the one hand, scholars focus on intangible outcomes of entrepreneurial learning, such as the development of an entrepreneurial mindset, or the raising of entrepreneurial awareness and intentions (Fayolle & Gailly, 2015; Gielnik et al., 2013). On the other hand, the role of contextualized experiences in entrepreneurship education is central to promote the development of knowledge and skills (Leitch, Hazlett, & Pittaway, 2012), where venture creation and success are often the expected outcomes of learning. For this reason, uncovering the interplay between entrepreneurship education and the different learning processes and outcomes is extremely relevant to understanding the determinants of entrepreneurship knowledge. However, the literature is scarce in demonstrating (a) what learning outcomes result from different configurations of entrepreneurship education (i.e., which settings and teaching approaches); (b) that entrepreneurship knowledge results in creating and managing effective, viable businesses, and (c) how the process of learning occurs in a dynamic setting over time. The purpose of this chapter is to propose a theoretical framework to be explored further in empirical research. The research questions we ask are: (1) what are the most important dimensions of entrepreneurial learning, particularly for young, first-time entrepreneurs, and (2) what instructional methods are most conducive for developing these dimensions of learning?

In other words, more research focusing on learning as the process linking entrepreneurship education and knowledge is necessary. Explaining how entrepreneurs learn and how their knowledge is related to education and specific experiences contributes to entrepreneurship research and practice, specifically to the entrepreneurship education literature. First, understanding dimensions of learning according to different types of education strategies can inform research to design studies specific for each educational context and strategy. Second, understanding that learning can be represented by different types of outcomes depending on the educational approach, will allow a more precise evaluation of entrepreneurship programs' success and outcomes.

With this study we explore a theoretical framework about how different configurations of entrepreneurship education result in different outcomes of learning and knowledge. Additionally, we suggest a research model to analyze the development of entrepreneurial learning along the new venture creation process from a multilevel perspective.

THEORETICAL BACKGROUND

Many scholars have focused on the topic of entrepreneurship education from different perspectives. Two of the most prominent questions within the entrepreneurship education literature are *what* and *how* entrepreneurship should be taught (e.g., Béchard & Grégoire, 2005; Kuratko, 2005). As for *what* should be taught in entrepreneurship education, Kuratko (2005) provides an overview of topics which are frequently related to entrepreneurs and the process of new venture creation. In our view, the topics listed by Kuratko fall into four major categories: individual level (psychological aspects of entrepreneurship; entrepreneurial awareness/spirit; risks and trade-offs of entrepreneurial career), organizational level (distinguishing entrepreneurship and managerial domains; venture financing; corporate entrepreneurship; entrepreneurship strategies), societal level (women and minority entrepreneurship; economic and social contributions of entrepreneurship), and research purposes-related topics (ethics and entrepreneurship; predictors of success). Although Kuratko describes the main topics of the field, agreement on whether these are the topics that should be taught in entrepreneurship education is not easily met. Moreover, there is not yet any evidence that these topics are relevant for the practice of entrepreneurship. Aldrich and Yang (2014) stress that if programs focus only on "know-what" knowledge, but do not approach a "know-how" perspective, they do not succeed in addressing the required tacit knowledge and complex procedures inherent to the activities that entrepreneurs need to learn. Fayolle (2013) expresses his concerns on the fact that the field of entrepreneurship education needs a strong intellectual and conceptual ground capable of strengthening entrepreneurship programs.

As for *how* entrepreneurship should be taught, there is agreement in the literature that universities are privileged arenas for entrepreneurship education (Block, Hoogerheide, & Thurik, 2011; Neck & Greene, 2011) and that higher education itself is a predictor of startup activity (Unger, Rauch, Frese, & Rosenbusch, 2011). Neck and Greene (2011) argue that entrepreneurship education should be viewed as a method. This method mainly focuses on entrepreneurship as a way of thinking, where students are given the opportunity to develop a portfolio of entrepreneurship competencies based on their critical experiences.

Other scholars consider that entrepreneurship education should also address the development of attitudes and affective predispositions towards entrepreneurship, rather than only tangible knowledge acquisition (Fayolle & Gailly, 2015; Shepherd, 2004). Additionally, there is growing evidence that entrepreneurial activity is a phenomenon which occurs at the team level (e.g., Harper, 2008; Neumeyer & Santos, 2019). Therefore, if entrepreneurs are instructed as discrete individuals and not in a team setting, where transactive memory can be created, programs are likely to fall short and not meet their goals towards knowledge development (Aldrich & Yang, 2014).

Other approaches focus on experimental methods within education, through which entrepreneurs can test hypotheses for their business (Ries, 2011). Although most authors believe that teaching entrepreneurship is better performed through experiential approaches and contact with examples, it is not fully established which methods are more efficient in entrepreneurship education. Fayolle (2013) argues that researchers and educators must deeply and critically reflect on their practices. However, which approaches to choose to teach entrepreneurship are not consensual among entrepreneurship educators, researchers, and entrepreneurs, and this is one of the main challenges in the field.

In summary, there seems to be agreement that entrepreneurship education should rely on the promotion of critical experiences, providing individuals the tools to transform these experiences into knowledge (Fayolle & Gailly, 2015; Politis, 2005, 2008). Experimenting with solutions for problems, learning by doing, critically reflecting upon theories, and engaging in real-life situations have been shown to have a higher impact on learning, the development of perceptions, and entrepreneurial intentions of students (Harrison & Leitch, 2005; Pittaway & Cope, 2007; Rasmussen & Sørheim, 2006). However, aside from a few examples (e.g., Corbett, 2007; Karia, Bathula, & Abbott, 2015), the literature is scarce in demonstrating whether entrepreneurship programs fully based on experiential learning approaches are effective in developing entrepreneurship knowledge and how that translates into venture performance outcomes.

Entrepreneurship education practices seem to be configured along a spectrum which ranges from raising theoretical and attitudinal notions about entrepreneurship (Bae, Qian, Miao, & Fiet, 2014; Fayolle & Gailly, 2015) to fully experiential, hands-on approaches focusing on venture launch and management (Honig, 2004). One extreme of the spectrum refers to educational approaches focusing on the main theoretical perspectives within entrepreneurship literature, with the goal of creating awareness and reflection about the phenomena. These practices may include some level of experience within the classroom and focus mainly on the development of the entrepreneurial mindset, i.e., a way of thinking which resembles that of entrepreneurs (Krueger, 2007). Therefore, these practices may rely on having contact with cases and examples, besides theoretical approaches to entrepreneurship. On the other side of the spectrum, entrepreneurship education practices focus on pure experiential methods, promoting experience in the field and hands-on practice with entrepreneurs (e.g., Santos, Neumeyer, & Morris, 2019). Naturally, the position of education programs varies along this spectrum, depending on the resources available, the goals of the programs, and the context in which they are developed. For this reason, we consider it important to understand the interplay between entrepreneurship education configurations with different dimensions of learning and knowledge.

METHOD OF REVIEW

To understand the interplay between entrepreneurship education configurations (focused on practice versus theory) with the different dimensions of entrepreneurial learning, we have analyzed ten conceptual and theoretical articles in relevant entrepreneurship journals based on Pearce II (2012), and in several additional outlets relevant for entrepreneurship and learning. Figure 8.1 describes in detail all the steps taken in the literature review.

Since the goal of this literature review is to integrate the theory on entrepreneurship education and learning, we focused solely on conceptual and theoretical articles, including reviews on one of the topics. This enabled us to have a broad overview of the literatures on both education and learning in entrepreneurship, and to understand the different perspectives described in these literatures regarding the acquisition of knowledge. Because entrepreneurship education has evolved greatly over time, passing through many changes in its configuration, we focused on the period 2000–15. As exclusion criteria, we have not included articles referring to entrepreneurship education as a setting to test other relationships. We excluded empirical articles as well, as indicated before, to get an overview of the bigger picture and the theoretical foundations. Our analysis included thus ten articles which are presented in Table 8.1. Based on these articles, we will discuss our findings in the coming section, where we map the dimensions of entrepreneurial learning over time (i.e., from before the initial business idea until after a company has been established) and according to the configuration of entrepreneurship education in which they are typically developed. To do so, we connect our findings with other important contents in entrepreneurship literature.

FINDINGS

Entrepreneurial learning occurs over time within the relationship between experiences and the educational context. Entrepreneurship education provides these experiences, as well as the basis to transform them into knowledge, both in formal and informal ways.

The literature states that the entrepreneurship process begins with the recognition of a feasible business idea (e.g., Baron & Shane, 2008). However, many studies focus on dimensions of learning which occur at a very early stage of the startup process, before a business idea is even identified. On the other

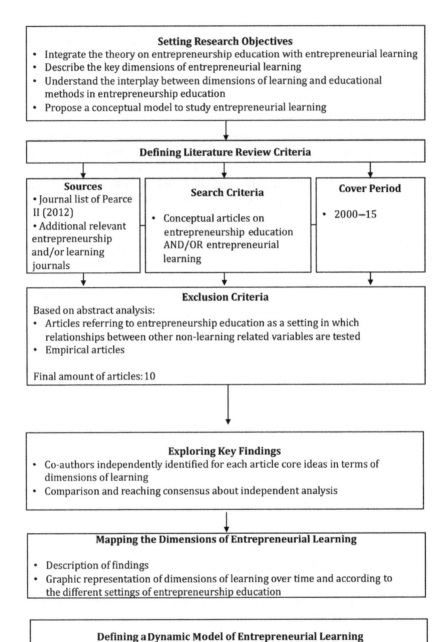

Figure 8.1   Roadmap of the study and literature review

Table 8.1   *Articles included in the analysis to map the configurations of entrepreneurship education and learning dimensions*

Author and year of publication	Title and journal	Core ideas of article included in the analysis
Honig, 2004	Entrepreneurship education: Toward a model of contingency-based business planning, *Academy of Management Learning and Education*	Comparison of pedagogical models for business planning education.
Kuratko, 2005	The emergence of entrepreneurship education: Development, trends, and challenges, *Entrepreneurship Theory and Practice*	Entrepreneurship is more than business creation. The author considers that entrepreneurship education and education institutions must embrace the fact that entrepreneurship is a way of thinking as a way to implement effective training strategies in their programs.
Harrison & Leitch, 2005	Entrepreneurial learning: Researching the interface between learning and the entrepreneurial context, *Entrepreneurship Theory and Practice*	The authors introduce a special issue aiming to explore topics which were scarce in the literature, among them being opportunity recognition and exploitation as a learning process.
Béchard & Grégoire, 2005	Entrepreneurship education research revisited: The case of higher education, *Academy of Management Learning and Education*	The authors conclude that the literature on the topic of entrepreneurship education evidences four main concerns: (1) related to the impact of entrepreneurial education in society and economy, as well as within the higher education institutions; (2) related to the systematization of entrepreneurship education; (3) related to the content to be taught; and (4) related to individual needs in structuring teaching programs. The authors emphasize that there are not many concerns related to social-cognitive or psycho-cognitive aspects of entrepreneurial education.
Politis, 2005	The process of entrepreneurial learning: A conceptual framework, *Entrepreneurship Theory and Practice*	Entrepreneurial learning presented as an experiential process where entrepreneurs' career experience, transformation process of experiences into knowledge, and entrepreneurial knowledge are at the core of the process.

Author and year of publication	Title and journal	Core ideas of article included in the analysis
Pittaway & Cope, 2007	Entrepreneurship education: A systematic review of the evidence, *International Small Business Journal*	Entrepreneurship education does have an impact on student propensity and intentionality towards entrepreneurship. There is, however, little consensus on the impact of entrepreneurial education in practice, creating more effective entrepreneurs. Future research should focus on key outcome variables to evaluate entrepreneurship education.
Holcomb, Ireland, Holmes, Jr., & Hitt, 2009	Architecture of entrepreneurial learning: Exploring the link among heuristics, knowledge, and action, *Entrepreneurship Theory and Practice*	Comparison between different learning contexts. The relationship between experience heuristics development and recognition of opportunities is explored.
Neck & Greene, 2011	Entrepreneurship education: Known worlds and new frontiers, *Journal of Small Business Management*	Suggestion of entrepreneurship teaching as a method which at its core provides the opportunity for students to practice entrepreneurship.
Fayolle, 2013	Personal views on the future of entrepreneurship education, *Entrepreneurship and Regional Development*	There is little consensus on what entrepreneurial education really is about and on which impacts the methodologies used have. There is a need for stronger intellectual and conceptual foundations of the practices adopted. Practitioners and researchers are called to reflect upon their practices on entrepreneurship education, which is not "taken for granted."
Aldrich & Yang, 2014	How do entrepreneurs know what to do? Learning and organizing in new ventures, *Journal of Evolutionary Economics*	The creation of viable and profitable ventures depends on the cognitive mechanisms of individuals, their past experience, and also on what entrepreneurs learn by doing and experimenting.

hand, scholars focus on learning dimensions that occur at an advanced stage of the process, after an idea has been identified and, in some cases, after venture launch. Because learning occurs over time and is a dynamic process (Kuratko, 2005; Politis, 2005), we mapped entrepreneurial learning dimensions along the venturing process, defining the moment of opportunity identification as a crucial milestone in this overview (see Figure 8.2). The learning dimensions developed along the startup process occur in entrepreneurship education settings that vary along a spectrum of theory and reflection oriented to practice and experiential learning (y axis in Figure 8.2). These settings can be formal (i.e., the classroom, service-learning projects, structured co-curricular events, boot camps) or informal (i.e., the activities developed in the university through which students learn about entrepreneurship in an indirect way). In the next section we discuss these findings and connect them to other important content in entrepreneurship literature.

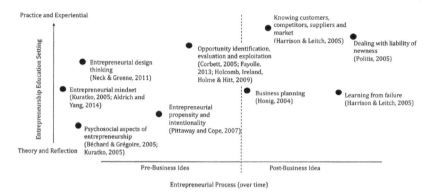

Figure 8.2   Dimensions of entrepreneurial learning

Dimensions of Entrepreneurial Learning Pre-Business Idea

During the pre-business idea stage, there is a set of learning dimensions which refer to the creation of awareness and thinking in a unique way. The development of an entrepreneurial mindset involves the creation of cognitive mechanisms, such as routines and heuristics, which enable potential entrepreneurs to learn better during later stages of the entrepreneurship process (Aldrich & Yang, 2014), or the development of future-oriented cognitive processes to imagine new ventures ideas (Frederiks, Englis, Ehrenhard, & Groen, 2019). Alongside these cognitive mechanisms which are relevant in entrepreneurship education (Santos, Costa, Neumeyer, & Caetano, 2016), there are other important psychosocial aspects of entrepreneurship that individuals need to develop before they identify a business idea (Béchard & Grégoire, 2005). Individuals need to know themselves, their motivations, and predispositions towards entrepreneurship. These two learning dimensions occur mainly at a theoretical and reflection level of entrepreneurship education. At this early stage, there are also practical and applied learning activities, which are crucial to create awareness of entrepreneurship. Entrepreneurial design thinking is a way of providing potential entrepreneurs with the necessary tools to think critically and divergently about their surroundings, which can result in the identification and creation of opportunities (Neck & Greene, 2011).

Most entrepreneurship education approaches have an impact on the startup intentions, although the literature lacks in evidencing if this intentionality results in actual venture creation and success (Pittaway & Cope, 2007). This learning dimension seems to be crucial to determine the effectiveness of education programs, although most evaluations are made at later stages of the process (Fayolle & Gailly, 2015). The propensity towards entrepreneurship and intention to engage in startup activities also occurs at a more theoretical level, in the sense that potential entrepreneurs may have these inclinations, but they are latent. These propensities, cognitive mechanisms, and the psychosocial aspects of entrepreneurship enable individuals to identify opportunities, which occur at a practice level. Opportunity identification, from a cognitive perspective, depends on the ability of individuals to analyze patterns of information and changes around them and recognize opportunities (Baron, 2006). Because this activity depends on individuals' cognitive structures and experience, opportunity identification can be learned (Costa, Ehrenhard, Caetano, & Santos, 2016; DeTienne & Chandler, 2004). Opportunity identification is best learned in experiential contexts (Corbett, 2005; Costa, Santos, Wach, & Caetano, 2018) and it is widely indicated in entrepreneurship education literature as a key dimension to be included in curricula (Fayolle, 2013). The fact that opportunity identification depends on the development of entrepreneurial cognition by individuals (Holcomb et al., 2009) demonstrates that these learning dimensions may change over time, but they prevail and connect with other learning dimensions occurring at later stages of the process. This suggests that entrepreneurial learning is a dynamic process where the competencies developed along the way need to be analyzed and assessed in terms of the outcomes that they produce. In this sense, analyzing the opportunity identification ability of potential entrepreneurs implies the study of other antecedents such as the mindset, cognition, and intentions. At the same time, opportunity identification will be a predictor of later learning dimensions in the process, as we discuss next.

Dimensions of Entrepreneurial Learning Post-Business Idea

After opportunity identification, decision making to further pursue that opportunity will determine whether a potential entrepreneur will act upon it or not (Baron & Shane, 2008). For a period of time, the opportunity exists only at the realm of the idea and it is not concrete (Costa et al., 2016). It is the decision to act upon the opportunity that will determine the unfolding of the rest of the entrepreneurship process. After this point, there are other learning dimensions that occur more at a practical, experiential setting. Business planning and business model design are tools that individuals use to test their business idea and to structurally plan the different activities for their venture. Business planning is very often a taught competence in entrepreneurship education (Honig, 2004). However, teaching what a business plan is purely at the theoretical level is unlikely to produce outcomes in terms of venture success. Several authors have argued that this dimension of learning is best learned in an experiential setting, where entrepreneurs can test the assumptions related to their business (Honig, 2004; Karia et al., 2015; Osiyevskyy, Costa, & Madill, 2016). While business planning requires a certain level of theoretical knowledge, other related activities require a complete experiential approach, such as interacting with customers (Harrison & Leitch, 2005). The experiences gained in these practical activities are transformed into knowledge because other dimensions of learning at the cognitive level had been developed before (Aldrich & Yang, 2014; Politis, 2005), evidencing the looping effect among these dimensions of entrepreneurial learning. These preconditions enable entrepreneurs to deal in a successful way with the liabilities of newness, i.e., avoiding failure after venture launch due to lack of financing or bad marketing (Politis, 2005). Entrepreneurs are thus better prepared at this point to suggest solutions to customers that fit the context within which they wish to act (Zhao, Libaers, & Song, 2015).

The remaining dimensions of learning, at a practical or theoretical level, enable entrepreneurs to respond successfully to the needs of the market where they plan to act. Dealing with the liability of newness includes the ability to suggest and design business solutions, but also the ability to present the business, apply for startup funding, and successfully market the business (Politis, 2005). Another important dimension is learning from failure, as individuals learn to think about alternatives to their activities (Cope, 2011). In the entrepreneurship process, and especially during the experiential activities, entrepreneurs learn a variety of aspects by testing what works and also what does not work out for their business (Harrison & Leitch, 2005).

The dimensions of learning described above do not occur as isolated events along the entrepreneurship process. On the contrary, they are interrelated and the earlier have an influence on later success. Some will work as predictors of knowledge while others may moderate the relationship between experiences and the transformation of those experiences into knowledge. Additionally, while the learning dimensions developed before business idea identification occur at the individual level (e.g., Baum, Frese, Baron, & Katz, 2007), the ones occurring after business idea identification are more likely to occur at the team level (e.g., West, 2007). Figure 8.2 depicts that at the beginning of the process most entrepreneurial learning dimensions are developed at predominantly theoretical and reflective settings, changing later into learning dimensions more focused on practical and experiential settings.

A Dynamic Model of Learning through Entrepreneurship Education

To understand better how entrepreneurs learn, the dynamic characteristics of the learning process as well as the resulting outcomes require close attention. While Figure 8.2 depicts the literature stream on entrepreneurship education and learning over time, our findings also suggest that learning is a dynamic process where different levels of analysis are considered and where knowledge is an observable outcome impacting future venture performance and success.

The notion that entrepreneurship can be learned derives mostly from the considerations of Peter Drucker (1985), who argued that entrepreneurship is a discipline and, as with all disciplines, can be learned (Kuratko, 2005). According to the perspective of Bandura (1986), education can prepare individuals to perform specific activities, one being "enterprising." Through knowledge acquisition and transfer, individuals are able to increase their self-efficacy and achieve success in startup activities (Anderson & Jack, 2008; Jack & Anderson, 1999). Therefore, entrepreneurship education provides students with frameworks through which they can understand and make sense of their experiences. In this view, entrepreneurial learning is seen as a process, rather than a single moment in time (Cope, 2005). Entrepreneurial learning is described by Politis as a continuous process that occurs throughout the lives of entrepreneurs and during the entrepreneurship process along which they transform those experiences into knowledge in a dynamic and interchangeable process between these two components: experience and knowledge (Politis, 2005). The literature also posits that entrepreneurial learning depends on different types of experience (such as past career experience, family background, education, and instruction) and other individual characteristics (such as cognitive style, predominant logic of reasoning, habits, routines, and emotions) (Politis, 2005; Aldrich & Yang, 2014). Finally, entrepreneurial learning is likely to be a dynamic process occurring at different levels of analysis (individual, team, and interaction between the two levels) (Aldrich & Yang, 2014).

Based on above, we propose a comprehensive research model to analyze entrepreneurial learning, which includes the different dimensions of learning over the startup process and the multilevel character associated with it (Figure 8.3).

In the model depicted in Figure 8.3, we suggest that each learning dimension is interrelated with another across the entrepreneurship process. This means that learning occurs in the interaction between the different learning settings and dimensions, and results in knowledge outcomes. Entrepreneurship knowledge is the outcome variable. It manifests along a time perspective and depends on the educational setting emphasized, as well as the learning dimension focused on those activities. Therefore, we draw the following propositions:

Proposition 1: Entrepreneurship educational settings focused on theoretical and reflective activities will increase knowledge related to the cognitive, psychosocial, and predispositions towards entrepreneurship.

Proposition 2: Entrepreneurship educational settings focused on practical and hands-on activities will increase knowledge related to operational entrepreneurship activities (opportunity identification, business planning, customer insight, dealing with liability of newness, and learning from failure).

As shown in Figure 8.2, it is likely that at an early stage of the startup process, cognitive, psychosocial, and predispositions towards entrepreneurship are developed in education settings that promote theoretical and reflective approaches. Because learning does not occur as a single event in time, these competencies developed at early stages are predictors of knowledge acquisition in later stages of the process, in settings promoting experiential activities. Therefore, we propose that entrepreneurial cognition (mindset, psychosocial aspects, and predisposition towards entrepreneurship) will enable the successful transformation of experiences into knowledge, in settings more related to practical activities. Subsequently, at later stages of the entrepreneurship process, individuals will not only demonstrate knowledge related to operational activities but this knowledge will also reflect on their venture success, such as acquiring financing and growth.

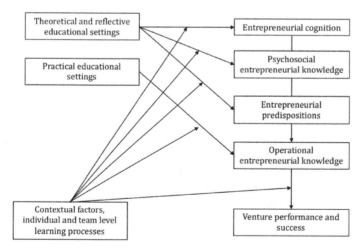

Figure 8.3   A dynamic model of learning entrepreneurial knowledge through entrepreneurship education

Proposition 3: Cognitive, psychosocial and predispositions towards entre-preneurship are predictors of knowledge demonstrated at later stages of the startup process, related to operational activities.

Proposition 4: Knowledge about operational startup activities are predictors of venture success.

In our proposed model, we consider characteristics of the context, of the individual, and of the team of utmost importance to understanding learning. Because learning occurs in close interaction with the context, these variables are likely to moderate the transformation of experiences into knowledge. Other important variables at the individual level are likely to moderate the learning process, such as past entrepreneurship experience, presence of role models, education, and learning style (Cassidy, 2004; Politis, 2008). Entrepreneurship activities are also usually developed within a team which makes team con-figurations and team learning behaviors potential moderators of the learning process (Savelsbergh, van der Heijden, & Poell, 2009). Therefore, we propose the following:

Proposition 5: Contextual factors, individual-level background variables, and team learning processes are moderators of the different phases of the learning process.

DISCUSSION

We have proposed a conceptual model for entrepreneurial learning based on the different configurations that entrepreneurship education can adopt. Specifically, we focused on the analysis of different formats of entrepreneur-ship education and the different dimensions of learning associated to these formats, as well as the expected outcomes. After mapping the different learn-ing dimensions mentioned in the literature, we have proposed a model, which accounts for the temporal and multilevel aspects of entrepreneurial learning.

Our study brings important implications for both research and practice. First, we have suggested several propositions which can be tested in empirical studies. For example, future studies can investigate the learning outcomes (knowledge) in different entrepreneurship educational settings. Additionally, early learning dimensions can be tested as predictors of entrepreneurship knowledge in later stages of the startup process. Because literature still lacks testing as to whether educational approaches result in more successful ven-tures, this relationship can be explored as well based on the model that we propose (Aldrich & Yang, 2014). The dynamic nature of our research model responds to a need for more multilevel and longitudinal research in entrepreneurship research (Akinci, 2015; Shepherd, 2011).

Second, our proposed model can provide important insights to the practice of entrepreneurship education. The literature has shown that there is a mismatch between the goals of the programs and the outcomes deriving from them (Fayolle, Gailly, & Lassas-Clerc, 2006). Most entrepreneurship education programs influence the formation of intentions towards entrepreneurship, but evaluations focus on venture launch and success (Fayolle & Gailly, 2015; Fayolle, 2013). Our proposed model can be used as a tool to evaluate entrepreneurship education programs. The model allows us to assess different types of knowledge according to the phase of the process being focused on in the program, as well as the educational configuration (theoretical or experiential) being used. This will allow a more precise evaluation of the success of entrepreneurship programs.

Understanding how entrepreneurs learn is crucial to understanding the venturing process and success thereof. Thus, with this study we aim to contribute to the entrepreneurial learning literature by providing a comprehensive and dynamic model which we hope will inspire future research.

REFERENCES

Akinci, C. 2015. Entrepreneurial learning through intuitive decision making. In D. Rae & C. Wang (Eds), *Entrepreneurial learning: New perspectives in research, education and practice*: 72–91. London: Routledge.

Aldrich, H. E., & Yang, T. 2014. How do entrepreneurs know what to do? Learning and organizing in new ventures. *Journal of Evolutionary Economics*, 24(1): 59–82.

Anderson, A. R., & Jack, S. L. 2008. Role typologies for enterprising education: The professional artisan? *Journal of Small Business and Enterprise Development*, 15(2): 259–73.

Bae, T. J., Qian, S., Miao, C., & Fiet, J. O. 2014. The relationship between entrepreneurship education and entrepreneurial intentions: A meta-analytic review. *Entrepreneurship Theory and Practice*, 38(2): 217–54.

Bandura, A. 1986. *Social foundation of thought and action.* Englewood Cliffs, NJ: Prentice Hall.

Baron, R. A. 2006. Opportunity recognition as pattern recognition: How entrepreneurs "connect the dots" to identify new business opportunities. *Academy of Management Perspectives*, 20(1): 104–19.

Baron, R. A., & Shane, S. A. 2008. *Entrepreneurship: A process perspective* (2nd ed.). Mason, OH: South-Western Cengage Learning.

Baum, J. R., Frese, M., Baron, R. A., & Katz, J. A. 2007. Entrepreneurship as an area of psychology study: An introduction. In J. R. Baum, M. Frese, & R. A. Baron (Eds), *The psychology of entrepreneurship*: 1–18. Mahwah, NJ: Lawrence Erlbaum Associates.

Béchard, J.-P., & Grégoire, D. 2005. Entrepreneurship education research revisited: The case of higher education. *Academy of Management Learning and Education*, 4(1): 22–43.

Block, J. H., Hoogerheide, L., & Thurik, R. 2011. Education and entrepreneurial choice: An instrumental variables analysis. *International Small Business Journal*, 31(1): 23–33.

Cassidy, S. 2004. Learning styles: An overview of theories, models and measures. *Educational Psychology: An International Journal of Experimental Educational Psychology*, 24(4): 419–44.

Cope, J. 2005. Toward a dynamic learning perspective of entrepreneurship. *Entrepreneurship Theory and Practice*, 29(4): 373–97.

Cope, J. 2011. Entrepreneurial learning from failure: An interpretative phenomenological analysis. *Journal of Business Venturing*, 26(6): 604–23.

Corbett, A. C. 2005. Experiential learning within the process of opportunity identification and exploitation. *Entrepreneurship Theory and Practice*, 29(4): 473–91.

Corbett, A. C. 2007. Learning asymmetries and the discovery of entrepreneurial opportunities. *Journal of Business Venturing*, 22(1): 97–118.

Costa, S. F., Ehrenhard, M. L., Caetano, A., & Santos, S. C. 2016. The role of different opportunities in the activation and use of the business opportunity prototype. *Creativity and Innovation Management*, 25(1), 58–72.

Costa, S. F., Santos, S. C., Wach, D., & Caetano, A. 2018. Recognizing opportunities across campus: The effects of cognitive training and entrepreneurial passion on the business opportunity prototype. *Journal of Small Business Management*, 56(1), 51–75.

DeTienne, D. R., & Chandler, G. N. 2004. Opportunity identification and its role in the entrepreneurial classroom: A pedagogical approach and empirical test. *Academy of Management Review*, 3(3): 242–57.

Drucker, P. F. 1985. *Innovation and entrepreneurship*. New York: Harper and Row.

Fayolle, A. 2013. Personal views on the future of entrepreneurship education. *Entrepreneurship and Regional Development*, 25(7–8): 692–701.

Fayolle, A., & Gailly, B. 2015. The Impact of entrepreneurship education on entrepreneurial ettitudes and intention: Hysteresis and persistence. *Journal of Small Business Management*, 53(1): 75–93.

Fayolle, A., Gailly, B., & Lassas-Clerc, N. 2006. Assessing the impact of entrepreneurship education programmes: A new methodology. *Journal of European Industrial Training*, 30(9): 701–20.

Frederiks, A. J., Englis, B. G., Ehrenhard, M. L., & Groen, A. J. 2019. Entrepreneurial cognition and the quality of new venture ideas: An experimental approach to comparing future-oriented cognitive processes. *Journal of Business Venturing*, 34(2), 327–47.

Gielnik, M. M., Barabas, S., Frese, M., Namatovu-Dawa, R., Scholz, F. A., Metzger, J. R. et al. 2013. A temporal analysis of how entrepreneurial goal intentions, positive fantasies, and action planning affect starting a new venture and when the effects wear off. *Journal of Business Venturing*, 29(6): 755–72.

Harper, D. A. 2008. Towards a theory of entrepreneurial teams. *Journal of Business Venturing*, 23(6): 613–26.

Harrison, R. T., & Leitch, C. M. 2005. Entrepreurial learning: Researching the interface between learning and the entrepreneurial context. *Entrepreneurial Theory and Practice*, 29(4): 351–71.

Holcomb, T. R., Ireland, R. D., Holmes Jr, R. M., & Hitt, M. A. 2009. Architecture of entrepreneurial learning: Exploring the link among heuristics, knowledge, and action. *Entrepreneurship Theory and Practice*, 33(1): 167–92.

Honig, B. 2004. Entrepreneurship education: Toward a model of contingency-based business planning. *Academy of Management Learning and Education*, 3(3): 258–73.

Jack, S. L., & Anderson, A. R. 1999. Entrepreneurship education within the enterprise culture: Producing reflective practitioners. *International Journal of Entrepreneurial Behaviour and Research*, 5(3): 110–25.

Karia, M., Bathula, H., & Abbott, M. 2015. An experiential learning approach to teaching business planning: Connecting students to the real world. In M. Li & Y. Zhao (Eds), *Exploring learning and teaching in higher education*: 123–44. New York: Springer.

Krueger, N. F. 2007. What lies beneath? The experiential essence of entrepreneurial thinking. *Entrepreneurship Theory and Practice*, 31(1): 123–38.

Kuratko, D. F. 2005. The emergence of entrepreneurship education: Development, trends, and challenges. *Entrepreneurship Theory and Practice*, 29(5): 577–98.

Leitch, C., Hazlett, S.-A., & Pittaway, L. 2012. Entrepreneurship education and context. *Entrepreneurship and Regional Development*, 24(9–10): 733–40.

Neck, H. M., & Greene, P. G. 2011. Entrepreneurship education: Known worlds and new frontiers. *Journal of Small Business Management*, 49(1): 55–70.

Neumeyer, X., & Santos, S. C. 2019. A lot of different flowers make a bouquet: The effect of gender composition on technology-based entrepreneurship teams. *International Entrepreneurship and Management Journal*, 16: 93–114.

Osiyevskyy, O., Costa, S. F., & Madill, C. 2016. Business sense or subjective satisfaction? Exploring the outcomes of business planning comprehensiveness in small and medium business context. *International Journal of Entrepreneurship and Innovation*, 17(1): 15–30.

Pearce, J. A. 2012. Revising manuscripts for premier entrepreneurship journals. *Entrepreneurship Theory and Practice*, 36(2): 193–203.

Pittaway, L., & Cope, J. 2007. Entrepreneurship education: A systematic review of the evidence. *International Small Business Journal*, 25(5): 479–510.

Politis, D. 2005. The process of entrepreneurial learning: A conceptual framework. *Entrepreneurship Theory and Practice*, July: 399–424.

Politis, D. 2008. Does prior start-up experience matter for entrepreneurs' learning? A comparison between novice and habitual entrepreneurs. *Journal of Small Business and Enterprise Development*, 15(3): 472–89.

Rasmussen, E. a., & Sørheim, R. 2006. Action-based entrepreneurship education. *Technovation*, 26(2): 185–94.

Ries, E. 2011. *The lean startup: How today's entrepreneurs use continuous innovation to create radically successful businesses*. New York: Crown Business.

Santos, S. C., Costa, S. F., Neumeyer, X., & Caetano, A. 2016. Bridging entrepreneurial cognition research and entrepreneurship education: What and how. In M. Morris and E. Liguori (Eds), *Annals of entrepreneurship education and pedagogy – 2016*: 83–108. Cheltenham, UK and Northampton, MA, USA: Edward Elgar Publishing.

Santos, S. C., Neumeyer, X., & Morris, M. H. 2019. Entrepreneurship education in a poverty context: An empowerment perspective. *Journal of Small Business Management*, 57(S1): 6–36.

Savelsbergh, C. M. J. H., van der Heijden, B. I. J. M., & Poell, R. F. 2009. The development and empirical validation of a multidimensional measurement instrument for team learning behaviors. *Small Group Research*, 40(5): 587–607.

Shepherd, D. A. 2004. Educating entrepreneurship students about emotion and learning from failure. *Academy of Management Learning and Education*, 3(3): 274–87.

Shepherd, D. A. 2011. Multilevel entrepreneurship research: Opportunities for studying entrepreneurial decision making. *Journal of Management*, 37(2): 412–20.

Unger, J. M., Rauch, A., Frese, M., & Rosenbusch, N. 2011. Human capital and entrepreneurial success: A meta-analytical review. *Journal of Business Venturing*, 26(3): 341–58.

West, G. P. 2007. Collective cognition: When entrepreneurial teams, not individuals, make decisions. *Entrepreneurship Theory and Practice*, 31(1): 77–102.

Zhao, Y. L., Libaers, D., & Song, M. 2015. First product success: A mediated moderating model of resources, founding team startup experience, and product-positioning strategy. *Journal of Product Innovation Management*, 32(3): 441–58.

9. Entrepreneurship ecosystem builders: philanthropy, entrepreneurs, universities, and communities working collaboratively

Deborah Hoover

INTRODUCTION

Philanthropy and entrepreneurship are inextricably linked. We know that entrepreneurship breeds philanthropy, but the reverse is also true – philanthropy in turn can breed entrepreneurship. Successful entrepreneurs develop skills that enable them to give back to their communities for compelling social causes in ways that reflect their passions. These days, entrepreneurs paying it forward seek to support entrepreneurship ecosystems, entrepreneurship support organizations, and entrepreneurship education to help other entrepreneurs succeed. They often blend their giving with the sharing of lessons learned based on both successes and failures.

The DNA that spawns the high level of activism and engagement prevalent among entrepreneurs positions them to take a more hands-on approach to deploying their philanthropic resources. They may be less inclined to approach their giving through traditional grantmaking (grant philanthropy) focused on providing financial capital to achieve a goal. Some take on mentoring roles that draw upon their skills and expertise with no direct financial investment (managerial philanthropy). Other entrepreneurs wish to fully immerse themselves and consequently infuse their giving with full-on involvement through venture philanthropy. Venture philanthropy involves the investment of financial resources coupled with expert advice grounded in the entrepreneur's own startup journey (Taylor, Strom, and Renz, 2014).

Still other entrepreneurs seek new ways to achieve their charitable goals through vehicles that disrupt traditional philanthropic means. For example, Mark Zuckerberg and Priscilla Chan, founders of the Chan Zuckerberg Initiative, a limited liability company (LLC) established in 2015, work at "the intersection of philanthropy, technology, and advocacy" to pursue the mission of building "a more inclusive, just, and healthy future for everyone."[1] In addition to their LLC, Chan and Zuckerberg also work through a more traditional philanthropic vehicle, a donor-advised fund at the Silicon Valley Community Foundation.[2]

Similarly, Washington, DC-based Case Foundation, established in 1997 by America Online founder Steve Case and his wife Jean, sought to work in ways that upend traditional approaches to philanthropy as the team pursued its mission "to invest in people and ideas that can change the world." Case harnessed "the best impulses of entrepreneurship, innovation, technology and collaboration to drive exponential impact."[3] Its strategies for social change encompassed "revolutionizing philanthropy, unleashing entrepreneurship, and igniting civic engagement" as the underpinnings for funding ecosystem building, inclusive entrepreneurship, accelerators and incubators, and social entrepreneurship. At the end of 2019, the Case family made a bold shift in the way they pursue social good. They stated that while they are proud of the foundation's accomplishments, they have decided to pursue their philanthropic goals through a new LLC that will focus its efforts on advancing impact investing, a means of achieving financial gains while simultaneously seeking social or environmental benefits.[4]

This chapter emphasizes the more engaged and disruptive roles philanthropists can play particularly in building entrepreneurship ecosystems. The first section will set the stage by discussing the significance and creation of entrepreneurship ecosystems. Equally important will be an exploration of the historical context for foundations as vehicles for innovation and social experimentation – risk capital – in order to find viable solutions to vexing problems. The chapter explores the emerging movement in the field of philanthropy embraced by successful entrepreneurs and other philanthropists taking big risks and injecting ingenuity into their social investments. This research highlights programs and strategies deployed by the philanthropists, both successful current and past entrepreneurs, who have worked together to drive this evolution, with emphasis on those funders bolstering ecosystems that operate in the higher education space. Lastly, this chapter explores the strategic roles philanthropists – and other champions – can play in building thriving ecosystems that connect campus to community.

ENTREPRENEURSHIP ECOSYSTEMS

Literature on entrepreneurship ecosystems has been growing over the last decade. Brad Feld, author of *Startup Communities: Building an Entrepreneurial Ecosystem in Your City* (Feld, 2012), is among the early promoters of the importance of rallying communities around entrepreneurs and the notion of being systematic in how they are supported and valued. Ecosystems provide the connective tissue that helps support entrepreneurs on their journey. The creation of entrepreneurship ecosystems is a new way of approaching economic development – starting and growing ventures rather than attracting them from elsewhere. Ecosystems involve partnerships, pathways, communication, and an array of players focused on different avenues of support for entrepreneurs (Figure 9.1).

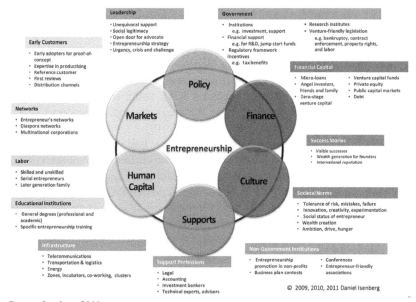

Source: Isenberg 2011.

Figure 9.1   *Domains of the entrepreneurship ecosystem*

Babson College's Entrepreneurship Ecosystem Project has been at the forefront of describing the elements of a thriving ecosystem, although we should not become too formulaic about ecosystem elements. Each ecosystem must grow from and be tailored to its own locale and culture. The broad headings include supports, culture, policy, finance, markets, and human capital, each of which can be easily assessed with an instrument from Liguori, Bendickson, Solomon, and McDowell (2019). Daniel Isenberg, founding executive director of the Babson Entrepreneurship Ecosystem Project, has said "[t]here is no one driver of an entrepreneurship ecosystem because by definition an ecosystem is a dynamic, self-regulating network of many different types of actors. In every entrepreneurship hotspot, there are important connectors and influencers who may not be entrepreneurs themselves" (Isenberg, 2014: 5). Philanthropy has become one of those players, although clearly the role of philanthropy looks different across the country depending upon the resources and dynamics present in each community.

Ecosystems are often geographically based and the ecosystem that informs much of this chapter is the northeast Ohio ecosystem – essentially the north-east quadrant of Ohio and home to four metropolitan areas – Cleveland, Youngstown, Akron, and Canton. This is a region rocked by economic chal-lenges of a shifting industrial base caused by manufacturing plant closing or relocation. While the region operates as an ecosystem, drawing state dollars to fund programming through JumpStart, a key entrepreneurship support organ-ization, these four cities are growing their own community-based ecosystems that connect into the larger regional ecosystem and its resources. Within the region are sub-ecosystems that focus on K-12 youth entrepreneurship and collegiate entrepreneurship connecting the programs and influencers to each other and to the regional ecosystem (Hoover, 2019).

Stories about the complexities of ecosystem building are conveyed in *Beyond Silicon Valley: How One Online Course Helped Support Global Entrepreneurs* based on the massive open online course (*Beyond Silicon Valley: Growing Entrepreneurship in Transitioning Economies*; Goldberg, 2018) ini-tiated by Michael Goldberg, director of Veale Institute for Entrepreneurship at Case Western Reserve University. He uses the struggles of northeast Ohio as a teaching platform to help people around the world working in transitioning economies understand how building an ecosystem is accomplished in places without the multitude of resources that exist in Silicon Valley. This volume is instructive in helping entrepreneurship champions comprehend how eco-systems differ and must capitalize on the assets at hand to assemble a team of dedicated ecosystem builders.

PHILANTHROPY AS ECOSYSTEM BUILDER

Ecosystem building has become an important strategy among entrepreneur-ship funders and is representative of innovative approaches foundations are employing to drive change (Meyers and Pope Hodel, 2017). Philanthropic funding of entrepreneurship is fueled by collaborative efforts among funders seeking to understand the field, be vocal advocates, and collaborate around shared goals. Northeast Ohio-based Burton D. Morgan Foundation is part of a growing community of entrepreneurship-focused foundations seeking to better understand the landscape of philanthropic entities serving as ecosystem builders and supporters. In an informal survey of a sample of entrepreneurship grantmakers completed in 2019 by Candid,[5] ecosystem building rose to the top of issue areas funded by these grantmakers in 2016 and 2017. When asked about the key support strategies deployed in these years, network building and collaboration also ranked high for this group of funders.[6]

For one of the nation's leading entrepreneurship funders, Ewing Marion Kauffman Foundation based in Kansas City, Missouri, bolstering the profession of ecosystem builder has become a focus of the foundation's work. Since 2017, Kauffman Foundation has been annually inviting aspiring and seasoned ecosystem builders to come together in Kansas City for the ESHIP Summit to explore how communities of people from diverse backgrounds can create thriving ecosystems that support entrepreneurs and local economies. Out of the summit has come the *Ecosystem Playbook*,[7] a handbook that evolves each year based on the lessons learned from diehard ecosystem builders working on the ground in communities across the United States. Kauffman Foundation has distilled its ecosystem building priorities into eight key elements. These elements are:

- *Entrepreneurs* who aspire to start and grow new businesses, and the people who support entrepreneurs.
- *Talent* that can help companies grow.
- People and institutions with *knowledge and resources* to help entrepreneurs.
- Individuals and institutions that serve as *champions and conveners* of entrepreneurs and the ecosystem.
- *Onramps* (or access points) to the ecosystem so that anyone and everyone can participate.
- *Intersections* that facilitate the interaction of people, ideas, and resources.
- *Stories* that people tell about themselves and their ecosystem.
- *Culture* that is rich in social capital – collaboration, cooperation, trust, reciprocity, and a focus on the common good – makes the ecosystem come alive by connecting all the elements together.

Philanthropy is just one of the influencers working collaboratively with entrepreneurs, creative professionals, investors, mayors, city council members, media, university leaders, policy makers, community developers, and corporate executives. This effort has given shape, identity, and a sense of professionalism to a field that is at the leading edge of a movement to support entrepreneurs. This is a critical development for our nation as the economy shifts and individuals must be prepared to assume more agency over their own work lives.

In cities across the country, philanthropy is enabling the deployment of ecosystem building skills to spark startup activity and play a vital role in changing the trajectory of ailing economies (Gose, 2018). In Chattanooga, Tennessee for example, two private foundations – Benwood Foundation and Lyndhurst Foundation – stepped up to lead an urban transformation rooted in entrepreneurship. The assets of both foundations stemmed from Coca-Cola executives at the helm of Chattanooga's first bottling plant established in 1899. In the 1980s, in the face of a decaying cityscape and crippling pollution, Benwood and Lyndhurst foundations partnered on pivotal projects that opened the city for new investment. Building on this success, in 2010 entrepreneurship ecosystem building moved into high gear. Benwood and Lyndhurst foundations were instrumental in establishing the Company Lab focused on connecting technology-focused entrepreneurs to the mentorship and investments they needed to grow. The two foundations also provided support for Chattanooga's Innovation District, created in 2013 with the Edney Innovation Center as a major driver. To achieve these milestones, Benwood and Lyndhurst supplemented grants with other ecosystem building efforts like convening stakeholders to help move the work forward. Ecosystem building efforts continue to advance, with Chattanooga bolstering diversity, equity, and inclusion programs for the startup community.

In this context, University of Tennessee at Chattanooga (UTC) established the Center for Innovation and Entrepreneurship in 2018 under the umbrella of the Gary W. Rollins College of Business. The new center is focused on engaging, equipping, and encouraging the university's innovators and entrepreneurs through the creation of a campus ecosystem and connecting that ecosystem and its players to Chattanooga's larger entrepreneurship community.[8] Entrepreneur and UTC graduate Gary Rollins gifted $40 million to the university in 2018 for scholarships, endowment, and faculty positions aimed at enhancing business and entrepreneurship programming on campus. Rollins is part of a movement that is reshaping how universities approach entrepreneurship on campus and connect to their communities.

REFRAMING THE CONVERSATION

Philanthropy is turning its attention to funding innovation and entrepreneurship as game-changing strategies for communities and institutions across the United States. While this direction has the appearance of being new and cutting edge, it actually harkens back to the earlier days of philanthropy when innovation in grant processes and goals was the norm for funders comfortable with experimentation and hoping for big wins as reward for testing bold ideas (Kasper & Marcoux, 2014). Funding innovation has gained traction among a cadre of forward-thinking funders, although most of these changemakers would still admit that it is more of an art than a science.

To understand the origins of this direction for philanthropy, we must first look to the donor-founders. In the world of foundations, donor intent is paramount and stated purposes for foundations reflect the donor's passions and interests. Application of the legal doctrine of *cy pres* (adhere as closely as possible to the donor's wishes) to foundation trusts was the premise that allowed donor intent to evolve over time as circumstances shifted and original purposes became outdated or impossible (Zunz, 2012). Many donors stated their purpose clauses in broad terms so the language provided future generations with flexibility to formulate strategies that reflected current societal challenges. For example, Rockefeller Foundation defined its purpose as promotion of "the well-being of mankind throughout the world" (Zunz, 2012). This broad language acknowledged that the future was uncertain and ongoing flexibility was a necessary characteristic for a perpetual entity.

Burton D. Morgan Foundation is an entity established in perpetuity and its intense focus on entrepreneurship stems from the passion of founder Burton D. Morgan (1916–2003), who believed that raising awareness about entrepreneurship as a career choice early in life would benefit students as they build their skills for the future. He articulated the foundation's grantmaking goals as "grants are to be made to institutions concentrating on entrepreneurial studies and to efforts supporting entrepreneurs" (Private Memorandum, 1994). Under this guidance, Morgan Foundation is focused on entrepreneurship, but with the latitude to adapt grantmaking priorities to fit the needs of the time. The foundation is funding and fostering ecosystems that support K-12 programming to instill the innovation and entrepreneurship mindset in children, curricular and experiential programming for college students, and an array of programs for adult entrepreneurs.

Morgan Foundation recently recalibrated through the creation of a strategic framework that removed some of the constraints of traditional grantmaking and instead incorporated more flexible practices that allow grantees to be nimble, better mirroring the entrepreneurship community they seek to grow. This shift in practices reflects one of the reasons foundations came into being in the first place as vehicles through which risk capital could be deployed and potentially transformational experiments could be piloted. While philanthropy has to some degree gotten stuck in funding safe and recognized programs, some foundations are boldly venturing into unknown territory. The *Stanford Social Innovation Review* notes that:

> a small group of funders have begun to return to their roots by deliberately reintroducing innovation into their philanthropic processes and portfolios. They seek out ideas with transformative potential, take risks on less proven approaches, open themselves to exploring new solutions, and recognize that innovation requires flexibility, iteration, and failure" (Kasper & Marcoux, 2014: 28).

It seems apparent that funding innovation and employing innovative approaches as a funder often leads to foundations acting themselves as pioneers in the field of philanthropy.

One such funder is Lemelson Foundation based in Portland, Oregon with a mission to improve lives through invention. Lemelson is the brainchild of inventor Jerome Lemelson (1923–97) who established the foundation in 1992 to promote invention and innovation around the world. Key initiatives funded by Lemelson Foundation include the Center for the Study of Invention and Innovation at the Smithsonian's National Museum of American History, established to inspire "creative invention" in children and teens. For university students, Lemelson has been a key supporter of the National Collegiate Inventors and Innovators Alliance, with more than 200 higher education members and support for the creation of invention-focused programs on their campuses. More recently, Lemelson has focused on building Oregon's entrepreneurship ecosystem. In cooperation with Oregon Community Foundation and other partners, Lemelson has established Invent Oregon to support the state's innovators of tomorrow. The 2019 Invent Oregon Collegiate Challenge welcomed more than 100 competitors from 17 Oregon colleges and universities to present prototypes and pitch ideas. The program is acting as a bonding force for higher education across the state to unite entrepreneurship champions around the elevation and mentoring of young entrepreneurs, including introducing high school students to the world of invention, innovation, and entrepreneurship.

Connection of philanthropy to universities and ecosystem building is not just an American phenomenon. The idea is gaining traction in other nations like Denmark, where Novo Nordisk Foundation and Carlsberg Foundation are taking leading roles in building Denmark's entrepreneurship and innovation ecosystems.[9] Novo Nordisk Foundation awards grants to promising university research initiatives that have the potential to address global challenges with sweeping innovations. The Carlsberg Foundation funds university-based scientific research projects that demonstrate social responsibility with an interest in supporting female researchers and entrepreneurs. Both foundations express interest in working together to strengthen connections across the ecosystem in support of a new generation of entrepreneurs and companies rising in Denmark.

GALVANIZING HIGHER EDUCATION AS ECOSYSTEM BUILDERS

The fusion of campus-based entrepreneurship ecosystems with regional ecosystems is a critical factor in the effectiveness of a community's ability to support its entrepreneurs. California's Silicon Valley–Stanford University region is often recognized as the pinnacle of ecosystems, possessing key elements that contribute mightily to its success – a risk-taking culture, talented and imaginative students, government support, abundant capital, robust collaboration with industry, and a community committed to giving back.[10] This environment reinforces a culture and ambition to change the world through new technology and products. The close proximity of high-powered educational resources like the d-school (Hasso Plattner Institute of Design at Stanford University) fosters collaboration and contributes to team-minded innovation and entrepreneurial endeavors. This environment offers access to generous alumni, successful entrepreneurs, and investors eager to give back to the community that spawned their success. They serve as speakers, mentors, and advisers. In addition, there exists a healthy exchange between the Stanford campus and industry operating through a formal program that promotes connection to university-driven research, conferences, and speakers. Industry also actively provides mentoring to students specifically related to their field of study.

Although the Silicon Valley–Stanford University phenomenon is revered as a model to be emulated, there are other ecosystems where universities are a driving force in sparking innovation and entrepreneurship. Pittsburgh's comeback story places its higher education institutions front and center.[11] Pittsburgh in the 1980s faced a bleak future as the steel industry retreated and unemployment rose to 18 percent. In the intervening years, the city shifted from a focus on its rivers and raw materials to an economy driven by innovation. The Pittsburgh Innovation District, with Carnegie Mellon University and University of Pittsburgh included in this 1.7 square mile beehive, is also home to startups, co-working spaces, and University of Pittsburgh Medical Center. Pittsburgh's ecosystem is doing many things right, connecting academic research to industry applications, and this fluidity is benefiting the local economy in critical ways. Yet as is true in cities across the country, Pittsburgh still faces many challenges ensuring that all citizens can tap into and build careers grounded in the innovation economy. To ensure that Pittsburgh's progress does not fizzle, Hillman Family Foundations in 2018 put its weight behind an ecosystem building effort known as InnovatePGH that draws together key players—industry, universities, non-profits, startups, government, and philanthropy—in a public–private partnership designed to develop plans that ensure Pittsburgh achieves its full "potential as a global innovation hub."[12]

As Pittsburgh's example demonstrates, ecosystem building is by no means an easy job. When Burton D. Morgan Foundation started working as an ecosystem builder in northeast Ohio more than a decade ago connecting universities to the regional ecosystem, the foundation felt like a lone wolf. Morgan Foundation was interested in encouraging connections, building synergies, and supporting entrepreneurs by connecting them to services. How the foundation went about this work was highly experimental. Year after year the foundation made grants, experimented with new ideas, and encouraged collaboration. When the foundation missed the mark, the team tried a different direction. Little by little the players emerged, the connections formed, leaders and champions gained experience, and good things started to happen. Eventually the elements of a regional ecosystem took shape as captured in ecosystem diagrams[13] for youth, collegiate, and adult entrepreneurship designed to facilitate navigation for those seeking services or ways to engage as mentors or ecosystem builders (Figure 9.2).

Burton D. Morgan Foundation was one influencer among many, but the bird's eye view the organization gained through its work supporting entrepreneurship across the region provided perspectives that allowed the foundation to help generate strategic connections for the emerging entrepreneurship ecosystem. The foundation formed partnerships with key players inside and outside the region also striving to become effective ecosystem builders. In 2006, Morgan Foundation entered into a pivotal partnership with Ewing Marion Kauffman Foundation through its Kauffman Campuses Initiative to build the Northeast Ohio Collegiate Entrepreneurship Program[14] focused on weaving entrepreneurship into a liberal arts curriculum. The partners selected five northeast Ohio colleges (Baldwin Wallace University, College of Wooster, Lake Erie College, Oberlin College, and Hiram College) to experiment with classroom-based and experiential entrepreneurship programs. This partnership not only served as an opportunity for Morgan Foundation to tap into Kauffman Foundation's vast intellectual capital, but also provided an early introduction to ways a network of entrepreneurship programs could amplify impact through shared learning and programming (Schneider, 2015). Following collaboration with Kauffman Foundation, Morgan Foundation established in 2012 a partnership with Blackstone Charitable Foundation aimed at introducing the LaunchPad (now in Ohio, named NEOLaunchNET) experiential entrepreneurship program on four northeast Ohio campuses (Baldwin Wallace University, Case Western Reserve University, Lorain County Community College, and Kent State University). Blackstone LaunchPad program, powered by Techstars, has grown to reach 500,000 students globally and evolved into its own ecosystem connected to the broader ecosystems in which the programs operate. LaunchPad "transforms students into entrepreneurs" capitalizing on campus assets, but also expands horizons by calling upon industry leaders, "mentors, networks, and brands."[15]

In northeast Ohio, intercampus networks in higher education are bolstered by connective tissue in the ecosystem that includes groups of colleges and universities partnering to offer extracurricular programs for students. An example of collaboration among northeast Ohio campuses is Entrepreneurship Education Consortium (EEC) comprising ten campuses focused on an intercampus idea competition and shared summer immersion program.[16] The 2019 summer program unleashed its team of talented students to solve real-world problems for companies and non-profits in the region. The purpose of EEC is "to provide practical 'experiential' and theoretical education to students

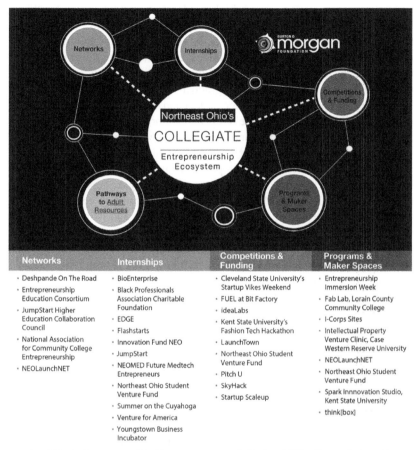

Networks
- Deshpande On The Road
- Entrepreneurship Education Consortium
- JumpStart Higher Education Collaboration Council
- National Association for Community College Entrepreneurship
- NEOLaunchNET

Internships
- BioEnterprise
- Black Professionals Association Charitable Foundation
- EDGE
- Flashstarts
- Innovation Fund NEO
- JumpStart
- NEOMED Future Medtech Entrepreneurs
- Northeast Ohio Student Venture Fund
- Summer on the Cuyahoga
- Venture for America
- Youngstown Business Incubator

Competitions & Funding
- Cleveland State University's Startup Vikes Weekend
- FUEL at Bit Factory
- ideaLabs
- Kent State University's Fashion Tech Hackathon
- LaunchTown
- Northeast Ohio Student Venture Fund
- Pitch U
- SkyHack
- Startup Scaleup

Programs & Maker Spaces
- Entrepreneurship Immersion Week
- Fab Lab, Lorain County Community College
- I-Corps Sites
- Intellectual Property Venture Clinic, Case Western Reserve University
- NEOLaunchNET
- Northeast Ohio Student Venture Fund
- Spark Innnovation Studio, Kent State University
- think[box]

In addition to the resources listed here, every campus in Northeast Ohio offers curricular and co-curricular entrepreneurship education for its students.

Once students are ready to launch ventures, a robust adult entrepreneurship ecosystem is ready to meet them. Click here for more resources available to budding entrepreneurs.

Last Updated July 26, 2019 - Please note this is not a comprehensive list of the resources available in the ecosystem.

Figure 9.2   Northeast Ohio collegiate entrepreneurship ecosystem diagram (2019)

in Northeast Ohio to prepare them to become entrepreneurs or intrapreneurs; create new ventures and jobs, and build wealth for the region."[17] The result is programming that draws together students, faculty, and community all with different life and educational experiences to learn and explore together.

Another collaboration among higher education institutions is Northeast Ohio Student Venture Fund (NEOSVF), started in 2010 and now a six-campus network focused on providing experiential opportunities for students seeking to learn the startup investment process by conducting due diligence on real companies and (with mentorship) making investments in these companies. NEOSVF "gives undergraduate and graduate students from higher education institutions an opportunity to better understand new ventures through experiential learning opportunities relating to entrepreneurship, venture capital, technology commercialization, and economic development."[18]

An overarching connector for entrepreneurship and higher education in the northeast Ohio region is JumpStart Higher Education Collaboration Council (JSHECC), a network of 22 campuses "jointly established in 2009 by JumpStart and Burton D. Morgan Foundation, operating to connect campus entrepreneurship programs to the region's ecosystem and its many assets."[19] While JSHECC was established to connect campuses to the ecosystem, it is now also serving as a dynamic learning community in the region that meets during the academic year to explore topics related to university-based entrepreneurship. The intersection of philanthropy and universities is having a meaningful impact on how higher education connects to the entrepreneurship ecosystem.

PHILANTHROPY AS DRIVER OF CHANGE ON UNIVERSITY CAMPUSES

Universities are feeling the shift as donors and philanthropic institutions press campuses to embrace innovation and entrepreneurship (Thorp and Goldstein, 2010). Such donors contribute in major ways to universities pursuing agendas that embrace the importance of innovation and the entrepreneurship mindset. These philanthropists are not typically looking for proven solutions, but rather "seek novel, valuable, high-impact solutions" (Thorp and Goldstein, 2010, 141). They are motivated by a desire for results, full engagement, and considerable leverage of donated funds. Gifts to universities in the era of venture philanthropy are frequently structured around pursuing a specific strategy. The new age of philanthropy is marked by a predilection for addressing big problems through innovation, team approaches, and a comfort level with failure. In these instances, gifts to support entrepreneurship are not usually in the form of perpetual endowment, but often seek to address challenges with expendable funds. Universities across the country are likely to have newly minted millionaires among their alumni and many would prefer to express their philanthropic aspirations with this sense of urgency and resolve.

Alumni donors to universities have often pursued an entrepreneurship path to success and their giving back reflects that lived experience. There has been an upsurge in the number of announcements about large entre-preneurship-focused gifts to higher education. One such announcement in 2018 came from Dartmouth College in Hanover, New Hampshire where Allison and Rick Magnuson pledged $20 million to establish the Magnuson Family Center for Entrepreneurship at Dartmouth College, a "dynamic hub for faculty, student and alumni connected to any department or school at Dartmouth."[20] The center adds to Dartmouth's growing focus on entrepre-neurship programming that reaches across the campus engaging students, faculty, and alumni developing ideas with promise. Rick Magnuson had been highly engaged with entrepreneurship support on campus prior to finalizing his commitment, reflecting the trend for philanthropy to be deeply involved in initiatives that bolster the goals of the gift. This gift builds on the momentum Dartmouth has achieved through its Dartmouth Entrepreneurial Network and reflects a desire among alumni givers to prioritize significant leverage as a key factor in their decisions to provide support of innovation and entrepreneurship.

Community colleges are also elevating the importance of entrepreneurship studies and their alumni are stepping up to support students pursuing asso-ciate degrees. Richard and Ann Kraft donated $300,000 to Richard's alma mater, Muskegon Community College in Michigan, as a way to recognize the know-how he gained in his early college years that propelled him to become a successful entrepreneur in the engineering field (Bass, 2017). These funds allowed the college to establish a rapid prototype lab for enterprising students. The next section of this chapter will highlight specific roles philanthropy can play in building connections from campuses to ecosystems and community resources.

PHILANTHROPIC STRATEGIES CONNECTING UNIVERSITIES WITH ECOSYSTEMS

Success of gifts for innovation and entrepreneurship rides on the ability to see the big picture and connect deployment of dollars to optimal connectivity in an ecosystem. Foundations can serve as conveners and consequently are uniquely positioned to help link together elements of an entrepreneurship ecosystem. Through partnerships, foundations can use many tools to help build and grow ecosystems that support universities and communities of entrepreneurs as they strive to reshape the startup landscape. This section explores three broad areas – grantmaking; collaboration and connectivity; and learning together – each offering multiple philanthropic tools that can build ecosystem strength, many of which can be deployed no matter what role supporters play in advancing ecosystem connectivity.

Grantmaking

Clarity of values

Burton D. Morgan Foundation sought to distill lessons learned over the years so they could be shared and built strategically and logically into the foundation's processes. The result is a system of values that reflect what the foundation has learned and woven together to emphasize the importance of ecosystem building activities.[21] The values are not static but evolve as the foundation and its partners learn and adapt through experimentation. Morgan Foundation values higher education programs that focus on the essence of the institutional culture; long-term sustainability; interdisciplinary reach; building the entrepreneurship mindset; inclusivity and diversity; mentorship; collaboration; evaluation, review, and feedback; ability to respond to change; and sharing lessons learned.

The values are integrated into questions posed in applications, the structure of interviews, and thus the very nature of the proposals submitted. Once a grant is awarded, the values are reflected in the metrics university grantees report and how the foundation and grantees pivot and adapt to changing circumstances. The values encourage behaviors that facilitate ecosystem building through collaboration, shared resources, and connections to community.

Listening and outreach

Listening to what is happening on the ground within ecosystems is emblematic of Kauffman Foundation's approach to staging its annual ESHIP Summit with activities designed to shine a light on the ecosystem builder's successes and challenges. To comprehend the intricacies of the ecosystem, foundations must engage in regular outreach to understand the nuances and persistent gaps in the ecosystem, including those on university campuses. Foundations can connect to ecosystem partners by conducting surveys, visiting grantee partners, attending events, scheduling meetings for deep dive conversations, and soliciting ideas. Ecosystem partners have perspectives based on their daily on-the-ground efforts and it is important to be attentive to what is happening since ecosystems must remain adaptive as needs and circumstances shift.

Competitive funding opportunities

Sometimes foundations utilize competitive processes to call attention to opportunities for innovation and encourage grantee partners to try fresh approaches. An example of competitive funding for ecosystem support is offered by Minneapolis-based Bush Foundation. Bush Foundation supports a variety of ecosystem projects including those focused on social business ventures. The program seeks to "[i]nspire, equip and connect people of all backgrounds to create and grow more successful social purpose businesses," and to "create a supportive ecosystem for business creators and growers and investors in social purpose businesses."[22] In 2019, Burton D. Morgan Foundation staged the Changemaker Grants Program, a competition among northeast Ohio's higher education institutions to identify projects that shape new ways of supporting entrepreneurship on campuses with particular emphasis on the generation of student pathways that enable seamless maneuvering among youth, collegiate, and adult entrepreneurship opportunities.[23]

Campus-based ecosystems

To promote the creation and evolution of campus ecosystems and connections to regional ecosystems, funders can prioritize the importance of strong networks to support entrepreneurs. Based in Hadley, Massachusetts, VentureWell works to "cultivate a pipeline of inventors, innovators, and entrepreneurs" and "fosters a growing network of individuals and institutions interested in moving the field forward and strengthening the innovation and entrepreneurship ecosystem."[24] VentureWell's Faculty Grants Program emphasizes for its university applicants the importance of having a "supportive entrepreneurial ecosystem for student teams to pursue commercialization."[25] Burton D. Morgan Foundation encourages ecosystem connectivity by requiring every higher education applicant to diagram the elements of their on-campus ecosystem.

Collaboration and Connectivity

Convening

The NC Idea Foundation, established in 2006, sponsors NC Idea Ecosystem, a grant program that provides funds across North Carolina to partners seeking to support entrepreneurs and willing to work with universities and other ecosystem partners. During Global Entrepreneurship Week 2019, NC Idea Foundation convened its ecosystem partners at an ecosystem summit in Raleigh to examine successes and address issues as they work in concert to support diverse entrepreneurs.[26] To be effective ecosystem builders, foundations can capitalize on their role as convener to bring together partners for important discussions at pivotal moments, for focus groups to collect perspectives, for events that present national experts and new ideas, and creation of learning communities.

Partnerships

Michigan-based William Davidson Foundation has been central to funding the efforts of Detroit's Wayne State University to connect the physical spaces that will form an Innovation District encompassing the university, TechTown Detroit, a new Industry Innovation Center, and the newly formed Detroit Urban Solutions.[27] Foundations do not do their work alone – partners are always critical to philanthropic success and the nurturing of healthy partnerships is fundamental to the effectiveness of philanthropy as an ecosystem builder. Partnerships with highest potential are grounded in mission fit, shared values, trust, and transparency, all adding up to relationships that allow for mutually agreed-upon pivots and shared learning.

Networks

Interconnected university-based entrepreneurship programs can capitalize on shared resources and learning opportunities. Blackstone LaunchPad provides a strong example of a national and international program with core principles articulated by Blackstone Charitable Foundation that guide the operation of the program and the connections among campuses. Northeast Ohio's interconnected campuses through such platforms as JSHECC have established the trust that underpins collaborative efforts among schools and strengthens the work of all participants.

Learning Together

Strategic learning

The roles a grantmaker can play to prompt strategic learning include convening, facilitation, capacity building, mentoring, and the organization of learning communities and communities of practice. Learning communities draw together groups of people who share a concern or question they hope to address together. Communities of practice involve colleagues coming together to exchange knowledge, learn new skills, and evolve standards of practice. Grantmakers are well positioned to bring engaged people together in an intentional way so that all participants benefit and contribute in meaningful ways.

Deshpande Symposium, a creation of Deshpande Foundation in partnership with University of Massachusetts-Lowell, has over the last nine years built a learning community among hundreds of university entrepreneurship faculty and program directors seeking to build strong programs on campus and connect to local ecosystems. A key thread of the symposium, "Developing Entrepreneurial Universities, Culture and Ecosystems,"[28] helps colleges and universities see the potential of bolstering the elements and connections of their campus ecosystem.

Philanthropic data

Foundations are in an ideal position to promote knowledge sharing and the power of strategic learning. While foundations regularly collect valuable information, these data have far less value if philanthropic entities only use the information internally. Instead foundations should interpret this information and send it into the world so others can use it. It is critical for foundations to work proactively and seek out opportunities to learn with colleagues in non-profits, campus settings, and grantmaking institutions.

CONCLUSION

More grantmakers and donors are emerging every year seeking to prioritize the role of ecosystem builders, with many focusing their energies on college and university campuses. Philanthropic entities are in a unique position to serve as engaged ecosystem builders connecting elements across the community, including those that reside on university campuses. Universities can play a critical role in influencing how institutional leadership works collaboratively to strengthen internal innovation and entrepreneurship programs and to create outward-facing elements that allow community entrepreneurs avenues of access to innovation, invention, and entrepreneurship support services. Philanthropic organizations and individuals can seed groundbreaking programs and set the stage for success through knowledge sharing, network creation, shared resources, and region-wide approaches. This style of philanthropic investment is growing in popularity and proving to be an effective way to develop meaningful experiences that deliver tools students need to be entrepreneurial thinkers and doers. It takes a community to hold up and support entrepreneurs on their journey and philanthropy can be an important player in this equation, investing not just financial resources, but also time and talent to heighten the learning for students and increase the chances of success for the ideas they generate and the ventures they create.

NOTES

1. https://chanzuckerberg.com/
2. www.forbes.com/sites/kathleenchaykowski/2018/11/10/zuckerberg-donates -214-million-to-silicon-valley-community-foundation-as-it-hires-new-ceo/ #122c5518550d
3. https://casefoundation.org/
4. https://ssir.org/articles/entry/fueling_the_momentum_of_impact_investing
5. Candid is a global resource for data and analytical tools focused on non-profits, foundations, and grants (candid.org).
6. Unpublished survey collected by Candid in 2019 for the Entrepreneurship Funders Network.
7. www.kauffman.org/ecosystem-playbook-draft-3/entrepreneurial-ecosystems #defininganecosystem
8. www.collegeconsensus.com/business/schools/university-of-tennessee-at -chattanooga/
9. www.youtube.com/watch?v=wx82ZGCUShM
10. www.kauffmanfellows.org/journal_posts/universities-and-entrepreneurial -ecosystems-stanford-silicon-valley-success

11. www.brookings.edu/research/capturing-the-next-economy-pittsburghs-rise-as-a-global-innovation-city/
12. https://hillmanfamilyfoundations.org/2018-annual-report/featured-grants/innovatepgh/
13. See www.bdmorganfdn.org/grant-focus to view youth and adult ecosystem diagrams.
14. www.bdmorganfdn.org/intersections-collegiate
15. www.blackstonelaunchpad.org/
16. www.bdmorganfdn.org/sites/default/files/editor/White%20Paper%20-%20Schmidt_Molkentin.pdf
17. www.eecohio.org/
18. www.neosvf.com/about.html
19. www.bdmorganfdn.org/jumpstart-higher-education-collaboration-council
20. www.bing.com/search?q=big+gifts+for+campus+entrepreneurship+&form=EDGSPH&mkt=en-us&httpsmsn=1&msnews=1&refig=57ff2d90b6544954822e52dc34653dde&sp=-1&pq=big+gifts+for+campus+entrepreneurship+&sc=0-38&qs=n&sk=&cvid=57ff2d90b6544954822e52dc34653dde
21. www.bdmorganfdn.org/collegiate-entrepreneurship
22. www.bushfoundation.org/social-business-ventures
23. www.bdmorganfdn.org/news/changemaker-grant-award-recipients-announced
24. https://venturewell.org/membership/
25. https://venturewell.org/faculty-grants/
26. https://ncidea.org/nc-idea-foundation-announces-inaugural-statewide-entrepreneurial-ecosystem-summit/
27. https://detroit.curbed.com/2019/8/13/20804304/wayne-state-university-detroit-urban-innovation-district
28. https://deshpandesymposium.org/

REFERENCES

Bass, D. (2017, Summer). "Revving Economic Engines at Community Colleges," *Philanthropy*, 18–25, 24.
Feld, B. (2012). *Startup Communities: Building an Entrepreneurial Ecosystem in Your City* (Hoboken, NJ: John Wiley & Sons).
Goldberg, M.E. (2018). *Beyond Silicon Valley: How One Online Course Helped Support Global Entrepreneurs* (Cleveland, OH: Michael E. Goldberg).
Gose, B. (2018). "Chattanooga: How 2 Foundations Helped Make This Down-on-Its-Luck City a Star of Tennessee," *Philanthropy and the City, The Chronicle of Philanthropy*, 31(2), 9–16.
Hoover, D. (2019). "The Ecosystem That Thrives," in *Community Colleges as Incubators of Innovation: Unleashing Entrepreneurial Opportunities for Communities and Students*, ed. Rebecca A. Corbin and Ron Thomas (Sterling, VA: Stylus Publishing), 85–101.
Isenberg, D. (2011). "The Entrepreneurship Ecosystem Strategy as a New Paradigm for Economy Policy: Principles for Cultivating Entrepreneurship," Babson Entrepreneurship Ecosystem Project, Babson College, www.innovationamerica.us/images/stories/2011/The-entrepreneurship-ecosystem-strategy-for-economic-growth-policy-20110620183915.pdf

Isenberg, D. (2014). "What an Entrepreneurial Ecosystem Actually Is," *Harvard Business Review*, May 12.

Kasper, G. and Marcoux, J. (2014). "The Re-Emerging Art of Funding Innovation," *Stanford Social Innovation Review*, 12(2) (Spring), 28–35.

Liguori, E., Bendickson, J., Solomon, S., & McDowell, W. C. (2019). Development of a Multi-Dimensional Measure for Assessing Entrepreneurial Ecosystems. *Entrepreneurship and Regional Development*, 31(1–2), 7–21.

Meyers, M.E. and Pope Hodel, K. (2017). *Beyond Collisions: How to Build Your Entrepreneurial Infrastructure* (Kansas City, MO: Wavesource LLC), 103–10.

Morgan, B.D. (1994). "Private Memorandum entitled 'Remarks on Mission.'"

Schneider, M. (2015). "Kauffman Campuses Initiative: A Study That Explores the Phenomenon of Cross-Campus Entrepreneurship" (Dissertation, University of Pennsylvania).

Taylor, M.L., Strom, R.J., and Renz, D.O. (2014). "Introduction," in *Handbook of Research on Entrepreneurs' Engagement in Philanthropy*, ed. Marilyn L. Taylor, Robert J. Strom and David O. Renz (Cheltenham, UK and Northampton, MA, USA: Edward Elgar Publishing), 1–8.

Thorp, H. and Goldstein, B. (2010). *Engines of Innovation: The Entrepreneurial University in the Twenty-First Century* (Chapel Hill, NC: University of North Carolina Press).

Zunz, O. (2012). *Philanthropy in America: A History* (Princeton, NJ: Princeton University Press).

10. Impact of entrepreneurship education: a review of the past, overview of the present, and a glimpse of future trends

Michela Loi and Alain Fayolle

INTRODUCTION

Drawing on an extensive review of the literature on entrepreneurship education effectiveness, Nabi, Liñan, Fayolle, Krueger, and Walmsley (2017) define the impact of entrepreneurship education as a change that we can observe through the following dimensions: (1) attitudes toward entrepreneurship; (2) intention, knowledge, and skills; (3) business creation; (4) performance; and (5) socioeconomic factors. Accordingly, these outcomes might encompass different levels of analysis, going from the individual level to the organizational and societal levels. Although this conceptualization implies an extended focus of analysis, previous literature reviews (e.g., Nabi et al., 2017; Rideout and Gray, 2013) and meta-analyses (e.g., Bae, Qian, Miao, and Fiet, 2014) have revealed that attitudes, and especially entrepreneurial intention, are the most frequently investigated outcomes. An implicit assumption of this trend, which is supported by the theory of planned behavior (TPB) (Kautonen, Van Gelderen, and Tornikoski, 2013; Kautonen, Van Gelderen, and Fink, 2015), is that if programs can foster attitudes and intentions, we can expect the entrepreneurial behavior, such as the creation of a new venture, to be more likely to manifest.

Has research produced evidence that entrepreneurship education programs foster attitudes and intentions? Are these variables still the core questions in recent research? What are the trends along which the topic has evolved? What understanding can be drawn from these studies, and how can it move the field forward? In addressing these questions, this work illustrates the core of interest characterizing the impact of the past and present research on entrepreneurship education and draws some reflections that might be of interest for forthcoming studies. In addition to the thematic overview, this work informs readers about the geographical origin of the contributions and explores the role played by scientific journals in the debate on the effectiveness of entrepreneurship education. Complementing the thematic overview, this analysis contributes toward planning future research collaborations.

The unit of analysis in this study consists of 132 papers published in entrepreneurship and education journals from 1990 to November 2019. To observe the trend, we have divided the entire period into three intervals: 1990–2003, 2004–16, and 2017–19. The choice of these time intervals allows us to have a deep focus on the most recent research (2017–19), and concurrently extend the temporal range of the systematic literature review on the impact of entrepreneurship education recently published by Nabi et al. (2017) that considered studies until 2016. The remaining period has been split into two parts.

As the main contribution, this chapter complements current overviews of the research on the impact of entrepreneurship education by updating and renewing them with different viewpoints. First, the study adopts a temporal perspective with three time intervals to examine contributions and observes them over two dimensions: one related to the descriptive characteristics of publications, notably focused on their geographical origin, co-authorship, and journals, and the other pertaining to the topics addressed. In so doing, this historical overview informs and orients future studies that aim to undertake new investigations on this topic.

The chapter is organized as follows. The first part describes the background of the research field, and the second part illustrates the studies' content along with the three time intervals. Guided by our four research questions noted above, the third part summarizes our reflections and suggestions for future research.

BACKGROUND OF RESEARCH FIELD ON IMPACT OF ENTREPRENEURSHIP EDUCATION

Brief Overview of Method

We selected our unit of analysis of 132 contributions from the ISI Web of Science, a database that is equipped with the necessary functions for bibliometric analysis (Orduna-Malea, Aytac, and Tran, 2019). We included journal articles and reviews and excluded proceedings and book chapters to map the topic in high-ranked journals. Following previous studies (e.g., Landström and Harirchi, 2018), we selected the journals according to the Association of Business Schools ranking (2018). Our list of entrepreneurship journals includes the following: *Entrepreneurship Theory and Practice, International Small Business Journal, Small Business Economics, Entrepreneurship and Regional Development, Journal of Business Venturing,* and *Journal of Small Business Management.* Among the journals that have an interest in education and learning, we included the following: *Academy of Management Learning and Education, Management Learning,* and *Studies in Higher Education.* We added three other journals that had published relevant contributions to the topic under inquiry: *International Entrepreneurship and Management Journal* and, following Nabi et al. (2017), we also considered the *Journal of Small Business and Enterprise Development* and the *International Journal of Entrepreneurial Behavior and Research.*

We used a set of keywords to combine the topic of entrepreneurship education to that concerning evaluation. For each topic, we identified synonyms to ensure complete coverage of the topic. Specifically, for entrepreneurship education, we also added enterprise education (Neck and Corbett, 2018) and entrepreneurial training (e.g., Gielnik et al., 2015). Training, in this work, is meant to represent a learning setting that might involve students as the educational setting does. This is in line with some entrepreneurship education studies that used the term training to refer to university entrepreneurship programs, involving graduates and undergraduates (e.g., Gielnik et al., 2015; Gielnik, Uy, Funken, and Bischoff, 2017; Rasmussen and Sørheim, 2006).

As regards evaluation, we considered the following synonyms: assessment, effectiveness, evaluation, impact, and learning outcomes.[1] We considered eligible all the 132 papers highlighted in the search, even if some of them touch upon the impact of entrepreneurship education only marginally (e.g., Chen, Greene, and Crick, 1998; Krueger, Reilly, and Carsrud, 2000; Obschonka and Stuetzer, 2017). We considered these papers important for our reflection because they provide interesting implications for the effectiveness of entrepreneurship education.

We used the available data from the ISI Web of Science to highlight the number of publications per year, authors' affiliation, and the distribution of publications in the scientific journals along with the three time intervals. In addition, we used a specific software to map the collaborations among authors across the globe[2] and visualize the temporal perspective among the publications that compose our unit of analysis.[3]

Descriptive Characteristics of Publications

Figure 10.1, which reports the number of publications per year, shows that the interest of highly ranked journals in the topic has grown considerably in the last five years, and the number of publications doubled in 2019, compared with the trend in 2015–18. This trend is in accordance with a recent literature review on entrepreneurship education showing that one of the most common topics in the field is the impact of entrepreneurship programs (Gabrielsson, Landström, Politis, and Hägg, 2018).

Figure 10.2 shows countries where authors have published works on the impact of entrepreneurship education. Canada, China, Europe, and the United

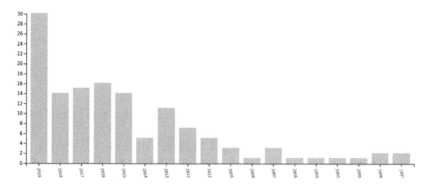

Figure 10.1   Publications per year

Figure 10.2   Publications and geographical areas

States (US) are actively engaged in this topic. Scholars from the US and United Kingdom have authored most of the studies. Among the European countries, apart from the United Kingdom, Spain and Germany contribute to the substantial development of the field.

Concerning the collaborations among scholars and their country affiliations,[4] Figure 10.3 shows that in Sweden and Italy, fewer interconnections exist with authors from foreign institutions. By contrast, in England, authors have more publications with co-authors from almost all countries that have scholars working on this topic, even though a European focus seems to prevail.

Figure 10.3   Co-authorship and countries

Germany and the US, which are central in the maps, have a high level of inter-connection with different countries.

Looking at the journals, as depicted in Figure 10.4, we can observe that the *International Journal of Entrepreneurial Behavior and Research* and the *Journal of Small Business Management* have published the highest number of publications dealing with the impact of entrepreneurship education. Moreover, these journals have maintained a constant interest in the topic over the last 10 years. Although the *Journal of Business Venturing, Entrepreneurship Theory and Practice*, and *Management Learning* have gradually disregarded the topic, in the last three years, *Studies in Higher Education* and the *Journal of Small Business and Enterprise Development* have intensified their publication activities about the effectiveness of entrepreneurship education.

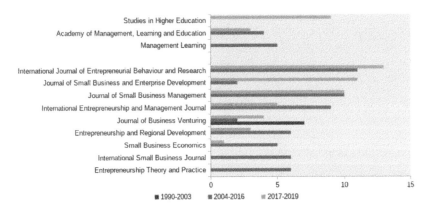

Figure 10.4   Journals publishing research on the impact of entrepreneurship education and time intervals

OVERVIEW OF THE CONTENT

To obtain a visual overview of the field that unfolds its temporal development, we performed a citation network analysis[5] (Van Eck and Waltman, 2014) of which the results are shown in Figure 10.5. Given our unit of analysis, the

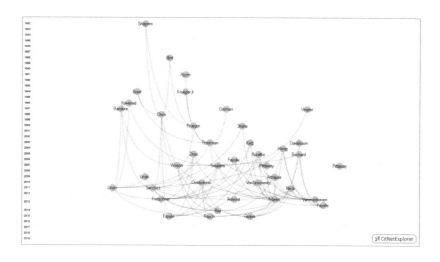

Figure 10.5   Citation network of impactful contributions (1990–2019)

picture shows the most important publications in the field, which have received at least 20 citations, and at the same time depicts how publications have built on each other over time. Therefore, the map visualizes the papers included in our unit of analysis and those that they cited. In so doing, this analysis allows having a temporal history of the most impactful references that constitute the theoretical bases of the topic, and recent publications that have become crucial at present. The most recent publications (2017–19) are not represented in the map because they have received few citations from the paper included in our unit of analysis.

According to this analysis, the contribution authored by Peterman and Kennedy (2003), which is central in the map, emerges as a foundational paper in the studies on the impact of entrepreneurship education. Another pivotal contribution is that by Souitaris, Zerbinati, and Al-Laham (2007), which has received citations from several contributions that are widespread in the map, which means that it is regarded as a general reference for this topic. If we consider the period from 2013 to 2016, further publications emerge as original papers in the field. Among them, the meta-analysis authored by Martin, McNally, and Kay (2013) is notable because of its relations with the other relevant contributions.

If we look at the publications before that by Peterman and Kennedy (2003), we can visualize the theoretical ground of the topic, centered on the entrepreneurial intention (Krueger et al., 2000; Ajzen and Fishbein, 2000) and primarily on the entrepreneurship event model (Shapero and Sokol, 1982).

In the following paragraphs, we comment on the perspectives brought by the pivotal works of our unit of analysis by examining them along with the three temporal intervals.

The Period 1990–2003

According to our unit of analysis, during this first period, the work by Peterman and Kennedy (2003) was the only contribution that empirically examined the effect of entrepreneurship education. They explored the impact of enterprise education on the feasibility and desirability perception of starting a business in adolescence. According to the incipit, "Despite the recognition that education and prior entrepreneurial experiences influence people's attitudes towards starting their own business, the impact of entrepreneurship or enterprise education, as distinct from general education, on attitudes or perceptions of entrepreneurship has remained relatively untested" (Peterman and Kennedy, 2003, p. 129). They adopted a pre-test/post-test control group design over a five-month period. Their study provided empirical evidence that the participation in the enterprise education program positively increases perceptions of desirability and feasibility. These results led them to claim that the inclusion of exposure in entrepreneurship or enterprise education in intention models is fundamental to enhance one's understanding of the entrepreneurship process.

Another important contribution is the work by Vesper and Gartner (1997) who adopted a macro perspective to critically examine how to evaluate the quality of entrepreneurship education programs. They proposed the Malcolm Baldrige National Quality Award Education Pilot Criteria as a ground to develop a comprehensive and detailed format for the identification of evaluation criteria that aim at surveying the results obtained by business schools in delivering entrepreneurship education programs. Overall, this framework is organized around the following seven dimensions: leadership; information and analysis; strategic and operational planning; human resource development management; educational and business process management; school performance results; and student focus and student and stakeholder satisfaction. According to Vesper and Gartner (1997), this framework gives insights on how to develop discernible and measurable criteria by which to evaluate an entrepreneurship program, helping to contrast the prevailing use of fluid and indeterminate criteria. Furthermore, this scheme of criteria might force scholars to become aware of the implicit goals, objectives, and pedagogical aspects related to entrepreneurship education design and delivery.

If we look at the evolution of entrepreneurship as a research field, we will not be surprised that the aforementioned contributions are among the first studies on the assessment of entrepreneurship education that have been published in high-ranked journals. As demonstrated by Landström and Harirchi (2018), the infrastructure of entrepreneurship started escalating in the 1990s through scholars from various research fields who imported various concepts and theories into the field. According to other studies, only in the 2000s did the field become legitimate (Meyer et al., 2014). This evolution seems appropriate to describe the trends underpinning the empirical and theoretical development of entrepreneurship education and its assessment.

The Period 2004–16

This period is crucial in the field, as several contributions have established the foundation of entrepreneurship education assessment. During this period, entrepreneurial self-efficacy and intention, as a proxy for entrepreneurial behavior, was introduced as essential outcomes to assess the effectiveness of entrepreneurship education. The first piece of empirical evidence was produced regarding the link between entrepreneurship programs and changes in attitude and intention toward self-employment (Wilson, Kickul, and Marlino, 2007; Souitaris et al., 2007). More importantly, findings revealed that, at the end of the program, the differences in the level of entrepreneurial self-efficacy between women and men disappeared, demonstrating the neutralizer effect of entrepreneurship education (Wilson et al., 2007). At the same time, contradictory findings emerged, raising concerns about the factual effect of entrepreneurship education (Oosterbeek, van Praag, and Ijsselstein, 2010; von Graevenitz, Harhoff, and Weber, 2010).

A prolific year for the topic was 2013, when a set of works appeared and became pivotal for the field. They include a literature review (Rideout and Gray, 2013) and a meta-analysis (Martin et al., 2013) that attested to the research preoccupation about producing empirical evidence regarding the effects of entrepreneurship education. In addition to these overviews of the literature, two other works are notable: one providing a general perspective on entrepreneurship education and specific comments on its evaluation (Fayolle, 2013), and the other presenting preliminary results of entrepreneurship education programs, specifically the Entrepreneurship Education Project, which carried out a longitudinal survey involving several countries around the world (Vanevenhoven and Liguori, 2013).

These studies emphasized that the field was in an early stage of development: "E-ed appears to be one of those phenomena where action and intervention have raced far ahead of the theory, pedagogy and research needed to justify and explain it" (Rideout and Gray, 2013, p. 346). Notably, they have shown that only weak signals have been produced in favor of a positive effect of entrepreneurship education and that changes in entrepreneurial intention may decay over time. Martin et al. (2013), for instance, based their analysis on 42 studies showing a positive relationship between entrepreneurship education interventions and an ensemble of outcomes, namely, positive perceptions about entrepreneurship, behavior such as nascence status, startup formation, and entrepreneurship performance, with a slightly positive impact on academic-focused entrepreneurship education programs.

A commonality among these contributions is the recognition of the methodological drawbacks of empirical works. Specific needs have been expressed to improve the research design, models to consider moderators, measures used to operationalize theoretical constructs, and statistical analysis to examine data. Furthermore, these studies have asserted the importance of formulating different and more complex research questions inspired by other academic disciplines such as education.

Partially addressing these concerns, Bae et al. (2014) looked specifically at the relationship between entrepreneurship education and entrepreneurial intention by analyzing 73 studies. They extended the previous meta-analysis (Martin et al., 2013), including moderators at the individual (background and gender), training (types of entrepreneurship education), and contextual levels (national culture), to effectively explain the dynamics underpinning the entrepreneurship education effect. Their work revealed that entrepreneurship education has a positive effect on intention, with a more positive impact on programs that focus on venture creation than business planning. As regards the role of moderators, they found that only cultural issues were able to strengthen the effects of entrepreneurship education on entrepreneurial intention.

In the ensuing years, essential advancements have emerged with three works providing theoretical lenses and rigorous assessments of entrepreneurship education. Through a quasi-experimental design with a control group and drawing on TPB, Rauch and Hulsink (2015) demonstrated the theory's robustness in predicting intention and behavior. They provided evidence of the relation between intentions and behavior 18 months after the end of a program that was mostly centered on active learning. Furthermore, Gielnik et al. (2015) introduced an action regulation lens to dig into the mechanisms connecting education to a consequent behavior. Extending the TPB, this randomized study showed that the strength of the relationship between an intended entrepreneurial goal and a consequent action depended on the plans to take action after the program. According to the action regulation theory (Frese and Zapf, 1994), these plans are important for the consequent behavior because they establish concrete steps to achieve an outcome that, in the case of this study, was represented by the creation of a new venture. Lastly, Fayolle and Gailly (2015) focused on attitude and intention to gather possible changes on these perceptual variables at the end and six months after a compulsory program. The researchers found that the initial level of entrepreneurial intention was negatively correlated with the impact of a program, noting that an intention is more likely to develop incrementally in students that are initially less attracted by entrepreneurship.

Overall, these studies have emphasized a set of issues requiring investigations which, if addressed, may provide the opportunity for the field to advance drastically. In particular, the temporal dimension necessary for an aspiring entrepreneur to show entrepreneurial behavior was highlighted as a question to address if we are to successfully assess the potential effect of entrepreneurship education. Furthermore, the contextual elements emerged as the missing items in the current models and were thought to moderate the relationship between intention and behavior. New mediators, such as the implementation intention, were mentioned as a critical connector between intention and consequent behavior. Lastly, identifying new theoretical lenses as an alternative to that of the TPB is necessary to explain contradictory findings among studies regarding the nexus of education–intention–behavior.

The Period 2017–19

Four years after the literature review authored by Rideout and Gray (2013), Nabi et al. (2017) published a systematic literature review on the impact of entrepreneurship education aiming at connecting training pedagogy to specific outcomes. Outlining the importance of exploring the reasons for contradictory findings, they have suggested different lines of inquiry for future research. These include introducing novel moderators (such as type of course, type of institution, and cultural values) to better understand how entrepreneurship education might work. In addition, using novel indicators related to emotion and mindset or to the transition of intention to behavior (such as dispositional optimism, the development of an entrepreneurial identity, and transition from entrepreneurial intentions into nascent or startup behavior) to gain a more holistic view of the impact of entrepreneurship education.

In exploring how these contributions have extended our knowledge, this study has observed some attempts to address the research suggestions posed by Nabi et al. (2017). Notably, we have observed two main tendencies. On the one hand, recent works have intensified country and cross-country inquiries, bringing a cultural perspective to the effect of entrepreneurship education (e.g., Ahmed, Chandran, and Klobas, 2017; Anosike, 2018; Arranz, Arroyabe, and de Arroyabe, 2019; Ferrante, Federici, and Parisi, 2019; Fietze and Boyd, 2017; Hunter and Lean, 2018; Muñoz, Guerra, and Mosey, 2019; Nyadu-Addo and Mensah, 2018; Zaring, Gifford, and McKelvey, 2019). Some of them also aim to understand the extent to which the entrepreneurial inclination varies depending on the national contexts, and how these differences influence the effect of entrepreneurship education in enhancing this spirit (e.g., Jabeen,

Faisal, and Katsioloudes, 2017; Nowiński, Haddoud, Lančarič, Egerová, and Czeglédi, 2019). In some of these studies, an important concern is the need to clarify the role of universities as drivers of entrepreneurial intention (e.g., Barnard, Pittz, and Vanevenhoven, 2019; Gieure, Benavides-Espinosa, Roig-Dobón, 2019; Roman and Maxim, 2017), entrepreneurial competences, identity, and learning processes (Kleine, Giones, and Tegtmeier, 2019). Furthermore, an interest emerges in studying the effect of entrepreneurship education in elementary and middle schools (e.g., Jónsdóttir and Macdonald, 2019; Pepin and St-Jean, 2019).

On the other hand, recent research has focused on the type of outcomes that entrepreneurship education might influence, expanding the consolidated view of looking at the increment of an entrepreneurial intent as a primary outcome of entrepreneurship education (e.g., Fretschner and Lampe, 2019; Gielnik et al., 2017; Hahn, Minola, Van Gils, and Huybrechts, 2017; Shirokova, Osiyevskyy, Morris, and Bogatyreva, 2017).

As regards the first tendency, looking at the United Arab Emirates, Jabeen et al. (2017) attempt to identify environmental and individual drivers that, within the university, might support students' choice to become entrepreneurs. They have found that the level of prior exposure to entrepreneurship education is crucial in fostering entrepreneurship because students are more likely to include starting a business among their career options. Another study conducted in the Visegrád countries (Czech Republic, Hungary, Poland, and Slovakia) corroborates this result, showing that students from countries that have been introduced to entrepreneurship education in high school show a higher level of intention than students who did not have the same experience. This policy is thought to strengthen the effectiveness of entrepreneurship education at the university level (Nowiński et al., 2019). To understand how universities might foster entrepreneurial intention through entrepreneurship education, other studies have highlighted the importance of education to promote emotional competence (Fernández-Pérez, Montes-Merino, Rodríguez-Ariza, and Galicia, 2019). Defined as an interrelated set of behaviors that individuals employ to recognize and manage their own emotions and those of others, emotional competence encourages entrepreneurship because it helps students to be more productive and creative and less risk-averse. This condition allows students to develop a positive attitude toward entrepreneurship.

As regards the second trend, Hahn et al. (2017) demonstrate that an inverse U-shaped relationship connects entrepreneurship education initiatives and learning outcomes (type of acquired knowledge), implying that at a certain point, the learning that results from education starts decreasing. They also show that prior founding experiences enable students to achieve higher levels of knowledge about entrepreneurship when they attend additional entrepreneurial education initiatives. The relationship is positively moderated by the practical-oriented pedagogy and by an opportunity-driven approach to entrepreneurship that characterizes a country's policy. Considering the logic applied to develop a business, Shirokova et al. (2017) show that prior exposure to entrepreneurship-related events and university offerings influence not only a student's choice to become an entrepreneur but also whether and when they use effectual or causal logic. Specifically, the findings demonstrate that experienced student entrepreneurs are more likely to adopt causal and effectual-oriented approaches than inexperienced students. Concentrating on the long-term training effects, Gielnik et al. (2017) scrutinize the role of passion in association with that of self-efficacy over 32 months after training. The findings reveal that entrepreneurship education has a positive effect on entrepreneurial self-efficacy by nurturing a passion that, in the long term, motivates an individual's effort to create a business. Lastly, Fretschner and Lampe (2019) emphasize the sorting and alignment effects on the level of entrepreneurial intention after an entrepreneurship program. Accordingly, rather than gathering the increment at the level of entrepreneurial intention, evaluation should determine the extent to which students gain a clear picture of their positive or negative position toward entrepreneurship (sorting effect) and adjust their entrepreneurial intention by moving to a less extreme position (alignment effect). Overall, they point out that the leading role of entrepreneurship education is to develop students' awareness of their genuine interest in becoming entrepreneurs, and this is the most important outcome to consider in an entrepreneurship education program. In accordance with this view, entrepreneurship education should aim to increase the fit between students and the possibility of becoming an entrepreneur. This fit might eventually influence the survival of the startup.

Overall, through the introduction of a cross-national perspective, recent studies have contributed to obtaining a holistic overview of the impact of entrepreneurship education. Furthermore, acknowledging some of the suggestions provided by Nabi et al. (2017), recent works have provided the field with the opportunity to expand the range of outcomes to evaluate entrepreneurship education, highlighting alternative objectives that entrepreneurship education programs might influence. Figure 10.6 summarizes the main perspectives characterizing each commented period.

A GLIMPSE OF FUTURE TRENDS

Altogether, these results highlight an ensemble of research areas that previous studies have proven to be critical for investigating the impact of entrepre-

1990 - 2003	
Need to evaluate the impact of entrepreneurship education	• Importance of using discernible and measurable criteria that can evaluate the important aspects of an entrepreneurship program (Vesper and Gartner, 1997). • Enterprise education has a positive influence on the perception of desirability and feasibility. Empirical findings suggest the need for incorporating the exposition to enterprise or entrepreneurship education in the intention models (Peterman and Kennedy, 2003).
2004 - 2016	
The research identifies important suggestions to improve the field	• The empirical analysis of entrepreneurship education as a driver of positive attitudes toward entrepreneurship, such as self-efficacy and entrepreneurial intention, is considered an important outcome of entrepreneurship education (Wilson et al., 2007; Souitaris et al., 2007; Vanevenhoven and Liguori, 2013). • Need for improving empirical methods to assess entrepreneurship education and to elaborate more complex questions (Fayolle 2013; Pittaway and Cope, 2007; Rideout and Gray, 2013). • Need for introducing moderators to explain the effect of entrepreneurship education, such as contextual variables (Bae et al., 2014; Martin et al., 2013). • Empirical and theoretical explanations of contradictory results, such as prior exposure to entrepreneurship education (e.g., Fayolle and Gailly, 2015). • Focus on middle and long-term results of entrepreneurship education (e.g., Fayolle and Gailly, 2015; Gielnik et al. 2015; Rauch and Hulsink, 2015).
2017 - 2019	
Development of a cultural perspective and alternative outcomes with respect to entrepreneurial intentions to assess entrepreneurship education	• National and cross-national perspectives on the effect of entrepreneurship education (e.g., Ahmed, Chandran, and Klobas, 2017; Anosike, 2018; Arranz et al., 2019; Ferrante, Federici, and Parisi, 2019; Fietze and Boyd, 2017; Hunter and Lean, 2018; Muñoz et al., 2019; Nyadu-Addo and Mensah, 2018; Zaring, Gifford, and McKelvey, 2019). • Effects of elementary, middle and tertiary education (e.g., Barnard, Pittz, and Vanevenhoven, 2019; Jónsdóttir and Macdonald, 2019; Pepin and St-Jean, 2019). • Adopting alternative outcomes to assess the impact of entrepreneurship education, instead of the increment of entrepreneurial intention (Nabi et al.,2017). A few examples are the learning curve (Hahn et al.,2017), effectual or causal logic (Shirokova et al., 2017), sorting, and alignment effects (Fretschner and Lampe, 2019).

Figure 10.6   Time intervals and research on the impact of entrepreneurship education

neurship education and, according to our understanding, still require further investigation. We can summarize the outcomes as follows:

• influence mechanisms of entrepreneurship education;
• circumstances under which entrepreneurship education is most effective; and
• temporal effects of entrepreneurship education.

Influence Mechanisms of Entrepreneurship Education

As regards the mechanisms by which entrepreneurship education influences specific outcomes, there is a need to develop in-depth understanding of the possible paths that connect training activities with the different phases of the entrepreneurial process. For instance, existing research has demonstrated that entrepreneurship education can neutralize background effects, attenuating the role of gender on self-efficacy and entrepreneurial intention (e.g., Wilson et al., 2007; Nowiński et al., 2019). Furthermore, entrepreneurship education fosters the relationship between intention and consequent behavior because it strengthens students' skills related to the planning of activities that are key to setting up a business (Gielnik et al., 2015). Lastly, entrepreneurship education might reinforce or adjust a previous idea regarding the choice of entrepreneurship as a career (e.g., Fretschner and Lampe, 2019). Future research, inspired by the objectives of entrepreneurship education systematized by Bechard and Toulouse (1998),[6] should dig deep into these various roles of entrepreneurship education and elucidate direct and indirect effects on perceptual and behavioral outcomes.

To synthesize this idea, Figure 10.7 highlights several examples of the mechanisms that have received initial empirical support and that future research should extend.

Entrepreneurship education is depicted as a moderator that can positively influence the acknowledged relationships between antecedents and intention rooted in TPB. However, it can also foster entrepreneurial behavior directly or indirectly by acting on other variables that mediate its effect. Future research should investigate deeply when and how entrepreneurship education may act as a moderator, and which other significant dimensions can be improved

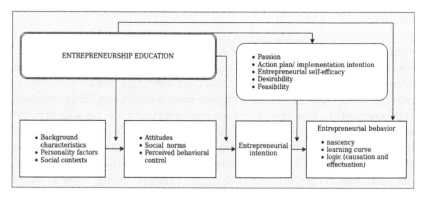

Figure 10.7   Entrepreneurship education: mechanisms of influence

with training to mediate the effect on entrepreneurial outcomes (including the intention and its transformation into action). For example, the motivational dimension, which concerns energy, direction, and persistence (Ryan and Deci, 2000), might play a crucial role as a mediator. Carsrud and Brännback (2011) have claimed that "motivations may be the spark that transforms a latent intention into real action and, therefore, is the missing link between intentions and action" (p. 12). According to the self-determination theory (Ryan and Deci, 2000), individuals are, by nature, inherently active, intrinsically motivated, and oriented toward self-development. Within this theoretical perspective, intrinsic motivation, which is understood as a precursor of psychological self-determination, is the principal component that explains human behavior. This is because people tend to satisfy three universal psychological needs, namely, needs for competence, autonomy, and relatedness, which are essential for their optimal development and functioning. The social environment plays an important role in fostering or hampering the achievement of these basic needs. Decades of research looking at these dynamics have produced empirical evidence that individuals might respond differently to the social contexts depending on the extent to which they perceive to be supported or not in achieving their need of competence or self-determination (Deci and Ryan, 2012). In entrepreneurship education, this stream of research might be particularly useful to better understand the dynamics behind its impact. Studies have demonstrated, for example, that elective courses are more effective than compulsory courses in increasing students' entrepreneurial intention (Karimi, Biemans, Lans, Chizari, and Mulder, 2016). Therefore, from a theoretical and empirical point of view, the exploration of intrinsic motivation emerges as an important aspect to be included in the entrepreneurship education future agenda.

Circumstances under which Entrepreneurship Education is Most Effective

Related to the need to investigate the mechanisms underpinning the relationships between education and outcomes, we need to understand the circumstances under which entrepreneurship education fosters or hampers entrepreneurial outcomes (from entrepreneurial intentions to behaviors, such as the creation of a new venture or career planning that better fits with personal aspirations). With circumstances, we are meant to identify personal characteristics, situational conditions, teaching approaches, and individuals' transition processes in life-long learning that might strengthen the role of entrepreneurship education. As noted in our analysis, for example, during the most recent period, research has emphasized the role of culture and that of the environment as critical elements in understanding the role of entrepreneurship education.

What seems unclear, however, is when entrepreneurship education maximizes its effect on perceptual variables and behaviors. This reflection indistinctly applies to an educational or training context as, in this work, they are both considered learning settings.

Therefore, looking at future research avenues, two different perspectives might be of some interest. The first is related to the need to identify how education interacts with demographic and context variables to figure out when this interaction causes different results. The second perspective is related to the need to optimize the fit between pedagogy, participants, and expected outcomes. The two perspectives in combination might provide a fine-grained overview of the impact of entrepreneurship education, emphasizing the questions of when and how entrepreneurship education works instead of looking at whether it works. This approach would help to build a system perspective on the assessment of entrepreneurship education that, drawn from the transfer of training approaches, may inspire a theoretical ground for new hypotheses (Loi, 2018).

Temporal Effect of Entrepreneurship Education

The temporal effect is another critical concern regarding the assessment of entrepreneurship education. Rideout and Gray (2013) affirm that the level of intention might decrease over time. However, studies on the stability of entrepreneurship education effects are limited, and no clear understanding exists on which outcomes deteriorate at the end of the programs. Furthermore, although prior studies have provided relevant contributions regarding the effect of entrepreneurship education at 6, 18, and 32 months after the training (e.g., Fayolle and Gailly, 2015; Gielnik et al., 2017; Rauch and Hulsink, 2015), there is a need to identify when the assessment of medium- and long-term results is appropriate.

We propose that to develop a clear theoretical proposition concerning the time issue, considering students' evaluations about the right moment to engage in entrepreneurial activity is useful. This suggestion is supported by recent research showing a different transition pattern from opportunity identification to intention and, ultimately, to the creation of a new business depending on how people approach the future as they get older (Gielnik, Zacher, and Wang, 2018). Gielnik and co-authors have observed that while young adults tend to switch from opportunity identification to entrepreneurial intention more often than older adults, older adults go to action through intention more often than young adults. In the case of young adults, a more expansive future time perspective, which is the perceptions of the remaining time before an important endpoint, explains the observed pattern. In the case of older people, their prior startup experience might facilitate the translation of an intention into the creation of a new business. This result suggests that for the assessment of entrepreneurship education the specificity of the transition process along the steps of the entrepreneurial process, which is related to prior experience and age, should be taken into account. Introducing a temporal perspective in the assessment approaches, therefore, is useful to better understand the moment in which it might be optimal to observe specific outcomes in the education and training context, where adults are more likely to be involved. Specifically, it would be interesting to investigate how entrepreneurship education interacts with the passing of time to affect the transition process, from opportunity identification to the creation of a new business. If we look at the education setting, Kwong and Thompson (2016), for example, have identified three types of students based on their intention to start a business immediately or in the future upon completion of their studies; these types are rapid, waiting, and doubtful potential entrepreneurs. The researchers have noticed that the most favored path is to work for others first and then become an entrepreneur at a later time. Another study has demonstrated that the attitude toward entrepreneurship has more explanatory power for intention among individuals who want to become entrepreneurs immediately after finishing their studies than among those who have other professional interests (Ramos-Rodríguez, Medina-Garrido, and Ruiz-Navarro, 2019). Therefore, further analysis is needed to understand whether entrepreneurship education persuades students to reschedule their entrance to entrepreneurship.

CONCLUDING REMARKS

Qualitative reviews of the literature on the impact of entrepreneurship education have pointed out relevant methodological drawbacks in prior studies that highlight the need for complex questions (Rideout and Gray, 2013) and fresh approaches to identify outcomes (Nabi et al., 2017). Recently, some authors have also affirmed that education research has not advanced at the same level of scholarship compared with general entrepreneurship research (Liguori, Winkler, Neck, and Terjesen, 2019; Neck and Corbett, 2018).

However, through our analysis, we have observed a tendency to improve research design that includes a longitudinal perspective and a control group. We have also recognized the scholars' effort to consider alternative outcomes to assess the impact of entrepreneurship education and explore medium- and long-term results. This overview might be biased by the criteria we have used to select our unit of analysis. Nevertheless, the research has progressed and future work, if inspired by previous contributions, may move the field forward. In this regard, we have positive expectations based on the trends observed from our temporal perspective.

Our analysis reveals that at the beginning of the 2000s, scholars built the theoretical foundation of entrepreneurship education, namely, the TPB and social cognitive theory as well as elaborating the entrepreneurship event model. We have recognized that during this period, two focal contributions influence entrepreneurship education, namely, the work of Peterman and Kennedy (2003) and that of Vesper and Gartner (1997). In the second period, meta-analyses and literature reviews have provided scholars with the opportunity to focus on the field, increasing their awareness of gaps and future lines of research. Relevant contributions have aimed to cope with the contradictory findings that emerged from empirical works. During the third period, new trends have emerged, emphasizing the need to consider the cultural contexts in which entrepreneurship education is delivered and widening the possible outcomes that may yield an improved understanding of the influence of entrepreneurship education.

Perceptual variables are at the heart of the research on entrepreneurship education assessment. Notably, entrepreneurial self-efficacy and intention are considered pivotal to evaluating the effect of entrepreneurship education. However, recent research has brought new perspectives, highlighting that the exposure of entrepreneurship education influences not only the career choice but also the logic people use to operate their own businesses and how they react to repeated participation in entrepreneurship education.

Our findings should be read in light of the study's limitation of relying on the choices that have guided the selection of our unit of analysis. Our overview is not meant to be as comprehensive as our research interest in understanding the evolution of the topic in highly regarded journals. Therefore, future research should complement this overview.

Drawing from this analysis, we have outlined reflections that might be of interest in forthcoming studies. First, we have argued the need for further investigation of the mechanisms by which entrepreneurship education influences perceptual and behavioral outcomes. Inspired by the self-determination theory, we have suggested considering the role of intrinsic motivation. Second, we can understand these mechanisms better if we look at the circumstances under which entrepreneurship education optimizes its positive influence. In this case, the question is to understand in which circumstances (personal characteristics, situational conditions, teaching approaches, and individuals' transition process in lifelong learning) entrepreneurship education better fits with an individual's self-development. Finally, a temporal perspective may enlighten the stability of the entrepreneurship education impact and the suitable time intervals for evaluating medium- and long-term results. Future research should explore how entrepreneurship education interacts with the passing of time to affect the transition along the phases of the entrepreneurship process, and whether or not it persuades student to reschedule their entrance in entrepreneurship.

In addition to conducting a thematic overview, this work has described the background of the research field. We have noticed that some regions in the world have actively participated in the development of the topic. The cultural perspective recently introduced in the field will probably contribute to expanding the interest in the topic worldwide, encouraging new collaborations among co-authors from different regions. This emerging emphasis could be relevant for understanding the contingency versus universal side of the impact of entrepreneurship education, opening a new research phase where scholars have to face critical theoretical challenges related to the role of contexts in enhancing entrepreneurship education effects. Building on the research in entrepreneurship, scholars might confront these research challenges more efficaciously (Gabrielsson et al., 2018), thereby contributing to the advancement of the entire field of entrepreneurship.

ACKNOWLEDGMENTS

We thank Manuel Castriotta for his support and expertise with VOS viewer and CitNetExplorer and Marco Cogoni for the geographical map.

NOTES

1. We truncated keywords with asterisks (*) to include any form of their appearance in the documents.
2. In this case, we used VOSviewer (Van Eck and Waltman, 2010).
3. In this case, we used CitNetExplorer (Van Eck and Waltman, 2014).
4. We obtained the figure with VOSviewer. In this case, the map is created using bibliographic data where the links represent co-authorship and the items represent the countries of authors' affiliations (Castriotta and Loi, 2017; Van Eck and Waltman, 2019).
5. The citation network analysis is performed with CitNetExplorer (Van Eck and Waltman, 2014), a software that was created to obtain a picture of the development of a field over time. It allows mapping the most important publications in a field, ordered by the year in which they appeared, and the citation relations between these publications. Each node represents a publication whose label corresponds to the last name of the first author. While the vertical location of a publication is determined by the publication year, the horizontal location is determined by the citation relations among publications. Accordingly, strongly related publications are closer to each other than those that are weakly related (Van Eck and Waltman, 2014). The curved lines among the nodes represent citation relations in which the older publication is always located above the citing publication.
6. Bechard and Toulouse (1998) proposed a didactic entrepreneurship model that combines three categories of objectives: (a) general, (b) specific, and (c) those related to teaching activities. In the general objectives, they have included entre-

preneurship awareness, the creation of a new business, and the development of a small business. In the specific objectives, they have mentioned as important elements those related to the situations, the skills, and the content. As regards the teaching objectives, they have included a list of components of which a few examples are administration, strategy, visionary process, and technical skills.

REFERENCES

Ahmed, T., Chandran, V. G. R., and Klobas, J. (2017). Specialized entrepreneurship education: does it really matter? Fresh evidence from Pakistan. *International Journal of Entrepreneurial Behavior and Research, 23*(1), 4–19.

Ajzen, I., and Fishbein, M. (2000). Attitudes and the attitude-behavior relation: reasoned and automatic processes. *European Review of Social Psychology, 11*(1), 1–33.

Anosike, P. (2018). Entrepreneurship education knowledge transfer in a conflict sub-Saharan African context. *Journal of Small Business and Enterprise Development, 25*(4), 591–608.

Arranz, N., Arroyabe, M. F., and Fdez. de Arroyabe, J. C. (2019). Entrepreneurial intention and obstacles of undergraduate students: the case of the universities of Andalusia. *Studies in Higher Education, 44*(11), 2011–24.

Bae, T. J., Qian, S., Miao, C., and Fiet, J. O. (2014). The relationship between entrepreneurship education and entrepreneurial intentions: a meta–analytic review. *Entrepreneurship Theory and Practice, 38*(2), 217–54.

Barnard, A., Pittz, T., and Vanevenhoven, J. (2019). Entrepreneurship education in US community colleges: a review and analysis. *Journal of Small Business and Enterprise Development, 26*(2), 190–208.

Bechard, J. P., and Toulouse, J. M. (1998). Validation of a didactic model for the analysis of training objectives in entrepreneurship. *Journal of Business Venturing, 13*(4), 317–32.

Carsrud, A., and Brännback, M. (2011). Entrepreneurial motivations: what do we still need to know? *Journal of Small Business Management, 49*(1), 9–26.

Castriotta, M., and Loi, M. (2017). *Entrepreneurship Education and the Rise of New Organizations*. Milan: Franco Angeli.

Chen, C. C., Greene, P. G., and Crick, A. (1998). Does entrepreneurial self-efficacy distinguish entrepreneurs from managers? *Journal of Business Venturing, 13*(4), 295–316.

Deci, E. L., and Ryan, R. M. (2012). Self-determination theory. In P. A. M. Van Lange, A. W. Kruglanski, and E. T. Higgins (Eds), *Handbook of Theories of Social Psychology*, pp. 416–37. London: Sage.

Fayolle, A. (2013). Personal views on the future of entrepreneurship education. *Entrepreneurship and Regional Development, 25*(7–8), 692–701.

Fayolle, A., and Gailly, B. (2015). The impact of entrepreneurship education on entrepreneurial attitudes and intention: hysteresis and persistence. *Journal of Small Business Management, 53*(1), 75–93.

Fernández-Pérez, V., Montes-Merino, A., Rodríguez-Ariza, L., and Galicia, P. E. A. (2019). Emotional competencies and cognitive antecedents in shaping student's entrepreneurial intention: the moderating role of entrepreneurship education. *International Entrepreneurship and Management Journal, 15*(1), 281–305.

Ferrante, F., Federici, D., and Parisi, V. (2019). The entrepreneurial engagement of Italian university students: some insights from a population-based survey. *Studies in Higher Education, 44*(11), 1813–36.

Fietze, S., and Boyd, B. (2017). Entrepreneurial intention of Danish students: a correspondence analysis. *International Journal of Entrepreneurial Behavior and Research, 23*(4), 656–72.

Frese, M., and Zapf, D. (1994). Action as the core of work psychology: a German approach. *Handbook of Industrial and Organizational Psychology, 4*(2), 271–340.

Fretschner, M., and Lampe, H. W. (2019). Detecting hidden sorting and alignment effects of entrepreneurship education. *Journal of Small Business Management, 57*(4), 1712–37.

Gabrielsson, J., Landström, H., Politis, D., and Hägg, G. (2018). Exemplary contributions from Europe to entrepreneurship education research and practice. In Fayolle, A. (Ed.), *A Research Agenda for Entrepreneurship Education* (pp. 105–26). Cheltenham, UK and Northampton, MA, USA: Edward Elgar Publishing.

Gielnik, M. M., Zacher, H., and Wang, M. (2018). Age in the entrepreneurial process: the role of future time perspective and prior entrepreneurial experience. *Journal of Applied Psychology, 103*(10), 1067–85.

Gielnik, M. M., Uy, M. A., Funken, R., and Bischoff, K. M. (2017). Boosting and sustaining passion: a long-term perspective on the effects of entrepreneurship training. *Journal of Business Venturing, 32*(3), 334–53.

Gielnik, M. M., Frese, M., Kahara-Kawuki, A., Wasswa Katono, I., Kyejjusa, S., Ngoma, M. … and Oyugi, J. (2015). Action and action-regulation in entrepreneurship: evaluating a student training for promoting entrepreneurship. *Academy of Management Learning and Education, 14*(1), 69–94.

Gieure, C., Benavides-Espinosa, M. D. M., and Roig-Dobón, S. (2019). Entrepreneurial intentions in an international university environment. *International Journal of Entrepreneurial Behavior and Research.*

Hahn, D., Minola, T., Van Gils, A., and Huybrechts, J. (2017). Entrepreneurial education and learning at universities: exploring multilevel contingencies. *Entrepreneurship and Regional Development, 29*(9–10), 945–74.

Hunter, L., and Lean, J. (2018). Entrepreneurial learning – a social context perspective: evidence from Kenya and Tanzania. *Journal of Small Business and Enterprise Development, 25*(4), 609–27.

Jabeen, F., Faisal, M. N., and I. Katsioloudes, M. (2017). Entrepreneurial mindset and the role of universities as strategic drivers of entrepreneurship: evidence from the United Arab Emirates. *Journal of Small Business and Enterprise Development, 24*(1), 136–57.

Jónsdóttir, S. R., and Macdonald, M. A. (2019). The feasibility of innovation and entrepreneurial education in middle schools. *Journal of Small Business and Enterprise Development, 26*(2), 255–72.

Karimi, S., Biemans, H. J., Lans, T., Chizari, M., and Mulder, M. (2016). The impact of entrepreneurship education: a study of Iranian students' entrepreneurial intentions and opportunity identification. *Journal of Small Business Management, 54*(1), 187–209.

Kautonen, T., Van Gelderen, M., and Fink, M. (2015). Robustness of the theory of planned behavior in predicting entrepreneurial intentions and actions. *Entrepreneurship Theory and Practice, 39*(3), 655–74.

Kautonen, T., Van Gelderen, M., and Tornikoski, E. T. (2013). Predicting entrepreneurial behaviour: a test of the theory of planned behaviour. *Applied Economics*, *45*(6), 697–707.

Kleine, K., Giones, F., and Tegtmeier, S. (2019). The learning process in technology entrepreneurship education: insights from an engineering degree. *Journal of Small Business Management*, *57*(S1), 94–110.

Krueger, Jr., N. F., Reilly, M. D., and Carsrud, A. L. (2000). Competing models of entrepreneurial intentions. *Journal of Business Venturing*, *15*(5–6), 411–32.

Kwong, C., and Thompson, P. (2016). The when and why: student entrepreneurial aspirations. *Journal of Small Business Management*, *54*(1), 299–318.

Landström, H., and Harirchi, G. (2018). The social structure of entrepreneurship as a scientific field. *Research Policy*, *47*(3), 650–62.

Liguori, E. W., Winkler, C., Neck, H. M., and Terjesen, S. (2019). Special issue on entrepreneurship education. *Journal of Small Business Management*, *57*(S1), 4–5.

Loi, M. (2018). Dealing with the inconsistency of studies in entrepreneurship education effectiveness: a systemic approach to drive future research. In Fayolle, A. (Ed.), *A Research Agenda for Entrepreneurship Education* (pp. 38–61). Cheltenham, UK and Northampton, MA, USA: Edward Elgar Publishing.

Martin, B. C., McNally, J. J., and Kay, M. J. (2013). Examining the formation of human capital in entrepreneurship: a meta-analysis of entrepreneurship education outcomes. *Journal of Business Venturing*, *28*(2), 211–24.

Meyer, M., Libaers, D., Thijs, B., Grant, K., Glänzel, W., and Debackere, K. (2014). Origin and emergence of entrepreneurship as a research field. *Scientometrics*, *98*, 473–85.

Muñoz, C. A., Guerra, M. E., and Mosey, S. (2019). The potential impact of entrepreneurship education on doctoral students within the non-commercial research environment in Chile. *Studies in Higher Education*, 1–19.

Nabi, G., Liñan, F., Fayolle, A., Krueger, N., and Walmsley, A. (2017). The impact of entrepreneurship education in higher education: a systematic review and research agenda. *Academy of Management Learning and Education*, *16*(2), 277–99.

Neck, H. M., and Corbett, A. C. (2018). The scholarship of teaching and learning entrepreneurship. *Entrepreneurship Education and Pedagogy*, *1*(1), 8–41.

Nowiński, W., Haddoud, M. Y., Lančarič, D., Egerová, D., and Czeglédi, C. (2019). The impact of entrepreneurship education, entrepreneurial self-efficacy and gender on entrepreneurial intentions of university students in the Visegrad countries. *Studies in Higher Education*, *44*(2), 361–79.

Nyadu-Addo, R., and Mensah, M. S. B. (2018). Entrepreneurship education in Ghana: the case of the KNUST entrepreneurship clinic. *Journal of Small Business and Enterprise Development*, *25*(4), 573–90.

Obschonka, M., and Stuetzer, M. (2017). Integrating psychological approaches to entrepreneurship: the Entrepreneurial Personality System (EPS). *Small Business Economics*, *49*(1), 203–31.

Oosterbeek, H., van Praag, M., and Ijsselstein, A. (2010). The impact of entrepreneurship education on entrepreneurship skills and motivation. *European Economic Review*, *54*(3), 442–54.

Orduna-Malea, E., Aytac, S., and Tran, C. Y. (2019). Universities through the eyes of bibliographic databases: a retroactive growth comparison of Google Scholar, Scopus and Web of Science. *Scientometrics*, *121*(1), 433–50.

Pepin, M., and St-Jean, E. (2019). Assessing the impacts of school entrepreneurial initiatives: a quasi-experiment at the elementary school level. *Journal of Small Business and Enterprise Development, 26*(2), 273–88.

Peterman, N. E., and Kennedy, J. (2003). Enterprise education: influencing students' perceptions of entrepreneurship. *Entrepreneurship Theory and Practice, 28*(2), 129–44.

Ramos-Rodríguez, A. R., Medina-Garrido, J. A., and Ruiz-Navarro, J. (2019). Why not now? Intended timing in entrepreneurial intentions. *International Entrepreneurship and Management Journal, 15*, 1221–46.

Rasmussen, E. A., and Sørheim, R. (2006). Action-based entrepreneurship education. *Technovation, 26*(2), 185–94.

Rauch, A., and Hulsink, W. (2015). Putting entrepreneurship education where the intention to act lies: an investigation into the impact of entrepreneurship education on entrepreneurial behavior. *Academy of Management Learning and Education, 14*(2), 187–204.

Rideout, E. C., and Gray, D. O. (2013). Does entrepreneurship education really work? A review and methodological critique of the empirical literature on the effects of university-based entrepreneurship education. *Journal of Small Business Management, 51*(3), 329–51.

Roman, T., and Maxim, A. (2017). National culture and higher education as pre-determining factors of student entrepreneurship. *Studies in Higher Education, 42*(6), 993–1014.

Ryan, R. M., and Deci, E. L. (2000). Self-determination theory and the facilitation of intrinsic motivation, social development, and well-being. *American Psychologist, 55*(1), 68–78.

Shapero, A., and Sokol, L. (1982). The social dimensions of entrepreneurship. *Encyclopedia of Entrepreneurship,* 72–90.

Shirokova, G., Osiyevskyy, O., Morris, M. H., and Bogatyreva, K. (2017). Expertise, university infrastructure and approaches to new venture creation: assessing students who start businesses. *Entrepreneurship and Regional Development, 29*(9–10), 912–44.

Souitaris, V., Zerbinati, S., and Al-Laham, A. (2007). Do entrepreneurship programmes raise entrepreneurial intention of science and engineering students? The effect of learning, inspiration and resources. *Journal of Business Venturing, 22*(4), 566–91.

Van Eck, N. J., and Waltman, L. (2010). Software survey: VOSviewer, a computer program for bibliometric mapping. *Scientometrics, 84*(2), 523–38.

Van Eck, N. J., and Waltman, L. (2014). CitNetExplorer: a new software tool for analyzing and visualizing citation networks. *Journal of Informetrics, 8*(4), 802–23.

Van Eck, N. J., and Waltman, L. (2019). VOS viewer manual. Manual for VOSviewer version 1.6.13.

Vanevenhoven, J., and Liguori, E. (2013). The impact of entrepreneurship education: introducing the entrepreneurship education project. *Journal of Small Business Management, 51*(3), 315–28.

Vesper, K. H., and Gartner, W. B. (1997). Measuring progress in entrepreneurship education. *Journal of Business Venturing, 12*(5), 403–21.

von Graevenitz, G., Harhoff, D., and Weber, R. (2010). The effects of entrepreneurship education. *Journal of Economic Behavior and Organization, 76*(1), 90–112.

Wilson, F., Kickul, J., and Marlino, D. (2007). Gender, entrepreneurial self–efficacy, and entrepreneurial career intentions: implications for entrepreneurship education. *Entrepreneurship Theory and Practice, 31*(3), 387–406.

Zaring, O., Gifford, E., and McKelvey, M. (2019). Strategic choices in the design of entrepreneurship education: an explorative study of Swedish higher education institutions. *Studies in Higher Education*, 1–16.

11. Cross-campus entrepreneurship through a general education strategy

Anthony Mendes, Jeffrey Hornsby and Andrew Heise

INTRODUCTION

General education curriculum has a long history addressing the intent of colleges and universities to develop comprehensive skills of students. The intent is to provide a program of education every student receives to develop personalities rather than specific skills of the student's major area of study. At the University of Missouri-Kansas City (UMKC), a novel approach was developed that partnered faculty from a discipline-specific area with an entrepreneurship professor. This way, both entities received credit for the course and students received the benefit of an entrepreneurship course focused on their discipline. The following is a description of this approach to general education and the enrollment impact over a three-year period.

The American Association of Colleges and Universities (AAC&U), the nation's largest organization with a focus on improving undergraduate education and advancing liberal education, is often considered a major informer for developing general education curricula. AAC&U general education initiatives aim to ensure every undergraduate student experiences a relevant and challenging general education curriculum. In addition to working with campuses to strengthen their general education programs overall or to reform specific aspects of them (e.g., science requirements or diversity requirements), AAC&U initiatives address strengthening general education for transfer students, embedding high expectations and meaningful assessment of student learning, and general education as essential for enhancing curricula and pedagogy (www.aacu.org/conferences/gened/2020, November 2019).

Most colleges and universities clearly state the purpose and intent of their general education curriculum. One example is California State University Northridge. On their website they state,

> The vision of General Education (GE) is to ensure that all CSUN students have a broad background in disciplines at the University level in order to appreciate the breadth of human knowledge and the responsibilities of concerned and engaged citizens of the world. Students must become lifelong learners and leave the University with a set of skills that includes the ability to read critically, to write and communicate orally with clarity and persuasiveness, to evaluate and draw appropriate inferences from limited information, and to access the wealth of technical, scientific and cultural information that is increasingly available in the global community. (https://catalog.csun.edu/general-education/, November 2019)

While there is some modification of these principles at every university, this statement clearly defines the overall intent of general education programs. Another example is the University of Arizona.

> The University-wide General Education Curriculum helps students attain the fundamental skills and broad base of knowledge that all college-educated adults must have, whatever their specific areas of concentration (i.e., the major and minor). The experiences of General Education encourage students to develop a critical and inquiring attitude, an appreciation of the interdisciplinary nature of subject areas, acceptance of persons of different backgrounds or values, and a deepened sense of self. The goal of General Education is to prepare students to respond more fully and effectively to an increasingly complex and ambiguous world. (https://gened.arizona.edu/, November 2019)

General education requirements are somewhat different at smaller liberal arts education institutions where students often have a wide range of course options. One example is Amherst College. "Amherst has no distribution requirements and no core curriculum. Instead, students choose the courses that matter most to them. Our open curriculum ensures that each classroom is filled with inquisitive, fully engaged students committed to the topic at hand." With this "open curriculum," students take responsibility for the breadth and focus of their education: "The open curriculum, is a complex dynamic of trust, communication, and experimentation on the part of both students and faculty. The open curriculum imposes one overriding requirement: that students take full responsibility for the courses they elect and that faculty take full responsibility for the courses they offer" (www.amherst.edu/academiclife/open-curriculum, November 2019).

Regardless of the approach to general education that a university might take, university accrediting bodies generally stipulate that a strong set of foundation courses are provided to students. Recently, there has been a push to include entrepreneurship in the general education curriculum, especially at schools that have a strong entrepreneurship focus. Including entrepreneurship as a general education course can be political since typically business courses have not been included in the general education program and its inclusion could lead to another course being omitted.

EARLY ATTEMPTS TO INFUSE ENTREPRENEURSHIP IN THE GENERAL EDUCATION CURRICULUM AT UMKC: CROSS-CAMPUS ENTREPRENEURSHIP

Those who attempt to expand entrepreneurship across all disciplines on a campus are aware of the many obstacles and roadblocks to the expansion. For some it is a territorial battle while for others it is the challenge of developing new curricula in disciplines where there is no room for additional courses, such as in health sciences and engineering. At UMKC, a novel approach has received considerable success. In collaboration with the UMKC Provost Office and Faculty Center for Excellence in Teaching, three general education courses have been developed to introduce concepts of entrepreneurship to a wide range of students from various colleges, schools, and departments.

In 2015, the Regnier Institute for Entrepreneurship and Innovation at the Bloch School of Management partnered with two academic units to offer unique general education courses to include domain expertise and entrepreneurship. The courses offered were: *Innovation and the Aging Population* (co-taught by faculty from the nursing school and entrepreneurship), and *Biological Innovation and Entrepreneurship* (co-taught by the biology and entrepreneurship faculty). The idea was to combine content from specific disciplines with entrepreneurship concepts where students worked in teams to propose new products and services for target markets. These courses were introduced in January 2015 and continue today. Brief descriptions of each course follow.

ANCH 199 – Biological Innovation and Entrepreneurship

Both observation and innovation lead to scientific achievement; adaptation of science often leads to economic achievement. In this course, we examine science, innovation, and value creation. We consider chains of discovery, including the innovations that fed them and those that led from them to the creation of economic wealth. This course intends to inculcate the entrepreneurial mindset in all students. Graduates distinguished by the ability to do things better, faster, cheaper, or simpler will create extraordinary value, achieving a high degree of economic self-determination, whether creating a new venture or working within an existing enterprise. Student learning objectives for this course include:

- Explain how an understanding of biology can lead to innovations that impact everyday life.
- Explain how to take an idea and develop a business model/strategic plan.
- Effectively present ideas for potential business development in both written and oral formats.

The majority of students who take this course are biology and health sciences majors. Approximately 20–25 students take this class per semester and class evaluations are favorable.

ANCH 310 – Innovation and the Aging Population

Students in this course will understand the implications of an aging United States population and what kinds of social changes will result. Moreover, they will learn to identify ways to do things better, faster, or more economically for that population, thereby serving society and achieving a high degree of economic self-determination. Students work in teams to develop new products and services for the aging population. Student learning objectives for this course include:

- Explain how an understanding of the aging population can lead to innovation that can impact everyday lives of aging United States citizens.
- Explain how to take an idea and develop a business model/strategic plan.
- Effectively present ideas for potential business development in both written and oral formats.

The foundational courses in the UMKC general education curriculum are referred to as Anchor courses. Students are required to take three Anchor courses offered in three phases, 100, 200, and 300 level courses. Students take the courses in sequence, reflecting their academic status, freshman, sophomore, junior, and senior levels.

This Anchor course is popular with students and every semester there is a waiting list to take the class. Enrollment is capped at 60 students. Students come from a wide range of disciplines.

In Spring 2017, another Anchor course was offered in collaboration with the UMKC Conservatory. This course, co-taught by a Bloch School of Management (entrepreneurship) professor with expertise in the arts and a professor in the Conservatory, was an extension of a cross-campus effort to expand the entrepreneurship curriculum. The course was an immediate success with significant enrollment and positive experiences reported by students.

ANCH 299 – Arts Entrepreneurship: The Music Business in Different Cultures and Industries

Students will explore culture and diversity through the lens of international music business entities, with a focus on entrepreneurship. Common themes will be identified across multiple industries and countries to provide an understanding of how to utilize one's talents and passions to create opportunities in a global context.

- Anchor 200 student learning objectives:
    - Students will be able to contextualize information and use the proper methods and theories as modes of understanding.
    - Focusing on specific problems and issues, students will demonstrate the ability to consider new modes of analysis drawn from a range of fields.
    - Students will demonstrate how thinking beyond disciplinary boundaries leads to innovation in all fields.
    - Students will draw on a variety of disciplines to develop an understanding of the complexities of human cultures, past and present, and come to an informed sense of self and others.
    - Students will describe a global culture that may include economic, environmental, political, and social issues facing all cultures.
    - Students will describe the factors defining cultural identities.
- Course-specific student learning objectives:
    - Demonstrate an understanding of the connections between performing arts and business.
    - Apply entrepreneurship methodology to pursue opportunities that align with talents and desires.

Early attempts to infuse an entrepreneurship curriculum in the general education curriculum were successful. Class enrollments have been at capacity and oversubscribed in some situations and students report favorable experiences. The Office of the Provost, where the general education administration is housed, continues to request entrepreneurship collaborations. Entrepreneurship faculty dedicate time to teach these courses and the revenue contributions to the Bloch School of Management is significant (enrollment data below). Entrepreneurship faculty have been recruited to assist in the advancement of the general education curriculum with an opportunity to develop new courses. While this approach to expand cross-campus entrepreneurship is effective, there are accreditation and workload issues to address. With three to four sections of Anchor courses being offered each semester with approximately 60 students in each section, one or two faculty members are required to cover the courses. These faculty are redirected from their business school courses to teach the Anchor courses. As such, the flow of tuition revenue, or lack thereof, back to the department has been an ongoing point of tension with the general education department. Additionally, Association to Advance Collegiate Schools of Business accreditation requires that scholarly academic or professional academic faculty classifications must teach 60 percent of their load in the business school in order to be "counted" for accreditation purposes.

COURSE ENROLLMENTS FROM NON-BUSINESS MAJORS

Prior to the offering of general education Anchor courses with entrepreneurship content incorporated, there was a small percentage of enrollment in business courses by non-business majors (15 percent). The majority of the non-business enrollments were in the Introduction to Entrepreneurship course. Since the introduction of entrepreneurship content in general education Anchor courses, non-business student enrollment has increased to 26 percent. This is significant for two reasons. First, it exposes non-business students to entrepreneurship concepts, primarily through business model development around creative new products and services. Second, it significantly increases the tuition flow through to the School of Management, where entrepreneurship is housed. From 2015 through 2018, 1,136 non-business students contributed tuition dollars from which the School of Management benefited. With the current general education tuition-sharing formula, the teaching faculty's department receives 80 percent of net tuition. With a conservative amount of $1,100 for a three-credit course, revenue flow to the entrepreneurship department is estimated to be over $1.2 million over a three-year period. Figure 11.1 shows total enrollment in all entrepreneurship courses and general education courses by semester from spring semester 2015 with tuition estimates based on a three-credit course.

Figure 11.2 shows enrollment in business entrepreneurship courses and enrollment in the general education Anchor courses. While business enrollments actually declined the general education courses with entrepreneurship content continued to increase.

As the data show, a correlation between enrollment in entrepreneurship-infused general education courses and an increase of non-business student enrollments in business entrepreneurship courses exists. The benefits of this is two-fold: increased enrollment in business courses and increased tuition revenue. This has led to leadership support for continued participation in the general education program. However, as is common with general education programs, revisions to the overall curriculum pose a threat to future growth in both enrollments and revenue share.

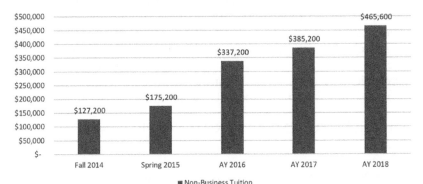

Note: No Anchor courses were offered in Fall 2014.

Figure 11.1   Non-business tuition

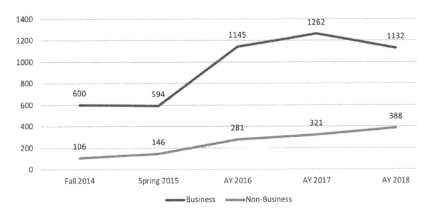

Note: First Anchor course offering began Spring 2015.

Figure 11.2   Course enrolments

GENERAL EDUCATION RECENT HISTORY AND DEVELOPMENTS AT UMKC: NEW OPPORTUNITIES

In July 2016, UMKC formed a General Education Task Force charged with the responsibility to review and redesign the university's general education program. The task force was guided by the requirements of the Higher Learning Commission and new requirements outlined in the Missouri House

Bill 2651: Higher Education Core Curriculum Transfer Act. During this transition period, revisions to the general education curriculum took place "while continuing to provide UMKC students with a high-quality, highly engaging educational experience that inspires curiosity, challenges intellectual capacities with curricular breath, depth, and interdisciplinary study that reflects the mission of the university," therefore the entrepreneurship Anchor courses continued to be offered. The core and emphasis of the newly developed general education program should also be an "articulated focus on skills, knowledge, and values that UMKC students should demonstrate at the conclusion of their studies to demonstrate competence as individual citizens, professionals and community leaders." Additional Program requirements included:

- Be driven by clearly stated and measurable student learning outcomes.
- Retain those elements of the current curriculum that demonstrate positive experiences for undergraduate students and remove those elements that do not add value to students' experience.
- Provide a baseline common denominator experience for undergraduate students in all degree programs.
- Provide experiences that will encourage students to demonstrate valued competencies guided by AAC&U LEAP outcomes including critical thinking, quantitative reasoning, communication skills, global thinking, cultural diversity, interdisciplinary thinking, civic engagement, ethical reasoning, problem solving, creativity, while also considering the university's commitment to developing within students the skills of innovation and entrepreneurship, and the capacity to experience failure with resilience.
- Encourage all academic and administrative units to work together to provide students with a broad, deep, and interdisciplinary experience reflecting the entire university.

A final meeting of the General Education 2.0 Task Force was convened in August 2017, and recommendations were submitted to Provost Barbara Bichelmeyer during the summer of 2017. The report was organized in three sections: Infrastructure, Student Experience, and Faculty Experience. The recommended implementation date, originally planned for fall 2019, was extended to fall 2020. In the interim, existing general education courses where entrepreneurship is a core component (described earlier in this chapter) were approved for continuation until the new curriculum is announced. Most importantly, and relevant to entrepreneurship as a core component of general education, is a process where new courses can be proposed to a curriculum review panel and approved by the provost. Faculty from the Regnier Institute are actively involved in creating and developing general education courses that will be available to a wider range of students at UMKC.

IMPACT OF GENERAL EDUCATION/ ENTREPRENEURSHIP COURSES: UNANTICIPATED OUTCOMES AND NEXT STEPS

The primary reason for the Regnier Institute to become involved in general education at UMKC was to expand the understanding and appreciation of entrepreneurship beyond the business school. The Bloch School of Management recognized the fact that students from all disciplines were pursuing entrepreneurship interests and departments across the campus were expressing interest in collaboration. In addition to the interest in course offerings, students were entering and winning awards in the Regnier Business Plan Competition and the Regnier Venture Creation Challenge. A cross-campus advisory board, made up of faculty and deans from various disciplines, was created to recommend ways to foster the spirit of entrepreneurship spirit on campus. This advisory board was, and continues to be, a major part of our cross-campus entrepreneurship strategy. In addition to early success, other opportunities emerged with implications for cross-discipline collaborations and entrepreneurship curriculum. These developments, both within the UMKC campus and with community partners, were not planned but evolved as a result of success in offering entrepreneurship as career enhancement.

Arts Entrepreneurship Certificate Program

As traditional career pathways for artists become more and more competitive, the ability of artists to create their own opportunities is a necessity. Entrepreneurship education for artists introduces students to new, innovative ways to think about how they create their artistic career. The format of a certificate was chosen for this program because most arts disciplines' curricula are lock step and inflexible. The proposed certificate is an achievable credential within these constraints and establishes a formalized program of study for students from the arts and students from business.

Student learning objectives:

- Students will understand how arts-based businesses create and capture value in society.
- Students will apply entrepreneurship methodologies to pursue opportunities to create and capture value that aligns with their talents and desires.
- Students will understand key management, marketing, financial, and economic principles necessary in an entrepreneurship career and an organization.
- Students will design, test, and execute a business model.

Course titles, descriptions, and learning outcomes

Entrepreneurial Mindset and Opportunity Recognition (3 credit hours)
This course teaches students how to develop an entrepreneurial mindset. Students will utilize play, creative problem solving, design thinking, and creativity tools while developing skills to mitigate risk and recognize opportunities.

- Identify characteristics of an entrepreneur.
- Understand the role of risk and reward in entrepreneurship and innovation.
- Recognize the role of creativity in entrepreneurship and innovation.
- Identify opportunities for value creation and value capture.

Entrepreneurship Toolkit (3 credit hours)
This course is for non-business majors (majors outside of the Bloch School) working towards an entrepreneurship minor. In this course students learn the basic elements of organizational functions including management, accounting, finance, and economics as foundational principles of entrepreneurship.

- Identify key management practices necessary to operate a venture.
- Apply basic marketing principles to effectively engage a target market.
- Analyze how shifts in supply and demand effect businesses.
- Illustrate how organizations keep records and the importance of this information.
- Describe the flow of money in a free enterprise economy.

Arts Entrepreneurship (3 credit hours)
This course will teach students how to design a business model, refine that business model, and take action. This course will take students through several models and frameworks that can be used to create new ventures (for-profit, not-for-profit, social ventures), create value within existing organizations, and pursue an entrepreneurship career in the arts.

- Students will be able to analyze an arts organization's business model for creating and capturing value.
- Students will be able to design effective business models to create and capture value in an arts context.
- Students will be able to create, evaluate, and execute a strategic plan that aligns with their talents and desires for creating and capturing value.

Principles of Arts Business (3 credit hours)
This course is in an online format and will provide an overview of the many different careers and business practices in the arts industries. The course

content will highlight the variables considered when creating, selling, and marketing a variety of items in different mediums.

- Students will identify and summarize the many different career opportunities in the arts economy.
- Students will distinguish between various sales and marketing channels, and the processes behind bringing a product or idea to market.
- Students will recognize and create components of effective media and communications designed to market and sell a product or idea.
- Students will summarize how the arts impact the economy.

Minor in Entrepreneurial Studies at Kansas City Art Institute

Through a unique partnership, UMKC Bloch School of Management has designed and is delivering a 16-credit hour minor in entrepreneurship for Kansas City Art Institute, a four-year college of art and design. In its initial launch, one-third of freshmen declared the minor further proving that entrepreneurship education is both necessary for and desired by art students.

Program-level learning outcomes:

- Pursue opportunities to create and capture value that aligns with their talents and desires.
- Understand key management, marketing, financial, and economic principles necessary in an entrepreneurship career and an organization.
- Design, test, and execute a business model.

Course titles, descriptions, and learning outcomes

Introduction to Art and Design Entrepreneurship (3 credit hours)
This is an introductory course to provide students with a foundational knowledge of what it means to work with a spirit of entrepreneurship. Topics include creative problem solving, entrepreneurship methods and practices, idea and business modeling, leveraging resources, and legal issues. This course counts as a liberal arts elective or open elective credit.

- Describe who entrepreneurs are, what they do, and why they do it.
- Apply frameworks and models of innovation and entrepreneurship to their own ideas.
- Define and evaluate the needs, problems, and demands of a market.
- Analyze the environmental, political, economic, legal, and ethical risks and rewards of entrepreneurship.

- Identify the financial, human, physical, and intellectual resources necessary, where to obtain them, and how to best utilize them, in order to pursue a venture opportunity.

Entrepreneurship Toolkit (3 credit hours)

Topics covered in this introductory business course include marketing, management, accounting and finance, economics, operations management, and personal finance through the lens of a creative enterprise. This course counts as a social science, liberal arts elective, or open elective credit.

- Identify key management practices necessary to operate an organization.
- Apply basic marketing principles to effectively engage a target audience.
- Analyze how shifts in supply and demand affect society and the business environment.
- Illustrate how organizations keep financial records and the importance of this information.
- Describe the flow of money in a free enterprise economy.

Creative Enterprise Studio (3 credit hours)

Topics covered in this course include opportunity recognition, venture modeling and design, and strategies for getting started. This course counts as an open elective.

- Apply creativity in the development of innovative business models.
- Evaluate business models and validate their components.
- Formulate a plan to implement a business model over time.
- Analyze markets and opportunities.

Entrepreneurship Experience (3 credit hours)

Students will pursue an internship or practicum experience in which they have the opportunity to use their newly acquired entrepreneurship skills alongside professionals and with the supervision of faculty. Or, if a student has a venture they have launched, they can further pursue their venture with additional coaching and mentoring. This course counts as a studio elective or an open elective.

- Apply an entrepreneurial mindset to a business scenario with real implications of risk and reward.
- Evaluate opportunities for value creation.
- Formulate a business model to create and capture value.
- Create a plan to validate and execute a business model.
- Assess the impact of their actions.

Professional Practice (3 credit hours)
The current required professional practice course within each major focuses on discipline-specific professional practice knowledge and experience. This course content varies by department. Each studio area at Kansas City Art Institute offers its own Professional Practice course.

Art and Design Entrepreneurship Seminar (1 credit hour)
This seminar requires students to engage in entrepreneurship events in the Kansas City community and come together to share their startup experiences. Students will also help promote the art and design entrepreneurship minor and serve as "ambassadors" for the program.

- Connect experiences to course content.
- Make connections across art/design and business/entrepreneurship disciplines.
- Apply knowledge, skills, and abilities gained in one situation to new situations.

GOING FORWARD: OPPORTUNITIES AND CHALLENGES

As part of the opportunity to create new courses, faculty from the Regnier Institute for Entrepreneurship and Innovation are designing a special course, "The Entrepreneurial Mindset." A series of three workshops are offered to develop the course, following specific guidelines and requirements of the general education curriculum. Once developed, the general education administrative team reviews and approves the curriculum. All new courses must begin fall 2020 and new courses will be part of the permanent general education curriculum. While the prospect of a general education course in entrepreneurship seems like an ideal way to expose all undergraduate students to entrepreneurship, it comes with certain challenges. Finding faculty to teach numerous sections of the course can be daunting. With new courses in entrepreneurship developed and offered in the Bloch School of Management, finding resources to an even greater opportunity can be overwhelming.

Preliminary meetings have recently occurred with deans and faculty from UMKC health sciences schools to explore collaborations in curriculum development. Initial plans include the possibility of an MD/MBA offering where medical students can complete their medical degree and a tailored MBA in seven years (UMKC has a six-year MD program). Other opportunities would also involve the School of Pharmacy, the Dental School, and the School of Nursing. Much of the interest in collaboration by non-business disciplines comes as a result of success in the general education initiatives and entrepreneurship programs offered to all students on campus.

12. Entrepreneurship education in Australia

Alex Maritz, Colin Jones, Dennis Foley, Saskia De Klerk, Bronwyn Eager and Quan Nguyen

INTRODUCTION

Entrepreneurship education (EE) has experienced rapid global growth in the past two decades (Jones, 2019a; Lackéus, 2019; Maritz, 2017), and although this growth has been identified as a moderate boom in Australia, there is evidence that such growth may have reached a plateau (Maritz, Nguyen, & Bliemel, 2019). Most of the research and scholarly writings on EE have been on programs, students, competencies, impact, scholarship, and outcomes of individual providers of such education (Liguori, Bendickson, & McDowell, 2018; Morris, Webb, Fu, & Singbal, 2013; Neck & Corbett, 2018), with scant research on national and international systems of entrepreneurship (Nabi, Liñán, Fayolle, Krueger, & Walmsley, 2017; OECD and EU, 2018; QAA, 2018; Wright, Mustar, & Siegel, 2019).

This chapter introduces insights into EE in Australia through the lens of scholars involved in the delivery of entrepreneurship programs at five prominent higher education institutions (HEIs), geographically representing five Australian states or territories. We propose emergent enquiry perspectives by providing an overview of EE in Australia, experiential education in entrepreneurship ecosystems and accelerators, place-based pedagogy in Australian EE, Indigenous Australian EE, competency EE models in Australia, and EE nuances across Australia. We believe this is a neoteric approach to a national discussion of EE involving emergent enquiry across such contexts.

Our aim is to extend the current literature on these perspectives, predominantly within the context of Australian higher education. In particular, we expand upon global scholarship discussions (Matthews & Brueggemann, 2015; Morris & Kuratko, 2014) within an Australian context on perspectives of EE programs (Maritz, 2017), entrepreneurship ecosystems and accelerators (Bliemel, De Klerk, Flores, & Miles, 2018; Spigel, 2017), placed-based pedagogy (Elmes, Jiusto, Whiteman, Hersch, & Guthey, 2012), Indigenous environments (Maritz & Foley, 2018), and competency models (Jones, Penaluna, & Penaluna, 2020). We further expand upon recent scholarship on embedding entrepreneurship in education in Australia.

We commence the discussion with an overview of recent research and scholarship on EE in Australia. We then proceed with insights on the perspectives mentioned above, culminating with nuances of EE specific to Australian higher education.

AN OVERVIEW OF ENTREPRENEURSHIP EDUCATION PROGRAMS IN AUSTRALIA

In recent research entitled "Boom or bust? Embedding entrepreneurship in education in Australia," Maritz et al. (2019) suggest that higher education institutions in Australia are experiencing a moderate EE boom, albeit marginally down on global EE transformational initiatives. What follows is an overview of this moderate boom, based upon the various courses and structures of EE in Australia, fluidity of EE in Australia, and substantive and symbolic foundations of EE. We are particularly mindful of the significant growth of EE globally (Nabi et al., 2017), recent global advances in the scholarship and impact of EE (Kuratko & Morris, 2018; OECD and EU, 2018; Morris et al., 2013; QAA 2018), and embedding of EE through EE ecosystems (Belitski & Heron, 2017; Bliemel, Flores, De Klerk, & Miles, 2019; Miles et al., 2017). To provide further contextualization, we refer to the dimensions of entrepreneurship education programs (EEPs), consisting of entrepreneurship ecosystems, outcomes, objectives, assessment, contextualization content, pedagogy, and audience (Maritz, 2017).

Courses and Structures of Entrepreneurship Education in Australia

In a longitudinal study on the status of EE in Australia (Maritz, Jones, & Shwetzer, 2015; Maritz et al., 2019), the authors identified a marginal decline in the number of EEPs. This is in stark contrast to the global growth in EEPs, yet mitigated by the significant growth of private-sector entrepreneurial training programs (many of which receive government funding and support), such as accelerators, incubators, co-working spaces, and event series (Bliemel et al., 2019; Renando, 2018; Spigel, 2017). The study examined EEPs across all 40 Australian HEIs, identifying full EE programs, major and minor EE specializations, subjects about and related to EE, delivery modes (such as online and blended), leadership of EE (such as centers and chairs in entrepreneurship), entrepreneurs in residence (which includes professors of practice), incubator and accelerator programs, entrepreneurship ecosystem integration, and HEI strategic intent to entrepreneurship (often associated with the entrepreneurship university). The 2019 study also included narratives from a few prominent HEIs, identifying best practice EE initiatives in Australia.

EEPs between 2014 and 2019 were identified as virtually identical (50 vs 54), EE with subjects significantly down (584 vs 462). Cognizance is, however, taken of the above-mentioned private-sector growth of entrepreneurship initiatives. It is noteworthy to observe that only four (out of 40) HEIs offer either full undergraduate or postgraduate programs in entrepreneurship (such as masters of entrepreneurship). A further 15 HEIs offer programs in entrepreneurship as a specialization, most often referred to as tagged degrees; such as masters of business (entrepreneurship). Nearly all HEIs offer subjects about (core) or related to entrepreneurship. Examples of core subjects include opportunity evaluation, lean startup, and business model design; whereas related subjects include innovation, creativity, and enterprise skills. Approximately 15 HEIs offer full online delivery in addition to blended and traditional EE. The online lag identifies either a lack of HEI support for this delivery mode, or lack of demand for such delivery.

From a leadership perspective, less than one-third of HEIs have a chair/ professor in entrepreneurship. This is further diminished by the notion that most of these chairs/professors were employed to boost research impact and outcomes, with lower-level academics usually tasked with managing most of the EE subjects. Research, despite being an integral and strategic component of HEIs, is not within the ambit of this chapter. We do however acknowledge the importance of theoretical underpinnings in EE. Entrepreneurs in residence, professors of practice, and associated EE enablers are somewhat lacking in HEIs, with less than 40 percent of HEIs employing entrepreneurs in residence, and only three HEIs employing professors of practice. The growth in accelerators and incubators directly associated to HEIs has grown significantly over the years, with over half of HEIs offering such support. Other entrepreneurship ecosystem initiatives were also evident in over half of the HEIs. There has been a significant growth in EE ecosystem initiatives including cross-branding, such as international collaborations and joint courses/subjects, international accelerator joint ventures, teaching/student exchanges, and scholarly EE academic consortiums.

An emergent enquiry perspective provided impactful evidence of associated innovative content aligned to EE, such as big data, virtual reality, sustainability, and artificial intelligence. Other initiatives identified included practitioner engagement, EE tools, micro credentialing, and HEI contextual initiatives (representing best practice EE within identified HEIs). From a HEI strategic intent perspective, less than 30 percent of HEIs espouse high levels of strategic entrepreneurship support when measured on the basis of navigational intent on entrepreneurship transformation. This may further highlight a significant absence of the entrepreneurship university across the sector.

Fluidity of Entrepreneurship Education in Australia

In contrast to aggregate EEP status from 2015 to 2019 in Australian HEIs, there remains a significant level of fluidity; not only between the years, but also within the HEI sector. This is evidenced by the significant growth in EE offerings from approximately 10 percent of HEIs, many not previously demonstrating EE leadership. Such offerings include newly appointed chairs/professors, innovative course/subject offerings, co-curricular advancements, directly aligned ecosystem initiatives, and strategic collaborations and alignments. Introspection further highlighted the effect of staff mobility, whereby entrepreneurship academics from previous leading HEIs are employed by other HEIs. This resulted in radically enhanced EEPs in the new institutions, a direct result of intellectual capital, experience, and expertise in EE. Overall, the fluidity and volatility can be interpreted as either emerging HEIs pushing out otherwise stable incumbents or incumbents simply lowering their EE offerings. Notwithstanding fluidity, the study highlights that 18 percent (seven HEIs) of Australian HEIs provide 78 percent of EEP initiatives. From a state perspective, Victorian HEIs dominate the EEP landscape, making the state a possible leader in the education sector.

Substantive and Symbolic Underpinnings

The strategic intent of HEIs in particular demonstrates the substantive and/or symbolic theoretical underpinnings to entrepreneurship university transformation. We posit here that such strategic intent is directly related to substantive underpinning (or lack thereof) in EEPs. Nguyen and Maritz (2019) provide insights to entrepreneurship as a strategic imperative in Australian HEIs, highlighting the disparity of the distribution of EEPs from a strategic perspective. Moderate to significant entrepreneurship transformation was only revealed by 42 percent of Australian HEIs, making it debatable which proportions of HEIs have substantive foundations, as only 28 percent of HEIs espouse high levels of support for EEPs. This may highlight that the majority of HEIs in Australia espouse significant symbolic underpinnings, underpinning strategic intentions towards entrepreneurship.

In the next section, we explore the notion of experiential EE and training in entrepreneurship ecosystems, with specific reference to accelerators in Australia.

ACCELERATOR PROGRAMS: LEARNING BY DOING

Researchers acknowledge that there is an increased "need to experiment with different ways of delivering experiential education" (Basu, 2014, p. 5).

Some also suggest that "Future research must progress to evaluate impact and identifying customised entrepreneurship provision to suit the requirements of specific regions and communities" (Jones et al., 2018, p. 553).

This section focuses on the learning experience through structured time-boxed events, e.g., incubators and accelerators that nurture, facilitate, and support the entrepreneurship learning experience. The entrepreneurship education ecosystem in this section is based on "'real time' or 'accelerated' approaches, [that] are considered crucial to the inception and development of 'entrepreneurship mindsets'" (Matlay, 2019, p. 1041) where the students learn by doing (Jones & English, 2004).

The entrepreneurship ecosystem is also described by Spigel (2017, p. 49) as the combination of "cultural outlooks, social networks, investment capital, universities, and active economic policies that create environments supportive of innovation-based ventures." In these entrepreneurship ecosystems, accelerators provide the infrastructure that facilitate entrepreneurship development. Even though there has been an increased focus on ecosystem research and programs that facilitate entrepreneurship and innovation in recent years, calls for "a more nuanced understanding of entrepreneurial ecosystems that takes into account local specificities" (Spigel, 2017, p. 67) remains.

Accelerators in Australia

In 2015, the Australian Federal Government rolled out a support program, the National Innovation and Science Agenda, with AUD$23 million aimed to support accelerators to develop and grow innovative startups (Australian Government, 2015). Since then there has been exponential growth of these programs and diversity in their focus on high-potential ventures to benefit the wider entrepreneurship ecosystem (Bliemel et al., 2018) in a specific region. These programs offer support in terms of education, connecting stakeholders, and providing physical infrastructure to help them succeed.

The incubators and accelerators offer emerging entrepreneurs (e.g., entrepreneurship students) the opportunity to be creative, experiment, and test ideas, almost like a laboratory. In science the use and importance of using laboratories as part of the curriculum and teaching activities is explained as "Laboratory activities have long had a distinctive and central role in the science curriculum... More specifically, they [academics] suggested that, when properly developed, inquiry-centred laboratories have the potential to enhance students' meaningful learning, conceptual understanding, and their understanding of the nature of science" (Hofstein, Shore, & Kipnis, 2004).

The main advantages of participating in these programs lies in the simulation of the real-life experience, building the idea from the ground up, acquiring necessary resources, management experience, and tapping into networks for opportunities (Qin, Wright, & Gao, 2019). It is essential to build future capacity, but these programs also build networks, by bringing all the entrepreneurial ecosystem stakeholders, e.g., policy makers (government, institutions), investors (venture capitalists, angel investors, mentors), entrepreneurs, educational institutions, and others together (Cohen, Fehder, Hochberg, & Murray, 2019).

Next, we contextualize an accelerator program, Teen Start-Up (www .teenstartupcamp.com.au/). This program is hosted by Lighthouse Innovations based in Canberra. We focus first on the context of Lighthouse Innovations and then we discuss the outcomes, objectives, content, assessment, pedagogy, and audience.

An Accelerator Program at Grassroots Level

To illustrate the use of accelerator-like programs in EE training, we focus on a single case to describe and analyse as well as reflect on multiple units of analysis that are embedded in the case (Yin, 2013). The context is the Teen Start-Up programs that run quarterly and is usually offered during the school holidays. The Lighthouse Innovation team launched the Teen Start-Up accelerator program in 2014 to give school-age students the opportunity to learn and develop entrepreneurial skills. Lighthouse Innovation chief executive officer, Anna Pino, explained that "Not every child will become an entrepreneur, but we can inspire every young person to have an entrepreneurial mindset – to think creatively and critically; to collaborate and communicate effectively; to focus, commit and have the grit to persevere when things get tough" (2018).

One of these events was held in collaboration with the School of Business at the University of New South Wales Canberra. Twenty-nine, 11- to 16-year-old students, including some who traveled interstate from Sydney, Brisbane, and the South Coast, took part in the two-day program. They had to work in entrepreneurship teams to complete a range of challenges, present their ideas, and complete activities to earn points as part of the Accelerator Start-Up Competition. The objectives of the program were to expose the students to the process of entrepreneurship, but also to develop an entrepreneurship mindset and entrepreneurial culture. Each of the activities was aimed at helping these students to develop their creativity, problem solving, teamwork, and business skills. The content of the workshops consisted of three broad activities each day. Each session was structured around a presentation (15–20 minutes) by an expert (e.g., researcher, scientist, local entrepreneur, engineer, psychologist, and architect) who introduced a potential startup topic (e.g., designing a game to help patients who had suffered a stroke; developing products from renewable resources, and designing a sustainable house for the Canberra climate). The guest speaker would present the topic, there would be some time for questions and answers, and then the teams would work on a solution and business model for each of these challenges. Facilitators would offer support and guidance. Having diverse actors involved in the accelerator program added to the learning opportunity, with stakeholders such as "classmates, peers or guest speakers" (Matlay, 2019, p. 1040).

This leads to the question on how they were assessed. With each activity the students would have to complete a quiz that covered the specific topic. The teams would also score marks for their planning efforts and how well they would approach the problem and business model development for each activity. Then the facilitators and guest speaker would assess the final product/service.

The pedagogical approach is based on experiential learning by taking the students through the process and "introduce[s] students to skills like creativity, problem solving and teamwork in a fun and interactive way" (Personal correspondence, January 14, 2018). Incubator and accelerator programs have a standardized offer to all teams, in a time-constraint program where only a limited and select cohort is accepted into the program. The program is structured and covers topics that develop entrepreneurship capabilities – design thinking, presentations skills, business strategy – and takes place in a dynamic setting with diverse operators, mentors, and guest speakers involved. The students are co-located in one space for the duration of the program and the individuals and teams are mentored to facilitate change, growth, and opportunities (Bliemel et al., 2019).

This accelerator program offers potential entrepreneurs to go through ideation, analysis, testing, execution, and reflection in a time-boxed and supportive environment. These programs provide the full spectrum of entrepreneurship development, but just in a shorter time frame and in a controlled environment (Bliemel et al., 2019). This then becomes the ecosystem where networking skill, proactiveness, and self-confidence (Mosey & Kirkham, 2019, p. 134) as well as entrepreneurs can be developed.

As accelerators provide a full spectrum of entrepreneurship development initiatives, they align closely with place-based pedagogy with regard to the interplay of community and environment, and we explore this integration in the next section.

PLACE-BASED PEDAGOGY IN ENTREPRENEURSHIP

In this section, we consider the concept of "place," embedding spatial context in EE, and a framework for place-based curricula innovation. We provide an example of the application of place-based pedagogy in an undergraduate EE program at an Australian university.

Place encompasses the interplay of community and environment within localized or distributed regions and can be thought of as the transformation of space (e.g., physical geography) through meaning making (Tuan, 1997). In an EE context, space can represent the location where knowledge transfer occurs, while place embodies community, networks, power relationships, as well as social and industry climates.

Diversity of place and spatial context is inherent in Australia's vast geography, with regional entrepreneurship activity influenced by actors' awareness of the rurality of entrepreneurship (Korsgaard, Müller, & Tanvig, 2015) and its enablers and constraints (Müller & Korsgaard, 2018). With place informing the development of rural citizenship (Corbett & Roberts, 2017), enhancing entrepreneurship students' spatial context competencies can assist in addressing local demands and shaping a region's future (Moffa, 2019).

While awareness of place-based entrepreneurship curricula is growing in Australia, the trend is largely unreflected in academic literature. One reason for this is that place-conscious curricula design likely occurs at an invisible level. For example, an entrepreneurship educator may design a social entrepreneurship project aimed at addressing local issues, yet he/she does not set the assessment through motive of place-based pedagogy.

In light of new venture creation not occurring in isolation to social context, embedding place-conscious design into curricula, and thus creating contextual awareness of community landscapes and network interactions, no doubt enhances the likelihood of launching products and/or services in regional and/ or international markets. Thus, place-based consciousness in curricular design need not occur to the detriment of providing students with an appreciation of global context; students can be educated to gain awareness of and critically evaluate global entrepreneurship efforts while innovating within regional locales. This in turn associates entrepreneurship outcomes with course development and content.

Elmes et al. (2012), advancing the work of Gruenewald (2003), offer four frames through which to consider place-conscious curricula design. The phenomenological frame acknowledges the role of human experience wherein place occurs via human perception and experience within space. The sociological frame views place through a network lens: commonalities connect people who then create locales based on shared identity. The critical frame draws on power relationships to understand social and physical structures, while the ecological frame recognizes physical location and place-based ecosystems. As illustrated in the example below, educators in Australia are implementing place-conscious curricula through multiple frames concurrently.

Place-Based Entrepreneurship Education at the University of Tasmania

At the University of Tasmania, a push for place-based pedagogy stems from the university's strategic direction: to be place-based and globally connected

(University of Tasmania, 2018). At the university, EE occurs in a regional island setting, which facilitates connection, and relationship building with local communities, as well as online offerings that allow for knowledge dissemination relating to Tasmanian-based endeavors beyond the state's geographical boundaries.

To illustrate a move towards place-based EE, we present an example of redesigning an undergraduate entrepreneurship unit in the College of Business and Economics. A place-based approach to curricula innovation was implemented through phenomenological and sociological frames (as introduced above; Elmes et al., 2012). The unit was first audited to examine whether weekly module topics adequately scoped the necessary entrepreneurship theory for students to satisfy accredited unit learning outcomes, and to determine if content was regionally, nationally, and/or globally connected. Given that the previous iteration of the unit was designed based on an American-centric textbook, many gaps were identified. Next, to impart knowledge of module topics, sources of content were acquired to ensure representation of entrepreneurship activity from regional, national, and global locales – acknowledging that place spans hyperlocal and globally networked regions. As students progressed throughout the unit, for each topic, they were thus presented with materials that provided awareness of global trends and current thinking as well as gaining appreciation of entrepreneurship in regional and national settings.

Implementing place-based curricula additionally aimed to foster positive career expectations and pathways (cf. social cognitive career theory: Lent, Brown, & Hackett, 2002) through presentation of case studies and educational materials featuring individuals who share regional proximity to the students. Place-based pedagogical approaches present an opportunity to inspire students towards imagined futures, which is pertinent in regional areas due to high national unemployment rates.

Place-based EE also introduces contextual EE scenarios, and in the next section we concentrate on the nuances of Australian Indigenous entrepreneurship.

INDIGENOUS AUSTRALIAN ENTREPRENEURSHIP ENVIRONMENTS

Indigenous entrepreneurship and enterprise education represent a significant opportunity for Indigenous people to enhance their entrepreneurship skills, in turn building vibrant Indigenous-led economies that support sustainable economic development and social well-being. Education programs that contain Indigenous business components, taught from and with Indigenous Australian EE content, create sustainable business environments.

Whilst the literature on mainstream entrepreneurship and ecosystem integration has developed significantly over the past decade or two, this has not been the case within the context of Indigenous entrepreneurship. Indicators reveal that the academic experiences of Indigenous entrepreneurs are markedly different to the mainstream or non-Indigenous entrepreneur (Shirodkar, Hunter, & Foley, 2018; Foley & Hunter, 2013). The social and economic disadvantages confronted by many Indigenous Australians is well known and understood and it stands to reason that the Indigenous entrepreneur or enterprise development can and is often markedly different to the non-Indigenous comparative (Maritz & Foley, 2018).

Dimensions that include community obligations, spiritual beliefs, racism, intergenerational poverty, low education achievements, and a lack of social capital generally severely hamper the nascent Aboriginal entrepreneur which directly negates short-term economic sustainability (Shirodkar et al., 2018). Lack of intergenerational capital continues to be a major restrictive element for the prospective Indigenous entrepreneur. We have seen the rise over the last decade of initiatives such as the Indigenous grassroots-driven Indigenous Chambers of Commerce lobbying for Indigenous business acceptance, skills training, and acting in advocacy roles. They are a voice for the nascent Indigenous Australian entrepreneur. This has led to the creation of Indigenous procurement policies with increased opportunities for the Indigenous entrepreneur via preferred supply contracts. The creation of the federally funded body Supply Nation provides a realistic intermediator between the corporate's large government supply contracts and the fledgling Aboriginal enterprise, yet they do not provide training and/or upskilling to the Indigenous operator (Loosemore & Denny-Smith, 2016; Shirodkar et al., 2018).

Cultural critics question this increase in Indigenous Australian involvement in enterprise within the dominant non-Indigenous economy as another form of colonization. We have well-documented examples of Aboriginal enterprise dating back 8,000 years, long before the establishment of similar large-scale distribution of value-added products in Europe, illustrating that entrepreneurship activity is an Indigenous practice, albeit not well known.

Whilst the current environment of the Indigenous Australian entrepreneur and enterprise is an exciting one, with the number of self-employed Indigenous Australians more than doubling in the last decade there remain severe hurdles to overcome (Hunter, 2018). Racism (Foley, 2003), a lack of business skills and formal business training are other impediments, and a lack of access to startup, working, and cash-flow capital.

Indigenous EE has identified the significant role of competency-based outcomes, and in the next section we further explore competency development in EE in Australia.

COMPETENCY DEVELOPMENT IN ENTREPRENEURSHIP EDUCATION

There are increasing calls for the development of comprehensive competency frameworks for enterprise and EE (see Bacigalupo, Kampylis, Punie, & Van den Brande, 2016; Gibson, 2006; Jones, 2019a; Morris et al., 2013; White, Hertz, & Moore, 2016) as a means of developing lifelong and life-wide learning capabilities (Barnett, 2011). While much of this work is occurring outside of the Australian context, it nevertheless has significant implications for the ongoing development of EE in Australian universities. One of the challenges that exist in this area is determining whether EE competencies are the aim of EE, or if competency development is a means to an end (such as value creation). Such debates, while interesting (see Jones et al., 2020; Lackéus, 2018; Lackéus, 2019), can be a distraction from the more important issue of how EE competencies are developed, and more importantly, how we can accurately assess their development. Here, we are very much interested in considering what practices are common in Australia regarding the development and assessment of EE competencies.

One of the more notable contemporary EE competency frameworks is EntreComp (see Bacigalupo et al., 2016). This model of entrepreneurship competencies has been developed with a range of potential future uses, including assisting individuals to start a venture, be intrapreneurs, and gain valuable employability skills. Aimed at students of all ages, this approach is organized through three competency areas, ideas, opportunities, resources, and into action. EntreComp is designed as a progression model, where learning activities are designed to engage students at four levels of mastery, foundation (discover and explore), intermediate (experiment and dare), advanced (improve and reinforce), and expert (expand and transform).

Nevertheless, like the earlier approach of Morris et al. (2013) and their startup focus (i.e., opportunity recognition, opportunity assessment, risk management, selling a vision, tenacity, creative problem solving, resource leveraging, guerrilla skills, value creation, adaptable focus, resilience, self-efficacy, and building and using networks), the issue of how to authentically assess the development of competencies remains problematic in EE (see Jones, 2019a).

Jones (2019a) incorporated the work of White et al. (2016) to raise the issue of whether or not an authentic performance situation is present during the attempted development of EE competencies. It is worth noting the sage advice given by Bloom (1956, p. 27) that "educational objectives must be related to a psychology of learning. The faculty must distinguish goals that are feasible from goals that are unlikely to be attained in the time available, under the conditions which are possible, and with the group of students to be involved." The concern being that if students of EE are merely completing pre- and post-self-assessments of competence development, then as an educational domain, EE is at risk of fully ignoring the advice of Bloom. This suggests the need for Australian EE practice to emulate best practice (often found in medical schools) when approaching the task of developing EE competencies.

Central to the development of EE competencies are three fundamental and interrelated dimensions, feeling, thinking, and acting (see Jones, 2019b). Any comprehensive pedagogy for EE (incorporating competence development) should aim to balance these three dimensions (Shulman, 2005). To the extent that such a balance does not exist, from Shulman's perspective, we could potentially be developing compromised pedagogies.

Consistent with the thinking of White et al. (2016), we posit that a performance situation is essential in developing and assessing authentic EE competencies. We anticipate that this explicit concern for reconciling any desired performance capability against evidenced student performance within a specific context may provide a serious challenge to educators in our domain. Nevertheless, we view as a weakness in the domain the extent to which existing competency approaches overly rely upon student self-assessment. A more desirable aim would be a combination of self-assessment combined with education observation and actual student performance against a known performance situation. Not merely to ensure triangulation of assessment measures, but also to enable students to receive multiple forms of feedback from which to improve performance.

While many Australian students are engaging entrepreneurship activities that would intuitively seem to align to the competencies in the EntreComp model (see Bacigalupo et al., 2016) and/or more traditional entrepreneurship competencies (see Morris et al., 2013), a lack of explicit assessment is also observed. It is common to encourage student engagement with activities designed to develop entrepreneurial competencies, within award programs and/or extra-curricular contexts, without assessment processes being designed with sufficient precision to capture pre-existing capability and/or developed capability. Such an observation suggests that EE in Australia is challenged by the same competence development issues observed elsewhere globally. Until such time that the process of constructive alignment is applied with precision to competence-related learning outcomes, it is quite likely this problem will remain.

NUANCES ACROSS AUSTRALIA

We provide a few examples of contextual EE across Australia, further highlighting applications discussed in the above sections.

The University of Canberra

EE foundations are spread throughout the university within the university's strategic plan titled "Distinctive by Design" (2018–22) which weaves together three overarching themes: empowerment of our diverse people; distinctive teaching and research; and an enriched living-learning environment on the Canberra campus and global locations.

A policy of innovation and entrepreneurship approaches to the pursuit of academic knowledge is interwoven within these three overarching themes. As an example, innovation is taught within the Faculty of Arts in the design (architectural) area in addition to the standard Management School areas. Where the University of Canberra is strategically different is it has adopted a policy of Indigenization combining the concept of entrepreneurship across the curriculum with Indigenization, providing faculties an opportunity to expand the concepts of EE to commensurately include an Indigenous component. In the entrepreneurship and innovation major, in the School of Management at third-year level, a subject on Indigenous entrepreneurship and culture has been introduced with no prerequisites investigating Indigenous entrepreneurship and enterprise over an 8,000-year time span attracting students from several disciplines outside of the Business School.

Students on the main campus in Bruce, Australia have the increased opportunity of EE by being successfully appointed to within-work integrated learning projects with Mill House Ventures. Mill House Ventures is committed to supporting the business growth and impact of Indigenous and social enterprise including not-for-profit and for-profit social ventures within the Australian Capital Territory. Mill House provides a place for new ventures to thrive, where external to the University of Canberra; clients can choose to work collaboratively through skills development initiatives in the Accelerator Program as well as access professional services through the student-led Mill House Clinic. EE is applied in a practical real-world situation in a challenging new business startup environment.

Mill House works with businesses that seek to trade for purpose. Entrepreneurs that are passionate about solving problems in the community often face barriers to business education and investment. Since inception and as an initiative of the University of Canberra, Mill House has worked with students, exposing them to the unique asset class that is a social enterprise. Students interested in learning EE learn about trading for a mission – an aspect of reflective learning what is unique about our way of doing business. Our EE students come from culturally and linguistically diverse backgrounds who provide insight into the barriers and opportunities associated with accessing meaningful and culturally appropriate work placements, creating meaningful professional services placements for students that is the foundation for EE.

La Trobe University, Melbourne

Although EE foundations are housed at La Trobe Business School (LBS), university-wide entrepreneurial university initiatives have met with rapid growth in entrepreneurship initiatives and outcomes. Foremost, the university introduced the *Entrepreneurship Essential*, whereby entrepreneurship is strategically infused across the university. Each and every degree or course in the university requires embedding entrepreneurship content and outcomes. This resulted in many cross-disciplinary subjects and EE initiatives campus-wide; from business, engineering, health sciences, law, and social sciences to horticulture. Within the Business School, every undergraduate student participates in a foundation entrepreneurship subject, providing a springboard for postgraduate EE. Further, related undergraduate entrepreneurship subjects are offered in various business degrees, particularly to enhance and develop enterprising skills and employability. From a postgraduate perspective, the Business School offers a masters of entrepreneurship and innovation-tagged degree, with postgraduate majors in cross-disciplinary degrees such as the masters of business information systems, master of management, and MBA. Students also participate in La Trobe Accelerator, an award-winning initiative, originally funded by LaunchVic as a state-wide initiative for participants to enhance their entrepreneurial skills to launch successful startups. The Business School has a PhD entrepreneurship stream, facilitating entrepreneurship research, teaching, and engagement. LBS is a 2019 recipient of AACSB accreditation, together with close affiliations to many ongoing international collaborations. The entrepreneurship discipline is led by a chair/professor of entrepreneurship, entrepreneurship academic staff members, a professor of practice, and an extensive network of part-time entrepreneurship lecturers and entrepreneurs in residence. These academics are leaders in global research, education, and engagement and all provide significant impact in their specific entrepreneurship specializations.

Queensland University of Technology, Brisbane QLD

A dynamic environment continues to develop that supports a wide variety of student needs. A growing partnership between the Queensland University of Technology (QUT) and MIT provides several opportunities for students to participate in high-level bootcamps and to also travel to Boston to collaborate and benefit from MIT's expansive entrepreneurship initiatives. The centralized coordination of activities through the QUT foundry provides the means to increase networking between students, academics, support staff, and external stakeholders. The foundry has footprints on both major campuses and a presence in the heart of Brisbane's startup precinct. Offering students a place to find themselves in ideation processes, speaker sessions, hackathons, pitching events, and startup weekends, the foundry is fast becoming the heartbeat of entrepreneurship at QUT. In terms of curriculum offerings, business students in both undergraduate and postgraduate courses can access a number of entrepreneurship units. Likewise, students in science and the creative industries also have entrepreneurship units tailored to meet the requirements of student development in those specific contexts.

University of New South Wales (Canberra) and Lighthouse Innovations, Canberra

From starting young (school-aged participants) in private university partnership programs (e.g. Lighthouse Innovations) to university accelerator programs (10x Accelerator UNSW), the broad spectrum of offerings all seem to focus on authentic, experiential learning environments and the inclusion and participation of the wider entrepreneurial ecosystem to solve real-world, but complex and grand challenges. This is proof that there is probably no "one size fits all" approach but rather a combination of different offerings to capture, nurture, and engage at all levels.

CONCLUSION

This chapter focused on extending the discussion, literature, and scholarship of EE within an Australian higher education context. First, we acknowledge the global growth in EE, despite moderate growth in an Australian context. This is further characterized by fluidity in Australian EE, in that the distribution of programs is scattered, with 18 percent of HEIs providing the lion's share of entrepreneurship offerings. From a strategic perspective, we identify significant symbolic underpinnings towards entrepreneurship program support. By espousing such significant symbolic underpinnings, HEIs in Australia do not, by nature, provide significant substantive foundations to support EE.

Second, when looking at accelerator and place-based pedagogy in an Australian context, we identify significant and encouraging initiatives at the institutions studied: this is, however, not widespread and significant throughout Australia. We note a significant growth of place-based entrepreneurship curricula in Australia, yet this is somewhat scant regarding scholarship in academic literature. Third, we identify the growth of global Indigenous EE, but this is by no means mirrored in an Australian context. Other than a lack of widespread Indigenous entrepreneurship programs, Australian Indigenous entrepreneurs have a distinct lack of access to startup capital. Fourth, competency development in EE has received much global attention, yet we identify a lag within the Australian context, predominantly due to a lack of constructive alignment to competence-related learning outcomes.

Finally, from a strategic imperative perspective, we identify a few avenues of supporting and encouraging EE initiatives. These include association with global entrepreneurship best practices (including co-branding), entrepreneurship ecosystem inclusion, strategic entrepreneurship initiatives (inclusive of entrepreneurial strategic intent and appointments), cross-disciplinary EE, and alignment to supportive research and engagement funding and collaboration. These implementations also enhance the relevance and sustainability of EE.

We believe the fluidity of EE in Australia may be attributable to a point in time, and we suggest longitudinal studies to examine EE developments over the foreseeable future. We further highlight the limitations of proximity and context in this chapter, suggesting a broader study consisting of additionally well-represented HEIs. Lastly, we welcome the scholarship and discussion for further global insights from Australian and international EE scholars. As this chapter was originally developed pre-COVID-19, we have not included any inference to the devastating economic and social consequences thereof, nor the effect on entrepreneurship programs at higher education institutions. This in itself would make for interesting research once we are back to the "new normal".

REFERENCES

Australian Government (2015). *National Science and Innovation Agenda*. Retrieved from www.innovation.gov.au

Bacigalupo, M., Kampylis, P., Punie, Y., & Van den Brande, G. (2016). *EntreComp: The Entrepreneurship Competence Framework*. Retrieved from https://publications .jrc.ec.europa.eu/repository/bitstream/JRC101581/lfna27939enn.pdf

Barnett, R. (2011). Lifewide education: A new and transformative concept for higher education. In N. Jackson (Ed.), *Learning for a Complex World: A Lifewide Concept of Learning, Education and Personal* (pp. 22–38). London: Authorhouse.

Basu, R. (2014). Entrepreneurship education in India: A critical assessment and a proposed framework. *Technology Innovation Management Review*, *4*(4), 5–10.

Belitski, M., & Heron, K. (2017). Expanding entrepreneurship education ecosystems. *Journal of Management Development*, *36*(2), 163–77.

Bliemel, M., De Klerk, S., Flores, R., & Miles, M. P. (2018). Emergence of accelerators and accelerator policy: The case of Australia. In M. Wright, I. Drori (Eds), *Accelerators Successful Venture Creation and Growth* (pp. 162–87). Cheltenham, UK and Northampton, MA, USA: Edward Elgar Publishing.

Bliemel, M., Flores, R., De Klerk, S., & Miles, M. P. (2019). Accelerators as start-up infrastructure for entrepreneurial clusters. *Entrepreneurship and Regional Development*, *31*(1–2), 133–49.

Bloom, B. (1956). *Taxonomy of Educational Objectives: The Classification of Educational Goals*. New York: Longmans, Green.

Cohen, S., Fehder, D. C., Hochberg, Y. V., & Murray, F. (2019). The design of startup accelerators. *Research Policy*, *48*(7), 1781–97.

Corbett, M., & Roberts, P. (2017). A small place: Education in rural Tasmania. *Australian and International Journal of Rural Education*, *27*(3), 1–8.

Elmes, M. B., Jiusto, S., Whiteman, G., Hersch, R., & Guthey, G. T. (2012). Teaching social entrepreneurship and innovation from the perspective of place and place making. *Academy of Management Learning and Education*, *11*(4), 533–54.

Foley, D. (2003). An examination of Indigenous Australian entrepreneurs. *Journal of Developmental Entrepreneurship*, *8*(2), 133–52.

Foley, D., & Hunter, B. (2013). What is an Indigenous Australian business? *Journal of Australian Indigenous Issues*, *16*(3), 66–74.

Gibson, D. (2006). *The E Factor*. London: Enterprise HQ.

Gruenewald, D. A. (2003). Foundations of place: A multidisciplinary framework for place-conscious education. *American Educational Research Journal*, *40*(3), 619–54.

Hofstein, A., Shore, R., & Kipnis, M. (2004). Providing high school chemistry students with opportunities to develop learning skills in an inquiry-type laboratory: A case study. *International Journal of Science Education*, *26*(1), 47–62.

Hunter, B. (2018). Recent growth in Indigenous self-employed and entrepreneurs. Working Paper 91/201. ANU Centre for Aboriginal Economic Policy Research. Retrieved from http://hdl.handle.net/1885/147840

Jones, C. (2019a). *How to Teach Entrepreneurship*. Cheltenham, UK and Northampton, MA, USA: Edward Elgar Publishing.

Jones, C. (2019b). A signature pedagogy for entrepreneurship education. *Journal of Small Business and Enterprise Development*, *26*(2), 243–54.

Jones, C., & English, J. (2004). A contemporary approach to entrepreneurship education. *Education + Training*, *46*(8/9), 416–23.

Jones, C., Penaluna, K., & Penaluna, A. (2020). Value creation in entrepreneurial education: Locating the start and finish lines. *Proceedings of the 10th ACERE Conference*, Adelaide.

Jones, P., Maas, G., Dobson, S., Newbery, R., Agyapong, D., & Matlay, H. (2018). Entrepreneurship in Africa, part 2: Entrepreneurial education and eco-systems. *Journal of Small Business and Enterprise Development*, *25*(4), 550–3.

Korsgaard, S., Müller, S., & Tanvig, H. W. (2015). Rural entrepreneurship or entrepreneurship in the rural – between place and space. *International Journal of Entrepreneurial Behavior and Research*, *21*(1), 5–26.

Kuratko, D. F., & Morris, M. H. (2018). Examining the future trajectory of entrepreneurship. *Journal of Small Business Management*, *56*(1), 11–23.

Lackéus, M. (2018). "What is value?": A framework for analyzing and facilitating entrepreneurial value creation. *Uniped*, *41*(1), 10–28.

Lackéus, M. (2019). Making enterprise education more relevant through mission creep. In G. Mulholland & J. Turner (Eds.), *Enterprising Education in UK Higher Education: Challenges for Theory and Practice* (pp. 199–214). London: Routledge.

Lent, R. W., Brown, S. D., & Hackett, G. (2002). Social cognitive career theory. *Career Choice and Development*, *4*, 255–311.

Liguori, E. W., Bendickson, J. S. & McDowell, W. C. (2018). Revisiting entrepreneurial intentions: A social cognitive career theory approach. *International Entrepreneurship and Management Journal*, *14*(67), 67–78. https://doi.org/10.1007/s11365-017-0462-7

Loosemore, M., & Denny-Smith, G. (2016). Barriers to Indigenous enterprise in the Australian construction industry. In P. W. Chan & C. J. Neilson (Eds.), *Proceedings* of the 32nd Annual ARCOM Conference, 5–7 September 2016. Manchester: Association of Researchers in Construction Management, pp. 629–38.

Maritz, A. (2017). Illuminating the black box of entrepreneurship education programmes: Part 2. *Education + Training, 59*(5), 471–82.

Maritz, A., & Foley, D. (2018). Expanding Indigenous entrepreneurship ecosystems. *Journal of Administrative Sciences, 8*(2), 1–14.

Maritz, A., Jones, C., & Shwetzer, C. (2015). The status of entrepreneurship education in Australian universities. *Education + Training, 57*(8/9), 1020–35.

Maritz, P. A., Nguyen, Q., & Bliemel, M. (2019). Boom or bust? Embedding entrepreneurship in education in Australia. *Education + Training, 61*(6), 737–55.

Matlay, H. (2019). Annals of entrepreneurship education and pedagogy – 2018. *Education + Training, 61*(7/8), 1040–2.

Matthews, C., & Brueggemann, R. (2015). *Innovation and Entrepreneurship: A Competency Framework*. New York: Routledge.

Miles, M. P., de Vries, H., Harrison, G., Bliemel, M., de Klerk, S., & Kasouf, C. J. (2017). Accelerators as authentic training experiences for nascent entrepreneurs. *Education + Training, 59*(7/8), 811–24.

Moffa, E. (2019). A paradox of place: Civic education in the rural south. *Social Studies Research and Practice, 14*(1), 105–21.

Morris, M. H., & Kuratko, D. F. (2014). Building university 21st century entrepreneurship programs that empower and transform. *Advances in the Study of Entrepreneurship, Innovation, and Economic Growth, 24*, 1–24.

Morris, M. H., Webb, J., Fu, J., & Singbal, S. (2013). A competency-based perspective on entrepreneurship education: Conceptual and empirical insights. *Journal of Small Business Management, 51*(3), 352–69.

Mosey, S., & Kirkham, P. (2019). Research opportunities considering student entrepreneurship in university ecosystems. In D. B. Audretsch, E. L. Lehmann, & A. N. Link (Eds.), *A Research Agenda for Entrepreneurship and Innovation* (pp. 155–67). Cheltenham, UK and Northampton, MA, USA: Edward Elgar Publishing.

Müller, S., & Korsgaard, S. (2018). Resources and bridging: The role of spatial context in rural entrepreneurship. *Entrepreneurship and Regional Development, 30*(1–2), 224–55.

Nabi, G., Liñán, F., Fayolle, A., Krueger, N., & Walmsley, A. (2017). The impact of entrepreneurship education in higher education: A systematic review and research agenda. *Academy of Management Learning and Education, 16*(2), 277–99.

Neck, H. M., & Corbett, A. C., 2018. The scholarship of teaching and learning entrepreneurship. *Entrepreneurship Education and Pedagogy, 1*, 8–41.

Nguyen, Q. A., & Maritz, A. (2019). Entrepreneurship as a strategic imperative in Australian universities. *Australian Centre for Entrepreneurship (ACE) Research Exchange Conference*, Sydney.

OECD and EU (2018). *Supporting Entrepreneurship and Innovation in Higher Education in the Netherlands*. Paris: OECD Publishing.

Pino, A. (2018). Personal interview conducted 14 January 2018. Canberra.

QAA (2018). Enterprise and entrepreneurship education: Guidance for UK higher education providers. Retrieved from www.voced.edu.au/content/ngv%3A60352

Qin, F., Wright, M., & Gao, J. (2019). Accelerators and intra-ecosystem variety: How entrepreneurial agency influences venture development in a time-compressed support program. *Industrial and Corporate Change, 28*(4), 961–75.

Renando, C. (2018). A map of the Australian Innovation Ecosystem 2.0. Retrieved from www.linkedin.com/pulse/map-australian-innovation-ecosystem-20-chad-renando/

Shirodkar, S., Hunter, B., & Foley, D. (2018). *Ongoing growth in the number of Indigenous Australians in business CAEPR working paper 125/2018*. Canberra: Centre for Aboriginal Economic Policy Research ANU College of Arts and Social Sciences.

Shulman, L. (2005). Signature pedagogies in the professions. *Daedalus, 134*(3), 52–9.

Spigel, B. (2017). The relational organization of entrepreneurial ecosystems. *Entrepreneurship Theory and Practice, 41*(1), 49–72.

Tuan, Y. F. (1997). *Space and Place: The Perspective of Experience*. Minneapolis, MN: University of Minnesota Press.

University of Tasmania (2018). University of Tasmania Strategic Direction. Retrieved from www.utas.edu.au/__data/assets/pdf_file/0004/1170409/UTAS-Strategic-Direction - Brochure.pdf

White, R., Hertz, G., & Moore, K. (2016). Competency based education in entrepreneurship: A call to action for the discipline. In M. Morris & E. Liguori (Eds.), *The Annals of Entrepreneurship Education and Pedagogy – 2016* (pp. 127–47). Cheltenham, UK and Northampton, MA, USA: Edward Elgar Publishing.

Wright, M., Mustar, P., & Siegel, D. (2019). Student startups, world scientific series. Retrieved from https://doi.org/10.1142/11494

Yin, R. K. (2013). Validity and generalization in future case study evaluations. *Evaluation, 19*(3), 321–32.

13. Donning their capes: women entrepreneurship students emerge as superwomen

Sara L. Cochran

INTRODUCTION

As the world weathered the storm of Covid-19 there were stories of women taking the charge in developing a vaccine (Givens, 2020) and making up the frontline of healthcare workers (Farrar & Gupta, 2020). This was a time when there were also many headlines of women arising as superwomen in fields traditionally dominated by men, such as running for political office (Gray, 2018), the first all-female spacewalk (Zraick, 2019), and women entrepreneurs reshaping the business world (Entrepreneur Staff, 2019). Women, however, face noteworthy challenges navigating traditionally men-dominated arenas, yet persistently show up as superwomen, "a woman of extraordinary or super-human powers" or "a woman who copes successfully with the simultaneous demands of a career, marriage, and motherhood" (Superwoman, 2020). These extraordinary powers are necessary for women to navigate challenging arenas and balance multiple roles. Women are needed in healthcare (Farrar & Gupta, 2020), politics (United Nations, 2020), space exploration (Whitman-Cobb, 2019), and certainly in entrepreneurship (Robb, Coleman, & Stangler, 2014).

Many entrepreneurs begin their training on college campuses (Cohoon, Wadhwa, & Mitchell, 2010) where the challenges for these students are similar to those of women entrepreneurs, causing them to show up as superwomen in extraordinary ways (Cochran, 2019a). As universities strive to prepare more women entrepreneurs, it is important to understand the experiences of these women. The purpose of this case study is to understand the gendered experiences of women entrepreneurship students while participating in a university entrepreneurship program with the specific research question, *What role does gender play in the academic experience of women participating in an entrepreneurship program?* The case study was conducted on a four-year university campus through the lens of Joan Acker's theory of gendered organizations

(1990, 1992, 1999, 2012) and a manuscript describing the study is published in the *Journal of Small Business Management* (Cochran, 2019b). This chapter is an adapted version of that paper and specifically focuses on a deeper dive into one of the themes of the findings, *superwomen*.

LITERATURE REVIEW

Women entrepreneurs face significant challenges (Kickul, Wilson, Marlino, & Barbosa, 2008), yet are needed because of their performance and contributions. Women perform better in crowdfunding campaigns (Johnson, Stevenson, & Letwin, 2018); women-led Fortune 1000 companies outperform the S&P 500 (Wechsler, 2015); women-owned enterprises are more likely to have a social impact (Stengel, 2016); and the future of American entrepreneurship and growth has been imagined in the hands of women entrepreneurs *if* they participate (Robb et al., 2014). So, despite challenges, women's participation in entrepreneurship is crucial to future economic and social prosperity.

Many entrepreneurs begin their training on college campuses (Cohoon et al., 2010) and research has been conducted on the most common types of entrepreneurship programs, best practices for programs, students' motivation for enrolling, learning outcomes, and even the purpose of role models in entrepreneurship education. However, very little is known about the experiences of entrepreneurship students. When looking specifically at women entrepreneurship students, who make up a distinct minority in entrepreneurship programs across the United States at a time when they are the majority of students overall (US Department of Education, n.d.), some studies separate parts of their data along lines of gender (Duval-Couetil, Gotch, & Yi, 2014), and others provide suggestions of strategies for attracting and nurturing women students (Gupta, Turban, Wasti, & Sidkar, 2009; Gupta, Turban, & Pareek, 2013; Lo, Sun, & Law, 2012). What remains needed is research on the experiences of these women students. This literature review provides highlights of the existing literature on entrepreneurship students.

ENTREPRENEURSHIP STUDENTS

As Wilson, Kickul, and Marlino (2007) stated, "In order to more fully capture the talents of women in new venture creation in the future, a vibrant 'pipeline' of potential entrepreneurs is required" (p. 388). Female[1] college students show a less positive view of entrepreneurship, regardless of their entrepreneurship education background (Lo et al., 2012). This could present a challenge for those educators attempting to recruit women into entrepreneurship programs.

Motivations to Enroll in Entrepreneurship Programs

Entrepreneurship students have reported various reasons for enrolling in entrepreneurship courses, such as having an interest in the subject matter (Duval-Couetil et al., 2014; Peterson & Limbu, 2010), having a specific business idea to pursue (Duval-Couetil et al., 2014; Menzies & Tatroff, 2006), as a requirement for an academic program (Peterson & Limbu, 2010), having a desire to see if they had what it takes to be an entrepreneur, or as a way to broaden their career prospects and choices (Duval-Couetil et al., 2014). Research suggests that men and women identify different reasons for pursuing an entrepreneurship program. Males are more likely to desire to become an entrepreneur or have a specific idea for a business (Duval-Couetil et al., 2014). Females, however, are more likely to indicate a desire to acquire knowledge, develop skills, network with local businesses (Petridou, Sarri, Kyrgidou, 2009), or value the courses as an additional educational credential (Duval-Couetil et al., 2014) or an added career prospect (Petridou et al., 2009).

Reasons for Not Enrolling in Programs

When asked their reasons for not choosing a concentration in entrepreneurship, men and women both indicated that it is a high-risk career, or it does not interest them (Menzies & Tatroff, 2006). Females, however, most strongly indicated that they did not think it fit their personality (Menzies & Tatroff, 2006). Further, women perceive a lack of support, fear of failure, and a lack of competency to be much more substantial barriers to pursuing entrepreneurship as a career than men students (Shinnar, Giacomin, & Janssen, 2012).

Entrepreneurship Student Characteristics

More than half of students in an entrepreneurship program reported having parents who were entrepreneurs (Peterson & Limbu, 2010) and college students who have family who were entrepreneurs are more likely to desire to start their own business (Pruett, Shinnar, Toney, Llopis, & Fox, 2009). The most influential reasons for those students who desire to start their own business are profit, independence, future opportunities, and achieving a satisfying lifestyle (Peterson & Limbu, 2010). In the area of entrepreneurship-related topics, students have been found to be most interested in learning about leadership, project management, and managing teams (Duval-Couetil et al., 2014).

INFLUENCE OF ENTREPRENEURSHIP EDUCATION

For college students, entrepreneurship programs have a strong influence on students' entrepreneurial intentions (Bae, Qian, Miao, & Fiet, 2014; Fayolle, Gailly, & Lassas-Clerc, 2006; Hsu, Shinnar, & Powell, 2014). Further, scholars have found entrepreneurship education to have a positive correlation with students' perceptions of an entrepreneurial career (Hsu et al., 2014; Lo et al., 2012; Packham, Jones, Miller, Pickernell, & Brychan, 2010) and assessments of their skills and abilities or entrepreneurial self-efficacy (Duval-Couetil, Reed-Rhoads, & Haghighi, 2002; Fayolle et al., 2006; Lo et al., 2012). Others have found there to be no significant correlation with self-efficacy, speculating that these courses give students a realistic view of the difficulty of starting and running a business (Muofhe & Du Toit, 2011).

While the influence of entrepreneurship education is broad, there are sometimes differences between men and women students. Entrepreneurship courses have been found to have a stronger influence on male students' desire to start a business (Packham et al., 2010) and their entrepreneurial self-efficacy (Sanchez & Licciardello, 2012). However, female students have been found to perceive more benefit from the learning experience in an entrepreneurship course than men do (Packham et al., 2010). In order to have more women students benefitting from the learning experience, scholars have looked towards ways of attracting and nurturing women students.

ATTRACTING AND NURTURING WOMEN STUDENTS

Entrepreneurship programs need to highlight female entrepreneurship in an attempt to change perceptions, encourage women to start businesses, and promote that female-owned businesses can be as and even more successful than male-owned (Gupta et al., 2013; Lo et al., 2012). In order to nurture female students, programs should include female role models in classroom visits, textbooks, and case studies, with special attention to those role models of similar background to the students in characteristics such as age, education, culture, gender, and business area (Gupta et al., 2009, 2013; Lo et al., 2012). There are also scholars who recommend textbook editors pay close attention to the way in which women entrepreneurship is presented (Nelson & Duffy, 2011).

Because students are more likely to desire to be entrepreneurs if their parents are entrepreneurs (Kickul et al., 2008), there is a unique opportunity for university entrepreneurship programs to reach out to those students who do not come from entrepreneurial parents and provide role modeling for prospects in the field of entrepreneurship (Peterson & Limbu, 2010). These programs should include promotion of women-owned businesses and foster women-owned student startups through female business model competitions, entrepreneurial workshops, and female mentoring programs (Lo et al., 2012; Riebe, 2012). Evidence suggests university women's mentoring programs are effective at attracting successful women to serve as mentors because those types of programs appeal to the women's sense of mission and desire to make the path easier for those behind them (Riebe, 2012) as they work to overcome negative gender stereotypes.

THE STUDY

The purpose of this case study is to understand the gendered experiences of women entrepreneurship students while participating in a university entrepreneurship program with the specific research question, *What role does gender play in the academic experience of women participating in an entrepreneurship program?* The case study was conducted on a four-year university campus in the Midwest through the lens of Joan Acker's theory of gendered organizations (1990, 1992, 1999, 2012) and used grounded theory methodology to analyze the data (Charmaz, 2014; Saldana, 2016).

Theoretical Framework

In order to understand the experiences of women students navigating a gendered organization, this study was conducted through Acker's model (1990, 1992, 1999, 2012). Acker (1992) argues that a gendered organization is one in which "gender is present in the processes, practices, images and ideologies, and distributions of power in the various sectors of social life" (p. 567). When an organization – or academic institution – is gendered, it means "advantage and disadvantage, exploitation and control, action and emotion, meaning and identity, are patterned through and in terms of a distinction between male and female, masculine and feminine" (Acker, 1990, p. 146). In this type of organization, gendering occurs in at least five interacting processes. The division of labor, behaviors, and power along the lines of gender; the construction of symbols and images that explain, express, and reinforce the divisions; interactions that reenact authority and hierarchy; the way the processes produce individual identity; and that of creating and conceptualizing social structures (Acker, 1990, 1992, 1999).

These five processes are interlocking and work together to produce a gendered substructure. This substructure becomes manifested in the arrangements of work, the rules regarding workplace behavior, and the interrelationship of workplace to home life (Acker, 1992).

In an academic program, evidence of these processes can be seen in the ways teams divide work responsibilities, the rules (spoken or unspoken) regarding behavior in the classroom or during program activities, or the interactions of students. Further, universities are gendered organizations (Gardner, 2013), which can impact students' choices to participate in various programs, as well as their participation experiences (Erickson, 2012). This theoretical framework was applied to look for patterns of gendering to understand the ways in which the program was gendered and influenced the experiences of the women students.

Research Method

This qualitative study was designed to explore the experiences of women in entrepreneurship education. This study was a case study design (Stake, 2006) as it allows for the study of a real-life, contemporary setting (Yin, 2013) using multiple types of data (Creswell, 2014). The specific research question was: *What role does gender play in the academic experience of women participating in an entrepreneurship program?*

This case study was embedded in a four-year institution of higher education in the United States with a well-established entrepreneurship program that not only included academic courses, but also supported an entrepreneurship center. Centers enhance the conceptual knowledge for students through experiential learning designed to bring course content to life (Kolb, 1984; Morris, Webb, Fu, & Singhal, 2013; Vanevenhoven, 2013). Entrepreneurship courses with extra-curricular aspects to enhance the coursework are recommended as an ideal learning environment (Morris et al., 2013). This institution was chosen because the strong entrepreneurship framework allowed the researcher to isolate and focus on the experiences of women students, which had not been explored extensively in current literature.

Data Sources

Four forms of data were collected: interviews/focus groups (with students and program faculty and staff), direct observations (of entrepreneurship courses), physical artifacts (recruitment materials, promotional materials, and the website), and documents (course syllabi) (Creswell, 2013; Yin, 2013). The individual interviews, using individual interview protocol,[2] were most relevant to the study as they allowed the participants to share their experiences, the phenomenon of the case study. The focus groups, using the focus group protocol[3] consisted of students and provided a forum to validate the participants' experiences with one another (Mertens, 2014) and for those an additional researcher was used to take specific notes on non-verbal communication. The perspectives of the program director and faculty, given during their individual interviews using the faculty and staff interview protocol,[4] were of particular relevance as the program had initiatives and efforts to attract more women students that were not publicized and provided background and context to further explain the site in which the case was embedded. Observing courses, using the class observation protocol,[5] allowed for seeing interactions and reactions of students who otherwise did not participate in the study. Analyzing the documents, using the data analysis protocol,[6] allowed an examination of gendered images in the photos and language used. Using multiple data sources also provided the opportunity for triangulation to enhance the trustworthiness.

To set up an appropriate environment for the study, the center director and other staff helped to identify potential participants as well as campus spaces convenient and private for the interviews and focus groups. The call was sent to the women students involved with the program with a request that those interested fill out a demographic survey via email.

For the interviews, a purposive sample is used. That is, only participants for whom the phenomenon being studied (e.g., participating in the program in one or more ways such as taking a course, being a member in the club, or working in the center) were recruited (Mertens, 2014). A heterogeneous group (Mertens, 2014) was determined from the information provided on the demographic survey, allowing variation in the sample so multiple perspectives were considered for the case (Creswell, 2013). Interviews were conducted until the data were saturated and redundant and no new themes emerged (Lincoln & Guba, 1985), yielding 10 usable interviews. Three additional interviews were not used as these women had not yet participated in any program activities. Respondents were also asked to participate in one of two focus groups.

During the site visit, the center director and two faculty members were invited to participate in individual interviews to gain their perspectives related to the research question (Stake, 2006). Also, direct observation of two foundational entrepreneurship classes were completed.

Data Analysis

Prior to data analysis, electronic recordings of the interviews and focus groups transcribed using Transcribe (www.transcribe.wreally.com) and notes were prepared from course observations and document review. A three-step grounded theory (Charmaz, 2014; Saldana, 2016) process was followed for data analysis, despite the desire to or amount of data needed to arrive at a new theory. This process is an emergent design, uses induction, and allowed me as a researcher to mitigate my preconceived notions about the study (Heppner & Heppner, 2003), as well as uses iterative strategies for an emerging analysis (Charmaz, 2014).

The first step was line-by-line coding through which each line or phrase was given a code or general description, with attention to using in vivo codes to preserve the meaning of the statement (Charmaz, 2014; Saldana, 2016). The next stage of coding, termed axial coding (Creswell, 2013) or focused coding (Charmaz, 2014), involved analyzing the codes to find themes, patterns, and categories to be sorted into groupings. These groupings were then sorted into smaller subcategories. The third component of grounded coding is selective coding (Saldana, 2016), which involved continuing to sort the categories of themes and determine the overarching themes, thus putting the codes together to determine the story they tell, the description of the case (Charmaz, 2014; Creswell, 2013) as shown in Figure 13.1.

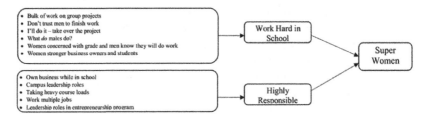

Figure 13.1   Data structure

These findings were then compared to existing literature for similarities and differences. In order to ensure the trustworthiness of my study, various measures were practiced to ensure confirmability, credibility, transferability, and dependability (Lincoln & Guba, 1985). Those measures included reflexivity through journaling, selecting an institution with which I was not affiliated, involving a peer reviewer on the focus groups, and debriefing with an outside mentor. Additionally, the interviewees were invited to participate in member checks of the interview transcripts (Creswell, 2014; Lincoln & Guba, 1985; Mertens, 2014).

RESULTS

In analyzing the data to answer the research question, *What role does gender play in the academic experience of women participating in an entrepreneurship program?*, the students involved in the program showed up as superwomen, which will be explored further in this section.

The Program

The entrepreneurship program was housed in the business school and included an entrepreneurship center and academic coursework, including an academic major that is only offered in conjunction with a second business-related major (curricular) and co-curricular programming. The center employed a woman director, two men faculty members, a man entrepreneur-in-residence, a woman graduate assistant, and several women student workers. The gender makeup of the program is explored further in Table 13.1.

The center provided programing for students, including a business model pitch competition, workshops to prepare for pitch competitions, and events in partnership with a regional organization that provided support to women entrepreneurs. Additionally, the center had an Innovation Corps (I-Corps) site, and a student entrepreneurship club with an annual idea pitch competition and biweekly meetings featuring speakers.

Table 13.1   Gender makeup of the program

Program aspect	Percentage of men	Percentage of women
University undergraduate population	41	59
Undergraduate business students	61	39
Declared entrepreneurship majors	69	31
Entrepreneurship club members	67	33
Entrepreneurship club officers	75	25
Recent pitch competition participants	83	17

The Participants

The student participants in the study were all undergraduate students with varying levels of involvement, as described in Table 13.2. These demographics, shown in Tables 13.2 and 13.3, were self-reported and based on the participants' interpretation of the demographic questions.

Superwomen

Student participants, as well as faculty participants, reported experiences that suggested that women students were "superwomen." These students were successful and performed very well in this man-dominated area, showing up with extraordinary powers being highly responsible and coping successfully with multiple simultaneous demands with schoolwork.

Table 13.2   Participant demographics

Pseudonym	Year	Age	Race	Major	Center employee	Owns a business
Brittany	4	22	White	Management and Marketing	Yes	Yes
Courtney	2	19	White	Entrepreneurship and Finance	No	No
Elizabeth	5	24	Hispanic White	General Business	No	No
Emily	4	26	White	HR and Marketing	Yes	Yes
Gabrielle	5	21	White	Liberal Studies	Yes	No
Georgia	3	28	White	Journalism	Yes	Yes
Jessica	2	19	White	Entrepreneurship and Management	No	No
Nicole	3	20	White	Marketing and Entrepreneurship	No	Yes
Olivia	4	21	White	Manufacturing	No	No
Samantha	3	20	Black	General Business	Yes	Yes

Table 13.3   Participant participation and business demographics

Pseudonym	Taken a course	In the club	Business interests
Brittany	Yes	Yes	Clothing resale, high-heel shoes, bakery, social business
Courtney	No	Yes	Food-related, automotive
Elizabeth	Yes	No	Clothing store, fashion-related
Emily	No	No	YouTube channel, art business, event space, cider mill, jewelry making, farm
Gabrielle	Yes	No	Clothing resale, coffee shop passport, making clothes
Georgia	No	No	Biography writing
Jessica	Yes	Yes	Bridal alterations, activism and ministry
Nicole	Yes	No	Bridal alterations, personal stylist, interior designer
Olivia	No	Yes	Environmental organization, not-for-profit, manufacturing
Samantha	No	Yes	Event space, bakery, public relations firm

Work hard in school

Participants described feeling devalued by men and other frustrations during group work. They shared that men often did not do the work or left the bulk of the group responsibility to women. During the focus group, Elizabeth stated that men were often in charge of the strategy or vision of a group project, but it was the women who took on the details and logistics of it all. Women tended to be faster to get to work on a group project. As Elizabeth described, they spent a few minutes greeting one another, and then got right to work delegating tasks and creating a timeline for the work.

Courtney told a story of a male classmate.

> One kid does not turn his stuff in at all on time. This is like three times, so I don't give him any work to do because I don't trust him. He is doing one thing and I've had to text him all week and be like "this is due on Tuesday." Cause that happened.

As she described her role in the group, I asked if she was designated the team leader by her professor or her peers. She said,

> By the peers. Everyone was put in their group and it was OK you guys have to choose who's gonna be the team lead. And, I was like I'm gonna do it. That's what I've done my whole life. I've been this way my whole life. So, I'll do it. (Individual interview)

> Brittany said she had a group member who would offer to help and then ask her to do the task. If he did do it, it would be done late, not well, or not at all. So, she would just take over the project and do the work herself. "I'm the type of person who just likes to do it myself, so I would kind of take it over." (Individual interview)

During the focus group, Nicole told of a group she was in at the time in which she would take over the responsibilities, "I think women are in general more contentious and thinking about all those millions of things all at once. So, when you're in a group with guys, you tend to. I tend to take over a lot of the responsibilities." She went on to tell of the way she thought that women took on all of the responsibilities.

> I think in general what I'm getting at is that in a lot of group projects when you're with guys and girls, the girl often ends up doing the editing and the writing and the communications side of things, and the organizational things, which kind of sounds like everything. And, I don't know, that's just been my experience and maybe I kind of want to control those things. But, especially like editing or writing, I find that girls do a lot of it.

As Nicole told this story, Jessica fiddled with her hands and Elizabeth bit her lip, both seeming uncomfortable and anxious to also speak of their experiences. I followed this story with the question, "So, what do males do?"

To which Nicole repeated, "What *do* males do?" Samantha immediately answered, "When I find out, I'll let you know. No, I'm kidding." Multiple participants laughed in response.

As the conversation in the focus group continued, Elizabeth shared specific stories about group work. One description she gave was about a time when a man student

> just literally did nothing and just expected us to do it and get it done. And, it was just the most frustrating thing, I was just like 'ugh.' But, then towards the end he was like, 'oh, but I want to have an opinion about something.' And, I was like, oh, I just wrote these ten pages, so you don't get an opinion anymore. Presentation is tomorrow, you're done.

Samantha further explained this type of scenario.

> I think the thing is with guys, if you're in a group and you present your idea, they're like ok I gave my two cents, I don't have to do anything because I know the girls are gonna do it. I know that you're gonna get it done, I know that you're concerned with your grade, I know that you're concerned with this, I know that you're concerned with that, so you're gonna do it whether you're supposed to be the leader or not.

Consistent with the women's experiences of setting high expectations for themselves and for working hard, Professor Smith described that although women students were much less likely to speak up in class, when he specifically called on women, they were much better prepared and "rich" in their responses than the men students. In describing a particular student, "she won't raise her hand, but if I call on her, she'll engage immediately" (Individual interview). He speculates this may be because they perceived that he had "given permission," as once he had called on a woman student, other women students would begin to speak up.

Professor Smith also said, "my experience so far has been that the females have been much stronger business owners and business entrepreneurs than the men have." When asked if this was reflected in their grades, he said, "Oh yeah, their grades reflect it. Their passion for what it is that they're doing and their drive and determination are different." I observed this as well. The students had been assigned a presentation in class. The women in the class presented carefully crafted scripts, thought-out responses, and presented within the assigned timeframe. They appeared much more prepared than the men in class who appeared more casual and less focused, often running over time for their presentations. Because the entrepreneurship major could only be pursued in conjunction with another major, those women who were pursuing the major were superwomen by taking on this extra work.

Highly responsible
The participants all reported having multiple responsibilities in their lives, including coursework, jobs, campus leadership, and family. Several of the participants were currently running their own business, which took up time beyond their university commitments. The women were very involved in campus leadership, including working as a sound technician for campus ministry, to serving on the campus judiciary board, to mentoring first-year students for the honors' college, and holding an officer position for the society of women engineers. The students also took heavy course loads.

Many of the students worked both on campus and off campus, sometimes working two jobs off campus. Many of the participants worked in the entrepreneurship center on campus, as well as off-campus locations such as a catering company, sewing and alterations, a yarn shop, a law firm, a restaurant, an outlet mall, babysitting, and doing freelance design work.

Although there were fewer women than men involved in the program, those who were involved took on leadership roles. When describing her peer, Brittany, Samantha said, "she's like a prime example of a student leader, what you would expect out of a student leader… I mean, she's pretty great" (Focus group) and Professor Smith described her as a "star entrepreneur." While fewer women compete in the pitch competitions, Professor Owens said that those who did were high performers and more likely to win.

The women students who were successful in the program were grateful for and took advantage of the resources provided. Brittany said she was not afraid to ask for help, which had served her well. She also stated that many of her women peers did not take advantage of the resources provided.

DISCUSSION

This theme of data included findings that represented the processes of Acker's (1990, 1992, 1999, 2012) theory of gendered organizations. The first process, the construction of divisions, was apparent with the women taking on the details and logistics of group projects; their instructor's reports of them being stronger students and business owners than the men; and their pursuit of much responsibility through heavy course loads, campus leadership, and family obligations, i.e., being superwomen. The construction of symbols and images was evident in the way women adapted, through taking on work, and dressing and acting "just right," which created more work for them relative to their men counterparts. The process of practices shaping identity was shown in that the women adapted to the appropriate identity of women in entrepreneurship: by performing very well in their work and taking on much responsibility.

Far from being gender neutral, it is clear that in this setting, the women in this study saw a distinct relationship between their identity as a woman and the appropriate roles or expectations in an entrepreneurship program, from class-room behavior to the seriousness with which their ventures were considered to a constant awareness of navigating men in their environment. The women coped with the process of creating and conceptualizing social structures by being superwomen and performing stronger than the men, as was evidenced by both their stories as well as their professors reporting that they worked harder and performed better than the men students. These processes are inter-locking and work together to produce gendered organizations in the form of the "gendered substructure" (Acker, 1990, 1999, 2012). These women were superwomen in order to navigate this organization.

Implications for Research

This study provides implications for both research and practice. First of all, the study should be replicated in both similar and different institutions to deter-mine the transferability of the themes, as well as in an entrepreneurship train-ing program outside of academia to determine how specific the findings are to university programs versus other training programs. The study should be repli-cated using men students to determine how specific some of the findings are to women rather than entrepreneurship students more generally. Future research should further tease out the idea of race and gender and the intersectionality of the two in the experiences of women students using Crenshaw's (1989) theory of intersectionality. Additionally, a future study could look at a program that is not tied to an entrepreneurship center to help understand the impact of the organizational structure when a program is tied to a center. A future study should also be conducted under the lens of Downing and Roush's (1985) theory of identity development to understand its impact on women's reported experiences related to a gendered organization. Furthermore, a future study could be conducted under the lens of entrepreneurial identity in entrepreneur-ship education similar to that suggested in Donnellon, Ollila, and Middleton's (2014) study.

Implications for Practice

This study provides implications for practice that can be implemented by edu-cators to address the influences of a gendered organization and better recruit and nurture women students. In order to help mitigate the women students' idea that entrepreneurship is not for them, it is important to provide role models by highlighting women entrepreneurs as class examples, in course materials, and as guest speakers. It is important to ensure that some of these women are in stereotypically masculine ventures and of similar age to the students.

In order to change the way that women operate in this gendered organization in things like taking on the "housekeeping" roles in group work and dressing more nicely than the men, vary the roles by assigning specific roles and tasks when assigning group work in class, or by providing a metric for checking in, ensuring that the students are graded based on their work towards the project, not on their peers' work. Create diverse teams with equal numbers of women and men students so that the women do not have to be outnumbered yet take on the bulk of the work. Additionally, dictate how students should dress for class, specifically having "professional" days, and thereby leveling the dress code.

CONCLUSION

This study explored the experiences of women students in a university entrepreneurship program at a four-year institution using Acker's (1990, 1992, 1999, 2012) theory of gendered organizations as a framework. As was highlighted in this chapter, the women showed up as superwomen to navigate this gendered organization. In order to address this in this and in similar programs, educators should level the playing field in ways they can manipulate by varying the roles for students, being intentional of finding women mentors and role models for the students, and encouraging relationships among the students and between students and program faculty and staff. Most immediately these steps can help women persist in a man-centered environment and increase the number of women thriving in these types of organizations.

NOTES

1. The vast majority of the literature surrounding this topic uses terms representing gender and sex interchangeably, such as woman and female and man and male, whether referring to sex or gender. This literature review is written to be consistent with the authors of the literature as the scope of this study is a broad exploration of the impact of gender roles in entrepreneurship education.
2. Available upon request (cochran9@iu.edu).
3. Available upon request.
4. Available from author.
5. Available from author.
6. Available from author.

REFERENCES

Acker, J. (1990). Hierarchies, jobs, bodies: A theory of gendered organizations. *Gender and Society*, *4*(2), 139–58.

Acker, J. (1992). From sex roles to gendered institutions. *Contemporary Sociology*, *21*(5), 565–9.

Acker, J. (1999). Gender and organizations. In J. S. Chafetz (Ed.), *Handbook of the sociology of gender* (pp. 171–94). New York: Springer.

Acker, J. (2012). Gendered organizations and intersectionality: Problems and possibilities. *Equality, Diversity and Inclusion: An International Journal, 31*(3), 214–24.

Bae, T. J., Qian, S., Miao, C., & Fiet, J. O. (2014). The relationship between entrepreneurship education and entrepreneurial intentions: A meta-analytic review. *Entrepreneurship: Theory and Practice*, 38(2), 217–54.

Charmaz, K. (2014). *Constructing grounded theory* (2nd ed.). Los Angeles, CA: Sage.

Cochran, S. L. (2019a). University resources: How prosperous women student entrepreneurs find their success. In V. Crittenden (Ed.), *Go-to-market strategies for women entrepreneurs: Creating and exploring success* (pp. 85–94). Bingley: Emerald.

Cochran, S. L. (2019b). What's gender got to do with it? The experiences of US women entrepreneurship students. *Journal of Small Business Management, 57*(S1).

Cohoon, J. M., Wadhwa, V., & Mitchell, L. (2010). *The anatomy of an entrepreneur: Are successful women entrepreneurs different than men?* Retrieved from www.kauffman.org

Crenshaw, K. (1989). Demarginalizing the intersection of race and sex: A black feminist critique of antidiscrimination doctrine, feminist theory and antiracist politics. *University of Chicago Legal Forum*, 139.

Creswell, J. W. (2013). *Qualitative inquiry and research design: Choosing among five approaches* (3rd ed.). Thousand Oaks, CA: Sage.

Creswell, J. W. (2014). *Research design: Qualitative, quantitative and mixed method approaches* (4th ed.). Thousand Oaks, CA: Sage.

Donnellon, A., Ollila, S., & Middleton, K. W. (2014). Constructing entrepreneurial identity in entrepreneurship education. *Journal of Management Education, 12*, 490–9.

Downing, N. E., & Roush, K. L. (1985). From passive acceptance to active commitment: A model of feminist identity development for women. *Counseling Psychologist, 13*(4), 695–709.

Duval-Couetil, N., Gotch, C. M., & Yi, S. (2014). The characteristics and motivations of contemporary entrepreneurship students. *Journal of Education for Business, 89*(8), 441–9.

Duval-Couetil, N., Reed-Rhoads, T., & Haghighi, S. (2002). Engineering students and entrepreneurship education: Involvement, attitudes, and outcomes. *International Journal of Engineering Education, 28*, 425–35.

Entrepreneur Staff (2019). Get to know the female entrepreneurs who are reshaping the business world. *Entrepreneur Magazine*, October 8. Retrieved from www.entrepreneur.com

Erickson, S. K. (2012). Women Ph.D. students in engineering and a nuanced terrain: Avoiding and revealing gender. *Review of Higher Education, 35*(3), 355–74.

Farrar, J. & Gupta, G. R. (2020). Why we need women's leadership in the Covid-19 response. *World Economic Forum*, April 3. Retrieved from www.wcforum.org

Fayolle, A. Gailly, B., & Lassas-Clerc, N. (2006). Assessing the impact of entrepreneurship education programmes: A new methodology. *Journal of European Industrial Training, 30*(9), 701–20.

Gardner, S. K. (2013). Women faculty departures from a striving institution: Between a rock and a hard place. *Review of Higher Education, 36*(3), 349–70.

Givens, D. (2020). Meet the Black woman taking the lead to develop a vaccine for Covid-19. *Black Enterprise*, March 26. Retrieved from www.blackenterprise.com

Gray, A. (2018). More women are running for political office in the US than before. *World Economic Forum*, August 28. Retrieved from www.weforum.org

Gupta, V. K., Turban, D. B., & Pareek, A. (2013). Differences between men and women in opportunity evaluation as a function of gender stereotypes and stereotype activation. *Entrepreneurship Theory and Practice, 7*, 771–88.

Gupta, V. K., Turban, D. B., Wasti, S. A., & Sidkar, A. (2009). The role of gender stereotypes in perceptions of entrepreneurs and intentions to become an entrepreneur. *Entrepreneurship Theory and Practice, 3*, 397–417.

Heppner, P. P., & Heppner, M. J. (2003). *Writing and publishing your thesis, dissertation, and research: A guide for students in the helping professions (research, statistics, and program evaluation)*. Belmont, CA: Cengage.

Hsu, D. K., Shinnar, R. S., & Powell, B. C. (2014). Expectancy theory and entrepreneurial motivation: A longitudinal examination of the role of entrepreneurship education. *Journal of Business and Entrepreneurship, 26*(1), 121–40.

Johnson, M. A., Stevenson, R. M., & Letwin, C. R. (2018). A women's place is in the... startup! Crowdfunder judgments, implicit bias, and the stereotype content model. *Journal of Business Venturing, 33*(6), 813–31.

Kickul, J., Wilson, F., Marlino, D., & Barbosa, S. (2008). Are misalignments of perceptions and self-efficacy causing gender gaps in entrepreneurial intentions among our nation's teens. *Journal of Small Business and Enterprise Development, 15*(2), 321–35.

Kolb, D. A. (1984). *Experiential Learning*. Englewood Cliffs, NJ: Prentice Hall.

Lincoln, Y. S., & Guba, E. G. (1985). *Naturalistic inquiry*. Newbury Park, CA: Sage.

Lo, C., Sun, H., & Law, K. (2012). Comparing the entrepreneurial intention between female and male engineering students. *Journal of Women's Entrepreneurship and Education, 1–2*, 28–51.

Menzies, T. V., & Tatroff, H. (2006). The propensity of male vs. female students to take courses and degree concentrations in entrepreneurship. *Journal of Small Business & Entrepreneurship, 19*(2), 203–23.

Mertens, D. M. (2014). *Research and evaluation in education and psychology: Integrating diversity with quantitative, qualitative, and mixed methods*. Thousand Oaks, CA: Sage.

Morris, M. H., Webb, J. W., Fu, J., & Singhal, S. (2013). A competency-based perspective on entrepreneurship education: Conceptual and empirical insights. *Journal of Small Business Management, 51*(3), 352–69.

Muofhe, N. J., & Du Toit, W. F. (2011). Entrepreneurial education's and entrepreneurial role models' influence on career choice. *SA Journal of Human Resource Management, 9*(1), 1–15.

Nelson, T., & Duffy, S. (2011). *Men, women, sex and gender in entrepreneurship education* (Working paper). Retrieved from www.researchgate.net

Packham, G., Jones, P., Miller, C., Pickernell, D., & Brychan, T. (2010). Attitudes towards entrepreneurship education: A comparative analysis. *Education and Training, 52*(8/9), 568–86.

Peterson, R., & Limbu, Y. (2010). Student characteristics and perspectives in entrepreneurship courses: A profile. *Journal of Entrepreneurship Education, 13*, 65–83.

Petridou, E., Sarri. A., & Kyrgidou, L. P. (2009). Entrepreneurship education in higher education institutions: The gender dimension. *Gender in Management: An International Journal, 24*(4), 286–309.

Pruett, M., Shinnar, R., Toney, B., Llopis, F., & Fox, J. (2009). Explaining entrepreneurial intentions of university students: A cross-cultural study. *International
Journal of Entrepreneurial Behaviour and Research, 15*(6), 571–94.

Riebe, M. (2012). A place of her own: The case for university-based centers for women
entrepreneurs. *Journal of Education for Business, 87*, 241–6.

Robb, A., Coleman, S., & Stangler, D. (2014). *Sources of economic hope: Women's
entrepreneurship*. Ewing Marion Kauffman Foundation.

Saldana, J. (2016). *The coding manual for qualitative researchers*. Los Angeles, CA:
Sage.

Sanchez, J. C., & Licciardello, O. (2012). Gender differences and attitudes in entrepreneurial intentions: The role of career choice. *Journal of Women's Entrepreneurship
and Education, 1–2*, 7–27.

Shinnar, R. S., Giacomin, O., & Janssen, F. (2012). Entrepreneurial perceptions and
intentions: The role of gender and culture. *Entrepreneurship Theory and Practice,
36*(3), 465–93.

Stake, R. E. (2006). *Multiple case study analysis*. New York: Guilford Press.

Stengel, G. (2016). Women entrepreneurs fuel social change and economic growth.
Forbes. Retrieved from www.forbes.com

Superwoman (2020). Retrieved from www.dictionary.com

United Nations (2020). Progress on the Sustainable Develepment Goals. www
.unwomen.org/-/media/headquarters/attachments/sections/library/publications/
2019/progress-on-the-sdgs-the-gender-snapshot-2019-two-page-spreads-en.pdf?la=
en&vs=5814

US Department of Education (n.d.). *Institute of Education Sciences, National Center
for Education Statistics*. Retrieved from http://nces.ed.gov/ipeds/

Vanevenhoven, J. (2013). Advances and challenges in entrepreneurship education.
Journal of Small Business Management, 51(3), 466–70.

Wechsler, P. (2015). Women-led companies perform three times better than the S&P
500. *Fortune*. Retrieved from www.fortune.com

Whitman-Cobb, W. (2019). What having more women astronauts could mean for space
exploration. *Fast Company*, July 11. Retrieved from www.fastcompany.com

Wilson, F., Kickul, J., & Marlino, D. (2007). Gender, entrepreneurial self-efficacy,
and entrepreneurial career intentions: Implications for entrepreneurship education.
Entrepreneurship Theory and Practice, 31(3), 387–406.

Yin, R. K. (2013). *Case study research: Design and methods*. Thousand Oaks, CA:
Sage.

Zraick, K. (2019). NASA astronauts complete the first all-female spacewalk. *New York
Times*, October 18. Retrieved from www.nytimes.com

14. A learning-by-doing approach to entrepreneurship education, student job creation and new venture incubation

Jeremy Woods and Peter M.W. Burley

INTRODUCTION

In this chapter, we outline a program for hands-on teaching of entrepreneurship while creating student jobs and startups at the same time. It is focused on training certain key skill sets and having students apply these skill sets on learning-by-doing (Rasmussen & Sørheim, 2006) projects (i.e., projects performing tasks for real small businesses in the community as part of the students' coursework). The students are then placed in paid, part-time jobs with local small businesses while they are in school to build resume material and get additional hands-on experience. The program also recruits students from the broader university population via a campus entrepreneurship club, delivering presentations, hosting speaker panels, and providing training and part-time job placement assistance in bi-weekly club meetings. This entire set of activities serves as a feeder system for selecting top student entrepreneurs who have concrete startup ideas or existing micro businesses for placement with our campus incubator, which delivers coaching, resources, and business development assistance to fine-tune minimum viable products, acquire paying beta customers, and attract initial capital infusion for exit from the incubator and subsequent growth.

It is important to provide a description of the skills training around which everything is based, including the pedagogical methods used to deliver the content. How these skills lend themselves to embedding students in learning-by-doing projects is illustrated along with growing these projects into paid part-time jobs. This leads to building students' critical thinking and problem-solving skills while replacing traditional minimum wage work. How all this activity encourages startup initiative to solve problems, create new value, and develop incubator ventures is considered.

ENTREPRENEURSHIP SKILLS TRAINING

The Journey from Practitioner to Educator

The entire program described here is a practice-based approach to entrepreneurship education (Neck, Greene, & Brush, 2014) inspired by my own experience as an entrepreneur and small business owner combined with the broader perspective and time for learning and experimentation associated with being back in academia (Elliott, 2017). As a small business owner, key activities I did out of necessity included web development, sales, traditional marketing, contract development, accounting, and administration. As part of my immersion in the world of learning and experimentation in academia, I have come to appreciate and master additional skills and activities such as software app development, patent/trademark/copyright research and paperwork, social media marketing, competitor research, industry research, best practices research, financial analysis, due diligence, and grant research and paperwork.

My own learning journey, like that of many practitioners-turned-educators, was borne out of setting aside my hubris as an entrepreneur and small business owner and opening my mind to a broader world of textbook publisher materials and other resources that I used to dismiss as a practitioner. While many educators do not have the real-world experience to be able to teach students how to apply theoretical concepts, practitioners can suffer from a different problem: being too closed-minded toward theory and new ways of doing things. My former attitude as a practitioner led me to quickly pass over information and tools because it seemed like they were irrelevant or would take too long to master. However, the setting aside of ego and openness to learning described above led to a growing intellectual curiosity and confidence that valuable information was always "out there" and relatively easy to identify, digest, and apply in a short period of time (Horrigan, 2016). It also led to a willingness to experiment with new technologies, eventually leading me to adopt all kinds of web and app development resources, social media marketing techniques, useful textbook publisher content, and digital tools for course management. My openness to adopting these wonderful pedagogical tools, which I once dismissed, has greatly increased my ability to transform from a practitioner into an educator (Pollitt, 2006). The result of this transformation was the birth of a program from which students, business owners, and the community could benefit.

The Skills Training Program

Since arriving at California State University, Bakersfield in 2014, I have focused heavily on student professional development, having nearly all the roughly 1,500 students taught over that time complete a professional development plan and develop a professional LinkedIn profile, which together are the starting point for the entire program described here. The skills training portion of the program then focuses on teaching the students eight specific skill sets which are applied on learning-by-doing projects with local small businesses. Finally, the students are placed in paid, part-time jobs with local small businesses after completion of their course projects.

The professional development plan pushes the students to articulate their work experience and current income and expenses, as well as their post-graduation and long-term professional and financial goals. All students have experience and natural skills and talents (Renzulli, 1973), but they need assistance to articulate their experience, skills, and talents in a way that resonates with small business employers. I help the students with this articulation by having every student tell me their current job, income level, and monthly expenses, their target job, income level, and expected expenses post-graduation, and their long-term professional and financial goals. I then work intensively with the students to do a "brain dump" of their work, classroom, volunteer, and hobby activities, the latter three of which most students don't think of when articulating their professional qualifications (Roulin & Bangerter, 2013). We include all of this information in the student's LinkedIn profile to showcase both their traditional and non-traditional experience and help them learn to articulate the deliverable value of the activities they performed in these experiences in terms of number of customers served, dollar value of transactions handled, dollar value of assets used or managed, time investment, and other metrics.

The students' work experience drives the specific skills development focus of each class, which in turn drives the learning-by-doing projects (described below). The students' professional and financial goals then drive the employment program part-time work placements (described below) to make the whole program sustainable.

As a result, classes are a mix of traditional lectures and hands-on class sessions featuring training on specific skill sets. All class sessions are recorded (audio and screen capture) and made available for students asynchronously. Additional training, troubleshooting, and grading feedback are delivered via virtual meetings, which are also recorded and made available for students. The skills training topics covered in class are: (1) web and software app development; (2) patent, trademark, and copyright research and paperwork; (3) sales outreach, social media marketing, and traditional marketing; (4) competitor research; (5) industry research; (6) administration and best practices research;

(7) accounting and financial analysis; and (8) capital acquisition due diligence and grant research and paperwork. The training content for each skill set is described below, along with Tables 14.1 and 14.2 providing additional details about each of the skill sets and Table 14.3 describing success stories and dollar amounts of value the program has created.

Web and software app development
For web and software app development, students are guided through the use of Wix, Photoshop, and various online app development and coding resources by focusing on a specific, no-nonsense, ever evolving list of deliverables. The current core of the web development deliverables focuses on training students in the use of a handful of key software features and a minimum, professional level of content and formatting. Students are coached in creating a website with, at a minimum, home, about, products/services, and contact pages, all of which have specific image and text guidelines for delivering a sufficiently robust and professional amount of content (Table 14.1).

The core of the graphic design deliverables focuses on a handful of key software features and content formatting guidelines (Table 14.1). Using this functionality, the students are coached in creating visual aids for illustrating concepts and processes. The core of the app development deliverables focuses on identification and use of user-friendly, off-the-shelf app and coding platforms (Table 14.1). Using these platforms, students are exposed to, and develop skills in, the creation of basic app functionality such as inventory management or user/content databases, augmented with short subroutines to produce Application Programming Interfaces in common programming languages.

Patent, trademark, and copyright research and paperwork
For patent, trademark, and copyright research and paperwork, students are mentored on how to navigate the United States Patent and Trademark Office's online patent and trademark databases, how to navigate Google Patents and the Global Brand Database, and how to navigate the United States Copyright Office's online copyright catalog. Again, the focus is on teaching the students to identify and prepare specific, no-nonsense deliverables which will be immediately useful for the learning-by-doing client company. The current core of the deliverables includes conducting an exhaustive prior art search for patents, trademarks, and/or copyrighted material similar to what the learning-by-doing client company has created. Students then assemble a list of the top five–ten "most similar" prior works with bullet points containing key, actionable information (Table 14.1). After gathering this information, students then learn to prepare patent applications for review by the learning-by-doing client com-

Table 14.1   Skill sets and training content

Skill set	Details	
Web and software app development	*Wix functionality* - Drag and drop user interface. - Add/delete/manage pages function. - Add text/image/button functions. - Upgrade capacity for hosting and domain name registration.	*Photoshop functionality* - Drag and drop user interface. - Layers organizing principle. - Insert/crop/rotate images function. - Insert text function. - Insert shapes function. - Visual aids illustrating concepts and processes saved as .png files and uploaded to Wix.
	Web content guidelines - *Home*: At least two images and two paragraphs profiling the company's top value. - *About*: At least three images/three paragraphs describing the company's history and leaders. - *Products/services*: At least three images/three paragraphs describing each major product or service the company offers. - *Contact*: A functioning physical address, email address, and phone number. - *General*: All pages interconnected with links.	*App development packages and languages* - *Packages*: Appery, Amazon Web Services. - *Languages*: Java, Python, PHP.

Skill set	Details	
Patent, trademark, and copyright research and paperwork	*Key patent information* - Name, identifying number, and abstract of the patent. - Key similar features from the background, description, summary, and claims sections of the patent to those of the patent the company wants to file. - Suggestions on how the company should differentiate itself from these features.	*Key trademark information* - Name (word mark), serial number, description of the mark, and goods and services code(s). - Suggestions on how the company should differentiate itself from these features. *Key copyright information* - Title, registration number, type of work, description, and contents. - Suggestions on how the company should differentiate itself from these features.
Sales outreach, social media marketing, and traditional marketing	*Contact pools* - The client company's existing customers. - The student's own friends, family, and associates. - My own contact network (instructor). - The general marketplace of users on the four major social media platforms (LinkedIn, Facebook, Instagram, and Twitter). *Key network-empowering social media platform branding features* - Consistent and professional page names. - Consistent and professional profile/cover pictures. - Consistent and professional company descriptions. - Strategic selection of company type and product/service categories. - Accurate contact information. - Links to the personal profiles of team members.	*Documentation and quantification of flyer, brochure, and poster marketing* - Photo and/or video documentation of the placement and distribution of materials. - Collection of a representative sample of basic demographics for the individuals to whom brochures and flyers are given and the "eyeballs" that walk by in the 15–30 minutes after the hanging of posters.

pany's lawyer and fill out and submit trademark and copyright applications directly on behalf of the learning-by-doing company.

Sales outreach, social media marketing, and traditional marketing

For sales and marketing, students learn how to undertake several extremely low-cost "guerrilla" marketing activities for learning-by-doing client companies. These activities teach students how to get out a clear, appealing, and consistent message to as many potential customers as possible through very specific targeting of demographic and psychographic characteristics. I always base my students' sales and marketing activities on what I like to call "the rule of 10." If there is one cardinal rule that I learned about sales and marketing from my years as a salesman, it is that customer acquisition is a numbers game (Kennedy, 2010). If you want one new customer, you need to reach out to at least 10 potential customers.

The four contact pools are listed in Table 14.1. For each project, the learning-by-doing client company is asked to give us access to their existing customers in order to understand and document those customers' demographics and psychographics and leverage their social networks. Students are encouraged to think broadly, do a "brain dump" of all the people they know, and document those contacts' basic demographics and psychographics, since many of the students think quite narrowly about networking not realizing how many potential customers they already know. Additionally, students have open access to my network of several thousand contacts, both in the local community and all over the world, through my social media presence and Outlook contact folder via Office 365. This way they can freely find email and phone details for these contacts and read my notes on the contacts to understand the context of my relationships with them. They can also write their own notes about their interactions with these contacts so that all can see the interactions everyone else has had with that contact. Finally, the general marketplace of social media platform users is accessible via extremely targeted advertising campaigns, leveraging these platforms' tools for selecting users who see the advertisements based on very specific customer characteristics.

Five marketing materials tools are developed. The first is a website, the setup of which was described above. The second is a basic social media footprint on Facebook, Instagram, LinkedIn, and Twitter, with special attention paid to creating an appealing, professional, consistent, and network-empowered brand message (Table 14.1). The third is the regular posting of brand message-consistent, value-added social media content which encourages likes, follows, and comments, which in turn encourage viral news feed activity. The fourth is meticulously quantified and documented brochure/flyer/poster development (Table 14.1). The fifth is preparation of email and text messages with appealing HTML features and links.

Five outreach activities are outlined. The first is contacting existing learning-by-doing client company customers and various friends and family in person and via phone, starting with a core of 10–20 contacts and expanding that to roughly 100 through networking. The second is "pushing" social media content out to top friends and contacts, sharing posts with 10–20 core contacts and asking those contacts to like and comment on the posts and share them with additional contacts, encouraging viral spread of the content. The third is leveraging automation software for email and text blasts to the same contacts described in the first two outreach activities, highlighting key value-added products, services, and information regularly to listservs of contacts' email addresses and cell phone numbers "newsletter style." The fourth is extremely targeted social media advertising, leveraging the demographic and psychographic profiles of existing customers and contacts to reach out to similar prospects in specific geographic areas. The fifth is distribution of posters, flyers, and brochures in high-traffic areas and at events likely to be frequented by the learning-by-doing client company's target customers.

Competitor research

For competitor research, students learn to leverage two databases that capture specific, actionable information (Table 14.2) on even the smallest of the learning-by-doing client company's competitors. This is augmented with additional information (Table 14.2) from the competitor's website, social media footprint, and online reviews and with outreach to some of the competitor's customers and current/former employees. While all the information sources other than the two databases are rather obvious, the key is teaching the students how to focus in on actionable information and explaining what the learning-by-doing client company can do with that information.

Students research the competitor in Reference USA, a database that contains practically every small business in the United States – even one-person shops that most national business databases overlook – gathering specific information which is actionable for the learning-by-doing client company. Afterwards, students augment this with legal and financial information from the Experian Commercial Risk Database. The students then visit the competitor's website and social media pages and search for online reviews about the competitor on sites such as Yelp and Glass Door. Finally, the students reach out to contacts they share in common with the competitor on social media. They also reach out to customers who reviewed the competitor via connections the students share in common with that customer on social media and reach out to former employees of the competitor identified through Glass Door to gather additional information. In the process, the students further develop their networking skills, often resulting in the acquisition of former customers of the competitor as new customers for the learning-by-doing client company.

Table 14.2   *Skill sets and training content, continued*

Skill set	Details
Competitor research	*Actionable information from Reference USA* - The address, phone number, and website of the competitor. - The names and titles of the competitor's key personnel. - Corporate linkages the competitor has to other companies. - The Standard Industrial Classification and North American Industry Classification System codes for business activities in which the competitor is involved. - The competitor's approximate number of employees and annual sales volume. - The approximate square footage of the competitor's facilities. - Estimated levels of the competitor's annual spending on accounting, contract labor, legal services, office equipment and supplies, payroll and benefits, rent and leasing, telecommunications, advertising, insurance, management and administration, package and container services, purchased print, technology, and utilities. *Actionable information from Experian* - The competitor's Doing Business As (DBA) definition. - Any judgments or tax liens filed against the competitor. - Any bankruptcies filed by the competitor. - A dollar estimate of the competitor's approved credit amount. - The competitor's approximate level of outstanding debts and payment history. - The competitor's overall Experian credit score and risk level.
Industry research	*Key first research information* - Critical issues, challenges, trends, and opportunities facing the industry. - Industry average financial ratios. - Important industry websites with additional information.

Skill set	Details
Administration and best practices research	*Contract language addressing key issues* - Language defining each contract partner (including what each partner does or wants or needs). - Language about who (each organization or individual person) does what (each job task or activity or the responsibilities of each organization or individual) in what location. - Language about insurance or liability (including what "bad" could happen, what insurance/money/etc. each organization or individual has to have in case something "bad" happens, and who has to do what if something "bad" happens). - Language about privacy or confidentiality (including descriptions of the exact information that is to be kept private by each organization or individual). - Language about pay or compensation (including who gives what to whom, exactly what the compensation is (money, benefits, academic credit, experience to put on your resume, or anything else), and who does what paperwork). - Language about characteristics, skills, or qualifications of partners/employees (including characteristics the partner/employee must have and characteristics such as race, ethnicity, gender/gender identity, sexual orientation, handicapped status, or anything else that can't be discriminated against). - Language about contract term and termination. - General provisions about amendments, assignment, entirety, governing law, and notices.

Skill set	Details
Accounting and financial analysis	*Basic accounting concepts*
	- Reviewing a sample general ledger for a year's worth of small business revenues, expenses, and capital transfers.
	- Sorting a general ledger into t-accounts.
	- Income statement and balance sheet preparation.
	- Writing up a statement of shareholder equity based on investor and founder ownership percentages.
Capital acquisition	*Key due diligence information*
Due diligence and grant research and paperwork	- Product/service offering, differentiation, and pricing.
	- Brand profile (including website and social media footprint).
	- Customer base and sales and marketing activities.
	- Human, tangible, and intangible resources (including intellectual property) and key partners.
	- Liquidity, credit rating, and historical/pro-forma financials.
	- Corporate form, the amount of capital sought, and the amount and form of equity offered.

Industry research

For industry research, the students learn to select key information from two key databases, First Research Industry Profiles and IBIS World. Most small business owners don't have the time to search and read through this material, leveraging students' time (Willem & Van den Broeck, 2007). The reports can be expensive for small businesses to acquire on their own, but they can leverage students' resources to gain these insights.

Administration and best practices research

For administration and best practices research, the students learn to develop contracts, administer basic human resources tasks, navigate the websites of various regulatory agencies for business registrations, licenses, and permits, conduct best practices research on various thought leadership websites, and generally "roll up their sleeves and do stuff" for the learning-by-doing client company.

For contract development, the students learn how to leverage the learning-by-doing client company's existing business relationships and contracts and integrate information from both of these sources with boilerplate text from Legal Zoom, Rocket Lawyer, and Nolo. In doing so, the students learn the major issues any contract must address (Table 14.2) and then apply this learning to prepare straightforward yet complete contracts which meet the learning-by-doing client company's basic needs but avoid the unnecessary and cumbersome language which often gets carried over from contract to contract.

For human resources, the students learn how to acquire a Federal Employer Identification Number and a State of California Employer Development Department number for a learning-by-doing client company, sign the company up with an appropriate workers' comp insurance vendor based on the company's industry and activities, file the appropriate documentation of that insurance, and fill out W4 and I9 forms with the company's employees. The students also learn how to administer the learning-by-doing client company's federal and state income tax withholding, federal social security and Medicare withholding and employer contributions, federal unemployment insurance contributions, and State of California employment training and disability insurance tax contributions using a handful of standard human resources software packages. Finally, the students learn how to maintain appropriate documentation and circulation of job application forms, employee handbooks, and statutorily required workplace informational posters.

For business registrations, licenses, and permits, students learn how to fill out and file state corporation (stock or non-profit), limited liability company, or limited liability partnership documentation, state sales and use permits, local business license and tax certificate forms, local fictitious business name and trading name filings, local building and zoning permits, and other documentation for the learning-by-doing client company.

For best practices research, the students learn to effectively surf Google, industry association websites, and thought leadership websites such as Startup Donut, PC Mag, Info World, Hiscox, and the Society for Human Resource Management. They learn to look for ways the learning-by-doing client company could "build a better mousetrap" with regard to day-to-day administrative areas like hardware and software solutions, business planning and reporting, physical facilities layouts, insurance coverage, employee training and empowerment, and more.

Accounting and financial analysis

For accounting and financial analysis, students are first given a "refresher course" on basic accounting concepts (Table 14.2), which many students do not remember well despite having studied these concepts in other courses. The refresher course begins with hammering home to students the importance of cash flow management. This focuses on the consequences of not paying loan, utility, and supplier payments and payroll in a timely manner, even if the company is expecting a big customer payment or capital infusion in the near future. The students then sort the transactions into t-accounts, learning that every debit always has a corresponding credit and vice versa. The students then learn to roll up the t-accounts into financial statements for the learning-by-doing client company.

The students are also taught how to do financial projections based on the learning-by-doing client company's customer demographics and psychographics, the detailed sales and marketing outreach activities outlined above, and market sizing data gathered from the United States Census Bureau's online resources for consumer market sizing and Reference USA for business market sizing. Finally, the students are given a basic understanding of cost accounting and encouraged to look for ways to reduce the learning-by-doing client company's expenses.

Capital acquisition due diligence and grant research and paperwork

For capital acquisition due diligence, the students are shown how to document and showcase key information about the learning-by-doing client company (Table 14.2) in an appealing format for lenders and investors. In particular, students learn how to demonstrate a meticulous level of detail to establish credibility while still presenting the information in a parsimonious, visually appealing manner. For grant research, students are taught how to recognize the positive impacts the learning-by-doing client company's activities have on the broader society and understand the company owners' personal philanthropic interests. The students then search for federal, state, local, non-profit, and foundation grants which seek to achieve these impacts and forward these interests using the Grantwatch and Pivot databases and conduct three key grant review tasks on selected grants (Table 14.2). If this review indicates that pursuing the grant is warranted, the students identify the required elements of the application, develop a timeline for completing the application, and work together with the learning-by-doing client company to prepare the application.

LEARNING-BY-DOING PROJECTS WITH LOCAL SMALL BUSINESSES

Like most university communities, Kern County, CA contains myriad small businesses which make up the overwhelming majority of the overall business population (Small Business Administration, 2009). Our particular area is home to over 25,000 small businesses in a wide variety of industries (roughly 20,000 with less than 10 employees and roughly 5,000 with 10–500 employees). Compared to the roughly 50 local businesses we have with over 500 employees, our small business community represents over 99 percent of the total local business population.

By utilizing these skills in a real-world scenario, students not only gain experience but also opportunities to interact with potential employers and network with skilled mentors. Furthermore, students are introduced into the local job market in a way which allows them to effectively showcase their skills and proficiencies. This ultimately leads to higher rates of employment by our students in more specialized positions. Over the past five years, over 200 free student learning-by-doing class projects with local small businesses have been delivered, generating nearly $200,000 in estimated value for the businesses.

The outreach for embedding students in learning-by-doing projects in this way is accomplished by having the students work on businesses their families and friends own and businesses of which they are frequent customers. Students who cannot identify a business are connected with small businesses in my database who are not yet capable of hiring employees, as well as with larger businesses which have "outside-the-box" needs for projects that don't fit within their existing hiring policies and procedures. My experience as a practicing entrepreneur and small business owner allows me to understand the problems many small businesses are facing, and my experience practicing sales techniques such as SPIN selling (Rackham, 1988) and helping clients succeed (Khalsa, 1999) allows me to help clients articulate their own labor needs in a way that leaves them enthusiastic about cooperation with my students. If you do not have such a background, you can approximate it by reading the two books cited above and then starting your own micro-business in any area you choose, running it for six months or a year, and trying to acquire customers.

STUDENT SMALL BUSINESS EMPLOYMENT PROGRAM

In order to further expand student involvement with local businesses and advance the students' careers, I eventually moved beyond doing free learning-by-doing projects in my classes to placing students into paid, part-time hourly work, and occasional full-time salaried work, with local small businesses. This has resulted in over 25 placements and over $175,000 in annualized[1] gross earnings for students over the past year, as well as a pipeline of roughly 75 additional open positions we're trying to fill, representing over $1.3 million in potential additional annualized gross earnings for students.

This activity was initiated through roughly three months of cold- and warm-calling outreach to local small businesses in certain key industry sectors identified through Reference USA. This outreach focused on the message that our students are available to do the tasks described in the skills training section above, asking questions about the challenges the businesses were facing, and mentioning selected success stories from the students' learning-by-doing projects related to those challenges. Based on the learning from these initial conversations, I then tailored email and social media messaging to reach out to a larger audience of both businesses and opinion leaders. This outreach eventually accelerated via word of mouth over the course of a year, to the point that I now get requests for new student workers nearly every week without any additional new outreach.

As the businesses began to request students, many of them wanted the students to work on learning-by-doing projects for free, since many of the success stories I circulated to the business community came from such projects. This was a great, and necessary, way to get many local businesses to sample our students' work over the first couple years of the program, and it led many of them to become somewhat dependent on our students' labor to accomplish their business goals. After this initial "free" period, however, I began explaining to the businesses that many of our students work 20+ hours per week in order to pay for school and living expenses. However, they largely work in traditional minimum-wage jobs in hospitality, retail, and manual labor which don't really leverage the skills knowledge they are acquiring in college. If the businesses could just pay for the opportunity cost of the students' time, I described, the students would much prefer to work applying their small business skill sets and could devote the time these businesses were requesting of them. Nearly all the businesses understood and agreed with this logic, allowing us to start our student small business employment program, the earnings and placements of which are highlighted in Table 14.3.

ENTREPRENEURSHIP INITIATIVE

All the activity described above encourages the students' initiative to solve problems and create new value, which has led both to growth for existing small businesses and to creation of new businesses in our community. Many of the small businesses our students have worked for, both via free learning-by-doing projects and paid part-time jobs, have generated additional revenues and undertaken new initiatives to improve and expand their operations as a direct result of our students' work. Some of these businesses are referred to the Small Business Administration-funded Small Business Development Center affiliated with CSUB for additional assistance in pursuing capital infusion and resource acquisition.

Some of the smaller businesses in which our students have worked are welcomed into the CSUB campus venture incubator (described in more detail below) to help them improve their minimum viable products and reach out to more customers and partners. Finally, getting students involved in delivering value on learning-by-doing projects and part-time jobs has inspired many of them to take initiative in developing their own entrepreneurship ideas into new businesses. Multiple students have "graduated" from our skills training program to join our incubator, develop a minimum viable product, acquire initial beta customers, partners, and resources, and achieve initial revenues.

ENTREPRENEURSHIP CLUB

The campus entrepreneurship club was established to extend the opportunity for skills acquisition and work with local businesses to business students outside of my classes and to students in other schools beyond the School of Business and Public Administration. The club allows these students to gain the skills described above, network with local businesses, and pursue their own new startups. It also allows for a space in which experts and fellow entrepreneurs can speak about their expertise and offer advice to students about both career development and entrepreneurship. Starting from zero a little over three years ago, we have built a leadership team of nearly 10 students, a core of roughly 50 active members, and a following of 2,000+ students on our listserv who have signed up with interest in working with local small and medium employers and building businesses.

Table 14.3   *Learning by doing*

Skill set	Learning-by-doing project success stories	Learning-by-doing project value creation 2014–19	Student part-time earnings 2019–20	Student part-time positions awaiting fulfilment 2020
Web and software app development	- Software development project focused on providing a logistics application for a car hauling company that successfully continued after conclusion of the class, eventually generating over 200 updated versions of the software and supporting 160 employees handling over 67,000 bills of lading.	137 projects completed, representing over $80,000 in comparable market value.	$16,000 (3 students)	$368,000 (19 positions)
Patent, trademark, and copyright research and paperwork	- Patent research project helped niche local aerospace company define differentiation from existing patents better on a collision avoidance system which could prevent over $5 million in potential damages for the client company and other similar aerospace companies.	4 projects completed, representing over $10,000 in comparable market value.		
Sales outreach, social media marketing, and traditional marketing	- Social media marketing campaign implemented for a real estate agency which resulted in two new clients in escrow within two months of the end of the project. - Poster advertising campaign implemented for a video gaming lounge which reached approximately 8,000 people daily. - Over 300 tickets sold for two different professional hockey games, representing roughly $15,000 in estimated revenues (ticket sales plus concession and merchandise sales). - Over 500 warm leads identified, over 200 warm leads contacted, and over 20 positive responses received via social media outreach, representing nearly $10,000 in potential new revenue for a water recycling business.	45 projects completed, representing over $70,000 in comparable market value.	$19,000 (10 students)	$349,000 (17 positions)

Skill set	Learning-by-doing project success stories	Learning-by-doing project value creation 2014–19	Student part-time earnings 2019–20	Student part-time positions awaiting fulfilment 2020
Competitor research	- Project helped better define three competitors' weaknesses and identified multiple, specific dissatisfied competitor customers possibly worth over $10,000 if attracted away from the competitor.	2 projects completed, representing nearly $2,000 in comparable market value.		
Industry research	- Industry structure and trend insights helped a small janitorial services company change its product/service mix, potentially opening a more appealing market worth over $100,000 annually.	1 project completed, representing nearly $1,000 in comparable market value.		
Administration and best practices research	- Students provided registration and logistical support for a local Chamber of Commerce event which raised over $10,000.	5 projects completed, representing over $4,000 in comparable market value.	$138,000 (12 students)	$476,000 (31 positions)
Accounting and financial analysis	- Negotiated roughly $10,000 in potential reduced costs with suppliers for a local restaurant.	4 projects completed, representing over $3,000 in comparable market value.		$112,000 (8 positions)
Capital acquisition Due diligence and grant research and paperwork	- Detailed grant funding application requirements identified for 14 different funding agencies disbursing approximately $30 million in annual state of California grant funding for a water recycling business.	5 projects completed, representing over $7,000 in comparable market value.	$3,000 (1 student)	$6,000 (1 position)

Bi-Weekly Meetings

The club is organized around a bi-weekly meeting routine. Meetings usually consist of having each attendee stand up and introduce themselves, including their major and any relevant career background, what they're hoping to get out of the club, any specific jobs they are interested in, and a brief "pitch" if they have a business idea. All of these introductions are captured by our club secretary in the meeting minutes so that we can follow up with the attendees and start helping them with their job interests and startup ideas. The meetings are also recorded in both audio and video and made available asychronously, and we've recently begun broadcasting the meetings sychonously as well to expand access to more students.

After introductions, the meetings feature training sessions on the skill sets described above. We also provide regular updates on new Student Small Business Employment Program job opportunities, instructions on how to get a business idea or existing micro-business into the Student and Faculty Venture Incubator, and updates on top incubator ventures.

Guest Lectures and Speaker Panels

We regularly invite professionals from the Kern County business community to guest lecture on a variety of topics. Our speaker panel series (inaugurated in 2018) is averaging roughly 70 attendees per event, and over the past academic year these panels have exposed students to hundreds of job opportunities. They have also featured discussions of 30 different new venture opportunities in demand with the major industry players in our region.

Our speaker panels focus on two main topics: job opportunities for entre-preneurship-minded students and business challenges facing the panelists. While we invite speakers from large companies as well as small ones, we try to have the large company speakers talk about jobs that they have a hard time hiring for through our campus career center – jobs that require passion-ate, outside-the-box problem solvers who are also humble, coachable, and diligent. This gives our club members a chance to learn about and pursue job opportunities that fit the skills and mindset with which we equip them. When we have the panelists talk about business challenges, we ask them to set aside solutions that people all over the state, the country, and the world are working on and instead focus on things that aren't being done right now that our student entrepreneurs should focus on doing.

Student Small Business Employment Program

The student small business employment program was already covered in some detail above, but it is a major feature of our entrepreneurship club, so it deserves mention again here. A student employment program is not nearly as common a feature in most entrepreneurship programs as the other elements of our entrepreneurship club (Ding & Jiang, 2017), but it is integral to the hands-on program of teaching entrepreneurship described in this chapter. In order to be successful including the student employment program in our entrepreneurship club, it has been critical to pursue the program with a certain mindset and develop a well-organized database of available students.

While building such a program requires some experience in entrepreneurship and sales, a results-oriented mindset is also essential. Small business job opportunities are relatively easy to identify if you follow the steps outlined above. What is difficult is motivating both the small business owner and potential student employees to move from "wishing" to "acting." This takes an achievement-oriented program manager (Finn & Zimmer, 2012) who is not satisfied until he or she has seen job opportunities through to an initiated project (often done for the first month with the student working probationally as an independent contractor) and then a stable, ongoing job (with the company either completing all the proper employment paperwork and setting up payroll withholding and contributions or running the job through a third-party staffing agency or payroll service). A well-organized database of students, cross-referenced by skill set, schedule availability, career interest, and earning goals is also essential. We usually have to email, text, and call each small business multiple times to get them to focus on actually getting a student started on a job, and we usually have to contact five or more students for every small business job we actually fill. Many of those jobs also have to be filled multiple times until the right match is found between student and employer.

Student and Faculty Venture Incubator

Our venture incubator provides hands-on, "in-the-trenches" assistance to students and community members with promising business ideas, as well as faculty looking to commercialize their research or technology, to stabilize their minimum viable products, delivering a combination of teaching, coaching, and mentoring to help novice entrepreneurs "solve problems." We then conduct outreach with, and provide referrals to, various resource providers, beta customers, partners, and funding sources necessary for turning the minimum viable product and the venture overall into a sustainable, healthy new business capable of significant revenue growth and job creation after its exit from the incubator. We bring new ventures into the incubator by having them answer five main questions: (1) what is the problem and why is it important to solve that problem; (2) what makes your solution sustainably differentiated from the competition; (3) what is your minimum viable product; (4) what is your sales and marketing plan; and (5) what are the financials. We then help each venture to hone and improve its answers to each of those five questions, connecting them with resource providers, beta customers, partners, and funding sources as the quality of the answers to those five questions warrants.

Over the past year, over 70 ventures were welcomed into our incubator and helped bring in roughly $150,000 in grant and seed funding for the top ventures, assisting them in targeting roughly $1.5 million in beta customer revenues for the year to come.

COMMUNITY-WIDE EXPANSION

To expand your program community-wide and meaningfully impact a local economy through significant numbers of business starts, earnings growth, and startup job creation, it is first necessary to build a coalition of investors, economic development partners, educational institutions, government partners, industry partners, small businesses, and leading entrepreneurs (Wolff, 2001). In our case, this coalition is called the Kern Initiative for Talent & Entrepreneurship (KITE). To build the KITE coalition, it was also necessary to create a shared vision (Howard, O'Brien, Kay, & O'Rourke, 2019), which for us is to turn Kern County, CA into a globally recognized hub for innovation at the intersection of the aerospace, energy, and agriculture sectors over the next decade. To achieve such a community-level vision, it is necessary to bring together a combination of federal, state, and/or foundation grant funding and matching donations from the community coalition members to hire dedicated staff and acquire facilities and resources. In our case, we are pursuing roughly $2 million in grants and matching donations. After acquiring this seed funding, we envision turning the Student Small Business Employment Program and the Student and Faculty Venture Incubator described above into self-sustaining entities through the introduction of an override charge of 10 percent of student earnings and 10 percent of beta customer revenues, paid by the local small businesses and incubator ventures, respectively. We project that these entities will be capable of turning out 40 new business starts ($3.75 million in beta customer revenues, $3.8 million in equity/debt/grant funding), 80 full-time jobs ($3.2 million in annualized earnings), and 500 part-time jobs ($3.75 million in annualized earnings) annually.

CONCLUSION

The hands-on program of teaching entrepreneurship while creating student jobs and startups described in this chapter is the culmination of a 25-year journey from practitioner to educator. It outlines a detailed pedagogical approach for helping students articulate their skills and experience, as well as their professional and financial goals, then equipping them with a toolbox of entrepreneurship skills, a quantified, deliverable accomplishment professional orientation, and a "roll up your sleeves" attitude. It then goes on to explain how to create jobs and new venture starts through learning-by-doing projects, then a student small business employment program, and a student and faculty venture incubator. Finally, the chapter offers a roadmap for how to grow the program campus-wide through a student entrepreneurship club and how to expand the program community-wide to make a significant impact on a local economy. It is an honor to have the opportunity to share this approach with you!

NOTE

1. Based on keeping each part-time job staffed with a student or combination of students for one year.

REFERENCES

Ding, H., & Jiang, L. (2017). Some typical problems of entrepreneurship education "popularization" in local universities and colleges. In *2017 International Conference on Education Science and Economic Management (ICESEM 2017)*. Amsterdam: Atlantis Press.

Elliott, J. E. (2017). Implications of emergent content, experimentation, and resources for outcomes assessment at Empire State College. In K. Jelly & A. Mandell, eds., *Principles, Practices, and Creative Tensions in Progressive Higher Education* (pp. 375–91). Rotterdam: SensePublishers.

Finn, J. D., & Zimmer, K. S. (2012). Student engagement: What is it? Why does it matter? In S. L. Christenson, A. L. Reschly, & C. Wylie, *Handbook of Research on Student Engagement* (pp. 97–131). Boston, MA: Springer.

Horrigan, J. B. (2016). *Lifelong Learning and Technology*. Pew Research Center, 22.

Howard, P., O'Brien, C., Kay, B., & O'Rourke, K. (2019). Leading educational change in the 21st century: Creating living schools through shared vision and transformative governance. *Sustainability*, 11(15), 4109.

Kennedy, J. L. (2010). Getting to "no" even faster. *Tribology and Lubrication Technology*, 66(10), 84.

Khalsa, M. (1999). *Let's Get Real or Let's Not Play: The Demise of Dysfunctional Selling and the Advent of Helping Clients Succeed*. Salt Lake City, UT: Franklin Covey Company.

Neck, H. M., Greene, P. G., & Brush, C. G. (Eds.) (2014). *Teaching Entrepreneurship: A Practice-Based Approach.* Cheltenham, UK and Northampton, MA, USA: Edward Elgar Publishing.

Pollitt, C. (2006). Academic advice to practitioners: What is its nature, place and value within academia? *Public Money and Management*, 26(4), 257–64.

Rackham, N. (1988). *SPIN Selling.* New York: McGraw-Hill.

Rasmussen, E. A., & Sørheim, R. (2006). Action-based entrepreneurship education. *Technovation*, 26(2), 185–94.

Renzulli, J. S. (1973). Talent potential in minority group students. *Exceptional Children*, 39(6), 437–44.

Roulin, N., & Bangerter, A. (2013). Students' use of extra-curricular activities for positional advantage in competitive job markets. *Journal of Education and Work*, 26(1), 21–47.

Small Business Administration (US) (2009). *Small Business Economy 2008.* Government Printing Office.

Willem, A., & Van den Broeck, H. (2007). Learning mode of small business owners. *Working Paper Faculteit Economie en Bedrijfskunde*.

Wolff, T. (2001). Community coalition building – contemporary practice and research: Introduction. *American Journal of Community Psychology*, 29(2), 165–72.

15. Difference Makers for college readiness

William Reisel and Robert Fanuzzi

INTRODUCTION

"Difference Makers for college readiness" is the signature, home-grown pre-college program of the St. John's University Staten Island campus. Directed by William Reisel, Professor of Management in the Tobin College of Business, the program operates under the Office of the Vice Provost and is guided by Associate Provost and Director of Civic Engagement Robert Fanuzzi as part of the university's network of community partnership programs. Founded in Brooklyn, St. John's University is a Vincentian institution. A robust network of local alumni, student volunteerism, mission-related service, academic service learning (ASL), and clinical and educational partnerships combine to keep St. John's firmly connected to its metropolitan communities and beyond through its global university presence.

Now in its fifth year, Difference Makers scales St. John's University's ASL curricula, administered by faculty with administrative support from the university's Vincentian Institute for Social Action, into a campus-level educational outreach program dedicated to high school students' college readiness. As a reflection and extension of the university's Vincentian mission of service, Difference Makers helps to define and distinguish the St. John's University's Staten Island campus's contribution to borough-wide college-readiness initiatives, which have brought together higher education institutions, the New York City Department of Education, and participating high schools in an effort to raise college completion and graduation rates on Staten Island.

Since its inception in 2016, Difference Makers has introduced high school students to a range of local social issues through ASL projects with not-for-profit partners in areas such as childhood cancer, immigration, HIV orphans in Zambia, anti-violence, childhood school tutoring, and food issues such as food insecurity and healthy snacks. For 2019, Difference Makers partnered with non-governmental organizations delivering services to African children, creating a global network. The program's ASL curricula educates students on social issues while strengthening their ability to scope and complete social enterprise projects in a three-month semester. Embedded in the Academy of Finance programs of participating high schools, Difference Makers teaches high school students pragmatic business strategies for effectuating social change and project management skills that benefit their not-for-profit partners while developing students' ability to plan and deliver research-based recommendations to their not-for-profit partner.

Difference Makers began as an internally-funded program of St. John's University that extended the ASL curricula of the Vincentian Institute for Social Action to a single high school Academy of Finance cohort in an effort to augment and enrich the campus's pre-college programming. Because it delivers measurable college admissions results that indicate high school business students' engagement with the institution's academic standards and mission-related goals, Difference Makers has grown to include three schools and is preparing a next phase of expansion within a network of participating public high schools in New York City.

Here we describe the theoretical research frameworks underpinning the Difference Makers program and identify their connections to entrepreneurship education and pedagogy. These frameworks include experiential service learning, ASL curricular outcomes, and non-cognitive variables of college readiness. Difference Makers employs the experiential learning strategies utilized in ASL projects in order to increase high school students' self-efficacy, confidence, socially responsible leadership, and character building. These measures represent non-cognitive evidence of college readiness, an increasingly important public policy consideration for addressing disparities in college admissions and preparedness (Sedlacek, 2011). We posit the pedagogical goals and outcomes of experiential learning, as applied through academic service learning, offer non-cognitive predictors of college success and can make measurable contributions to higher education's equity and inclusion initiatives.

To the extent that Difference Makers identifies and measures non-cognitive variables of college readiness, the program draws on entrepreneurship education to contribute to those goals. Access to higher education and completion of a degree are unequivocally associated with improved economic outcomes (weekly income) for United States students (Torpay, 2018). We believe entrepreneurship education, as applied through the ASL curricula of the Difference Makers program can generate supplemental measures of underserved students' non-cognitive college readiness and should be considered an important part of higher education's recruitment and preparation of underserved students. In sum, Difference Makers offers a proof of concept, a funded program, theoretical frameworks, and a research model for the next generation of higher education access strategies while directly connecting admissions and recruitment to the institution's mission.

ENTREPRENEURSHIP EDUCATION

The research frameworks employed by Difference Makers represent important linkages to entrepreneurship education. They contribute important benchmarks and outcomes for the measurement of entrepreneurial self-efficacy, an important variable in determining the efficacy of entrepreneurship education in the academy (Al-Awbathani, Malek, & Rahman, 2019). Entrepreneurship learning focuses on opportunity identification and capacity to address new topics and challenges (Politis, 2005). These skills are transferable to future activities to address social entrepreneurship and, presumably, are relevant to addressing challenges in college. Students in Difference Makers are responsible for serving a need identified by a not-for-profit partner. They prepare for this by working in teams, each of which structures into simulated parts of a not-for-profit organization such as marketing, operations, and finance.

EXPERIENTIAL LEARNING THEORY

Difference Makers is guided by several research frameworks and learning theories that are useful in determining the role of entrepreneurship education in the classroom and in society. A theoretical foundation of Difference Makers is experiential learning theory (Dewey, 1938; Kolb & Kolb, 2005). The Kolbs call this the "process whereby knowledge is created through the transformation of experience" (194). Experiential learning involves, at its core, student interactions with the environment that evoke thoughts, feelings, and behaviors. The learning environment is the surrounding community with its own pressing set of endemic social issues such as gang violence, illness, and hunger, which loom large and are outside of students' control. Yet, through participation in the program, students study major social issues and learn leadership skills, which they use to conceptualize solutions to social problems. To bring about these experiences, Difference Makers places the student in the center of the decision-making processes with guidance provided by professors, who serve more as consultants than as instructors. Moreover, the pairing of high school students with professors further prepares student expectations about what it is like to prepare for college. All of this is consistent with entrepreneurship education's recognized need for engaging and experiential learning (Kassean, Vanevenhoven, Liguori, & Winkel, 2015).

ACADEMIC SERVICE LEARNING, RETENTION, AND EQUITY

To facilitate experiential learning, Difference Makers employs academic service learning as its pedagogical and curricular backbone. Difference Makers adopts its definition of ASL from the National Community Service Act of 1990:

> a method (A) under which students or participants learn and develop through active participation in thoughtfully organized service that (i) is conducted in and meets the needs of a community; (ii) is coordinated with an elementary school, secondary school, institution of higher education, or community service program, and with the community; (iii) and helps foster civic responsibility; and (B) that (i) is integrated into and enhances the academic curriculum of the students, or the educational components of the community service program in which the participants are enrolled; (ii) and provides structured time for the students or participants to reflect on the service experience (42 U.S.C. § 12511). (National Community Service Act, 1990)

Difference Makers also adopts the program and learning outcomes model developed for St. John's Vincentian Institute for Social Action for its graduate and undergraduate ASL curriculum. As employed by St. John's University, ASL aligns students' learning experience with the mission of the university, which is to serve the underserved, but creates five benchmark principles to seamlessly connect to the academic curricula and faculty member's course requirements: (1) it is part of a course or program, (2) it targets a community need or problem, (3) it uses a partnership with a not-for-profit, (4) there is no financial reward to students or faculty, (5) a reflection statement is required of students. The reflection statement is also a required culminating aspect of Difference Makers to show what students have learned and, in certain instances, elicit expressions of the student's transformational experience. Kiely (2005, p. 6) summarizes the thinking about reflection as a means "to connect experience with concepts, ideas, and theories and generate new and applicable knowledge in concrete 'real-life situations,'" a pivotal connection to experiential learning theory. As applied through Difference Makers, ASL also follows the pathways of experiential learning theory in that students are given concrete challenges. They generate both specific solutions and broader reflections on how their learning experience relates to institutional goals and social needs. The reflection statements are a required culminating aspect of ASL. Students report profound feelings of accomplishment through participation in the program.

ASL is associated with many positive student success outcomes, including student engagement and retention (Gallini and Moely, 2003). Difference Makers adopts ASL and the research findings of its contribution to these two critical areas in order to create a predictive model of college readiness for high school students. Asti, Vogelgesang, Ikeda, & Yee (2000) conducted a longitudinal study of ASL and found multiple positive outcomes: "academic performance (GPA, writing skills, critical thinking skills), values (commitment to activism and to promoting racial understanding), self-efficacy, leadership (leadership activities, self-rated leadership ability, interpersonal skills), choice of a service career, and plans to participate in service after college." In a further large-scale study of socially responsible leadership capacity of college-aged students, Dugan and Komives (2010) suggested that community service develops student leadership capacity and peer discussions about social issues. Importantly, they found that the relationships between students and faculty as mentors is supportive of socially responsible leadership capacity. This suggests that the mentoring by college professors of high school students can also facilitate socially responsible leadership. ASL makes a strong contribution to college students' retention by facilitating high rates of peer-to-peer contact as well as quality engagement with their college professor.

In doing so, ASL promotes students' social integration, which is "achieved when students have developed some friendships with other students, have had positive and personal contact with teachers and staff members, perceive the university as concerned with their growth and development as students, and are committed to the institution." As recounted by Yob, social integration is "about fit with the groups the student cares about, both inside and outside the university" (2000, p. 41). Using Tinto's model of college students' retention, Yob recounts research finding that an individual "will persist in college if he is engaged and actively participates as a student, as a friend, and as a citizen of the larger community" (p. 41). As reported by Yob,

> students who took a service-learning class had higher four-year and five-year graduation rates, even when controlling some of the other factors that could have an influence such as gender and ethnicity; although, a student's preparation for college had a stronger influence than participation in service-learning (2009). The more immediate impact of the service-learning course taken during the first year increased the odds of returning for the second year by 1.474, regardless of SAT and high school GPA scores (2009, p. 4). (Yob, 2014, p. 48)

Difference Makers uses the ASL model and its research underpinning to create a comparably high level of student–faculty engagement for high school students. Since our program outcomes, we propose that the findings, which indicate a strong correlation between students' ASL participation, academic performance, and retention in college, are also are evidence of high school students' college readiness. Indeed, we believe that ASL can operate as a predictive model for high school students' college readiness precisely because of its demonstrated impact on entering college students' adaptation to college life. ASL helps

> explain why some [college] students integrate academically and socially while others do not. The model describes psychological attributes that contribute to academic performance and social integration: self-efficacy; coping strategies; and locus of control (i.e., attribution). Specifically, students make efforts toward degree completion if they believe that they are capable, can cope with problems using approaching rather than avoiding methods, and see themselves in control of their successes and failures... In addition, consistent with the premises of retention theories, academic goals, institutional commitment, social involvement, and social support also have been found to be positively related with student retention and GPA. This suggests that involvement in college and the growth in psychological attributes both contribute to students' educational success. (Song, Furco, Lopez, & Maruyama, 2017)

To the extent that the ASL program of Difference Makers makes a positive and documented impact on these psychological attributes among participating high school students, we believe that the research findings that articulate a positive correlation between ASL participation and retention among college students can also be used to predict a high rate of high school students' college readiness.

This correlation is especially promising for predicting and programmatically establishing effective pre-college and college-readiness interventions among high school students belonging to underrepresented groups. Data from the New York City Department of Education shows that high school graduation rates are extremely variable, depending on demographics and location; graduation rates at our participating high schools range from 79 to 92 percent (NYC DOE, 2019). Table 15.1 provides a profile of the three high school demographics and college readiness.

Table 15.1   *Sample high school demographics and college readiness*

	Curtis High School	**Susan Wagner High School**	**Tottenville High School**
Graduation rate	79	89	92
College enrollment	65	76	74
Asian	7	15	5
African American	36	10	2
Hispanic/Latin	41	27	12
White	13	46	80

Note: All figures are percentages based on New York City Department of Education data.

As delivered through Difference Makers, ASL addresses inequity in college readiness, as many of the students in the program are attending public high schools that come from underserved communities and rarely interact with college professors to perform a full-semester ASL project (St. John's University, 2018). Research indicates that ASL can equalize disparities in college readiness as measured by incoming students' SAT scores. As Yob (2014) reports, "The more immediate impact of the service-learning course taken during the first year increased the odds of returning for the second year by 1.474, regardless of SAT and high school GPA scores" (p. 48). Disparities in SAT scores have been linked to disparities in level of SAT test preparation, which are often parallel with income disparities. We find that when ASL is reserved for enrolled and tuition-paying college students, it deprives under-represented high school students of a learning model statistically and strongly associated with academic attainment among their cohort. Song and Furco conclude that ASL

> may have the greatest potential for promoting underrepresented students' educa-
> tional success insofar as it offers them opportunities to connect with diverse commu-
> nities and address societal issues that matter to them... [Academic] service-learning,
> which engages students in actions that link their college life to community issues
> through course-based community-based learning experiences, has the potential of
> mitigating feelings of uncertainty and disconnection that underrepresented students
> often feel when entering college. (Song and Furco, 2017)

Ranghout and Gordon hypothesize that ASL can predict underrepresented students' academic success to the extent that it enables them to see beyond statistical measures of their efficacy and reorient the goals of formal learning to better approximate the community and human values found among members of their cohort. They identify the ability to develop social insights into their own educational experience and institution as an important "border knowledge" that will enable students from underrepresented groups to better navigate the demands of predominantly white institutions of higher education and incorporate knowledges and abilities they do not incorporate or recognize (p. 9).

NON-COGNITIVE VARIABLES OF COLLEGE ADMISSION

Difference Makers also adopts the theoretical framework of "non-cognitive variables" from studies of predictive admission criteria of underrepresented college students' success. In doing so, we discuss new models of college readiness and admission policies. Sedlacek (2005) describes non-cognitive variables as "relating to adjustment, motivation, and student perceptions, rather than the traditional verbal and quantitative." While non-cognitive variables are useful for all students, they provide frameworks for fairly assessing the abilities of people of color, women, international students, older students, students with disabilities, or others with experiences that are different from those of young, white, heterosexual, able-bodied, Eurocentric males in the United States (traditional students). Sedlacek's eight non-cognitive variables lay out an alternative framework for student evaluation: positive self-concept, realistic self-appraisal, navigation of the system, building and pursuing long-range goals, reliance on a strong support person, leadership, community, and acquisition of non-traditional knowledge (Sedlacek 2011).

Research into the impact of non-cognitive variables on college admissions and success emerges from studies of minority students' college completion in historically black colleges and universities and predominantly white institutions (PWI). Nasim writes, "While traditional merit-based approaches have not entirely failed, they have tended to dismiss the unique contextual and institutional barriers that many ethnic minorities must negotiate in order to compete and be academically successful" (p. 344). Among the most important of Sedlacek's variables, according to Nasim, Roberts, Harrell and Young, is

> the ability to establish community ties, which refers to participation in community service and extracurricular activities; a desire to interact with others within the campus community; and feeling comfortable and accepted within one's environment (Sedlacek, 2011). Participation in community service is significantly related to academic success for African American students (Fleming, 1984). Young and Sowa (1992) cite that establishment of a sense of belonging to the community as demonstrated through involvement in community service is a moderate predictor of college GPA for African American student-athletes in their second year at a PWI. This suggests that establishment of a sense of belonging within the university setting is an important factor to consider when examining the achievement and retention of African American students at PWIs. (Nasim et al., 2005, p. 347)

The ethnic and class diversity of high school students participating in Difference Makers guide our adoption of non-cognitive variables as a research model and theoretical framework for the program. We are cognizant of disparities in awareness of and access to SAT preparation among high school students but are inspired by the wide support and facility for community service among college-bound high school students, regardless of their race and income. Difference Makers brings diverse students a service-based program that allows them to develop high levels of confidence and accomplishment, as measured by their reflection essays, excerpts from which appear later in this chapter, and their rate of acceptance to St. John's University.

PROGRAM DESCRIPTION

Difference Makers operates as a place-based civic engagement program that aligns private higher education, the New York City Department of Education, participating high school administrations, local foundations, and New York State educational policies, helping to engage the many actors in the entrepreneurship ecosystem. High school students, high school administrators, university faculty members and leadership, city and state educational leaders, and local non-profit representatives work closely and collaboratively across sectors.

Difference Makers gives the participants in this institutional framework a common civic purpose: helping underserved and underrepresented students prepare for college. College readiness has become a top priority of the Office of the Mayor of the City of New York, the New York City Department of Education, and the local high school principals. Staten Island's three higher education institutions, St. John's, the College of Staten Island/City University of New York, and Wagner College launched 30,000 Degrees: College Readiness for a Stronger Staten Island with four local high schools to align and leverage participants' college-readiness programs. College readiness is also a priority of local private foundations, such as the Staten Island Foundation, which has a clear mission to support student success, particularly underserved students (e.g., Staten Island Foundation, 2019). St. John's has longstanding internally and externally funded college-readiness programs, such as the dual-credit College Advantage program and Special Opportunity programs, in addition to Difference Makers (St. John's University, 2019).

Difference Makers capitalizes on St. John's University's commitment to ASL, adding two aspects that are generally not used at the college level but central to entrepreneurship education: (1) high school students, working in teams, build a simulated social enterprise that partners with an actual community-based not-for-profit organization (Light, 2006); and (2) students conduct fundraisers to support their community partners. The design of a social enterprise by the student teams involves dividing the organization's functions into marketing (e.g., social media), operations (what they do to deliver service), and finance (how they will conduct their fundraiser to support their not-for-profit partners). The fundraisers that the students lead largely take place at school. To date, the students have sold approved snack bags or other items for about one dollar each. Usually the profits are about 50 cents per item sold. Some students perform their own fundraisers outside of school. In 2019, the students raised funds selling "Difference Makers" imprinted bracelets and raised $1,760, which was evenly divided and donated to five community partners at our January completion ceremony.

High school student recruiting for the program takes place in the spring and ends in September. The program launches with an orientation meeting on the Staten Island campus of St. John's at the beginning of October. Schools transport their students to campus to meet with faculty, administrators, and to hear from participating community partners. The on-campus orientation is a key part of the participants' college readiness, as it familiarizes them with a college campus and allows them to visualize themselves as a first-year student. Starting in 2019, students came to St. John's Staten Island campus three times, providing a local university touchpoint during their college search.

After the orientation, St. John's University faculty members teaching in the Difference Makers program visit the high schools once per week for 90 minutes at each school usually starting in early October and concluding at the end of January. Students are required to log 15 hours during the fall meetings and 15 hours outside of meetings when they work on fundraising. During the first meetings in October, community partners come to the schools to talk about their organizations and task students with projects that raise their awareness. For example, members of True 2 Life, an anti-gang violence program funded by Staten Island's Central Family Life Center, met with Difference Makers students, teaching them about community violence and violence interruption programs, such as Chicago's Cure Violence (Cure Violence, 2020). In one high school visit, True 2 Life leaders, many of whom are former gang members, victims of violence, and therefore "credible messengers," marked 1,000 violence-free days in their Staten Island community, rallying the students to their anti-violence cause. Difference Makers students heard about the dangers of community violence from anti-violence program leaders and created an Instagram social media campaign (2020) to reach Staten Island youth with anti-gang messages.

Once representatives of Difference Makers' community partners have visited the high schools, the students select their project and form groups to study the issue through online research and build their simulated social enterprise. The program syllabus makes all Difference Makers learning activities and resources accessible through digital platforms, allowing students to take control of the project and divide their enterprise into marketing, operations, and finance. Students divide the labor among the departments and appoint leaders of each area to study the project requirements. By the end of December, all groups prepare presentations which they deliver at the annual certificate ceremony and dinner held at St. John's in late January.

Participating university faculty in Difference Makers have prior ASL experience and certification, in addition to subject matter expertise. Both the authors of this chapter are recipients of St. John's presidential Academic Service-Learning Award, given to one university faculty per year. Critical to the pedagogy is the culminating reflection statement, which is the fifth and final requirement of an ASL project. Students typically enter the program with transactional goals, such as fulfilling community service hours required for graduation. They enroll in Difference Makers as a means to that end but by the time the program concludes, their reflection statements show that they feel transformed by the experience of helping others in need, particularly because many of the students are also from underserved backgrounds.

Difference Makers sets up GoFundMe pages (2020) for the students' social enterprises. They sell approved items such as bracelets and snacks to raise funds for their community partners. Since 2016, Difference Makers students have raised $7,677, with 100 percent of the funds delivered to their community partners. The funds are given to leaders of the not-for-profit organization at the culminating Certificate Ceremony when all student participants are honored in front of their guardians, teachers, principals, Difference Makers sponsors, and St. John's University leadership.

A great amount of expense and effort goes into celebrating the accomplishments of the students at the annual Completion Ceremony. St. John's hosts the event in January in its largest facility on the Staten Island campus, providing students, teachers, and their parents and guardians a buffet dinner and academic ceremony led by St. John's University academic leaders. Central to the evening is the awarding of the certificates of completion and the student ASL project presentations. Since 2016, 762 students have received certificates. In 2020, the program also distributed 10-Star medals showing the torch of knowledge and a dedication for distinguished service. Parents, teachers, and principals all attend and are served a buffet dinner. Community partner representatives and high school students offer testimonials of the value of their enterprise.

Difference Makers evolves by adding new features each year. In 2018, social media accounts on Instagram and YouTube were established to support Difference Makers and provide reference points for progress, including photos and videos of meetings with community partners. Difference Makers' social media accounts build a sense of community among students from different high schools and dedicates them to their social enterprise.

CURRENT OUTCOMES

The central goal of Difference Makers is to develop students' college readiness. College counselors in participating high schools view Difference Makers as an important contributor. One high school counselor stated, "The Difference Makers Program has provided my students with a valuable service-learning experience that not only enhances their college applications and resumes, but also helps them understand the impact that a few people can have on many." Principals of the high schools also speak of the value of the program. David

Cugini, principal of Susan Wagner High School, stated, "Difference Makers speaks to a core value that I have as an educator which is service learning… This program allows our children to understand their capacity to be an agent of change, to show how much they are needed."

A meta-analysis of 382 ASL studies shows that participation in ASL is highly predictive on socially responsive knowledge, self-efficacy and self-esteem, compassion, and political participation (Conway, Amel, & Gerwien, 2009). Figure 15.1 adopts this model to articulate outcomes.

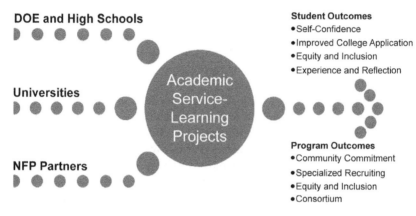

Figure 15.1   Difference Maker outcomes

Difference Makers invites participants to attend college open houses, including St. John's University's Staten Island campus, and apply to St. John's. An analysis of the acceptance rate to St. John's provided by the Office of Admissions showed that for fall 2020, Difference Makers student participants enjoyed a 76 percent acceptance rate. University leadership welcomes Difference Makers student participants' applications because they are already aligned with the Vincentian mission of the university to serve the underserved. St. John's President Conrado Gempesaw commented, "I am pleased to know that an increasing number of students participating in the program are now applying to St. John's. Your support from the High School principals will also help in the recruitment of their overall student body."

Public and private grantors recognize that Difference Makers is filling a gap in students' college readiness and have funded the program in successive years. The New York State Department of Education has supported Difference Makers through its End of School Day grant for the past three years. Three local private foundations – The Staten Island Foundation, Richmond County Savings Foundation, and Northfield Bank Foundation – support the program, with additional support coming from Consolidated Edison and National Grid. Internal funding comes from St. John's University's Provost's Office, Office of Admissions, and the Vincentian Institute for Social Action. Difference Makers has reached a point of sustainability.

All supporters of Difference Makers receive an annual report that records the number of student participants, the number of projects, and the number of community partners. It includes testimonials from participating students as well as from leaders of community-based organizations.

Difference Makers has also gained visibility and support from colleagues at conferences. Reisel has presented the program at meetings of St. John's Vincentian Institute for Church and Society and at the annual meeting of the United States Association of Small Business and Entrepreneurship, where he was a finalist for Excellence in Pedagogical Innovation. Reisel and Fanuzzi presented the program to participants at the annual meeting of the Coalition of Urban and Metropolitan Universities in 2017.

In 2019, St. John's University's Vincentian Institute for Social Action awarded the authors a Faculty Research Consortium grant to develop, determine, and deliver a quantitative measurement of college readiness outcomes among Difference Makers participants. For this research, we adopt the theoretical frameworks of ASL, non-cognitive variables of college admission, and entrepreneurship education for the creation of survey instruments, which will be delivered to students, parents, and high school counsellors. Our research design includes eight hypotheses: (1) participants in the Difference Makers program will be positively correlated with perceived college readiness, social and personal efficacy, and positive citizenship attitudes; (2) participants in the Difference Makers will have lower absentee records than their grade-level absenteeism; (3) participants will rate contact hours with college professors as positively related to their college readiness; (4) school guidance counselors will rate student participation in Difference Makers as contributing to improved college readiness; (5) school employees (guidance counselors and/ or teachers) will rate student participation in Difference Makers as a factor that strengthens the participant's college application profile; (6) participant reflections will be strongly associated with positive attitudes towards community service, social skills, and self-efficacy; (7) participation in Difference Makers is strongly related to participants' beliefs about their future increased likelihood of volunteering and contributing to their community; and (8) participation in Difference Makers through trips to college campuses is correlated with a better understanding of what is required to succeed at college. With this empirical research, Difference Makers can offer predictive analysis of college success by linking improved outcomes of college applications to improved learning outcomes for college students engaged in ASL.

FUTURE DIRECTIONS FOR THE PROGRAM CURRICULUM

Each year, Difference Makers strives to enhance the students' experiences in ways that are consistent with the goals of entrepreneurship education and experiential learning. Because of support for student-led research, we intend to scale the research component of the Different Makers curriculum into quantitative research reports that can be included and published in a Difference Makers Annual Report to students' administrators and teachers. In addition, we are preparing an article that includes Difference Makers student participant research for St. John's ASL journal, *Journal of Vincentian Social Action.*

Furthermore, Difference Makers can help high school teachers and administrators affiliate their students with the learning community and New York City Career and Technical Education programs within their schools in order to facilitate college readiness. To accomplish this, we are expanding the "tracks" of Difference Makers from its current home within the Academy of Finance and business education learning communities of participating high schools to include learning communities that prepare students for careers in education and environmental studies. With teacher recruitment among students from underserved communities a priority for the New York City Department of Education, we believe that Difference Makers can offer an ASL curriculum that prepares students for the rewards of teaching careers and provides them with experiential learning opportunities suitable for strong college applications.

SCALING DIFFERENCE MAKERS FROM SCHOOLS TO UNIVERSITIES

We consider two models for scaling the current business model of Difference Makers: "deeper" and "wider." A deeper approach is to open multiple citywide cohorts of Difference Makers within a single school. Currently, Difference Makers reaches about 75–100 students out of 10,000 students attending the three high schools. Each school has a cohort of approximately 30 students. By expanding Difference Makers to additional learning communities and to more sections of our current learning communities, we can increase the number of cohorts within a single school. This "deeper" engagement within each school utilizes the program's record of accomplishment and internal support from within the school, including student and parent support organizations. As Difference Makers becomes "school-wide," high school college counselors can encourage students to include participation in Difference Makers on the "additional information" section of the college common application and to highlight the program to college admissions officers with whom they liaise.

A "wider" expansion model allows Difference Makers to keep its current social enterprise model and expand it to more schools at the other four boroughs of New York City. This is consistent with the funding model of Difference Makers, which is largely supported by New York State grants that are distributed to local school districts, principally what are known as community schools. Difference Makers is a service provider under this fiscal program. With empirical evidence of high school participants' college readiness, New York City Department of Education leaders can adopt the program by district, bringing it to multiple schools, and potentially to city-wide post-secondary readiness or equity and inclusion offices. Under an accelerated horizontal growth strategy, the program can scale from 3 to 15 high schools and serve roughly 500 students up from 75–100. Such a growth goal over the course of two years will require the Difference Makers to add an administrative layer and a training component to ramp up skills for new professors as well as greater fundraising capacity to support the larger cost structure of the program.

A third model for the growth of Difference Makers expands the program from St. John's University to other institutions. Although St. John's Office of Advancement has allocated time and effort, the cost burden of Difference Makers has never been carried by the institution. Our current business model is a social enterprise in that we seek external funding and develop new campaigns among alumni and other local stakeholders to make the program self-funded. To the extent that it reaches that goal, Difference Makers offers a positive return on investment for the institution, considering that a single student can have a substantial impact in terms of net tuition revenue over an estimated four years of attendance. As we develop and prove the business case for Difference Makers to our institution, we create a replicable model for quality admissions recruiting that includes not only the non-cognitive variables so important to evaluating college applications from diverse applicants but an ASL curriculum with proven impact on college student retention.

CONCLUSION

Difference Makers has helped underserved high school students in New York City to improve their college readiness via participation in ASL led by college professors. The program, which launched in 2016, has attracted funding and support from grantors in private, public, and corporate sectors and in-kind support from St. John's University. A major goal of the program is the introduction of non-cognitive outcomes for consideration by college admissions officers. Our anecdotal evidence is supportive of the program goal and Institutional Review Board-approved research is under way to validate the program's contribution to high school student college readiness. Moreover, Difference Makers is consistent with the literature's call for more research into underrepresented domains and populations (Liguori, Corbin, Lackeus, & Solomon, 2019).

Difference Makers attributes its research in improved learning outcomes and college readiness of underserved high school students to the theoretical frameworks for entrepreneurship education. We believe that experiential learning theory, linked to the pedagogical frameworks of ASL, helps to explain the success of entrepreneurship education in this context. Difference Makers promotes entrepreneurial self-efficacy, a crucial outcome of entrepreneurship education and an important cross-referent with the non-cognitive variables that are changing the college recruitment metrics across the country. Difference Makers demonstrates that entrepreneurship education can contribute to the increasingly productive debate over college readiness and the responsibility of higher education to goals of diversity, equity, and inclusion.

REFERENCES

Al-Awbathani, R., Malek, M. M., & Rahman, S. A. (2019). The role of informal institutions in moderating the relationships between entrepreneurial self-efficacy, entrepreneurial outcome expectations, and entrepreneurial career choice: A conceptual perspective. *Journal of Entrepreneurship Education, 22*, 1–7.

Asti, A. W., Vogelgesang, L. J., Ikeda, E. K., & Yee, J. A. (2000). How service learning affects students. *Higher Education, 144*. Retrieved from: http://digitalcommons .unomaha.edu/slcehighered/144

Conway, J. M., Amel, E. L., & Gerwien, D. P. (2009). Teaching and learning in the social context: A meta-analysis of service learning's effects on academic, personal, social, and citizenship outcomes. *Teaching of Psychology*, 36: 233–45.

Cure Violence (2020). Retrieved from: https://youth.gov/content/cure-violence-chicago -illinois

Dewey, J. (1938). *Education and Experience*. New York: Simon and Schuster.

Dugan, J. P., & Komives, S. R. (2010). Influences on college students' capacities for socially responsible leadership. *Journal of College Student Development, 51*, 525–49.

Gallini, S. M., & Moely, B. E. (2003). Service-learning and engagement, academic challenge, and retention. *Michigan Journal of Community Service Learning*, Fall, 5–14.

GoFundMe (2020). Retrieved from: www.gofundme.com/f/difference-makers-of -staten-island

Helms, J. E. (2009). Defense of tests prevents objective considerations of validity and fairness. *American Psychologist, 64*, 283–4.

Instagram (2020). Retrieved from: www.instagram.com/statenisland_differencemakers/

Kassean, H., Vanevenhoven, J., Liguori, E. W., & Winkel, D. E. (2015). Entrepreneurship education: A need for reflection, real-world experience and action. *International Journal of Entrepreneurial Behavior and Research, 21*(5), 690–708.

Kiely, R. (2005). A transformative learning model for service-learning: A longitudinal case study. *Michigan Journal of Community Service Learning*, 5–22.

Kolb, A. Y., & Kolb, D. A. (2005). Learning styles and learning spaces: Enhancing experiential learning in higher education. *Academy of Management Learning and Education, 4*(2), 193–212.

Langhout, R. D., & Gordon, D. L. (2019). Outcomes for underrepresented and misrepresented college students in service-learning classes: Supporting agents of change. *Journal of Diversity in Higher Education,* http://dx.doi.org.jerome.stjohns.edu:81/10.1037/dhe0000151.

Light, P. C. (2006). Reshaping social entrepreneurship. *Stanford Social Innovation Review*. Retrieved from www.ssir.org

Liguori, E. W., Corbin, R., Lackeus, M., & Solomon, S. J. (2019). Under-researched domains in entrepreneurship and enterprise education: Primary school, community colleges and vocational education and training programs. *Journal of Small Business and Enterprise Development, 26*(2), 182–9.

Nasim, A., Roberts, A., Harrell, J. P., & Young, H. (2005). Non-cognitive predictors of academic achievement for African Americans across cultural contexts. *Journal of Negro Education, 74*(4), 344–58. Retrieved from https://jerome.stjohns.edu/login?url=https://search-proquest-com.jerome.stjohns.edu/docview/222066198?accountid=14068

National Community Service Act of 1990, Pub. L. No. 101-610, 104 Stat. 3127 (Nov. 16, 1990).

NYC DOE (2019). 2018–19 school quality guide – online edition. Retrieved from: https://tools.nycenet.edu/guide/2019/?utm_source=InfoHub&utm_medium=Public_Page&utm_campaign=SQR_InfoHub_Page

Politis, D. (2005). The process of entrepreneurial learning: A conceptual framework. *Entrepreneurship Theory and Practice, 29*, 399–424.

Sedlacek, W. E. (2005). The case for non-cognitive measures. In W. Camara and E. Kimmel (eds.), *Choosing students: Higher education admissions tools for the 21st century* (pp. 177–93). Mahwah, NJ: Lawrence Erlbaum Associations.

Sedlacek, W. E. (2011). Using noncognitive variables in assessing readiness for higher education. *Readings on Equal Education, 25*, 187–205.

Song, W., Furco, A., Lopez, I., & Maruyama, G. (2017). Examining the relationship between service-learning participation and the educational success of underrepresented students. *Michigan Journal of Community Service Learning, 24*(1), 23–37. Retrieved from https://jerome.stjohns.edu/login?url=https://search-proquest-com.jerome.stjohns.edu/docview/2013522312?accountid=14068

St. John's University (2018). Tobin professor receives prestigious award for academic service-learning work. Retrieved from: www.stjohns.edu/about/news/2018-09-06/tobin-professor-receives-prestigious-award-academic-service-learning-work

St. John's University (2019). College advantage program. Retrieved from: www.stjohns.edu/admission/other-programs/college-advantage-program

Staten Island Foundation (2019). Mission. Retrieved from: http://thestatenislandfoundation.org/about-us/

Torpay, E. (2018). Measuring the value of education, Bureau of Labor Statistics. Retrieved from: www.bls.gov/careeroutlook/2018/data-on-display/education-pays.htm

Yob, I. M. (2014). Keeping students in by sending them out: Retention and service-learning. *Higher Learning Research Communications, 4*(2), 38–57. Retrieved from https://jerome.stjohns.edu/login?url=https://search-proquest-com.jerome.stjohns.edu/docview/1545527714?accountid=14068

16. The art of teaching arts entrepreneurship

Caroline Vanevenhoven and Jeff Vanevenhoven

INTRODUCTION

There is a small, but slowly growing body of literature focusing on arts entrepreneurship and an even smaller compilation that pursues the pedagogical approaches to teaching arts and creative industries students the skills they need for self-sustainability and success (Gangi, 2017; Pollard & Wilson, 2014; White, 2017). Arts education scholars acknowledge that – given arts professionals can be as much as three to five times more likely to be self-employed or freelance – entrepreneurship skills are necessary (Bridgestock, 2012; Friedrichs, 2017). However, within literature, there is a lack of consensus on the most effective teaching tools and what arts entrepreneurship curricula look like (Arizona State University PAVE Program, 2016; Beckman, 2007; Gangi, 2017). This chapter examines recent studies on entrepreneurship education from a traditional "college of business" point of view as well as those from an arts point of view. Using the five themes proposed to develop an arts-focused entrepreneurship mindset by Pollard and Wilson (2014), this chapter discusses mindset development goals from both a business and an arts perspective while exploring the nexus between them.

PARALLELS AND GAPS

When surveying the literature on business entrepreneurship education (BEE) and arts entrepreneurship education (AEE), noticeable parallels exist with regard to the overall skill-specific needs for entrepreneurship education into arts programs. However, previous research has noted a gap that exists between the two disciplines (Chang & Wyszomirski, 2015). Exploration of co-disciplinary literature could help administrators and educators to better understand how best to teach AEE skills. One possible explanation for such a gap – beyond the inherent differences between disciplines – could be the resulting difference in the common goals of entrepreneurs and those of artists/ creative industries professionals. The fact is that, by and large, entrepreneurs actualize their visions for the purpose of generating revenue and successful companies while artists may choose to actualize their visions to make a living from their artistic passions and talents (Bridgestock, 2012). As these two sets of goals can be quite different, AEE cannot always directly translate from a traditional entrepreneurship class or course. Arguably, the list of potential entrepreneurship competencies and skill developments beneficial to arts and creative industries students is sizable. This chapter presents a framework of startup behaviors and competencies to guide arts and arts entrepreneurship educators. This framework can then strengthen the curriculum and peda- gogy of unique skills for arts students and empower them to choose to be self-sustaining and/or self-employed.

Connecting entrepreneurship teaching methods from business and translat- ing them to artistic entrepreneurship methods like Gangi (2017) explores is just one important step towards a centralized conceptualization of AEE (Gangi, 2017) and BEE (Vanevenhoven & Liguori, 2013). Increasingly, people are accepting that arts non-profits and arts organizations have significant influence on the economic health of communities. Art and culture are important on an individual, community, national, and global level for revitalizing both urban and rural communities (Duxbury, Campbell, & Keurvorst, 2011); strength- ening local economies (Bryan, Hill, Munday, & Roberts, 2000); creating appealing places to work and live (Sterngold, 2004); and acting as a space for individual growth and expression (Holden, 2009). Additionally, research has shown that exposure to art and music can positively impact both the academic and social success of children (Kisida, Bowen, & Greene, 2018) In redefining what culture looks like today, specifically with regard to the development of the internet, Holden (2009) puts art and culture into three intertwined categories and describes the result "as a networked activity, where funded, homemade, and commercial culture are deeply interconnected" (Holden, 2009, p. 451). Training artists and culture keepers how to be self-sufficient and sustainable is then key to ensuring the continual development and preservation of art. In fact, as arts graduates interviewed by Arizona State University's PAVE Program in the Arts responded when they asked, "What do you wish you had learned?" (2016), the majority reported marketing, communication, networking, and entrepreneurship skills. In a small study of participants from North Carolina attending the 5th Annual Southern Entrepreneurship in the Arts conference, 36 percent of respondents reported lack of startup or other managerial skills had hindered their artistic career in one way or another (Welsh, Onishi, DeHoog, & Syed, 2014). Further conclusions from the aforementioned study also rec- ommended that arts entrepreneurship should be approached holistically, and include learning opportunities in both venture creation and entrepreneurship mindset particularly when "Many artists have already established their businesses when they realize they need entrepreneurial business skills beyond starting the business and creating a feasibility and business plan" (p. 22). To this end, coming to a resolution on which entrepreneurship skills are key and how to teach them to arts students will competitively strengthen fine arts curriculum. The goal would then be to help lessen the challenges arts graduates face as they strive for employability and success in their chosen career paths.

As mentioned, gaps exist in the knowledge of AEE best practices and established research in the best methods to teach the skills necessary for artists to make a living as practicing artists. The learning paths of arts students are often unique and individualized just as the genres of arts themselves, thereby also necessitating individualistic entrepreneurship learning. One important gap to explore is defining arts entrepreneurship and identifying learning methods. It is difficult to imagine, however, what AEE is when BEE scholars point out they themselves need to have a firmer sense of the definition and context of entrepreneurship education and pedagogy (Gangi, 2017; Kassean, Vanevenhoven, Liguori, & Winkel, 2015; Liguori et al., 2018; Matthews, 2018; Neck & Corbett, 2018; Solomon & Matthews, 2014; Vanevenhoven, 2013). More investigation into the thoughts of entrepreneurship scholars and educators focusing on what they are teaching in their classrooms and the methods they are using could be useful information for fine arts scholars and educators wanting to incorporate entrepreneurship in their curricula. If fine arts programs in colleges and universities feel they have tools they can use and methods they can employ, then logically more of them can adopt AEE curricula. While arts programs enhanced with entrepreneurship skills will certainly benefit the colleges and universities on a broad level, the students becoming professionals in those programs will be most rewarded by having obtained a more complete education in how to make a living as an artist. There are endless famous quotes regarding the innate *goodness* of art, and it can be argued that when art succeeds everyone benefits.

Current business entrepreneurship literature is enthusiastically exploring methods, definitions, and paradigms. As the scholarly field, entrepreneurship is relatively new by comparison to disciplines such as finance or management; there is debate over how best to define and teach entrepreneurship skills. Topics and books such as experiential learning, Business Model Canvas (Osterwalder, 2008), Lean Startup (Ries, 2011), bootcamps, and startup weekends are generating excitement and at times heated debate. In a recent *Annals of Entrepreneurship Education and Pedagogy*, Matthews (2018) charges his colleagues with what he believes are five key explorations. First, scholars must define the lexicon of entrepreneurship. What words should be used, how should they be defined, and how should they be used in the context of entrepreneurship? Second, end the misuse of the word "entrepreneurial" to mean creative or innovative. True entrepreneurship goes beyond a creative idea just as a work of art is not merely a vision in the artist's mind, but a true manifestation of that idea brought to life. Third, find new benchmarks for measuring student success. Not starting a new venture does not equate to failure. Fourth, "Integrate research more closely with entrepreneurship education" (Matthews, 2018, p. xxi). This suggests reflectively integrating theory, research, and practice into the entrepreneurship curriculum. Perhaps most surprising is the fifth and final charge to ban the word *entrepreneurial* temporarily until there can be more of a consensus on what exactly that means (Matthews, 2018).

REACHING BEYOND THE TRADITIONAL

Other scholars are reaching into fields such as neuroscience (Krueger & Welpe, 2014); Jungian and Whole Brain Theory (Thomas, McDonagh, & Canning, 2014); self-efficacy (Shekar, Huang-Saad, & Libarkin, 2018); entrepreneurship mindset (Pollard & Wilson, 2014); and expanding on Sarasvathy's (2001) Effectual Theory (Gangi, 2017). Effectual entrepreneurs "engage in creative processes based on: a.) who they are; b.) what they know; and c.) who they know" (Read, Sarasvathy, Dew, Wiltbank, & Ohlsson, 2011, p. 4). While all the action and attention entrepreneurship is receiving is producing great dialogue, innovative teaching methods, and new connections with other social sciences, substantial work in tested theories about entrepreneurship education derived from entrepreneurship theories appear to be missing from the literature. Using Gartner's (1990) Delphi panel method, Neck and Corbett (2018) interviewed 17 respected entrepreneurship educators. The authors questioned whether there is or should be a difference between andragogy and pedagogy in the paradigm of entrepreneurship education. Their findings led them to suggest looking at Boyer's (1990) lens of scholarship of teaching and learning in order to build entrepreneurship education and building theory (Neck & Corbett, 2018).

A particularly current theme is that of experiential learning and game play. "Experiential learning… centers on the idea that students can learn entrepreneurship theories, principles, and concepts by applying themselves to projects and activities rooted in real-world practice" (Schindehutte & Morris, 2016, p. 161). The main argument being that students cannot passively learn entrepreneurship skills from reading case studies and listening to lectures. If educators expect students to start ventures they need to go out and actually start them, fail, and learn to reflect on and pivot from failure. The authors go on to state that if the student is more engaged, the experience will be richer and more meaningful. The crucial part of engagement is maintaining a balance between what knowledge and skillset a student possesses and how much the student is challenged in learning new skills. Think of it like a Goldilocks principle: challenge cannot be too little, or too much, it needs to be *just* right to create "high engagement and an energized focus, where emotions are positive and aligned with the task at hand" (p. 163).

WHAT IS CURRENT LITERATURE SAYING ABOUT ARTS ENTREPRENEURSHIP?

It is little wonder that if business entrepreneurship scholars have difficulty in finding consensus in their discipline, arts and creative industries educators are struggling to incorporate entrepreneurship into their curricula. "As new as entrepreneurship is to business schools, '*arts* entrepreneurship' is a much newer academic discipline, and one even less clearly defined" (Essig, 2009, p. 117). In a literature review seeking definitions of art entrepreneurship, Gangi finds the answers vary. Art entrepreneurship is defined as a process of management, a tool for social value creation, synergistic actions that result in sustainable art, and methods of training arts and creative industries students to be self-sufficient in order to build social as well as economical value within communities (Gangi, 2017). Interestingly, of the literature reviewed by Gangi, the oldest dated back only eight years suggesting the field is only just emerging. However new the field, there are scholars who have keen focus on what they believe should be the goals of AEE. One such is Ben Toscher, whose work introduces his conceptual framework for teaching entrepreneurship skills to music students. He examined the relevance of entrepreneurship education to musicians, explored "artistic and entrepreneurship career identities, social cognitive career theory, and arts entrepreneurship education to suggest some of the contextual and cognitive barriers music students may face" (Toscher, 2019, p. 4). Toscher goes on to evaluate the entrepreneurship competencies and types of learning in order to then present his framework of specific learning activities and the concepts they teach music students.

SIMILARITIES BETWEEN TWO DISCIPLINES

Bridgestock states that fine arts and creative industries professionals are three to five times more likely to be self-employed or working short-term and freelance jobs (Bridgestock, 2012). Three skill categories, and specific skills within those categories, that are essential for higher education arts programs to incorporate into their curricula are outlined. The author goes on to propose a three-year plan of study that would incorporate the aforementioned skill categories, drawing on Beckman's (2007) view that "arts entrepreneurship programs should ideally be built upon a foundational shift in thinking from 'money ruins art' to 'money enables art'" (as quoted in Bridgestock, 2012, p. 127). Some sage advice given to readers is to be mindful that: "Entrepreneurship is not a sub-topic within a business-related curriculum, but is a set of qualities, beliefs, attitudes, and skills that underpins all areas of working life" (p. 135). Given that, it does not seem a far reach to suggest that entrepreneurship skills and arts skills may not be so different. Think back several paragraphs to Schindhuette and Morris (2016) who suggest that learning from failure is an essential element to entrepreneurship education. Now picture a potter at the wheel. Even the most experienced artist working in clay will have a seemingly perfect vessel collapse and cause the creator to start the process all over again. An equally likely scenario is the potter pivoting mid-throw towards a vessel completely different from the original design. Similar examples can be seen in any other artistic medium which illuminates a most thrilling fact: artists spend each day failing, learning, and trying again until "it" works. Essig points out that it takes a change in just two words of Peter Drucker's definition of entrepreneurship to tailor it to become both more palatable and more relevant to artists: "Creativity (formerly 'innovation' in Drucker's statement) is the specific instrument of entrepreneurship. It is the act that endows resources with a new capacity to create value (formerly 'wealth' in the Drucker definition)" (Essig, 2009, p. 118). It is thrilling to see that artists and creative students are already trained with a growth mindset that is ripe and receptive for learning entrepreneurship skills.

One final parallel found in the literature is between the practice-experimen t-skill-building process most artists, dancers, musicians, and creatives go through in learning, and Neck and Greene's practice of teaching entrepreneur-ship as a method rather than a process. The authors point out that although entrepreneurship can be taught as a linear, step-by-step process, it is more effectively taught as a method whereby the student builds skills and tech-niques, creativity, and their "toolkit" via iterative and practiced experimenta-tion (Neck & Greene, 2011). As this process is already strikingly similar to the way artistic students hone their natural talents it seems a natural possibility to explore further as a method of teaching arts entrepreneurship.

ARTS ENTREPRENEURSHIP MINDSET

Drawing inspiration from Beckman (2007) is a qualitative naturalistic inquiry on developing an arts entrepreneurship mindset (Pollard & Wilson, 2014). From interviews with educators, the authors find five common themes of skills the interviewees found important for arts and creative industries stu-dents should graduate knowing or having been exposed to. The themes found were the ability to think strategically and analytically, having confidence in one's abilities, the ability to collaborate and communicate effectively, and an understanding of how to infer current arts contexts (p. 3). The authors go on to propose that an arts entrepreneurship mindset can be built upon two main principles. First, as procuring a job in the arts industry can be much different than in other industries, arts students need to be taught how to be employable. Second, skills, examples, and experience should be taught out in real-world settings and situations and not just the college theater, the arts studio, music practice rooms, or classrooms. They remind readers that it is not personality traits that make entrepreneurs, mindset is ultimately individualistic and personal, and finally that even the word *entrepreneurship* can be a turn-off to an arts student. It is suggested that it is better to call it "creative practice" instead (p. 19).

Equally worth exploring is the difference between fixed and growth mindsets, or the perception of whether a certain skill or ability is something that can be honed and developed. Dweck (2010) maintains that "Individuals with a fixed mindset believe that their intelligence is simply an inborn trait – they have a certain amount and that's that. In contrast, individuals with a growth mindset believe that they can develop their intelligence over time" (p. 16). In contrast, those with a growth mindset tend to persist and demonstrate resilience even when faced with failure (Hochanadel & Finamore, 2015). Exploring students' perceptions on whether certain abilities have more of a fixed mindset or more of a growth mindset, Anderson found that the middle school students had a growth mindset and the college students tended to be undecided regarding artistic skills. The author theorized that this difference could be representative of research that has shown two differing perceptions on creative abilities. "Some people define creative abilities as representing a 'trait' found only in rare circumstances. For example, they would think of artistic ability as existing among famous artists. In others, it is the learned skills that improve over time. For example, they may picture a friend who practices artistic abilities regularly and has shown improvements" (Anderson, 2018, p. 60).

HOW SHOULD ARTS ENTREPRENEURSHIP BE TAUGHT?

While there seems to be much agreement among scholars and educators as to which skills arts and creative industries students should have, there is little literature on how best to teach those skills. Essig maintains that "there are basic skills of venture creation that can be taught across all disciplines. But to teach arts entrepreneurship *to artists* means to teach them to recognize or create opportunity, manage, and direct their careers, and launch their artistic enterprise" (Essig, 2009, p. 119). A recent trend in arts education has been a keen focus on social media. In light of the current world health, economic, and climate conditions, seeking virtual outlets on which to share, discuss, and learn about art and culture seems a logical progression. Recent research has shown that as we move into a more digitally participative culture, students who incorporate types of social media into learning art skills are able to build their own confidence through multiple interactions with other individuals (Castro, 2012). Additionally, incorporating the dynamic and multi-faceted elements of social media extends what Castro terms "emergence." Castro further states, "The kinds of knowledge that merge through these kinds of learning (via social media) could never originate from any one individual, including the teacher. Emergence in the type of learning is only possible through social participation" (p. 155). There is also a strong argument to be made for incorporating social media learning, as nearly two thirds of faculty members responding to a national survey sent out by Babson College Survey Research Group reported already using social media to some degree in their current courses (Moran, Seaman, & Tinti-Kane, 2011).

Purpose

The purpose of this qualitative study is to discover and explore some methods, styles, thoughts, and examples within BEE as given by some leading entrepreneurship educators and educational research scholars. This chapter seeks to explore thoughts and opinions on: What skills do scholars and educators believe arts and creative industries students should have/will need? What is the definition of entrepreneurship mindset? Given that arts professionals often have vastly different career paths and goals, how can business entrepreneurial mindset be taught effectively from an arts perspective to reflect learning style and goals?

Analysis

Table 16.1 shows the responses pertaining to the skills and abilities an arts entrepreneur should possess. Given how important the arts can be for community and economy, it is interesting that the ability to collaborate was not ranked more importantly.

In response to the question of how best to define *entrepreneurship mindset*, 16 initial themes emerged. The matrix in Figure 16.1 shows the evolution of the categorization from the initial sort to the resulting three major themes.

A final analysis found that three common themes emerged from the responses: business skills, personality traits, and behavioral skills. Table 16.2 shows the three most common themes were recorded in literature in response to variations of the question: How do you characterize or define *entrepreneurial mindset*?

Table 16.1   *Arts entrepreneur skills and abilities*

Skill/ability	Very important (%)	Somewhat important (%)	Important (%)	Slightly important (%)	Not important (%)
Self-efficacy	60	33.33	6.67	0	0
Ability to collaborate	31.25	68.75	0	0	0
Communication	62.5	37.5	0	0	0
Ability to think creatively/ strategically	68.75	31.5	0	0	0
Understanding of current industry	62.5	37.5	0	0	0

Note: Responding to the question, 'How important are the following abilities for an arts entrepreneur to have'?

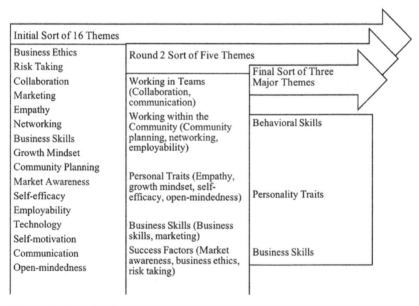

Figure 16.1   *Evolution of grouping*

Table 16.2   Themes discovered

Theme	Number of times used in definition
Business skills	13
Personality traits	9
Behavioral skills	8

How do you characterize or define *entrepreneurial mindset?*

Business skills: General business skills, marketing, market comprehension, technology skills

Personality traits: Empathy, growth, mindset, self-efficacy, perseverance, self-motivation, open-mindedness, risk taking

Behavioral skills: Networking, communication, community planning, collaboration, employability

DISCUSSION

Reviewing literature published by both business entrepreneurship and arts entrepreneurship scholars reveals a rich knowledge base of themes, teaching methods, and paradigms. There is consensus between the two disciplines as to what sorts of entrepreneurship skills arts and creative industries students need for success in their chosen careers. Amongst both arts educators and the arts community, there is a strong motivation to banish the stigma of the "starving artist" and to build business ecosystems and communities that support the arts. However, there has been little collaboration between business and arts scholars in general, and even less attention paid to *how* to teach arts entrepreneurship and *how* arts students learn best. Expanding on such frameworks as Toscher (2019), frameworks for other arts disciplines can take shape and develop. One limitation to this study is the literature and data that have yet to be explored. A further limitation is the need to include arts leadership educators and scholars. We recommend future research on this topic to follow the well-trodden paths provided by our friends and colleagues in related disciplines. Also important is examining how the recent shift towards a more digital culture has affected arts entrepreneurship skillsets.

CONCLUSION

There are connections just waiting to be made, curricula and methods just waiting to be developed, and learning styles to be explored and established. This chapter is a beginning for outlining where BEE and AEE concur. From here, educators must continue collaborating with each other, developing shared best practices, building ecosystems and community, all of which should be done in an accelerated way with measurement mechanisms built in (cf., Hessling, Robinson, Capps, and Gallardo-Williams, 2018; Liguori,

Bendickson, Solomon, and McDowell, 2019). Of great importance is studying learning styles and methods of arts students, and connecting teaching exercises and methods to certain startup skills. New and expanded frameworks for dance, fine arts, theatre, and creative industries programs should be created in order to develop curricula aimed at including entrepreneurship skills in beneficial ways. Finally, arts-specific templates should be developed geared toward giving arts students employability skills. Many creative individuals possess a sense of humor, a sense of adventure, and great courage. Do we, as educators, mentors, and coaches, possess the same character and fortitude? The foundation for strong AEE exists. It is up to us to continue growing it and making it better.

REFERENCES

Anderson, H. (2018). Fixed and growth mindsets: All abilities are not perceived equally. *NCUR 2018*, pp. 54–62.

Arizona State University PAVE Program (2016). *How It's Being Done Report: Arts Business Training across the US*, prepared by L. Essig and M. Flanagan. Retrieved from https://herbergerinstitute.asu.edu/sites/default/files/arts_business_training _across_the_u.s._-_hibd_2016.pdf

Beckman, G. D. (2007). Adventuring arts entrepreneurship curricula in higher education: An examination of present efforts, obstacles, and best practices. *Journal of Arts Management, Law, and Society, 37*(2), pp. 87–112.

Boyer, E. L. (1990). *Scholarship Reconsidered: Priorities of the Professoriate.* Lawrenceville, NJ: Princeton University Press.

Bridgestock, R. (2012). Not a dirty word: Arts entrepreneurship in higher education. *Arts and Humanities in Higher Education, 12*(2–3), pp. 122–37.

Bryan, J., Hill, S., Munday, M., & Roberts, A. (2000). Assessing the role of the arts and cultural industries in a local economy. *Environment and Planning A, 32*(8), pp. 1391–408.

Castro, J. C. (2012). Learning and teaching art through social media. *Studies in Art Education 53*(2), pp. 152–69.

Chang, W. J., & Wyszomirski, M. (2015). What is arts entrepreneurship? Tracking the development of its definition in scholarly journals. *Artivate: American Journal of Entrepreneurship in the Arts, 4*(2), pp. 11–31.

Duxbury, N., Campbell, H., & Keurvorst, E. (2011). Developing and revitalizing rural communities through arts and culture. *Small Cities Imprint, 3*(1), pp. 111–22.

Dweck, C. S. (2010). Mind-sets. *Principal Leadership, 10*(5), pp. 26–9.

Essig, L. (2009). Suffusing entrepreneurship education throughout the theatre curriculum. *Theatre Topics, 19*(2), pp. 117–24.

Friedrichs, A. M. (2017). Suggestions for incorporating entrepreneurship education in the classical performance studio. *Artivate: American Journal of Entrepreneurship in the Arts, 6*(1), pp. 27–40.

Gangi, J. J. (2017). Towards a consensus: Suggested foundational building blocks for arts entrepreneurship research and pedagogy. *Artivate: American Journal of Entrepreneurship in the Arts, 6*(1), pp. 46–62.

Gartner, W. B. (1990). What are we talking about when we talk about entrepreneurship? *Journal of Business Venturing, 5*(1), pp. 15–28.

Hessling, P. A., Robinson, E. E., Capps, J. A., & Gallardo-Williams, M. T. (2018). Cross-disciplinary reading circles: Community building, collaboration and professional growth. *Journal of Faculty Development, 32*(3), pp. 19–24.

Hochanadel, A., & Finamore, D. (2015). Fixed and growth mindset in education and how grit helps students persist in the face of adversity. *Journal of International Education Research, 11*(1), pp. 47–50.

Holden, J. (2009). How we value art and culture. *Asia Pacific Journal of Arts and Cultural Management, 6*(2), pp. 447–56.

Kassean, H., Vanevenhoven, J., Liguori, E., & Winkel, D. E. (2015). Entrepreneurship education: A need for reflection, real-world experience and action. *International Journal of Entrepreneurial Behavior and Research*, pp. 690–708.

Kisida, B., Bowen, D. H., & Greene, J. P. (2018). Cultivating interest in art: Causal effects of arts exposure during early childhood. *Early Childhood Research Quarterly, 45*, pp. 197–203.

Krueger, N., & Welpe, I. (2014). Neuro-entrepreneurship: What can entrepreneurs learn from neuroscience? In M. H. Morris (Ed.), *Annals of Entrepreneurship Education and Pedagogy*, pp. 60–90. Cheltenham, UK and Northampton, MA, USA: Edward Elgar Publishing.

Liguori, E., Bendickson, J., Solomon, S., & McDowell, W. C. (2019). Development of a multi-dimensional measure for assessing entrepreneurial ecosystems. *Entrepreneurship and Regional Development, 31*(1–2), pp. 7–21.

Liguori, E., Winkler, C., Winkel, D., Marvel, M. R., Keels, J. K., van Gelderen, M., & Noyes, E. (2018). The entrepreneurship education imperative: Introducing EE&P. *Entrepreneurship Education and Pedagogy, 1*(1), pp. 5–7.

Matthews, C. H. (2018). Preface: Three key challenges to advancing entrepreneurship education and pedagogy. In M. H. Morris & E. Liguori (Eds.), *Annals of Entrepreneurship Education and Pedagogy*, pp. xvi–xxiv. Cheltenham, UK and Northampton, MA, USA: Edward Elgar Publishing.

Moran, M., Seaman, J., & Tinti-Kane, H. (2011). *Teaching, Learning, and Sharing: How Today's Higher Education Faculty Use Social Media*. Boston, MA: Pearson.

Neck, H., & Corbett, T. (2018). The scholarship of teaching and learning entrepreneurship. *Entrepreneurship Education and Pedagogy, 1*(1), pp. 8–41.

Neck, H., & Greene, P. (2011). Entrepreneurship education: Known worlds and new frontiers. *Journal of Small Business Management, 49*(1), pp. 59–70.

Osterwalder, A. (2008). *Business Model Innovation Matters!* New York: Wiley.

Pollard, V., & Wilson, E. (2014). Entrepreneurial mindset in creative and performing arts education in Australia. *Artivate: Journal of Entrepreneurship in the Arts, 3*(1), pp. 3–22.

Read, S., Sarasvathy, S., Dew, N., Wiltbank, R., & Ohlsson, A. V. (2011). *Effectual Entrepreneurship*. New York: Routledge.

Ries, E. (2011). *The Lean Startup*. New York: Crown Business.

Sarasvathy, S. D. (2001). Effectual reasoning in entrepreneurial decision making: Existence and bounds. *Academy of Management Proceedings, 1*, pp. D1–D6.

Schindehutte, M., & Morris, M. (2016). The experiential lean portfolio in entrepreneurship education. In M. H. Morris & E. Liguori (Eds.), *Annals of Entrepreneurship Education and Pedagogy*, pp. 161–75. Cheltenham, UK and Northampton, MA, USA: Edward Elgar Publishing.

Shekhar, P., Huang-Saad, A., & Libarkin, J. (2018). Examining *differences* in students' entrepreneurship self-efficacy in curricular and co-curricular entrepreneurship education programs. In M. H. Morris & E. Liguori (Eds.), *Annals of Entrepreneurship Education and Pedagogy*, pp. 218–36. Cheltenham, UK and Northampton, MA, USA: Edward Elgar Publishing.

Solomon, G. T., & Matthews, C. H. (2014). The curricular confusion between entrepreneurship education and small business management: A qualitative analysis. In M. H. Morris (Ed.), *Annals of Entrepreneurship Education and Pedagogy*, pp. 91–115. Cheltenham, UK and Northampton, MA, USA: Edward Elgar Publishing.

Sterngold, A. H. (2004). Do economic impact studies misrepresent the benefits of arts and cultural organizations? *Journal of Arts Management, Law, and Society, 34*(3), pp. 166–87.

Thomas, J., McDonagh, D., & Canning, L. (2014). Developing the arts entrepreneur: The "learning cloud." *Design Journal, 17*(3), pp. 425–43.

Toscher, B. (2019). Entrepreneurial learning in arts entrepreneurship education: A conceptual framework. *Artivate: A Journal of Entrepreneurship in the Arts, 8*(1), pp. 3–22.

Vanevenhoven, J. (2013). Advances and challenges in entrepreneurship education. *Journal of Small Business Management, 51*(3), pp. 466–70.

Vanevenhoven, J., & Liguori, E. (2013). The impact of entrepreneurship education: Introducing the entrepreneurship education project. *Journal of Small Business Management, 51*(3), pp. 315–28.

Welsh, D. H., Onishi, T., DeHoog, R. H., & Syed, S. (2014). Responding to the needs and challenges of arts entrepreneurs: An exploratory study of arts entrepreneurship in North Carolina higher education. *Artivate: Journal of Entrepreneurship in the Arts, 3*(2), pp. 21–37.

White, J. C. (2017). Analyzing entrepreneurship in the United States art sector. *Artivate: Journal of Entrepreneurship in the Arts, 6* (1), pp. 8–32.

PART II

Model university entrepreneurship programs

17. Florida State University Jim Moran College of Entrepreneurship

Susan Fiorito and Wendy Plant

INTRODUCTION

In December 2015, Jan Moran and the Jim Moran Foundation gave a $100 million gift to establish the nation's largest interdisciplinary, degree-granting school of entrepreneurship and to support the statewide growth of the Jim Moran Institute for Global Entrepreneurship. The Jim Moran School for Entrepreneurship (JMS) had the full support of Florida State University's (FSU) president and provost, deepening its commitment to innovation and entrepreneurship as the first pillar in the university's newly adopted strategic plan.

The JMC opened its doors to students as the Jim Moran School in August 2017, creating the nation's first stand-alone entrepreneurship school at a public university. With its mission of "Inspiring innovation, instilling compassion and igniting an entrepreneurial mindset in the next generation of leaders," the college greatly expands upon entrepreneurship courses taught since 2008 in the College of Business in the Department of Entrepreneurship, Strategy and Information Systems.

In November 2019, President John Thrasher and Provost Sally McRorie announced that the JMS would become the Jim Moran College of Entrepreneurship (JMC). This transition represents the university's profound commitment to entrepreneurship education across all disciplines at FSU and is further evidence of the importance of entrepreneurship to its growth in co-curricular offerings and degree programs.

The JMC's goals are to build an interdisciplinary curriculum that will provide students with the skills to think entrepreneurially. In other words, through all that we do in the college, we encourage students to follow their passions, learn competences in creative problem solving, encourage resilience in the face of failure, and learn to work with teams of people who may be from different backgrounds, disciplines, and lifestyles. The mission of the JMC is to be a world-class organization that provides a profound impact through dissemination of knowledge, support, and inspiration for our students in a way that will enable them to achieve their fullest potential.

Dr. Susan S. Fiorito, who was named the founding director of the Jim Moran School in February 2016, continues as Dean of the JMC. Dr. Fiorito oversees activities of the college, including the development of curricula and programming. She sits on the Academic Deans' Council and reports directly to the provost.

With the opening of the then-JMS, Wendy Plant, Director of the InNOLEvation® Center for Student Engagement, moved from the Jim Moran Institute to the JMS. The student incubator, speaker events, competitions, and other programs for entrepreneurial students became part of the school.

In January 2018, the JMS also became the administrative home to FSU's long-standing Retail Merchandising and Product Development Program. Retail entrepreneurship became the school's third major, along with commercial and social entrepreneurship, and has greatly enhanced its curricular and co-curricular offerings.

In February 2018, the administrative staff moved into the newly renovated 19,000 square foot Jim Moran building, in downtown Tallahassee, a few blocks from the State Capitol. The building features a new state-of-the-art student incubator called the Greenhouse, which is open to FSU students from all disciplines who have started a business. The close proximity of the college and the institute allows for even greater access and connections between the students and the surrounding professional and governmental communities.

In the fall of 2018, the faculty, support staff, and advisors also moved into new facilities on the FSU main campus, with dedicated offices, a classroom, and co-working space. This has quickly become the on-campus heart of entrepreneurial activity while still allowing students easy access to the other hubs of design and innovation on campus.

FSU's Innovation Hub, which opened in January 2018, is closely aligned with the college. The 14,000 square foot space includes a Design Lab featuring a Makerspace and Virtual Reality Lab, robust collaborative workspaces, meeting and program rooms that feature the latest technologies to support design thinking, innovation, and entrepreneurship. The Innovation Hub assists students who need help prototyping and building their ideas into reality. The JMC has helped sponsor internships for 14 student interns from seven disciplines who work in the Innovation Hub assisting other students and faculty with 3D printing, augmented reality, virtual reality, and laser printing.

CURRICULUM

Students receive a bachelor of science degree in entrepreneurship from the JMC. Currently the undergraduate majors include commercial entrepreneurship, social entrepreneurship, and retail entrepreneurship, and soon a science, technology, engineering, and mathematics (STEM) major beginning in fall 2021. The goal is to expand the curriculum to include additional majors, possibly creative arts and allied health. A master of science degree in retail entrepreneurship with a major in textiles and apparel entrepreneurship was launched in fall 2019.

The college also offers classes to more than 400 students annually who are minoring in entrepreneurship in conjunction with various colleges and majors across the campus. Some of these minors include retail operations, commercial, social, hospitality, STEM, and computational science.

With a focus on creating a cohesive group of entrepreneurs with a desire for shared success, the JMC expects students to work together to promote the success of each other's ventures and to demonstrate leadership by actively engaging and supporting entrepreneurial activities across campus.

The college offers students case-study learning while providing opportunities for innovative, hands-on application. Students take introductory courses in entrepreneurship and specialized courses in technology commercialization, strategy formulation, organizational design, and venture finance. The curriculum is designed by full-time faculty who all have their own entrepreneurial experience, tenure-track or specialized faculty in retail and product development, plus entrepreneurs in residence (EIR) from colleges across campus. They teach students project planning and how to launch, manage, and generate income from a venture. The foundation of the JMC is its creative and dynamic interdisciplinary curriculum focused specifically on entrepreneurship and innovation (E&I).

The undergraduate degree prepares tomorrow's entrepreneurs for a challenging financial, ethical, legal, and global competitive future. The JMC's programs maximize a student's ability to analyze and respond effectively to these issues, improve critical thinking, and build up the discipline needed to compete in today's challenging and potentially lucrative field of entrepreneurship.

Entrepreneurship faculty advise the student chapters of the Collegiate Entrepreneurs' Organization at FSU, Collegiate DECA, Tamid, Enactus, and the Society for Advancement of Management. In addition, the JMC hosts an entrepreneurship summer camp for high school students. This is an opportunity to expose high school students to the entrepreneurial community, showing them the resources available to them to start a business.

UNIQUE ASPECTS AND FEATURES

With over 23 full-time faculty, 16 EIR, approximately ten experienced adjuncts, and faculty associates from academic units across campus, the JMC is able to influence students from all disciplines. Currently, EIR and faculty associates are housed in the Jim Moran College; College of Criminology and Criminal Justice; College of Engineering; the Florida State library system; College of Law; College of Social Sciences and Public Policy; College of Medicine; College of Motion Picture Arts; College of Human Sciences; College of Nursing; and the College of Arts and Sciences. All EIR and faculty associates are members of the Council for Entrepreneurship, whose mission is to facilitate student success and support the university's focus on entrepreneurship. Aside from teaching classes in the entrepreneurship major and minor, the EIR mentor students, serve on the JM Micro Grant committee, judge the InNOLEvation® Challenge business plan competition, develop co-curricular experiential events, and more.

All entrepreneurship majors are required to have an internship and are all strongly encouraged to have an international experience before graduation. The JMC provides several $2,500 scholarships for study abroad programs. In addition, FSU's International Programs has partnered with the college to match this amount, providing a total of $5,000 for many students.

The college offers a free faculty/staff class each semester for up to 40 faculty or staff across the FSU campus to learn more about how to start their own business. This class meets over lunch hours to not affect their workday. Faculty/ staff range in age, ethnicity, and gender, and are from various departments and colleges. A direct result of the inaugural spring 2016 class is Damfino's, a new restaurant in Quincy, FL, that improves access to fresh, healthy food and supports local, small-scale farms by providing an outlet for their products. This restaurant now has five full-time employees and five part-time employees. It opened in December 2016 and is thriving.

INNOLEVATION® CENTER FOR STUDENT ENGAGEMENT

The college's InNOLEvation® Center for Student Engagement offers a variety of co-curricular programs for any FSU student interested in entrepreneurship, such as business model and pitch competitions, micro grants, speaker events, and the Greenhouse student business incubator.

The college partners with Domi Station, a local community business incubator, Tallahassee Community College, Jim Moran Institute for Global Entrepreneurship, and others in the Tallahassee entrepreneurial ecosystem on Startup.com and OnceHub for a mentor platform that allows FSU entrepreneurship students to get advice and support from a large pool of qualified mentors. Students can make appointments to talk with vetted subject matter experts that are shared by the other affiliates. Additionally, the college works with local program partners to give students numerous opportunities outside of the university. Students are encouraged to pitch at 1 Million Cups Tallahassee, which is held in the Jim Moran Building.

The Greater Tallahassee Chamber of Commerce has also partnered with the JMC to help students secure internships and other benefits. Students are provided "courtesy" memberships with the Chamber of Commerce so they can connect more easily with local business leaders. The Chamber pairs students with mentors, who offer business advice and organize internships in the Tallahassee workforce. The partnership between FSU and the Chamber is also intended to help local businesses retain top talent and boost local entrepreneurs. Students have had the opportunity to attend a day-long seminar called Opportunity Tallahassee where participants were acquainted with the physical, social, economic, and educational structure of Tallahassee and also attend the annual Chamber's Entrepreneurial Forum Breakfast which connects them with the community.

Additionally, other stakeholders include the college's Education Fellows, who represent a community of professional and scholarly individuals from a wide array of backgrounds and professions who share their experience, perspective, and expertise with aspiring student entrepreneurs.

FOSTERING A COMPETITIVE SPIRIT

Relationships with colleges across campus allow for collaborations on many events throughout the year that are open to all enrolled students at FSU and the FAMU-FSU College of Engineering. For example, the JMC sponsors FSU's Digitech Shark Tank competition where students across campus apply to pitch in front of a panel of judges to win $1,000. The college also sponsors the $2,000 prize for the FAMU-FSU College of Engineering's Shark Tank competition, and engineering students are required as a part of their senior design capstone course to compete in the annual InNOLEvation® Challenge business model competition. Engineering majors pair up with students from other majors during the first several workshops to form teams before the application deadline. InnoVenture Weekend is a collaboration between four colleges and departments and is open to all students. Students are provided a list of problems faced by a group of people ahead of time, and they must form teams to develop viable solutions to one of the problems during the course of the weekend. The college is also a major sponsor of FSU's annual hackathon, HackFSU.

ENTREPRENEURSHIP AND INNOVATION LEARNING COMMUNITY

The JMC launched the E&I Learning Community in fall 2018, and the students live together in a section of one of FSU's newest residence halls. It is designed to immerse 36 first-year students in E&I at FSU and expose them to all of the exciting things happening around campus and in Tallahassee. Through speakers, coursework taken as a cohort, shadowing opportunities, and a one credit hour E&I colloquium, students are encouraged to explore their own interests and ideas, look for ways to solve problems, and develop a project based on these interests.

Students form groups of passionate innovators and build friendships that last throughout their time at FSU and beyond. E&I Learning Community students develop their creative, technical, and practical entrepreneurial skills and are exposed to campus and community resources that support these efforts. The E&I Learning Community gives the students the perfect place to study, work, and live together and create an energetic environment for idea generation, brainstorming, and development.

AWARDS AND RECOGNITIONS

In January 2019 the then-JMS was recognized with the United States Association for Small Business and Entrepreneurship's Model Emerging Program Award. In September 2019 the Global Consortium of Entrepreneurship Centers presented the school with the Exceptional Activities in Entrepreneurship across Disciplines Award. It was the only program to receive this honor.

In fall 2019 FSU soared eight spots to no. 18 among national public universities in the latest *U.S. News & World Report* rankings, meeting and well exceeding its goal of joining the Top 25. It's the greatest single-year improvement in university history. "It's an incredible accomplishment for Florida State University," said President John Thrasher. "The credit goes to so many people – our faculty, our staff, and certainly, our great students. I couldn't be prouder."

In November 2019, the president and provost also announced that the JMS would now be the JMC. "It was the $100 million gift from Jan Moran and the Jim Moran Foundation in 2015 that allowed us to establish the JMS," said President Thrasher. "In just a few short years, Susan Fiorito has overseen the growth of the school to a point where today the University Board of Trustees designated it as the JMC. This is truly a historic day in FSU's history as we add another college, further demonstrating how transformational this gift continues to be," the president added.

FUTURE GOALS

One of the JMC's goals is to provide an opportunity for all students in the major to study abroad with funding provided by the college. Currently, entrepreneurship courses are offered at FSU study centers in London, Valencia, Florence, and Panama City.

Another initiative is to solidify more partnerships with departments across FSU's campus. There is a STEM entrepreneurship major being developed in collaboration with the FSU/Florida Agricultural and Mechanical University (FAMU) College of Engineering, with classes currently being offered. The creative arts major is being proposed to begin in fall 2022. This will also allow for more students interested in different fields to collaborate on business ideas, participate in competitions together, and create more diverse teams.

In addition to the JMC's first master of science degree in textiles and apparel entrepreneurship that launched in fall 2019, two new graduate programs will start in fall 2020: masters degree in entrepreneurship with a major in product development and an online masters in hospitality entrepreneurship. In collaboration with the FSU/FAMU College of Engineering, the masters in product development advances the knowledge and skills of students so that they can bring unique value to companies of any maturity level that are working in new product design and development. The face-to-face classes offered in this program provide students with a hands-on engaging experience to develop abilities in innovation and commercialization.

The masters hospitality major is an online degree program in collaboration with the Dedman School of Hospitality. It provides an advanced curriculum focused on the importance of leadership and innovative thinking, and graduates will be fully prepared to start their own ventures or pursue careers in the private or public sectors, including government and academic professions. Students are also encouraged to take courses at FSU's international study centers, with entrepreneurial lodging offered in Florence, supply chain in the Republic of Panama, and hospitality management in Valencia.

Finally, a Ph.D. in entrepreneurship is under development to be launched in fall 2022.

18. The Georgetown University Entrepreneurship Initiative

Jeff Reid

INTRODUCTION

The Georgetown Entrepreneurship Initiative is founded on a core belief that entrepreneurship is one of the world's most powerful forces for positive change. Georgetown Entrepreneurship's three-part mission is:

1. to instill an entrepreneurial mindset in students and foster an entrepreneurial culture across the university;
2. to support the successful growth of alumni ventures; and
3. to leverage the power of entrepreneurship to make an impact in the world beyond Georgetown.

The Initiative began in 2009 with the hiring of founding director Jeff Reid, who had previously founded the Center for Entrepreneurship at the University of North Carolina at Chapel Hill. Over its first several years, limited resources were focused almost entirely on student programs. While housed in the McDonough School of Business, the goal from the outset was to create one campus-wide focus of activity for entrepreneurship across Georgetown University. Early highlights include the creation of a campus-wide pitch competition, speaker events, mentor programming, summer incubator, and enhanced course offerings.

In 2017, the Initiative hit an inflection point with the creation of an advisory board made up of prominent alumni and other business leaders. This advisory board helped to garner support from university senior leadership (most importantly with deans and the provost), and also led to an expansion of the mission to go beyond the student focus, adding the second (alumni) and third (impact the world beyond Georgetown) pillars to the mission statement. The broader mission along with expanded financial support from donors led to a period of dramatic growth with overall programming, budget, and staff size more than tripling between 2017 and 2019 and an expectation of continued growth beyond 2020. Descriptions of selected offerings and future ambitions are included later in this chapter.

OUR GUIDING PHILOSOPHY: BUILD CULTURE AND COMMUNITY

Our overarching goal is to create a culture and community that support entrepreneurial thinking and activity across Georgetown University. The paradigm we embrace is that of *leading a movement*, as opposed to simply offering a set of programs and activities. Thus, our programming is done in service to the longer-term goals of fostering community and influencing culture change. Our ultimate ambition would be for every single Georgetown student – across all of our various schools and degree programs – to develop an entrepreneurial mindset that they would actively use to improve their own lives and the communities they live in no matter what career path they pursue. Some ways this "movement" philosophy is manifested include the following.

Opportunistic, Innovative, and Inclusive

Entrepreneurship is not considered a traditional discipline in most academic structures, much less at a 240-year-old Catholic university in a traditional government town, so we often find resistance to new approaches. Simultaneously, we see unlimited opportunities to do new things yet have limited time and other resources available. Therefore, we adopt a long-term view allowing us to focus efforts on areas we can influence today while keeping an eye on the future when resources grow and/or resistance fades.

One example: we met initial resistance to creating a minor in entrepreneurship, but a few years later growing student demand and a constant cultivation of champions resulted in unanimous approval of the minor by the business school faculty.

One successful mechanism for building support across campus among faculty and staff is a regular lunch series we call our Georgetown Entrepreneurship Exchange. A free lunch and informal gathering has regularly attracted dozens of university employees with an interest in entrepreneurship to attend and become part of our community, helping us to identify and cultivate future champions.

Deliberately Marketing-Oriented

We exert considerable effort on marketing campaigns designed to engage students, alumni, and our broader community who might not initially self-identify with an affinity for entrepreneurship. Our more effective methods include a weekly e-newsletter, robust web site, and active social media. We get strong results from spreading our "Create the Future" tagline around campus through fliers, news screens, t-shirts, water bottles, and other SWAG. Creative new efforts include a 25-foot inflatable branded light bulb displayed at various outdoor events and a podcast series featuring the stories of student and alumni entrepreneurs (viz., *Venture Forward*, available on iTunes and other podcast platforms).

Play to Our Strengths

While not known for technology development or engineering, Georgetown does have significant competitive advantages such as the globally minded talent of our student body, our location in Washington, DC, and the Jesuit values that animate the university. Georgetown attracts ambitious students who want to change the world; our role is to help them learn how entrepreneurial thinking can help them. The nation's capital offers its own robust startup ecosystem as well as connectivity to global business, international development, and policy-related opportunities. Values, ethics, and personal reflection are key elements of entrepreneurship that Georgetown can highlight perhaps more than other institutions.

Jesuit Roots Give Us a Competitive Advantage

The Order of the Society of Jesus which founded Georgetown can be viewed as a role model for innovation since its origin nearly five centuries ago in Paris as a "social entrepreneurship startup created as a dorm project by college classmates." Among many Jesuit values that influence our entrepreneurship initiative are that every human has value, and everyone should strive to find the calling that allows them to make the best impact on the world around them. All of our campus pitch competitions include judging criteria evaluating how well the student team incorporates Jesuit values, and our courses often explore the many ethical challenges of entrepreneurial pursuits.

We Believe in Diversity and Inclusion

We constantly and deliberately seek diversity of all kinds among our faculty, mentors, competition judges, guest speakers, and student leaders with an understanding that our diverse students are often looking for role models with which they can identify. Inclusion also means having a diverse group of students actively participate in the design and delivery of our programs, ensuring that we stay relevant to our key audience. We strive to ensure that students outside the business school and first-generation students feel welcomed into our programs, and frequently partner with relevant campus organizations. Some results of these efforts include:

- Roughly 80 percent of the prize money awarded at Georgetown pitch competitions over the last three years went to women-only or women-led teams.
- Female general partners at United States venture capital funds are more likely to have attended Georgetown than any other school after Harvard (Women Leading Venture 2019 Report).
- Awarded the 2018 Student Engagement Award by the Global Consortium of Entrepreneurship Centers.

PROGRAMMING HIGHLIGHTS

Brief highlights of selected programs within each of the three pillars of our mission are provided here.

Strategic Pillar 1: Instill an entrepreneurial mindset in students and foster an entrepreneurial culture across the university.

Entrepreneurship Minor and Fellows Program

The minor is currently available to undergraduate business majors. Non-business students can take the same classes to earn an entrepreneurship fellowship.

Content Entrepreneurship

Professor Eric Koester offers a unique course in which students write and publish books (or other creative works) as a way to learn and practice entrepreneurship. The vast majority of students in this course become best-selling authors and describe the experience as "life-changing." This course won the USASBE 2018 Excellence in Entrepreneurship Education Award and was detailed in the 2018 Annals of Entrepreneurship Education and Pedagogy. Over the last two years, Professor Koester has scaled the course to reach hundreds of participants and dozens of other universities, earning him recognition as the 2020 USASBE Entrepreneurship Educator of the Year.

Georgetown Venture Fellows Program

An eight- to twelve-month apprenticeship within a local venture capital firm. Students work part time during the school year and full time during the summer, gaining valuable experience working alongside active investors for an extended period of time. Originally created for MBA students, the program has grown to include undergraduates, with 15 total fellows placed in 2020.

MBA Concentration in Entrepreneurship

A series of electives for MBA students on various topics, offered along with a robust suite of co-curricular programs. In 2019 and 2020, recruiters answering the *Bloomberg Businessweek Global MBA Recruiter Survey* recognized Georgetown MBAs as no. 1 most creative, no. 3 exceptional entrepreneurial skills, and no. 4 overall reputation for entrepreneurship.

Entrepreneurs in Residence

One of our most powerful initiatives has been the creation of entrepreneurship in residence (EiR) program, now numbering around 24 EiRs each year. Our EiRs commit to engaging with students and alumni on a regular basis in a variety of formats including one-to-one coaching, group mentoring, guest speaking, student club advising, and competition judging. Each EiR receives a modest monetary stipend to formalize the engagement, but their primary motivation is to give back to students and other entrepreneurs.

Venture Capital Investment Competition

The Venture Capital Investment Competition is a global competition in which students from nearly 100 top-ranked universities compete as teams of venture capitalists. Georgetown has won two national championships at the undergraduate level along with four of the last seven global championships at the graduate level. We run a multi-round internal competition to select our teams, and then provide extensive training.

Pitch Competitions

Georgetown offers multiple pitch competitions, each designed to engage students in a unique way. Of note, all of these competitions include criteria evaluating how well the teams incorporate Jesuit values into their venture.

Rocket Pitch Competition
Two-minute pitch in a quick-hitting format for 30 teams each semester. Often an entry point for students with an entrepreneurial idea.

Ventures and Values Competition

As part of a required sophomore-level business course titled *Ethical Values of Business*, students form teams and pitch startup ideas. The instructors use these "startups" as case studies to explore various ethical issues in business, and the teams then compete in a pitch competition. This course often introduces entrepreneurship to students who previously had not considered it.

Georgetown Entrepreneurship Challenge

Our most expansive event, the Challenge annually engages nearly 100 student teams from across the campus to pitch in 10+ preliminary events held within different schools (e.g. Law, Medicine, MBA) in order to attract more participants. Twelve finalist teams compete for a share of $35,000 and additional in-kind services. The championship round also serves as an end-of-year celebration bringing our community together.

Leonsis Family Entrepreneurship Prize/Bark Tank Competition

Our "biggest stage" each year features eight selected teams pitching in our "Bark Tank" competition (named as a nod to *Shark Tank* and our university's bulldog mascot). $100,000 in prize money is available each year due to the generous support of the Leonsis family. Winning teams have generally achieved significant traction, and the event draws over 300 attendees with significant "campus buzz" and press attention. Many of these teams have subsequently grown successful companies. Also of note, top prize winners in recent years have all been women-led businesses.

Summer Launch Incubator

Around 15 student ventures participate in our Summer Launch Incubator, a four-week intensive program consisting of dedicated coaching, customer discovery, and minimum viable product creation. Most students receive a stipend so they can fully engage without concern for lost wages during a time of year when financial aid is generally unavailable.

Entrepreneur Mental Health and Wellness

In 2019, we engaged Jessica Carson as our first expert in residence for mental health and wellness. With a background in both entrepreneurship and psychology, Carson brings to our program a unique understanding of how entrepreneurs relate to mental health and wellness issues.

Strategic Pillar 2: Support the successful growth of alumni ventures.

To serve our alumni community, the Georgetown Entrepreneurship Initiative partners with the Georgetown Entrepreneurship Alliance, a volunteer-driven affinity group within the Georgetown University Alumni Association. In recent years, we have significantly ramped up support for alumni in their pursuit of entrepreneurial success, recognizing that the entrepreneurial "seeds" planted while someone is a student may not sprout until many years later, but whenever it does Georgetown will be there to help.

Georgetown Venture Lab

Dozens of alumni-led growth companies are members of our Georgetown Venture Lab, made possible by a gift from the Leonsis family. The Lab provides a robust community of fellow entrepreneurs in a shared co-working space in downtown Washington, DC.

Georgetown Angel Investment Network

Launched in 2019, GAIN has already invested over $1.5 million in several ventures. Members are generally alumni who are accredited investors looking for attractive investment opportunities in Georgetown-related startups and growth companies.

Mentorship and Coaching

EIRs and experts on call engage as coaches, mentors, or advisors for alumni.

Alumni Awards and Pitch Competition

Annual awards honor outstanding alumni such as the founders Halo Top Ice Cream, Cvent, and Sweetgreen. A pitch competition supports aspiring alumni entrepreneurs.

> Strategic Pillar 3. Leverage the power of entrepreneurship to make an impact in the world beyond Georgetown.

While we continue to build new programming for students and alumni of Georgetown University, we are also growing our impact on the world beyond our campus.

Georgetown Pivot Program

Certificate in business and entrepreneurship created specifically for formerly incarcerated individuals.

Dog Tag Bakery

Certificate in business and entrepreneurship along with an experiential learning program created specifically to empower veterans with service-connected disabilities.

Global Entrepreneurship Training

Executive education offerings for aspiring entrepreneurs from around the world. Our first cohort from Sardinia, Italy completed the TalentUP program in 2019.

Entrepreneurship Policy

Building on our university's natural strengths in policy, government, and diplomacy, and in partnership with the United States Small Business Association, Georgetown hosted the first Global Roundtable on Entrepreneurship Policy featuring diplomats from 30 countries discussing how to enact policies to support entrepreneurial growth in their countries. This event kicked off a continuing effort now housed under the Startup Nations initiative of the Global Entrepreneurship Network.

FUTURE AMBITIONS

As Georgetown Entrepreneurship looks to the future, plans include:

Greater Research Emphasis

We recently hired a world-class academic leader who is expected to greatly enhance our research impact.

Get in the Core Curriculum

Georgetown Entrepreneurship has recently been invited by leaders in both the business school and the provost's office to propose innovative ways to inject entrepreneurial thinking and activity into the experience for all Georgetown undergraduate students. We also seek to open our entrepreneurship minor to all undergraduate students.

Central Campus Space

We have initial plans to build a central space on our main campus to house many of our student activities.

Launch new "Hacking for Humanity" Initiative

Building on our current "Hacking for Defense" course, we plan to greatly expand our utilization of Steve Blank's lean startup methodology to solve important problems for the benefit of mankind under the banner of "Hacking for Humanity" or "H4H." In H4H classes, interdisciplinary student teams will collaborate with state, local, and national government agencies, non-profits, and other stakeholders as they engage in the ultimate experiential learning exercise of solving big, meaningful societal problems. H4H will connect current students with alumni, the marketplace, and the world as a living expression of the entrepreneurial mission-driven spirit of Georgetown.

19. Iona College Hynes Institute for Entrepreneurship and Innovation

Christoph Winkler, Lendynette Pacheco-Jorge and Jarlyne Batista Monzon

INTRODUCTION

In 2017, the Hynes Institute started with a vision to bring new learning opportunities to Iona College by helping students develop an entrepreneurial mindset. Almost three years later, this vision is visibly alive at the intersection of our learning spaces, our students who engage in those spaces, and the programs that support our students in those spaces. While our first year focused on building the foundations for the Hynes Institute, the second year allowed us to implement a broad range of curricular and co-curricular programs. Now, as we are in the midst of our third year, we strive to redefine entrepreneurship education spaces by integrating curricular, co-curricular, and community engagement program elements. Our students are at the center of everything we do. They are our most valuable asset as we continue to build and grow our program not only *for* our students, but also *with* our students. To us, it is most gratifying to see our students take ownership of their learning as they set out to translate their college experiences into successful futures.

BACKGROUND AND MISSION

The Hynes Institute for Entrepreneurship and Innovation was established in 2017 thanks to the generosity and record $15 million gift to Iona College from James P. Hynes '69, '01H and Anne Marie Hynes. The gift was informed by a design team who led the charge in researching and developing a comprehensive business plan that became the underpinning of the transformational entrepreneurship program. The Hynes Institute strives to have lasting and far-reaching impact for all Iona students regardless of their school, discipline, or major. Funds have been allocated to support startup costs, the buildout of two state-of-the-art learning spaces, as well as an endowment fund. The goal is to operate a fully self-sustaining academic program within the first five years of operation.

The vision for the Hynes Institute is broad with a mandate to provide entrepreneurship education opportunities for all Iona students and the surrounding community. The Hynes Institute, which reports directly to the provost, operates its interdisciplinary program both independently and collaboratively with the two respective schools on campus, the LaPenta School of Business and the School of Arts and Science. "The mission of the Hynes Institute for Entrepreneurship & Innovation is to create and foster an interdisciplinary community of Iona students who engage in entrepreneurial learning opportunities to develop an entrepreneurial mindset."

The Hynes Institute is unique since it was able to implement a program that, by design, has the primary objective to serve the entire campus community of approximately 4,000 students. Although still in its early development stages, the Hynes Institute team has already built a robust curricular and co-curricular program that provides students with an environment that fosters an entrepreneurial mindset through practice and creative problem solving across all disciplines and schools. It aims to ensure that students develop the knowledge, skills, and experience required to create, innovate, and lead in a global economy.

Within its second year of operation, the Hynes Institute engaged 667 students and 56 faculty members on campus as well as in its temporary collaborative workspace GaelVentures (its future incubator space). With the start of its third academic year in fall 2019, the Hynes Institute established a campus presence by opening a new home and state-of-the-art 3,700 square foot collaborative learning space. To date, the Hynes Institute team is comprised of endowed professor and founding program director, assistant director, community manager, administrative support, assistant professor (tenure-track), entrepreneur in residence, adjunct faculty (six), graduate assistants (two), and student leaders/interns (eight).

PROGRAM DESCRIPTION

Curricular Programming

Before the founding of the Hynes Institute, entrepreneurship education was virtually absent from Iona College's academic offering. One of the first tasks of the founding program director was the formation of a 14-member interdisciplinary curriculum committee. The committee was tasked to develop the foundational curricular program elements that are geared to engage Iona students in entrepreneurial learning, regardless of their school, discipline, or major. The Hynes Curriculum Committee, which has since transformed into a smaller committee, has accomplished the following curricular program elements to date:

1. Integration of two one-hour modules (entrepreneurial thinking and action) in Iona's freshmen seminar, the Columba Cornerstone.
2. Development of an Integrated Core Theme (ICT) with the title "Innovation and the Creative Mind." An ICT is comprised of four core curriculum courses (one humanities center piece course, three integrated courses) offered since fall 2018.
3. Development of an introductory core curriculum course in entrepreneurship and innovation (*ENT 200: Intro to Entrepreneurship and Innovation: Practice and Mindset*). Between spring 2018 and fall 2019 we offered a total of 14 sections with a total of 335 students enrolled.
4. Development of an Academic Learning Community (ALC) for incoming freshmen that links *ENT 200* to Iona College's *Columba Cornerstone* freshmen seminar.
5. Development of a *Living Learning Community* (LLC) in entrepreneurship and innovation. This LLC is an ALC for freshmen who are living together in one of our dorms. An essential component of each LLC is a dedicated resident assistant, who works closely with the Hynes Institute to link and integrate freshmen in our various co-curricular programs.
6. Development of a 15-credit undergraduate minor in entrepreneurship and innovation that engages students in topics such as ideation, design thinking, ethical leadership, business modeling, internships, and entrepreneurship in practice.
7. Development of five graduate courses that guide them through the development of an entrepreneurial venture, including ideation, design thinking, business modeling, and financing. Courses can be taken to complete a 15-credit advanced certificate program, or as electives of Iona College's MBA.
8. Development of two interdisciplinary undergraduate majors: bachelor of arts in entrepreneurial leadership and BBA in entrepreneurship.

CO-CURRICULAR PROGRAMMING

One of the most critical elements of our interdisciplinary approach to entrepreneurship education are our various co-curricular program offerings. These programs link students to entrepreneurial learning opportunities at the Hynes Institute, as well as existing programs on campus that started to infuse entrepreneurship into their own disciplines. Our emphasis has been on building an entrepreneurial culture of innovation on campus by engaging faculty and students in the development of these programs. The following list gives an overview of the various program elements:

1. *Co-working* is a collaborative workspace at the Hynes Institute where Iona students can work with fellow students, mentors, and faculty to develop ideas, work on projects, and discover their entrepreneurial potential. Co-working is open to all Iona students and there is no RSVP required.
2. *Entrepreneur Talks* offer the entire Iona community the opportunity to learn from entrepreneurs, intrapreneurs, and industry leaders on a variety of topics (e.g., financing your business, learning from failure, launching a business, networking).
3. The *Hynes Distinguished Speaker Series* features prominent entrepreneurs.
4. *Student Workshops* allow students to engage in experiential learning to enhance their problem-solving abilities. Topics include storytelling, intellectual property, 3D printing, networking, ideation, problem/need identification, and business model canvas.
5. The *Iona Innovation Challenge* gives Iona students the opportunity to design solutions that address real-world problems. Over the course of the semester, students are not only able to work on their ideas by completing a series of milestones (video pitch, executive summary, pitch deck), but also gain valuable feedback by working with our growing mentor network (facilitated by our entrepreneur in residence) from a variety of fields. The two-month competition concludes with a final event where students compete for $6,000 in prizes.
6. *The Entrepreneurship Club*, a Collegiate Entrepreneurs' Organization chapter, was launched in fall 2017. The student club has 30 active members and organizes regular meetups, speaker events, workshops, and off-campus excursions.
7. Since fall 2018, six students of our entrepreneurship club have been accepted to *University Innovation Fellows*, a program of Stanford University's Hasso Plattner Institute of Design. Students apply the design thinking process to support the entrepreneurship and innovation ecosystem at Iona College. Our first cohort worked on an initiative to engage student clubs around campus to improve their inter-club collaborations through a competition, the Changemaker Challenge. The second cohort is currently working on designing a freshmen community engagement and retention project.
8. Our *entrepreneurial interns* are integral members of our team and assist with events, provide programming support, engage in student out-reach, and lead many special projects. One example of such a project is our *Ionavation Podcast*, which features alumni, entrepreneurs, and fellow students to share and discuss a broad range of entrepreneur-

ship topics. These podcasts are exclusively produced, hosted, and promoted by our student interns and available on YouTube and iTunes.

FACULTY DEVELOPMENT AS AN ESSENTIAL BUILDING BLOCK

In addition to its native programming (above), the Hynes Institute provides ample opportunities for Iona faculty to build capacity for entrepreneurial learning opportunities within their respective disciplines. In order to do so, we developed a series of faculty development and funding opportunities that serve as a catalyst for curricular innovation across the college.

An essential element of our faculty outreach, development, and collaboration efforts have been our monthly *Lunch and Learn Seminar* series for faculty and staff across the college. The seminars are held four–five times per semester and include topics such as 3-D printing, design thinking, redesigning learning spaces, agile, service learning, social entrepreneurship, or storytelling.

Building off our Lunch and Learn seminars, we launched the *Hynes Faculty Fellowship Program* to provide Iona's full-time faculty with an opportunity to develop and implement entrepreneurial learning innovations within their disciplines. We apply a broad definition of entrepreneurial learning innovations to foster creativity amongst faculty and push the boundaries of our growing field of entrepreneurship education. Proposals must demonstrate how the proposed project (1) supports the development of an entrepreneurial mindset amongst students, and (2) goes above and beyond existing educational practices at the college. For instance, learning innovations could be (but are not limited to) the development of a new course or the modification of an existing course by infusing entrepreneurship/innovation content through innovative pedagogies into that course (e.g., design thinking, experiential learning, service learning, etc.); an entrepreneurial class project or co-curricular program (e.g., club, speaker events, workshops series); or entrepreneurial service learning projects. The following breakdown illustrates the overall structure and timeline for our second (2019–20) funding cycle:

- January 2019: Announcement of program and request for proposal.
- February–April 2019: faculty are required to attend at least one out of five one-hour faculty development seminars.
- April 5, 2019: Hynes Faculty Fellows Symposium at Iona College.
- April 30, 2019: Deadline to submit project proposals.
- May 2019: Awards notifications (range $1,000–$4,000) to Fellowship Cohort 3.
- Summer and/or fall 2019: Project preparation.

- Fall 2019 and/or spring 2020: Project implementation.
- April 2020: Presentation of project outcomes at a Hynes Faculty Fellows Symposium at Iona College and submission of one-page project reflection/ report for symposium proceedings.
- April 30, 2020: Kick-off of new fellowship cycle.

During its first two funding cycles, the Hynes Institute has awarded $21,643 to 11 projects from 10 departments (mathematics, occupational therapy, media and strategic communication, biology, chemistry, fine arts, performing arts, psychology, speech communication, finance). Projects, which are often cross-disciplinary collaborations between faculty members, range from student-run social ventures (e.g., Community Sales Initiative: students reducing waste by collecting gently used items from residential students during move-out day and selling them to incoming students at the beginning of the fall semester), to academic freshmen service-learning projects (e.g. Designing your Future: Iona freshmen teaching multi-lingual 2nd–5th graders how to 3D print as part of an afterschool program), to new course developments (e.g. The Art of Curating: a course that teaches students how to successfully stage and run an art exhibit). These fellowship projects create a transformative impact and serve as a catalyst to introduce entrepreneurial learning across the college in ways we never could have imagined possible.

It is also important to note that an essential element of these faculty fellowships is a clear pathway towards scholarship by encouraging faculty fellows to document, present, and disseminate their work beyond Iona College. For instance, faculty fellows are invited to submit their work to the Annual USASBE Conference (www.usasbe.org) following each program cycle. The Hynes Institute provides conference travel support to faculty fellows in addition to the initial award, if accepted to the conference. We piloted this program for the first time when we co-hosted the 2020 USASBE Conference with the theme "Interdisciplinary and Experiential Entrepreneurship Education" in New Orleans. The results of this pilot have been incredible. A total of eight faculty fellows attended the conference showcasing and discussing their work with fellow entrepreneurship educators.

CONCLUSION

The Hynes Institute is quite unique given its positioning at the college, as well as its transformative and interdisciplinary approach to entrepreneurship education at a small liberal arts institution. As evidenced above, the Hynes Institute has already accomplished a lot within a short amount of time and has impacted many college stakeholders. Given that the Institute has not been conceived as an entity under a specific school or program, we were able to start a transformation that has already yielded a substantive change in the college's culture. Entrepreneurship and innovation have been embraced as important pedagogical elements to support student learning at every level at the college, from freshmen learning communities to graduate courses.

20. Millikin University Center for Entrepreneurship

Julienne Shields

INTRODUCTION

Millikin University had an early commitment to entrepreneurship that harkens back to the founder James Millikin who was an entrepreneur with a vision for an institution of higher learning that embraced industry and practicality as equals with the literary and classical. That vision has led to a campus with eyes to the sky and feet on the ground, where entrepreneurship students and faculty alike collaborate to dream and deliver on that promise. This mindset influences our pedagogical paradigm within the classroom, and we call it "performance learning." Performance learning is more than experiential learning. It incorporates a component of external validation. We apply this to our entrepreneurship curriculum by including tangible market validation, revealing performance learning and entrepreneurship have a great deal of alignment by reinforcing academic relevance.

HISTORY

The Small Business Center was launched within the Tabor School of Business in 1997, by Jack Gaston, and in 1998 Sharon Alpi became the founding director of the Center for Entrepreneurship. Sharon is regarded by many as a force of nature and inspirational mentor who worked tirelessly to build an entrepreneurship ecosystem rare for an institution the size of Millikin University.

The long-standing relationship with the Coleman Foundation was essential to the development of the Center and its multi-disciplinary programs. While the $2.5 million in investments over 15 years was vital, the mentorship from Michael Hennessy, chief executive officer of the Coleman Foundation, was indispensable and the relationships developed among the Coleman Fellows' schools was critical to the development and sustainability of the program.

In 2010, Millikin University and the Center embarked on a $1 million endowment campaign called Project Confirm to support the sustainable programming of the Center for Entrepreneurship on Millikin's campus. That successful effort has led to the ability for the Center to experiment with new initiatives, to support the educational initiatives of the Center, the students, entrepreneurship faculty and fellows, and the community.

In 2012, Millikin received a Global Consortium of Entrepreneurship Centers award for Exceptional Activities in Entrepreneurship across Disciplines, and in 2013, Millikin received the Outstanding Specialty Entrepreneurship Program Award from the United States Association of Small Business and Entrepreneurship for its arts entrepreneurship program. These recognitions were primarily due to the commitment to broad types of student-run ventures.

In 2018, Millikin hired its first full-time, tenure-track entrepreneurship professor, to develop and strengthen the research capabilities of the program.

CURRICULAR COMMITMENT

Millikin University has an entrepreneurship major, an entrepreneurship minor for non-business majors, an arts entrepreneurship certificate, and an entrepreneurship certificate. The certificates are differentiated because artists are often looking for business-related functional skills not taught in arts classes, while business students are often seeking more creative and design competencies not taught in business classes.

The major, minor, and certificates are particularly flexible when it comes to accepting courses from non-business disciplines that infuse learning goals across disciplines. In 2020, there are 32 courses outside of the business school that formally infuse entrepreneurship learning goals into the course. We encourage our business and entrepreneurship students to take classes in other contexts and disciplines so they can apply what they learn in those courses to their course of study and future entrepreneurship intentions.

A notable feature of the Tabor School of Business Core that all business students are required to take is a set of courses called Business Creation and Team Dynamics where students are put into teams to develop an in-depth business model of a new, creative business. At the end of the course project, they are able to use their work to compete for substantial academic travel scholarships while they are enrolled at Millikin.

STUDENT-RUN VENTURES

Although Millikin University was not the first to embrace the concept of student-run ventures as entrepreneurship pedagogy, it has arguably "riffed" on the concept more than any other institution. What started with one student-run venture in 1998, First Step Records – a student-run record label – has expanded to 15 unique ventures within nine disciplines in 2020.

There are a few important elements of student-run ventures to consider when it comes to their proliferation on Millikin's campus. Within the disruption often experienced within academia, the reality that Millikin continues to support student-run ventures is a testament to their value as distinctive, effective, and extraordinarily energizing despite the additional efforts and resources required to continue them.

One important distinction from other incarnations of student-run ventures is that Millikin's student-run ventures are in no way critical to the functioning of the business of the university. For example, they are not part of the bookstore, athletics, or food and beverage operation on campus. There is not an automatic set of customers that support the ventures because of a university need. Funding does not flow from university "customers" to the ventures in any meaningful way. The students on the management or founding teams of these ventures must appeal to and discover their customer base.

Student-run ventures are wildly popular with many students on campus. We have had discussions at the administrative level about why students are taking multiple student-run venture classes. "Didn't they already learn entrepreneurship in First Step Records? Why did they sign up for two more?" or "Why is she signing up for Blue Satellite a fifth time?" While these are reasonable questions, and fiscally responsible ones, what we have learned from having a variety of ventures from which to choose include three key takeaways. (1) Students are profoundly interested in experimenting or testing theories learned in the classroom in a practical setting with a faculty member alongside them. (2) Students also love to learn the hard way – through failures – so that they pay attention to the course work in other classes. (3) Ventures tend to offer excellent opportunities for peer-to-peer learning.

There are also structural lessons learned for faculty throughout the comparing and contrasting of various ventures. (1) There is no one right way to structure a venture; (2) the ventures are distinct experiences from one semester to another given the unique mix of students who enroll; and (3) each faculty member brings his/her own strengths and talents to each venture which yields different emphases to the kinds of lessons learned from the ventures. Student-run ventures also yield opportunities for creative destruction as well. There is never a dull moment. For example, a student-run venture that is not able to generate sufficient customer interaction for learning opportunities may suffer a couple of fates: (1) enrollment wanes causing students and faculty to reimagine the venture through new product or service offerings; or (2) the venture is discontinued, and the lessons learned are celebrated. The second can be a tough one to swallow, and careful cultivation of positive messaging is recommended.

FACULTY AS EDUCATIONAL ENTREPRENEURS

Most faculty teaching entrepreneurship competencies are outside of the business school and infuse creativity, innovation, and startup concepts, learning objectives, and projects into their courses. They are the lifeblood of our multi-disciplinary program.

Faculty autonomy is a particularly critical feature of Millikin's ecosystem. The faculty that are dreaming, experimenting, forging ahead, and even failing alongside the students are the engines of entrepreneurship on Millikin's campus. Their willingness to explore, their eagerness to launch and relaunch ventures, and their commitment to a philosophy of detachment so students can appreciate the risk and reward of the effort are all essential to the continued desirability of students to enroll in the ventures.

Millikin University faculty are educational entrepreneurs who are encouraged to infuse entrepreneurship into their courses by their chairs and deans, and aided by relatively streamlined course approval processes. Again, the commitment to performance learning at Millikin is pervasive and policies and procedures support this.

Another important attribute of Millikin is its commitment to creating continuously unique experiences as educators. Our faculty by-in-large expect to teach a 4-4 load, and yet a number of those teaching entrepreneurship across diverse disciplines agree to teach an overload to test pilot a student-run venture or a course in which they are able to infuse an entrepreneurship pillar. Overwhelmingly, when the question arises, "how do you get your faculty to teach entrepreneurship?" the response is, "I have no idea as I have never had that problem." The emotions, agency, pride, camaraderie, and celebrations (of both failures and successes) among faculty who embrace and teach entrepreneurship across campus is palpable.

MULTI-DISCIPLINARY APPROACH

Whereas the Center for Entrepreneurship at Millikin has a strong commitment to arts entrepreneurship on Millikin's campus (Millikin is ranked as a top 10 school in the country for musical theater by *College Magazine*), we observed that there were distinctive types of entrepreneurship functions within the arts – singular artists and troupes of artists – that were engaging in new ventures. Conversely, we noticed business students with wonderful skills, but little passion and talent that the artists brought to the conversation.

We were experimenting with multi-disciplinary teams in classes for years, and in 2016, we started working on ways to develop and promote multi-disciplinary teams as consulting teams and as competitive teams. We adapted Agile methodologies and Scrum to these multi-disciplinary projects with art majors, history majors, biology majors, physics majors, and more. While Agile has been in information technology for years, we started adapting it and translating it primarily using language more tailored to arts and humanities.

PIPELINE EFFECT

In a small town like Decatur, Illinois, it is necessary to have strategies for engaging youth who will hopefully attend Millikin and for developing relationships with community entrepreneurs for whom our students can practice the entrepreneurship skills they have learned and honed on campus. The Center has engaged throughout the past years in a number of local youth entrepreneurship initiatives including a collaborative a high school summer program called CampCEO, a middle school program for our public school district called SMASH Camp, the iSmartGirls event for innovative girls, and more.

Millikin University was also the first four-year institution to spearhead a partnership with IncubatorEdu – a high school entrepreneurship program with impressive results – to provide proficiency credits for graduates of their programs upon enrollment at Millikin. Much more than a recruiting strategy, watching the effects of the curriculum on the high school students is helping inform future curricular innovations at Millikin.

At the other end of the spectrum, we work with local entrepreneurs who need help with innovative projects. We pull together multi-disciplinary teams for short sprints to help the local entrepreneurs. This allows our students to develop interdisciplinary appreciation, practice Agile principles, problem solve with real situations, and make professional connections. These relationships have spawned post-project internships and friendships.

FINAL THOUGHTS

Millikin University's entrepreneurship program advances conversations, collisions, and creativity. We are fortunate to be able to leverage our size, resources, and institutional commitment to performance learning to be a nimble and bold program that continues to deliver entrepreneurial experiences and impact to our students, faculty, institution, and community.

21. University of Missouri-Kansas City Regnier Institute

Jeffrey Hornsby, Anthony Mendes and Andrew Heise

INTRODUCTION

The University of Missouri-Kansas City (UMKC) provides a variety of programs and course offerings focused on entrepreneurship. The Regnier Institute for Entrepreneurship and Innovation provides programs for both students and community members, while the Department of Entrepreneurship and Management provides academic offerings for students. Both are housed within the Bloch School of Management on the UMKC campus. One person acts as the department head and director of the institute. Staff is cross-hired as program administrators and instructors. This allows us to streamline efforts and be more responsive to our environment. Figure 21.1 provides a summary of our program impact.

Our Department and Institute team is made up of highly experienced academic scholars and practitioners. As of 2019, the Institute consists of four PhD tenure/tenure-track faculty, four managing directors (who oversee venture development, arts entrepreneurship, student programs, and cross-campus relationships), two assistant directors (who oversee our mentor and venture workshops), a program manager, and a venture coach.

PROGRAM DESCRIPTION AND UNIQUE ASPECTS

Curricular and Cross-Campus Academic Programs

Our academic credit-bearing programs are offered through the Department of Entrepreneurship and Innovation. Over the last four years, the department increased its production of student credit hours by 33.56 percent. This increase is a result of better marketing across campus and the addition of our general education courses that are discussed below.

Degrees/Coursework	E-Scholars	Cross-Campus Partnerships	Mentor Program
Formal degrees: PhD, MBA Option, Major Emphasis and Minor	Since its inception in 2011, the E-Scholars program has demonstrated significant results:	Partnerships Across Campus:	153 mentors in database
25 courses offered each semester	100+ ventures launched	Innovation and the Aging Population: 60 students per semester	Added 23 new mentors in 2017–2018
Currently 7 online courses	70+ have received external funding from competitions, grants, loans, and investors	Biology, Innovation and Entrepreneurship: 30 to 60 students per semester	Added 8 new attorneys up 4 from last year to provide pro bono work for E-Scholars
Courses revised in fall 2018 with Entrepreneurial Mindset and Opportunity Recognition, Designing the Business Model, and Entrepreneurial Finance forming the core of both our minor and BBA emphasis area	50+ have hired employees or used outside contractors	Arts and Entrepreneurship: 40 students enrolled	Volunteered over a 1000 hours per year toward our programs and with our students
		New Venture Creation:	
		Collaboration with the Law School	
Participant Quotes:	Participant Quotes:	Developed a partnership with the Kansas City Arts Institute	Participant Quotes:
"Without my knowledge of Entrepreneurship that I gained at the Regnier Institute, I would not be able to play the role in corporate innovation and technology that I have in Kansas City."	"Before E Scholars, we felt like we were playing "entrepreneur". Through E Scholars we became entrepreneurs, and we now feel prepared for the next chapter of our venture."	Participant Quotes:	From an E-Scholar: "Having a mentor there who has been through it before, and basically made all of mistakes before you, that you can draw from, is very comforting and gives you the confidence going forward. "
"I get to be creative in the entrepreneurship programs here, and my success is a team effort at the Bloch School."	"E Scholars gave me the tools and guidance I needed to turn my dream of being an entrepreneur into a reality. If it weren't for the amazing faculty and staff I would have never been able to conceptualize, launch and scale my business so quickly."	"I definitely recommend this course to other students. It's a much needed course for all [arts students]."	From a mentor: "They have dreams and it's a good reminder for me that there are big ideas out there. If you can help nurture them, they can help inspire you too. "
		"Extremely important practical information about how to think like an entrepreneur"	From a mentor: "Really it's an exchange of energy between the mentors and scholars. It's an opportunity to give back to Kansas City through helping these ventures grow."
		"This is extremely important for anyone wanting to make a living off their artistic practice."	

Figure 21.1　Entrepreneurship and innovation impact

For fall 2018, we fully revamped our undergraduate curriculum to further embrace project-based learning, play, and creative problem solving in every course. Based on the latest research and best practices in the field, our entrepreneurship curriculum focuses on risk mitigation, opportunity alertness, resource leveraging, reflection, teamwork, peer review, design thinking, and creativity tools. Successful completion of courses can lead to formal degrees in entrepreneurship (PhD, MBA Option, Major Emphasis, and Minor).

To accommodate student demand and offer flexibility in our curriculum, seven undergraduate entrepreneurship courses are now offered online with plans to add other undergraduate courses within the next year. Curriculum flexibility enables students from a wide range of disciplines such as engineering, the arts, health sciences, and social sciences to take courses in entrepreneurship – providing valuable skills and resources to enhance their academic accomplishments.

Anchor Courses in the General Education Program/Cross-Campus Courses

In partnership with faculty from various disciplines, we offer general education courses that infuse entrepreneurship in the arts, biological sciences, and humanities curriculum. Nearly 300 students enroll in these courses annually. Courses offered include:

- ANCH 310 – Innovation and the Aging Population: 60 students per semester.
- ANCH 199 – Biology, Innovation and Entrepreneurship: 30 to 60 students per semester.
- ANCH 299 – Arts Entrepreneurship: 40 students per semester.

Arts Entrepreneurship

The goal of our Arts Entrepreneurship Initiative is to incorporate entrepreneurship education into various arts disciplines including music, theatre, dance, and visual arts. We offer two classes in partnership with the UMKC Conservatory, "Arts Entrepreneurship" and "Principles of Arts Business". Launched fall 2019, we have also developed a partnership with Kansas City Arts Institute to offer a business and entrepreneurship minor to art and design students. A Certificate in Arts Entrepreneurship in partnership with the UMKC Conservatory launches fall 2021.

STUDENT AND COMMUNITY CO-CURRICULAR PROGRAMS

Entrepreneurship Scholars

The Regnier Institute offers a program called Entrepreneurship Scholars (E-Scholars). E-Scholars is a comprehensive program for early-stage entrepreneurs, through which we help them take their business ideas from concept to reality. Participants are both students and community members. Because the program focuses on early-stage ventures, we work with a wide variety of industries and technologies including enterprise software and mobile apps, consumer products, medical devices, culinary ventures, and not-for-profits. Student participants in the program can take E-Scholars for up to six credit hours towards their minor or major.

E-Scholars has two main components: content and mentorship. E-Scholars work with academic and practitioner lecturers in areas including business strategy, marketing and sales, finance, idea feasibility, product-market fit, legal, project management, and operations. Students also work with a network of over 150 mentors who provide both ad hoc and ongoing coaching. Mentors are principally concerned with educating entrepreneurs and assisting ventures to be commercially successful. Applying their collective experience to student ventures, they provide considerable expertise, helping to advance student ventures through strategic coaching.

Beginning January 2019, specialized tracks designed to give more dedicated attention to each business according to their focus was launched. This includes a New Product track covering 3D design, 3D printing, and manufacturing processes; a Technology track for those developing businesses around software as a service, web applications, or mobile applications; and a Services track, for those who plan to launch a business whose primary offering is a service (to include not-for-profits).

Since 2017, we have offered an online version of E-Scholars. In 2017 we piloted an online session for 10 ventures and based on our experience and feedback, we revised the course and offered the online version to over 20 student ventures across the University of Missouri System. By offering the program online, we can expand our reach and include people outside of the Kansas City area. This could include students from other universities, people from other parts of the United States, and across the globe.

Since its inception in 2011, E-Scholars has supported more than 300 entrepreneurs. More than 100 ventures have launched, including more than 70 who have received external funding from competitions, grants, loans and investors, and more than 50 who hired employees or used outside contractors.

Highlighted E-Scholars success stories

Mobility Designed

For years, Mobility Designed founders Max and Liliana Younger had an idea for a better crutch. The traditional under-arm crutches that everyone is familiar with went essentially unchanged for 150 years. As product designers, both Max and Liliana knew what it took to design successful products that solve real problems. What they did not have was the business background to build their plan to turn a great product idea into a great business. They took the leap and joined the E-Scholars program to put together a plan and launch the venture. Max and Liliana took first place in the 2015 Regnier Venture Creation Challenge, taking home a $15,000 cash prize to help them further develop their venture. In April 2016, Mobility Designed went viral online, generating more than 30 million views of their video after a positive mention from an influential tech website. This newly garnered attention resulted in a flood of pre-orders and interest in their product.

Integrated Roadways

Tim Sylvester is a graduate of UMKC's School of Computing and Engineering, as well as the inaugural (2011) cohort of the Regnier Institute's E-Scholars program. He created Integrated Roadways, which is rethinking the traditional model for developing and deploying roadway transportation networks. Sylvester founded Integrated Roadways to develop and deliver factory-built, precast pavement sections with embedded intelligent transportation systems (or "smart pavement"). The company delivered its first product to the Kansas Department of Transportation in 2012, and its second product to UMKC's new Bloch Executive Hall in 2013. Integrated Roadways was selected in 2015 to receive a $50,000 LaunchKC grant, and in 2016 was selected by the City of Kansas City as one of its first participants in the Innovation Partners Program.

E-Scholars testimonials

The E-Scholars program has been phenomenal this term, hitting three main aspects of becoming a successful entrepreneur perfectly. From the period of instruction led by an astounding team and guest speakers, how could one not learn and further their own insight into their venture and entrepreneurship? These insights and ideas are furthered by the peer group in E-Scholars. (From Aware Vehicles, formerly Agrivalence – Kris Mahan)

E Scholars gave us the road map we needed to move forward with our venture and the guidance from community mentors was key in bringing all the pieces together. Before E-Scholars, we felt like we were playing "entrepreneur." Through E-Scholars we *became* entrepreneurs. (From Travel Hive – Jillian Carlilie and Kim Rosen)

Mentor Program

The Regnier Mentor Program consists of a network of over 150 professionals from almost every industry and skillset. Mentors are primarily focused on coaching entrepreneurs and assisting ventures in becoming commercially successful. Mentors volunteer as one-on-one E-Scholar coaches, guest lecturers, mentor in residence, and judges for competitions.

Our mentors collectively provide over 1,000 hours of their time each academic year to our programs and students. Here are a few ways they volunteered in 2017–18:

- 12 mentors facilitated workshops in the Venture Hub.
- Seven mentors had regular office hours at the Venture Hub working with students or walk-ins from the community.
- Five mentors helped with E-Scholars practice pitches.
- Six mentors provided instructional content to E-Scholars.
- Over 50 mentors served as judges for our competitions.
- 28 mentors provided one-on-one counseling to E-Scholars.

Venture Hub

The UMKC Bloch Venture Hub is the next step in our efforts to nurture Kansas City area entrepreneurs. The programs are a "hub" where students and community entrepreneurs can develop their ventures from concept to launch and scale. The location in one of the largest co-working organizations provides low-barrier access to many of UMKC's entrepreneurship resources and physical meeting spaces for idea-stage entrepreneurs to access entrepreneurship resources, programming, and mentoring. In 2018 we hosted over 30 workshops for over 500 people.

Competitions

During the 2018–19 school year we offered two pitch/business plan competitions for students.

Entrepreneur Quest

Entrepreneur Quest is a University of Missouri System competition. Students made an initial pitch for a venture idea. The top 10 teams from two of the four System schools participated in our E-Scholars online to further explore their idea and create a business plan. The top 10 teams from each of the four Missouri System schools made presentations around their business plans in March 2019 at their home university. The top three venture teams took home

$30,000 in prizes and were invited to compete in a system-wide competition in April 2019 for another $30,000 in prizes. A team from UMKC took 2nd in the System competition.

Regnier Venture Creation Challenge
Since its inception in 2011, the *Regnier Venture Creation Challenge* (RVCC) has been open to students from any school in the region. Students compete in the preliminary round by pitching their business model and participating in our venture fair. Judges select semi-finalists who present a business plan slide deck. Through a newly formed partnership with Blue Cross-Blue Shield of Kansas City, we offer a special track for medical or healthcare startups. The competition awards $75,000 in total prizes. In RVCC 2019, over 70 venture teams from seven different universities competed.

First Wednesdays Speaker Series

On the first Wednesday of each month during the academic year, the Regnier Institute hosts a special speaker event to inspire Bloch students to launch new ventures. Monthly, this event brings together over 150 students and community members. Past speakers include Henry Bloch, David Hall, Barnett Helzberg, panels of young entrepreneurs, and many others. These speakers allow students to hear the startup stories and struggles from the region's most famous companies.

Summer Scholars

Summer Scholars is a two-week intensive course for approximately 20 incoming freshmen and transfer students. Students earn three hours of course credit for our Entrepreneurship Mindset course and are introduced to the entrepreneurship department, the Regnier Institute, and the Kansas City entrepreneurship community.

Enactus

Enactus is a cross-campus organization supported by Regnier Institute staff. Students use the entrepreneurial processes to implement social change. Our Enactus chapter currently has more than 90 students participating. Approximately 50 percent are students with the Bloch School of Management and 50 percent are majors from other parts of campus.

More than 75 students participate in one of 11 student-developed projects. These projects impact almost 6,000 people. Here is a sampling of their projects and impact:

- Arts and Entrepreneurship helps local artists learn skills to better equip themselves for the business world. Through their efforts, 32 artists are better prepared to turn their passion into a career.
- FeedKC identified the dual problems of food waste and hunger in Kansas City. Students diverted over 2,300 pounds of edible meals to organizations and people in need. They are now taking the additional step of creating a scalable mobile application to create a sustainable model.
- Strategies for Success taught workshops on financial literacy, planning for after high school, and career and educational opportunities to 360 high school students.
- 400 students in Ogwugwu, Nigeria gained access to clean water and soon will gain access to sanitary facilities. Student-led fundraising efforts made these improvements possible.
- 100 students and startups connected to improve the entrepreneurial ecosystem in Kansas City.
- Students partnered with the Kansas City Economic Development Corporation to support trade with Changsha, China.

UMKC Enactus accomplished a top 16 finish at a national competition out of over 500 university chapters in the United States. *In 2019, our Enactus chapter finished in fourth place nationally.*

High School Programs

We actively work to promote our programs and offerings to high school students and teachers. We partner with two school districts to offer dual credit courses. We offer a variety of workshops on innovation to high school groups visiting campus including DECA and KC Prep. During the 2018–19 school year, we hosted approximately 300 high school students. We also offer workshops for business and entrepreneurship teachers.

Research

Theoretical and applied research has been a foundation of the Regnier Institute since its inception over 10 years ago. Three research-active tenured professors are Jeff Hornsby, Mark Parry, and Brian Anderson, who have cumulatively 150+ journal articles and seven books.

Funding

Our academic programs are supported by the Bloch School of Management, named after Henry W. Bloch, founder of H&R Bloch. His foundation supports many educational initiatives within the Regnier Institute and the Bloch School. Our co-curricular programs are supported by an endowment from the Regnier Family Foundation, the Kauffman Foundation, and our annual Entrepreneur of the Year Awards banquet. We also receive private donations. Our annual budget is ~$900,000.

FUTURE DIRECTIONS

The Regnier Institute for Entrepreneurship and Innovation has existed since 2008. Its programs have grown extensively to include cross-system (the University of Missouri System consists of four universities) cross-campus, and community outreach programming and courses. Like most successful entrepreneurship centers, the entrepreneurship landscape across our campus and in our communities is constantly changing. To that end, we have embarked on a new strategic plan to position us in a way to meet these challenges and impact entrepreneurs (traditional, corporate, and social) over the next five years.

PART III

Best practice innovations inside and outside the classroom

22. *Are you the one?* A game for encouraging classroom diversity

Shelby Solomon and Otis Solomon, Jr.

INTRODUCTION

Many entrepreneurship professors, among others across disciplines, desire to encourage students to break out of their social circles and engage in diverse interactions in and outside of the classroom. Moreover, embracing diversity is important for nascent entrepreneurs, as outsiders and loose social network ties serve as a vital source of new knowledge and potential providers of resources (e.g., investors, customers, employees, domain experts, channel partners, and so forth) (Larson & Starr, 1993). To date many routine attempts at encouraging diversity take an excessively paternal approach, such as forcing students into prespecified groups based upon student majors or some other readily observable difference. We view such attempts to encourage diversity as undesirable because paternal tactics limit individual freedom restraining students from the opportunity to strategize, tinker, and learn from the process.

To respect individual autonomy while encouraging diversity, we offer a game based on MTV's reality series *Are You the One* (AYTO henceforth). The game encourages diversity through the use of group incentives, thereby preserving autonomy and inspiring social exploration. Playing AYTO also helps students to hone their problem solving and cooperative skills, as the game requires the class work as a collective in figuring out the solution to a semester-long challenge. Finally, running the AYTO class game is a novel way for professors to approach the subject of diversity and enliven the class.

GAME ORIGIN, OVERVIEW, AND OBJECTIVE

AYTO at its core is a game designed to push individuals to learn about each other and make assessments as to how they relate to one another. Before attempting to run this game in your class, we suggest that you watch a few episodes of the MTV series to get an idea of the rules and nature of the game. The MTV series AYTO[1] is available for streaming through a number of services.

In the MTV version of AYTO, an even number of singles (e.g., 10 males and 10 females) are brought to a villa where they are told that one of the members of the opposite sex is their perfect match based upon a compatibility algorithm. The singles are then told that they will be given $1 million dollars ($50,000 each) if they can all identify their perfect matches by the end of the season. The process unfolds across ~10 weekly matching ceremonies where each sex takes turns attempting to pair up with their perfect matches (i.e., males and females alternate leading matching ceremonies). At the end of each ceremony the host tells the group how many matches they got correct, but does not let them know who those matches were. To aide in this process the singles are also allowed to use the *truth booth* each week, where they can ask if one prospective couple is a match and receive a yes or no answer. The objective of the classroom version of AYTO is very similar, however, the class attempts to figure out matches based upon deep-level diversity (e.g., personality or attitudes) not dating compatibility. Moreover, students are playing for extra credit points as opposed to money.

ORGANIZING THE GAME FOR CLASS

The professor starts the game by administering personality tests to a class. The professor should inform the students that the personality tests will be used for a class diversity game that will be played for extra credit. We suggest using the Big 5 inventory (e.g., Donnellan, Oswald, Baird, & Lucas, 2006) to measure personality, in addition to a few other measures of the professor's choosing (e.g., Rokeach's (1973) values survey or Snyder & Gangestad's (1986) self-monitoring survey). We do not recommend telling the students how the game is played until after they have taken the test, as students can take screen shots of the test and use them to cheat if they know how they game works. Furthermore, we propose offering a sizable extra credit reward (~3 percentage points), because raising the stakes makes the game far more entertaining for everyone in the later stages.

Next, the professor creates a correlation matrix between all of their students' responses, as a means to quantify differences. The professor then uses an algorithm to match students into two maximally different sets based upon their correlations with each other. This is slightly different from the MTV series AYTO, because the students are placed into maximally different sets rather than matched to who is most different from them—as matching students to who are most different results in multiple matches.

If given an even number of students that need to be paired,[2] consider a matrix for which the rows and columns correspond to students (Appendix A). The intersection of a column and row contains the correlation coefficient of the student whose name appears at the head of the row and column.

We view the problem as a graph with students as nodes in the graph containing edges between all pairs of students labelled with their correlation. A matching is a subset of edges in which no node occurs more than once. Thus, the problem is to find a matching for which the sum of the correlations is the minimum. The Python 3 (python.org, 2018) package NetworkX contains a function called max_weight_matching to find the matching for which the sum of the correlations is maximum. To translate our problem to a maximum problem, change the correlations from r to 1-r. The NetworkX min_weight_matching() algorithm finds the derangement of minimum correlation. For further instructions on running the algorithm refer to the sample code and data listed in Appendix B.

After running the algorithm and creating the unique sets of maximally different matches the professor can explain the game to the students. We recommend building a table of potential matches for students to use as a visual aide. The professor can make this table by taking the list of matches and sorting each column alphabetically to scramble the matches. The professor may project the table while playing to remind students who their potential match could be. The professor is now able to explain the challenge to their students – that is, to match themselves with the other students in the class who are diverse from themselves such that the two groups are maximally different from each other. Most of the time there will be a handful of students in the class who have seen the show and the class will catch on very quickly. We try to avoid getting hung up on the complexities and constraints placed upon the task of algorithm in making derangements and maximally distinct sets, and simply state that their goal is to find their perfect matches in terms of who is most diverse from them given the constraints of the class setting.

Once the students understand how to play the game, the professor gives them one truth booth and one matching ceremony per week. If the students correctly identify a match in the truth booth, then the pair is removed from the matching ceremonies and subsequently counted as correct. As previously stated, it is important that the professor does not say which matches the class got right, and only says how many were correct each week. Additionally, any time the class is allowed to assemble into groups for other activities and assignments the professor can remind them of the extra credit at stake in playing AYTO to suggest that they should use the group work as a way to get to know people. This pattern is carried out until either the students guess all their matches during a single ceremony and win the extra credit or the semester ends, at which point, they lose. Depending on class size the number of ceremonies may need to be adjusted – try to give them a number of ceremonies and truth booths that equals the number of matches in the class.

OUTCOMES OF PLAYING *ARE YOU THE ONE?*

In playing AYTO with students we find much to be learned through the activity. One of the first things that students begin to recognize, and that we find intriguing, is the fact that some people who are close friends are actually strikingly different from each other. This finding even surprised us in designing the game and running the preliminary data as we expected the similarity attraction paradigm to rule out such instances as common place. Another rewarding aspect of playing the game is the level of engaged problem solving that students put forth to play. As the game progresses and the stakes become higher, the students begin to have very intellectual discussions of decision making, risks, and how to make the most out of limited information. Finally, students enjoy playing the game, it serves as an amusing daily ice breaker to start class, and provides a great topic of discussion for the times when students want to talk about something other than work.

NOTES

1. We note that the rules of the game on MTV change slightly from season to season, and rules outlined in this chapter are most consistent with Season 1. Hence, what we describe in this chapter may not be representative of later seasons of the MTV series.
2. In the event that you have an odd number of students, we recommend withholding a student from the algorithm at random, and then matching them with whoever shares the lowest correlation with them – creating a group of three where two people work as a pair.

REFERENCES

Donnellan, M. B., Oswald, F. L., Baird, B. M., & Lucas, R. E. (2006). The mini-IPIP scales: tiny-yet-effective measures of the Big Five factors of personality. *Psychological Assessment*, 18(2), 192–203.

Larson, A., & Starr, J. A. (1993). A network model of organization formation. *Entrepreneurship: Theory and Practice*, 18, 5–15.

python.org (2018). Python Software Foundation. Python Language Reference, version 3.8. Available at www.python.org.

Rokeach, M. (1973). *The nature of human values*. New York: Free Press.

Snyder, M., & Gangestad, S. (1986). On the nature of self-monitoring: matters of assessment, matters of validity. *Journal of Personality and Social Psychology*, 51(1), 125–39.

APPENDIX A

Table 22A.1   Sample data

Sample Data										
	0	**1**	**2**	**3**	**4**	**5**	**6**	**7**	**8**	**9**
Participant 0	1.00									
Participant 1	0.33	1.00								
Participant 2	0.50	0.36	1.00							
Participant 3	0.50	0.51	0.38	1.00						
Participant 4	0.29	0.53	0.37	0.38	1.00					
Participant 5	0.27	0.74	0.13	0.50	0.52	1.00				
Participant 6	0.57	0.43	0.57	0.59	0.51	0.42	1.00			
Participant 7	0.04	0.48	0.00	0.23	0.59	0.53	0.22	1.00		
Participant 8	0.67	0.47	0.57	0.57	0.39	0.43	0.67	0.25	1.00	
Participant 9	0.59	0.68	0.38	0.52	0.46	0.61	0.62	0.22	0.56	1.00

APPENDIX B

```
import math
import networkx as nx
from networkx.algorithms.matching import max_weight_matching

# Input correlation data in long form listing each possible pairing. This is the only piece of code that needs
to be modified to run the algorithm.
weighted_edges=[
                (0,1,1-0.33),
                (0,2,1-0.50),
                (0,3,1-0.50),
                (0,4,1-0.29),
                (0,5,1-0.27),
                (0,6,1-0.57),
                (0,7,1-0.04),
                (0,8,1-0.67),
                (0,9,1-0.59),
                (1,2,1-0.36),
                (1,3,1-0.51),
                (1,4,1-0.53),
                (1,5,1-0.74),
                (1,6,1-0.43),
                (1,7,1-0.48),
                (1,8,1-0.47),
                (1,9,1-0.68),
                (2,3,1-0.38),
                (2,4,1-0.37),
                (2,5,1-0.13),
                (2,6,1-0.57),
                (2,7,1-0.00),
                (2,8,1-0.57),
                (2,9,1-0.38),
                (3,4,1-0.38),
                (3,5,1-0.50),
                (3,6,1-0.59),
                (3,7,1-0.23),
                (3,8,1-0.57),
                (3,9,1-0.52),
                (4,5,1-0.52),
                (4,6,1-0.51),
                (4,7,1-0.59),
                (4,8,1-0.39),
                (4,9,1-0.46),
                (5,6,1-0.42),
                (5,7,1-0.53),
                (5,8,1-0.42),
                (5,9,1-0.61),
                (6,7,1-0.22),
                (6,8,1-0.67),
                (6,9,1-0.62),
                (7,8,1-0.25),
                (7,9,1-0.22),
                (8,9,1-0.56)]

G = nx.Graph()
G.add_weighted_edges_from(weighted_edges)
G.edges
s = nx.max_weight_matching(G)
sum_of_correlations=0.0
number_pairs=round(len(s)/2.0)
print("Match  Correlation")
for i in range(0,len(s)):
    if(i < s[i]):
        print("(%d, %d) %.2f" % (i,s[i],1.0-G.edges[i,s[i]]['weight']))
        sum_of_correlations=sum_of_correlations+(1.0-G.edges[i,s[i]]['weight'])
print("Sum of correlations:",sum_of_correlations)

# See output below based on the sample data

Match  Correlation
(0, 7)  0.04
(1, 6)  0.43
(2, 5)  0.13
(3, 9)  0.52
(4, 8)  0.39
Sum of correlations: 1.5100000000000002
```

Figure 22B.1   Sample Python 3 code

23. Assume less, observe more: the toothbrush design challenge

Doan Winkel, Justin Wilcox and Federico Mammano

INTRODUCTION

Identifying, and testing, hidden assumptions is a critical skill for any entrepreneur. This fun and high-energy exercise, which won the 2019 *USASBE 3E Excellence in Entrepreneurial Exercises Award*, utilizes children's toothbrushes to help students see how easily they can make hidden assumptions that hinder the success of a project. Then the exercise introduces students to customer observations, a tool that can be used to mitigate the consequences of hidden assumptions. Overall, this is an engaging design-thinking exercise that encourages students to assume less, and observe more.

Understanding the role hidden assumptions play in the failure of businesses is important for students, but it's a difficult concept for students to internalize until they've experienced it themselves. This exercise, a part of the award-winning Experiential Entrepreneurship Curriculum (www.teachinge .org), gives students the experience of making hidden assumptions, and demonstrates how doing so often leads to a project's failure. The exercise also introduces students to design thinking's customer observations, which they can use to discover hidden assumptions and turn them into validated learnings that improve a product's design.

The exercise begins by organizing students in teams of four, and giving each team an adult-sized toothbrush, as well as the dimensions of an average adult's hand, and dimensions of an average child's hand. Teams are given five minutes to design a new, bestselling toothbrush for children, after which they report on their designs, including the dimensions of their toothbrushes (Figure 23.1).

Almost universally, teams will create toothbrush designs for children that are proportionally smaller than adult-sized toothbrushes, not realizing they are making hidden assumptions about the fine motor skills of children. Next, educators can play a short video from Tom Kelley of IDEO (http://bit.ly/

Figure 23.1   Designing a child's toothbrush

ExECToothbrush), where he tells the story of how toothbrush manufacturers made the same incorrect assumptions for years, and how they identified, and rectified, that assumption with a simple set of customer observations resulting in a new innovative, and best-selling, toothbrush design.

After reflecting on their designs, and those described in the video, students will understand not only how easy it was for them to make hidden assumptions, but also how easy hidden assumptions can be to prevent. Finally, students are given an assignment to hypothesize problems students are facing on campus, and then go observe students at that location to test their hypotheses. When students come to the next session of class, they collectively reflect on the hypotheses they validated, invalidated, and any new problems they discovered, demonstrating the efficacy of customer observations.

Observing customers in natural settings is a powerful experience for students. They discover new business opportunities. They increase their customer empathy. They hone their behavioral analysis skills. All critical entrepreneurial competencies!

Students going through this exercise learn a technique to gain insight into the small details of a customer's interaction with their environment that a customer may not think to express in interviews.

THE EXERCISE

Form teams of three or four students. Give each team an adult toothbrush (Figure 23.2).

Figure 23.2   Adult toothbrush

Their assignment is to design a child's toothbrush in five minutes. The design must include at least the following elements:

1. Color scheme
2. Dimensions.

The color scheme element is really a red herring. The colors they choose are irrelevant. We include the color scheme requirement to ensure students are not solely focused on the dimensions element. The dimensions are where students will unearth hidden assumptions, and create an ineffective product based on those hidden assumptions.

Hidden assumptions will likely cause students to design a toothbrush with the wrong dimensions for children. They will assume a smaller hand needs a proportionally smaller toothbrush. Display Figure 23.3 that contains hand size data. To emphasize their importance, tell students the hand dimensions that are on the slide: the average adult male hand, is 7.44 inches long (measured from the tip of the middle finger to the wrist) and 3.30 inches wide (measured across the palm). The average adult female hand size is 6.77 inches long and 2.91 inches wide. The average child hand size is 5.5 inches long and 2.75 inches wide. Tell teams they have five minutes to design the best-selling toothbrush for children, and they must include the dimensions.

Average Hand Sizes

- **Adult Male:**
  - Length: 7.44"
  - Width: 3.30"
- **Adult Female:**
  - Length: 6.77"
  - Width: 2.91"
- **Child:**
  - Length: 5.5"
  - Width: 2.75"

Adult Toothbrush

- Length: 7.25"
- Width: 0.5"

Figure 23.3   Hand dimensions

THE DEBRIEF

After five minutes, ask teams to report on what design challenges they made. Specifically, ask all groups whether their child's toothbrush was larger or smaller than an adult's. Most teams will end up making a smaller toothbrush. This is a very natural and logical assumption based on the hand size data we presented (to bias) them. It is the assumption very experienced product designers at toothbrush manufacturers made, so your students are in good company!

Your students likely designed a child's toothbrush that would fail in the market based on hidden assumptions. Show the video (http://bit.ly/ ExECToothbrush) where IDEO partner Tom Kelley drives home the importance of acknowledging and testing hidden assumptions.

Reflect on what hidden assumptions they made, and why they made them. Emphasize that it is natural to assume smaller people need smaller toothbrushes, but that the students' assumptions make for bad toothbrushes, and even worse businesses.

Show on a slide: *Entrepreneurs can't trust numbers alone. In order to improve the world, we must see, feel, and experience it for ourselves!* Point out that many toothbrush manufacturers made the same invalid assumptions many of them made in terms of a smaller hand needs a smaller toothbrush.

Discuss how students could test their assumptions to determine their validity. Steer them toward observing customers using a product or service, and toward prototyping the product or service. This exercise is fast, fun, and engaging for students. It is a flexible experience that you can use to introduce various topics including why companies fail, planning versus experimenting, and the business model canvas.

LEARNING OUTCOMES AND KEY TAKEAWAYS

This fun and interactive exercise will help educators engage their students in learning a concept critical to successful entrepreneurs in a memorable way, that students can apply immediately, with just a handful of toothbrushes.

Using this exercise will achieve the following learning outcomes:

- Students discover how easy it can be for them to make hidden assumptions.
- Introduce students to a powerful tool to gather information on customer experience in real-life situations. This allows students to avoid predicting customer behavior by actually observing it.
- Students practice how to listen with their eyes in order to understand what people value and care about, and what they don't.

Through this exercise, educators can:

- Introduce students to a powerful tool to gather information on customer experience in real-life situations. This allows students to avoid predicting customer behavior by actually observing it.
- Learn how students can practice how to listen with their eyes in order to understand what people value and care about, and what they don't.
- Provide a common reference experience for expanding on topics later in the course.

CONCLUSION

This experiential exercise can be useful to any educator teaching design thinking, lean startup, business model generation, customer development, or any course associated with new venture creation. Students enjoy the experience, and leave with an internalized experience of how easy hidden assumptions are to make, and a practical tool to combat them. Moreover, it is well grounded in best practice research for entrepreneurship education (cf., Pittaway & Cope, 2007; Kassean, Vanevenhoven, Liguori, & Winkel, 2015; Neck & Corbett, 2018; Vanevenhoven & Liguori, 2013).

REFERENCES

Kassean, H., Vanevenhoven, J., Liguori, E., & Winkel, D. E. (2015). Entrepreneurship education: a need for reflection, real-world experience and action. *International Journal of Entrepreneurial Behavior and Research*, 21(5), 690–708.

Neck, H. M., & Corbett, A. C. (2018). The scholarship of teaching and learning entrepreneurship. *Entrepreneurship Education and Pedagogy*, 1(1), 8–41.

Pittaway, L., & Cope, J. (2007). Simulating entrepreneurial learning: integrating
experiential and collaborative approaches to learning. *Management Learning*, 38(2),
211–33.

Vanevenhoven, J., & Liguori, E. (2013). The impact of entrepreneurship education:
introducing the entrepreneurship education project. *Journal of Small Business
Management*, 51(3), 315–28.

24. The Small Enterprise Education and Development Program

Daniel Holland and Michael Glauser

INTRODUCTION

The Small Enterprise Education and Development (SEED) Program provides a transformative international learning opportunity for students at Utah State University (USU). The SEED students spend 12 weeks in a developing country to teach entrepreneurs fundamental business building principles, help secure funding through strategic partners, and provide ongoing mentoring as the entrepreneurs strive to grow their small businesses.

Students strengthen their entrepreneurial skills through a three-pronged approach: learning, teaching, and mentoring. First, they study entrepreneurship fundamentals in a classroom setting. Second, they travel to their assigned country and teach the principles to many local nascent entrepreneurs. Finally, they work side by side with entrepreneurs, supporting and mentoring them through the startup or growth process.

Learning in a classroom provides the foundation for the students participating in the program. However, the depth of learning is greatly enhanced as they teach basic entrepreneurship classes to scores of clients. Research has shown that students that spend time teaching what they have learned gain a better understanding of the topic and improve their confidence and attitude toward the subject matter (Cohen, Kulic, & Kulic, 1982). Experiential learning (Kolb, 1984) is the capstone of the program, as students work with their clients to implement the entrepreneurship principles that they were taught. They are able to participate in the experience, reflect on the outcomes, draw conclusions, and plan new ways to achieve the new venture goals. By learning, teaching, and doing, students return from their SEED experience with a deeper understanding of entrepreneurial principles and can more effectively use those skills in their own ventures or in other employment.

SEED PROGRAM OVERVIEW

SEED started over 10 years ago when the Jon M. Huntsman School's Center for Entrepreneurship partnered with DanPer Corporation to provide education and funding to nascent entrepreneurs in Trujillo, Peru. The SEED program currently targets necessity entrepreneurs in five developing countries: Peru, Ghana, Philippines, Dominican Republic, and Guatemala. The Center for Entrepreneurship sends students to SEED locations during fall, spring, and summer semesters to teach entrepreneurs fundamental business building principles, help secure funding through strategic partners, and provide ongoing mentoring as the entrepreneurs strive to grow their small businesses.

SEED PROGRAM GOALS

The goals of the SEED program include:

- Empower underserved individuals and families with the skills of enterprise creation and development through a long-term commitment of education and mentorship.
- Provide safe in-field learning experiences for students through partnerships with reputable organizations in select regions of the world.
- Maintain sustainability through a variety of funding arrangements.
- Support up to 100 students each year from a wide variety of majors.
- Enable students to master the skills of business development through teaching and mentorship.
- Provide a transformative life experience through helping others.

LOCATION AND PARTNER SELECTION

Locations are selected based on several criteria. First, the location must be rated as a level 1 or level 2 for safety by the Department of State. Second, we only choose locations that are accessible to airports, transportation, hospitals, and other critical services. Third, we must find partners that will provide clients, facilities for teaching, funds for lending, and in-field supervision. Current partners include DanPer Corporation, Mentors International, Operation Underground Railroad, Lifting Generations, and other organizations. These partnerships are an integral part of the success and sustainability of the SEED program.

HOW SEED WORKS

There is a minimum of four students in each country during any given semester. Over the course of the year, we will send up to 24 students to Peru, 36 to the Philippines, 18 to Ghana, 30 to the DR, and 12 to Guatemala. There is significant demand for SEED internships and students must prepare early in their academic career to secure a position. The basic program process includes:

- Students complete a rigorous application and interview process to be accepted into SEED. Language skills are required for Spanish-speaking countries.
- Students in any major can meet the education requirements by taking a course in the fundamentals of entrepreneurship. To date, 53 different majors have been represented in the program.
- During the semester before leaving for their destination country, SEED students complete a business consulting course that prepares them for the experience.
- The in-country experience lasts for approximately 12 weeks.
- Students are provided safe housing and a stipend for airfare, resulting in minimal out-of-pocket expenses during their semester abroad.
- Students may earn a minor in entrepreneurship or up to nine internship credit hours for a project they choose to complete during the experience.
- Students work with our partner organizations to connect with local entrepreneurs. The services they provide include teaching entrepreneurship curricula, helping to vet business opportunities, assisting in writing simple business plans/models, preparing basic financial statements, securing funding through the partner, developing sales and marketing plans, and ongoing mentoring and monitoring of progress toward business objectives.

PROGRAM SOURCES OF FUNDING AND SUSTAINABILITY

In the early years, SEED loan funds were generated by USU students raising money in service-learning projects and from donations from friends and alumni of the Huntsman School of Business. In 2014, we transitioned to a model of relying on our in-country partners for loan funds. This model is sustainable for our partners because of the high repayment rate they realize. The program has distributed hundreds of thousands of dollars in small loans with an average annual repayment rate of over 98 percent. With partners handling the lending, it has allowed us to dedicate 100 percent of the generous gifts to the program towards student expenses. Recently, the Huntsman School received a $1 million gift from Gail Miller, a prominent Utah entrepreneur, which has ensured the sustainability of the program for years to come.

GROWING THE PROGRAM BEYOND USU

Other schools can replicate the SEED program by selecting a safe location, securing housing, and seeking out key partners for funding and in-field support. We are happy to share our training program for students, our curriculum for clients, and the lessons we have learned. In addition, and perhaps more valuable, we invite other universities to partner with us and take advantage of our existing program, partnerships, and infrastructure. Students from other universities have been participating in the SEED program for the past two years. They are selected by their universities, go through the training materials, work with our in-field partners, and live in the apartments with our USU students. The total cost for non-USU students is approximately $3,000, which includes housing, airfare, and in-country expenses for a full semester. Other universities who join us typically find funding for their students who participate.

SEED OUTCOMES AND IMPACT

Over the life of the program, SEED has genuinely impacted the lives of thousands of local entrepreneurs in the destination countries and hundreds of USU students. We provide a brief summary of outcomes below.

Client Impact

- More than 4,500 people have been taught foundational business principles by SEED students.
- Over 700 new businesses have been launched and supported.
- Household income improved significantly for most clients (nearly 100 percent average increase across all locations).
- Family nutrition improved because of increased household income (more nutritious foods and less alcohol and trans fats).
- Many clients have been better able to support their children in high school and university programs, affecting generations.

Student Impact

- Over 400 students have participated in the program.
- More than 50 different majors have been represented.

- International experience changes students' perspectives and mental models.
- To teach is to learn twice – students learn business principles at a deeper level by teaching to others.
- Development of relevant career skills.
- Strengthening language skills.
- Greater employability upon graduation.
- Meaningful relationships with clients and partners.
- Seeing lives change through the power of entrepreneurship.
- A personal transformational life experience.
- Well prepared to start their own business.

STUDENT FEEDBACK

Student feedback regarding the SEED program has been overwhelmingly positive. Christian Hobbs found that the SEED program was a differentiator in his job search.

> When I asked what set me apart from the other unbelievable candidates, they explained without hesitation that it was my experience in Peru with the SEED Program. The SEED Program set me apart at the national level and was the perfect platform to launch me into my future.

Marissa Barlow explained how the SEED program helped her with her own startup.

> Working with strong female entrepreneurs in the Philippines every day taught me something a classroom never could: how to think outside the box. They are perfect examples of "bootstrapping" a business, and I have definitely applied that to my own company, Nani Swimwear, since being home.

Michael Scott Peters shared that the SEED program prepared him for an incredible opportunity at the United Nations.

> This program captures the true meaning of the Huntsman Difference by combining classroom knowledge with outside-the-classroom opportunities. Thanks in large part to the SEED program and our work with victims of human trafficking, I was able to secure a position with the United Nations as the United States Youth Observer.

Jared Black revealed how this opportunity changes the lives of the women who had been rescued from sex trafficking by our partner Operation Underground Railroad.

> One girl described the hopelessness and fear that she had once felt and told us that she now had hope because she had proved to herself that she could make an honest living and provide a better life for herself and her son. These girls had passed through some of the worst horrors a person can experience, and entrepreneurship became a tool for them to restore their self-confidence and rekindle their hope for a better future.

CONCLUSION

Entrepreneurship scholars have long called for a greater level of action and practice in entrepreneurship education (Neck & Greene, 2011). Vanevenhoven (2013, p. 468) argued that "we need to send our students into the actual environments that they are studying." Experiential learning allows students to participate in "real-world" projects and reflect on the processes and outcomes. It strengthens the propensity to act entrepreneurially and develops the skills and abilities that increase performance (Kassean, Vanevenhoven, Liguori, & Winkel, 2015). Action is a critical component of entrepreneurship and educators will do well to provide students with the opportunity to "do" as well as to "learn."

The SEED program introduces a stimulating method for teaching the skills of entrepreneurship. It combines classroom training and practice with real-world application of the skills students learn. By learning, teaching, and mentoring, SEED interns empower less fortunate individuals and families to improve their standard of living in a sustainable way. In doing so, the students strengthen their own knowledge of entrepreneurial principles, problem-solving skills, and vision of a global community. The SEED method provides students with the experience and skills they need to create value in new venture creation or as a member of any organization they may choose to join.

REFERENCES

Cohen, P. A., Kulik, J. A., & Kulik, C. C. (1982). Educational outcomes of tutoring: A meta-analysis of findings. *American Educational Research Journal*, 19, 237–48.

Kassean, H., Vanevenhoven, J., Liguori, E., & Winkel, D. E. (2015). Entrepreneurship education: A need for reflection, real-world experience and action. *International Journal of Entrepreneurial Behavior and Research*, 21(5), 690–708.

Kolb, D. A. (1984). *Experiential learning: Experience as the source of learning and development*. Englewood Cliffs, NJ: Prentice Hall.

Neck, H. M., & Greene, P. G. (2011). Entrepreneurship education: Known worlds and new frontiers. *Journal of Small Business Management*, 49(1), 55–70.

Vanevenhoven, J. (2013). Advances and challenges in entrepreneurship education. *Journal of Small Business Management*, 51(3), 466–70.

25. What does entrepreneurship mean to you? Using "implicit entrepreneurship theory" in the classroom

William B. Gartner, Katarina Ellborg and Tina Kiefer

INTRODUCTION

This exercise aims to explore the unacknowledged beliefs and assumptions that students have about entrepreneurship in general, and about the characteristics of entrepreneurs and their entrepreneurial actions in particular. It is suitable at the beginning of a course (or seminar), as a way to generate discussion about student assumptions and preconceptions about entrepreneurship. The exercise uses drawing as a technique to elicit ideas and insights, and thereby engages students in group work when exploring entrepreneurship in an educational context.

No student enters an entrepreneurship class, course, or program without some personal definition of entrepreneurship and understanding of what entrepreneurs do. These viewpoints matter in the learning process (Nabi, Liñán, Fayolle, Krueger, & Walmsley, 2017). Part of the challenge of enabling students to learn new things about entrepreneurship, and to gain deeper entrepreneurial skills and capabilities, is that they often have to "unlearn" prior knowledge and beliefs (Fayolle, Verzat, & Wapshott, 2016). So, we start where students are rather than where we want them to be. And, we work to enhance those views and beliefs that sensitize students to their own situations and how the context they are in significantly influences the kinds of opportunities and capital (human, financial, and social) they can identify with and engage in.

This exercise is based on methods and insights from "Implicit Leadership Theory" (Schyns, Kiefer, Kerschreiter, & Tymon, 2011; Schyns, Tymon, Kiefer, & Kerschreiter, 2013) in which visual methods are used to raise awareness of the implicit assumptions and beliefs that individuals have about leaders, particularly about how leadership involves matching individual behaviors to specific social contexts (Day, 2001). Visual methods are proven tools in learning and research, where participants gain new insights and perspectives from trans-mediation, that is, moving between various sign systems (for example between language and pictorial representation) (Siegel, 1995).

This classroom exercise is an excellent way to begin a first class session. It quickly engages all students in group discussions and the drawing process enables students to sketch their ideas and enhances overall class discussion as the student groups present and discuss their visualizations.

EXERCISE FORMAT

The exercise would typically take between 60 to 75 minutes to conduct. Timing depends on the number of groups in the class, the length of the group presentations allowed, as well as how long the instructor wants to engage in class discussion.

Individual Reflection

The instructor asks students to spend five minutes, individually, listing out the characteristics that they associate with entrepreneurs, as well as the kinds of activities that they think entrepreneurs engage in. We begin with this instruction: List the characteristics of an entrepreneur and their actions. (5 minutes)

Group Illustration

After students generate their lists, the instructor forms groups (four to five students per group) to DRAW their understandings of an entrepreneur. The drawings are poster size (e.g., A1 size paper) that can be attached to the walls of the room for presentation to the class. The drawings should not contain any words, but illustrations, symbols, and visual representations that provide a visualization of the characteristics and activities of an entrepreneur that the group agrees on. Figures 25.1 and 25.2 show sample drawings. (20 to 30 minutes)

First Impressions and Presentations

The drawings are introduced, one by one, to the rest of the participants. In this way, the members of the class get a chance to reflect on their first impressions of the visualization. The instructor asks the class members what interpretations they make from the drawing, before asking the group that has made the drawing to present their interpretation. Each group does no more than a three-minute presentation of their drawing. They should point out what all of the visual elements of the drawing mean. (Some examples of student drawings are presented at the end of this exercise.) It is likely that the instructor will need

Figure 25.1   Sample drawings

Figure 25.2   More sample drawings

to step in to ask questions about the drawings so that all of the visual elements are identified and discussed. Assumes six groups are presenting. (20 minutes)

Discussion and Analysis

The instructor utilizes the remaining time during the class to discuss the similarities and differences among the drawings as a way to explore the various beliefs that the class, as a whole, holds about entrepreneurship and entrepreneurial behavior. This discussion provides a way to use the drawings to offer insights into what the course (program, seminar, etc.) will focus on, and what the class will not focus on. (15 to 30 minutes)

LEARNING OUTCOMES AND KEY TAKEAWAYS

Through the trans-mediation process, the students can quickly voice their ideas about entrepreneurship and entrepreneurs, engage in a discussion with others about these views, and get feedback about whether their ideas and viewpoints will be emphasized in the class in later sessions. This is a great way for the instructor to engage students in group work, get them to "prototype" their ideas in pictorial representations, and offer insights into ideas on critical issues the course is likely to address. Ideas about entrepreneurship vary, and as we know, academics seem to disagree on what entrepreneurship is and what entrepreneurs do (Gartner, 1990), and this is especially true in educational settings where entrepreneurship turns into a learning context (Neck & Corbett, 2018). This exercise provides a quick and entertaining way for students to articulate their implicit theories about entrepreneurship, and for the instructor to relate these to the content of the course.

Finally, as the drawing examples illustrate (Figures 25.1 and 25.2), students visualize different aspects of entrepreneurship and entrepreneurial action. While some drawings illustrate the entrepreneur involving others, nearly all drawings depict the idea (e.g., the light bulb), and most drawings describe aspects of the entrepreneurial journey. Instructors can utilize the images to highlight aspects of the course and both challenge and affirm certain assumptions that students have about entrepreneurship and entrepreneurial behavior. This makes the exercise both a starting point for each student's learning journey and a way to deal with traditional or even normative perspectives on entrepreneurship.

REFERENCES

Day, D. V. (2001). Leadership development: A review in context. *Leadership Quarterly*, 11, 581–613.

Fayolle, A., Verzat, C., & Wapshott, R. (2016). In quest of legitimacy: The theoretical and methodological foundations of entrepreneurship education research. *International Small Business Journal*, 34, 895–904.

Gartner, W. B. (1990). What are we talking about when we talk about entrepreneurship? *Journal of Business Venturing*, 5(1), 15–28.

Nabi, G., Liñán, F., Fayolle, A., Krueger, N., & Walmsley, A. (2017). The impact of entrepreneurship education in higher education: A systematic review and research agenda. *Academy of Management Learning and Education*, 16, 277–99.

Neck, H. M., & Corbett, A. C. (2018). The scholarship of teaching and learning entrepreneurship. *Entrepreneurship Education and Pedagogy*, 1, 8–41.

Schyns, B., Kiefer, T., Kerschreiter, R., & Tymon, A. (2011). Teaching implicit leadership theories to develop leaders and leadership: How and why it can make a difference. *Academy of Management Learning and Education*, 10(3), 397–408.

Schyns, B., Tymon, A., Kiefer, T., & Kerschreiter, R. (2013). New ways to leadership development: A picture paints a thousand words. *Management Learning*, 44(1), 11–24.

Siegel, M. (1995). More than words: The generative power of transmediation for learning. *Canadian Journal of Education/Revue Canadienne de l'éducation*, 455–75.

26. Scale up, scale back: an experiential exercise in scaling

James Hart

INTRODUCTION

Students sometimes struggle to understand the concept of scaling up and the importance of being able to scale back, when necessary. This exercise helps students, experientially, understand how to scale a business. Simultaneously, students learn a technique to ideate, understand their concept potential, and create from a minimum viable product or service.

NEED ADDRESSED

Lee Breuer, the legendary Pulitzer Prize-nominated avant-garde New York theatre director and artistic director of Mabou Mines theatre company, has done with his company what many arts organizations struggle to do – survive for decades. When I asked him how he has managed to keep his company alive for so long, he said that Mabou Mines is the "ever-shrinking and expanding company." He went on to communicate that when resources are available, they will do large-scale productions – like *The Gospel at Colonus*, which appeared on Broadway, had a 90-person gospel choir, and starred Morgan Freeman. When Mabou Mines has limited resources, they scale back and do very simplistically designed and executed performances.

Perhaps intuitively, Breuer was speaking about the entrepreneurial concept of "scaling up and scaling back." Simultaneously, he was referencing an idea that is now known as a minimum viable product (or service).

Most businesses do not survive over a long-term period (Marmer, Herrmann, Dogrultan, & Berman, 2011, p. 4). However, those that are highly adaptable and have the ability to both scale up and scale back and start with a minimum viable product or service, so as to reduce costs and risk, likely have a greater potential to succeed. By being so adaptable, an organization increases its chances of surviving the storms of recessions, dwindling resources, changes that come with time, and the volatility of the market.

LEARNING OBJECTIVES

- Students are able to design a minimum viable product or service.
- Students can both scale up a business and scale back, as the need arises.
- Students can ideate, developing concepts that have the potential to scale.

REQUIREMENTS

Time
This exercise typically takes between 20 and 30 minutes to complete.

Space
Most in-person learning environments will suffice.

Materials Needed
None.

Number of Students
This exercise requires at least two people participating. Beyond two, any number of students can engage in this exercise.

GAME/EXERCISE DESCRIPTION

1. Instructors should guide students through the concepts of scalability and minimum viable product.
2. Divide students into pairs.
3. Ask them to identify who will be A and who will be B.
4. Inform students that they will work with an entrepreneurial concept they have devised. Note: If students have not yet developed entrepreneurial ideas, guide them through an ideation process (see Hart, 2018 for examples).
5. Inform them that A will share their entrepreneurial concept with B.
6. B will then tell A to "scale up."
7. A will articulate a concept that is larger in scale than their initially articulated concept.
8. As A articulates their scaled-up concept, B will again ask them to scale up and will do so three more times (five times in total). Each time B asks A to "scale up," A's idea will expand in scale.
9. Once B has asked A to scale up five times, A will return to their initial idea that they articulated, before imaginatively scaling up.
10. A will share their original concept.

11. B will ask A to "scale back."
12. A will articulate a simpler version of their initial concept.
13. B will continue asking A to scale back four more times (five times in total). A will consistently articulate a simpler version of their concept, as B requests.
14. Once A has scaled up five times, gone back to the initial idea, and then scaled back five times, it is B's turn to scale up and back.
15. B articulates their concept.
16. A then repeats the process they underwent with B. A asks B to scale up five times, then go back to the original concept B articulated. A then asks B to scale back five times.
17. Once each party has both scaled up and back, the instructor will reiterate the concept of minimum viable product or service and the benefits of creating such. The instructor can note how an entrepreneur's vision may become far more expansive than first devised.
18. The exercise concludes with the instructor summarizing what has been covered and addressing any questions students may have.

BRIEF SUMMARY OF EXERCISE

* A and B are paired.
* A shares an original concept with B.
* B asks A to scale up their idea five separate times.
* A returns to original idea.
* B asks A to scale back their idea five separate times.
* Partners switch turns and the process starts again.
* The instructor reviews, discussing scalability and the concept of minimum viable product.

EXAMPLE OF A CONCEPT THAT IS BOTH "SCALED UP AND BACK" AND HOW THIS EXERCISE MAY UNFOLD

A: My idea is to create a large coffee shop that enables me to create quality coffee for a large range of local customers.
B: Scale up.
A: Ok, I will do all I said before but will also feature and sell local artists' works. Profits will be allocated to each of the artists with a 10 percent commission going to the coffee shop.
B: Scale up.
A: I will accomplish what I said before but also engage the services of a local roaster so I can have coffee beans roasted that feature original recipes I come up with.

B: Scale up.

A: I will do all that I said before but will buy my own roasting equipment and sell gourmet roasted beans customers can purchase in bean form or ground.

B: Scale up.

A: I will create original recipes for roasting coffee beans, will outsource roasting, and distribute my beans nationwide. A portion of profits will be distributed through a foundation I create that offers grants to artists in my home state.

B: Return to your original idea.

A: My original idea was a large coffee shop that makes coffee with a series of quality presses.

B: Scale back.

A: Instead of a brick-and mortar-coffee shop, I will sell coffee through a portable kiosk at the local airport. Simultaneously, I will offer a subscription service of delivered hot coffee for other businesses in the airport.

B: Scale back.

A: Alright. I will make and sell coffee at events like sports venues and festivals with a small portable quality coffee maker that fits on the back of my pick-up truck and operates off of a generator. Simultaneously, I will offer a subscription service for hot coffee delivered to area businesses.

B: Scale back.

A: Instead of operating from a truck, I'll buy used portable coffee containers, pre-make hot coffee from home, and deliver to area businesses that have a subscription with my company.

B: Scale back.

A: OK, I will create pre-made ice coffee from home, which I will market as locally made. I will sell this product during the summer at area community tailgate parties, festivals, and other public and private events.

TIPS AND THOUGHTS

It is up to the instructor to foster a learning environment in which students feel they can both play and explore their ideas without being judged by the instructor or peers. To help them fully engage with the exercise, consider offering an example of how this exercise might occur. They will then likely use the instructor's example as a model in their decision-making process. Furthermore, if an instructor releases students from the need to appear innovative in their decision making, students are more likely to make bold decisions, to play, and accept the degree of improvisation this exercise requires.

When engaging students in this exercise, an instructor should expect a considerable amount of energy and volume to occur in the room.

Encourage discussion once the exercise concludes. By asking them to articulate what they experienced and learned, students can reflect and further participate in their learning.

REFERENCES

Hart, J. D. (2018). *Classroom Exercises for Entrepreneurship: A Cross-Disciplinary Approach*. Cheltenham, UK and Northampton, MA, USA: Edward Elgar Publishing.
Marmer, M., Herrmann, B. L., Dogrultan, E., & Berman, R. (2011). *Startup Genome Report Extra on Premature Scaling*, p. 4. https://integral-entrepreneurship.org/wp-content/uploads/2016/07/Startup-Genome-Premature-Scaling.pdf

27. Entrepreneurship finance over coffee

Pedro Tonhozi de Oliveira and Whitney Peake

INTRODUCTION

In most basic entrepreneurship courses, there is at least one student team each semester that wants to open a coffee shop – or a food truck, pizza place, the list goes on and on. While it seems like an easy idea to pursue for an entrepreneurship project, oftentimes those teams – and even entrepreneurs starting this kind of business – lack basic understanding relative to the costs involved and pricing of their products and services. The Entrepreneurial Finance over Coffee Exercise promotes activity-based learning through a mini-consulting exercise to help strengthen students' skills in the areas of basic pricing and pricing strategy. This exercise helps students learn how to use market research to make decisions, and gives students experience in practicing consulting work, which is important as they work to think critically about pricing problems.

PRICING STRATEGY, MARKET RESEARCH, AND CONSULTING

Entrepreneurial Finance over Coffee helps strengthen students' skills in areas of basic pricing and pricing strategy, which are critical but often deficient. It helps students learn how to use market research to make decisions, and how such activity can affect the bottom line and break-even projections. Further, students gain experience in practicing consulting work, which is important both within entrepreneurship and beyond, as students work to think critically about pricing problems. This exercise promotes activity-based learning, with immediate application of material for undergraduate or MBA students in basic entrepreneurship, small business management, or venture-planning courses.

The first outcome achieved in the classroom with this exercise is that students learn to create a realistic vision of pricing in the small business setting. Next, they understand the costs behind opening a business (in this case a coffee shop). Finally, through work with a consulting mindset, students often provide innovative solutions. Students understand fundamental pricing concepts, including elasticity, value (perceived pricing), as well as the effect of contextual factors. This is a fun way to address some complicated concepts.

THE CHALLENGE

The entire class pitches in to brainstorm categories of products sold in a coffee shop. The instructor selects some categories and instructs different teams to work on each category and conduct market research on the products, and pricing (estimated sales price and cost of goods sold) of them. Then, a plot twist is introduced as each member is remixed into new teams, composing product specialists in each category. Each new team is a consulting company team competing for a contract with the instructor and will develop a full product line-up and pricing strategy for the business. Each team then presents its findings and the instructor judges the best one, based on the assumptions, to create the income statement and calculate the time to break even.

So What?

Understanding pricing is an issue we see in many entrepreneurship classes, ideas, and business plan competitions, and with early-stage entrepreneurs in general. Research in entrepreneurship pedagogy suggests that students do not sufficiently improve understanding of entrepreneurial finance issues after completing traditional business plans in courses (Karia, Bathula, & Abbott, 2015). They often understand the purpose of market research related to financial concepts but need to obtain data points to make valid estimates.

Given these issues, entrepreneurial finance and accounting are critical topics for students to practice and develop continually. Additionally, as Generation Z continues to move on to university, instructors must find ways to engage this entrepreneurial generation, which is focused on the immediate application of concepts to real-world problems (Povah & Vaukins, 2017; Seemiller & Grace, 2017). This exercise was designed to fill this gap.

PART 1: THE MARKETING RESEARCH

In preparing for the exercise, the instructor should discuss the different market research methodologies important to the course. In the beginning of the exercise, the only instructions needed are the outcomes that are needed from them – product line-up with estimated sales price and cost of goods sold – and it is important for the instructor to emphasize that every member of the group may be called to present. Students can use any resource they desire and even call or go to a coffee shop to ask questions.

PART 2: THE CONSULTING BUSINESS

When the time for the first part is up, the instructor will introduce the plot twist assigning students to new teams. The first task is to come up with a name for their coffee shop. The second is to design the full menu of products they want to sell – or you might limit teams to two or three of each category. The final deliverable is a simplified income statement and break-even time calculation.

Table 27.1   Sample comparison table of income statement for teams

Product	At cost	Low price	At competition	A little above	Airport/hotel
Brewed coffees	0.75	1.25	2.50	3.00	7.00
Premium coffees	1.50	3.00	4.25	4.50	10.00
Pastries	1.50	2.00	3.00	3.50	12.00
Whole bean roast	8.00	10.00	13.50	14.00	20.00
Merchandise	10.00	12.00	14.00	15.00	20.00
Income statement	**At cost**	**Low price**	**At competition**	**A little above**	**Airport/hotel**
Sales	154,190.00	239,080.50	360,260.50	384,795.00	281,957.00
COGS	149,704.00	144,161.50	136,561.00	129,775.00	47,617.25
Gross profit	**4,486.00**	**94,919.00**	**223,699.50**	**255,020.00**	**234,339.75**
Salaries and wages	120,000.00	120,000.00	120,000.00	120,000.00	120,000.00
Business expenses	50,000.00	50,000.00	50,000.00	50,000.00	50,000.00
Operating income	**(165,514.00)**	**(75,081.00)**	**53,699.50**	**85,020.00**	**64,339.75**
Income taxes			10,739.90	17,004.00	12,867.95
Net profit (profit)	**(165,514.00)**	**(75,081.00)**	**42,959.60**	**68,016.00**	**51,471.80**
Initial investment	169,900.00	169,900.00	169,900.00	169,900.00	169,900.00
Break even (years)	**Never**	**Never**	**4.0**	**2.5**	**3.3**

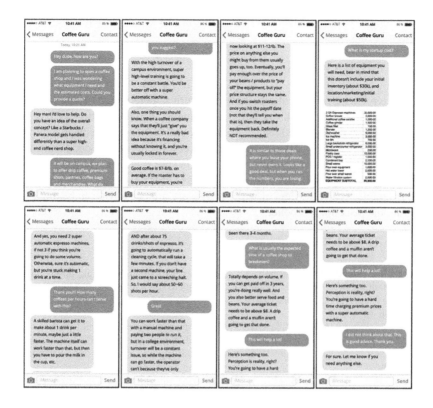

Figure 27.1   Chat with coffee specialist

THE ASSESSMENT

The way we assessed the exercise was developing a table to calculate the comparison between the teams. For reference see Table 27.1. This is a simplified version, but with relevant concepts, of an income statement.

Some questions that are important to ask during the presentation are:

- Why would someone prefer your coffee shop over Starbucks?
- How did you come up with this margin?
- How much is your startup cost? What did you consider in your calculation?
- What is the market size?

Beyond being a fun exercise for students to work with realistic numbers and compete with one another for the consulting contract, this exercise is designed as an interactive way to teach key principles of pricing for students and novice entrepreneurs.

KEY TAKEAWAYS

This exercise helps students see how net profit is determined, as well as the break-even time based on the initial investment. In running this exercise in class, break even (in years) ranges from 1.2 years to 4.3 years, with an approximate three-year expectation (based on market information provided from the coffee shop specialist shown in Figure 27.1). This is an opportunity to show students how pricing strategy influences time to break even, and how unrealistic assumptions – regardless of whether they are high or low – can be made in setting the price for a product.

REFERENCES

Karia, M., Bathula, H., & Abbott, M. (2015). An experiential learning approach to teaching business planning: connecting students to the real world. In Mang Li and Yong Zhao (Eds.), *Exploring learning & teaching in higher education* (pp. 123–44). Berlin: Springer.
Povah, C., & Vaukins, S. (2017). Generation Z is starting university – but is higher education ready? *The Guardian*, July 10, retrieved from www.theguardian.com/higher -education-network/2017/jul/10/generation-z-starting-university-higher-education -ready
Seemiller, C., & Grace, M. (2017). Generation Z: education and engaging the next generation of students. *About Campus*, 22(3), 21–6.

28. Using interactive video vignettes to teach customer discovery

Michael Dominik and Daniel Cliver

INTRODUCTION

The use of interactive video vignettes (IVVs) as an active learning pedagogical tool in United States higher education is a relatively recent phenomenon, with no work published to date on this topic in entrepreneurship education. The most prevalent examples of this approach come from work sponsored by the United States National Science Foundation in the fields of biology (Wright, Newman, Cardinale, & Teese, 2016), physics (Laws, Willis, Jackson, Koenig, & Teese, 2015), and information systems mobile applications (Oakley & Church, 2018). IVV deployment in these educational settings can take different forms, but they typically feature online delivery of short duration video content (one- to three-minute "vignettes") accessed through a web browser, with the ability for students to use their pointing device to interact with the content, for instance, to select chapters and to answer questions. Different than passively watching an instructional video, the learner is required to take action to appropriately use an IVV. Moreover, IVVs are conveniently accessible, familiar in their use of web browser software, and most importantly, can be individualized and action-driven, making them well suited for the modern entrepreneurship classroom. Accordingly, this chapter describes the development of a prototype interactive video vignette for entrepreneurship education (IVV-EE) designed to teach entrepreneurial customer discovery and interviewing skills.

IVV usage is grounded in education research and incorporates insights from how people learn. A well-designed and well-produced IVV should promote experiential learning, bring forth real-world situations, provide scaffolding support in using multiple instructional techniques to progress students toward deeper understanding, and offer feedback as learners progress (Bransford & Schwartz, 1999). More specifically, film can be a highly experiential medium with high efficacy in facilitating student learning given experiences effectively bridge theory and practice; the act of experiencing facilitates the connection between action and thought (Liguori, Muldoon, & Bendickson, in press).

The use of IVVs can enable a method of learning that brings students virtually to off-campus locales, settings, and produced situations, that can be used to illustrate topical principles and provide a basis for exercises, activities, assignments, and other means of learning. It can provide the students with a story, a set of characters with whom they can identify and to whom they can refer when they conduct exercises or analyses. IVVs can be used to supplement textbook reading, as homework assignments, pre-class tutorials, and flipped classroom engagements where students can replay IVV content and review them at their own pace. Using short segment videos only a few minutes long is also more engaging for students, with research showing that short videos (up to three minutes) yield the highest levels of engagement (Guo, Kim, & Rubin, 2014).

IVV-EE NEED

The development of customer discovery skills is an important lesson for entrepreneurs and students of entrepreneurship. Engaging prospective customers as part of problem validation before building a solution helps ensure the entrepreneur will build a product people actually want by learning the features and benefits that customers seek, and validating the assumptions and hypotheses adopted by the entrepreneur (Neck, Neck, & Murray, 2018; Ries, 2011).

Teaching customer discovery interviewing skills in the classroom through lecture, written description, and even video-recorded example can be suboptimal, especially when students are unable to visualize situations, because they are in a classroom setting, or are learning as part of an online class. To drive experiential learning, students could be instructed to conduct customer interviews by going outside the classroom and observing or interacting with real "customers" who are not class colleagues. This approach, however, presents barriers because of logistics, legalities, and scheduling challenges related to student engagement of real-world persons outside of the immediate college campus. On campus, students might also be instructed to conduct audio and even video capture of their interviews, enabled and enhanced through the ready availability of mobile device recording capabilities, but this results in delayed feedback only given to the student some time after having conducted the actual interview. Another option is to use available online simulation solutions, such as Venture Blocks (VentureBlocks.com), a paid subscription-based solution that helps students learn how to conduct informative interviews and translate findings into customer insights for potential business opportunities, and which aids in helping students learn what kinds of questions to ask. The

IVV-EE approach presents a novel way to guide students in the development of customer discovery skills.

IVV-EE CONCEPT

The concept for the IVV-EE was to use customized high-quality but non-commercial quality video production, in order to take the student virtually "outside" the classroom while they remained in the physical classroom or in an online presence. This was expected to be particularly beneficial as an adjunct teaching tool in a course where entrepreneurial mindset development is but one of several learning objectives, for instance in a course principally based around an entirely different discipline, such as computer science. For purposes of entrepreneurship education, the IVV-EE would be designed for students to learn principles of customer discovery by observing an interview in a recorded video and then being prompted as to whether the interview questions observed were good or bad. Instructors could then optionally conduct a corollary activity, such as classroom discussion or online dialogue.

The IVV-EE concept featured several design elements: (1) vignettes would be of varied lengths, ranging from under one minute up to three minutes; (2) vignette lessons would be modular, such that an instructor would be able to use topics in any order; (3) vignettes would be in MP4 file format, so that instructors could embed them into classroom material to provide their own tailored introduction and post-viewing instructions; (4) vignette videos would be delivered through the internet using a web browser user interface, and compatible with YouTube and its requirements; (5) vignettes would be filmed in the local region around Rowan University.

The IVV-EE purpose and goal was expressed in the prototype as:

> This interactive video lesson will give you, the entrepreneur and innovator, the chance to make choices regarding the best types of questions to ask prospective customers, so that you can learn and validate what you see as the problem, discover more about your prospective customers, and apply what your prospective customers say to your solution. The hypothetical situation you are about to interact with has been created to improve the questions you ask when you interact with prospective customers.

IVV-EE PROTOTYPE CREATION

The situational topic selected for the hypothetical entrepreneurial customer discovery action originated from a Rowan University summer entrepreneurship "bootcamp" program, a two-week college-level entrepreneurship course for local high school students from underrepresented and underprivileged populations. One bootcamp student group explored an entrepreneurial concept to address sunscreen application problems; as such, the IVV-EE prototype interviews were targeted to be done in a public setting at a seaside town 50 miles away.

Delsea Regional, one of the secondary schools participating in the Rowan bootcamp program, had the requisite skills and resources for high-quality non-commercial video production, and a collaboration was proposed that would fit with their summer schedule under a Rowan University grant project. The video capture, editing, and final production of the vignettes was done by Delsea, who provided the professional video equipment, operators, and editors, and students as would-be entrepreneur actors, and was responsible for video capture and video editing, including web programming to enable interactivity.

A storyboard was collaboratively developed, along with scripting and flow sequence. Actors were recruited who would pose as college students considering a new venture based on the sunscreen application problem. The actors were scripted to present themselves as would-be young entrepreneurs conducting interviews in order to validate their assumption that people who go to the beach are not sufficiently aware of how to apply sunscreen. The production team set up during the summer at a local beach town, and approached a diverse set of persons to solicit their voluntarily participation in the recordings for the project. Actors were provided with dialogue to pose specific questions to the volunteers, with some questions intentionally developed as "good" and others as "bad," with the intention that IVV-EE learner students would watch both types of questions and select responses as either "good question" or "bad question". For filming, 15 question sets were developed, and 12 volunteers agreed to be interviewed, with each asked at least three interview questions by the actors, and each of the 15 questions asked at least two times. For final editing, 11 questions were retained.

For example, one question posed by the actors was, "About how many times have you been to the beach this summer?," which was intended to be a good question. As programmed for interactivity, if the learner chose "good," a narrator was presented on the screen and advised the learner, "You're right! This is a good question because it helps the entrepreneur understand how often potential customers might need a solution for applying sunscreen." If the learner chose "bad," the narrator advised, "Sorry, that's not the best answer! It's a good question because it helps the entrepreneur understand how often potential customers might need a solution for applying sunscreen."

Post-production work was done over a period of several weeks and included the use of Final Cut Pro for audio and video editing, with web-programming tools to provide the interactive elements. The IVV-EE prototype requires hosting with an online platform such as a Google shared drive for multiple discrete video segments and associated html programming to enable the interactive functionality. The introduction and other video segments of the prototype have been posted on YouTube (https://youtu.be/3kvifK-xEAw) as a non-interactive demonstration.

FUTURE PROMISE: IVV-EE DEVELOPMENT AND APPLICATION

The IVV-EE prototype was meant to be a learning aid for students with little entrepreneurship background, and secondarily to assist instructors with little entrepreneurship education experience. Because it focused on a topic that can be challenging for students and entrepreneurship educators to learn experientially, it incorporated simple direct examples and language. Possible applications for this IVV-EE prototype include offering it as a homework assignment, as an exercise to prepare for a class lecture or tutorial session, as a prompt for in-class discussion, or to prepare for a quiz or exam.

The IVV-EE offers promise as a novel and informative way to deliver entrepreneurship education. As a prototype, it advances knowledge in the use of IVVs as an entrepreneurship education tool and provides an opportunity to study its efficacy and impact on learning, and to understand where and how it can be applied inside and outside the classroom setting. Its experiential nature, connection to the real world, and facilitation of deliberate practice make its use aligned with best practices for entrepreneurship education (e.g., Kassean, Vanevenhoven, Liguori, & Winkel, 2015; Neck & Greene, 2011).

REFERENCES

Bransford, J., & Schwartz, D. (1999). Rethinking transfer: A simple proposal with multiple implications. *Review of Research in Education, 24*, 61–100.

Guo, P. J., Kim, J., & Rubin, R. (2014). How video production affects student engagement: An empirical study of MOOC videos. In *Proceedings of the first ACM conference on Learning@ scale conference* (pp. 41–50), March. ACM.

Kassean, H., Vanevenhoven, J., Liguori, E., & Winkel, D. E. (2015). Entrepreneurship education: A need for reflection, real-world experience and action. *International Journal of Entrepreneurial Behavior and Research, 21*(5), 690–708.

Laws, P. W., Willis, M. C., Jackson, D. P., Koenig, K., & Teese, R. (2015). Using research-based interactive video vignettes to enhance out-of-class learning in introductory physics. *Physics Teacher, 53*(2), 114–17.

Liguori, E. W., Muldoon, J., & Bendickson, J. (in press). "Experiential entrepreneurship education via U.S. films: Why and how." *Journal of Small Business and Enterprise Development.*

Neck, H. M., & Greene, P. G. (2011). "Entrepreneurship education: Known worlds and new frontiers." *Journal of Small Business Management, 49*(1), 55–70.

Neck, H., Neck, C., & Murray, E. (2018). *Entrepreneurship: The practice and mindset.* Thousand Oaks, CA: Sage.

Oakley, R. L., & Church, M. (2018). Engaging students with mobile application IS concepts through creating video vignettes. *SAIS 2018 Proceedings*, 38.

Ries, E. (2011). The lean startup: How today's entrepreneurs use continuous innovation to create radically successful businesses. Crown Publishing Group: New York.

Wright, L. K., Newman, D. L., Cardinale, J. A., & Teese, R. (2016). Web-based interactive video vignettes create a personalized active learning classroom for introducing big ideas in introductory biology. *Bioscene: Journal of College Biology Teaching*, *42*(2), 32–43.

29. The Technology Commercialization Academy: fueling student startups

Bruce Teague and Yanxin Liu

INTRODUCTION

The Technology Commercialization Academy (TCA) is an intensive eight-week summer co-curricular program in which undergraduate students develop working commercialization plans based on patented technologies. This immersive co-curricular program allows students to experience the process of developing unique business applications from existing licensed intellectual property (IP). Students work hands-on with the inventors to understand the range of potential applications. Following this brainstorming phase, they form teams that spend the remainder of the program developing plans to commercialize and launch the best ideas generated.

The Eastern Washington University (EWU) Center for Entrepreneurship has run the TCA for two summers. Results have been extremely positive. Student participants learn and practice important entrepreneurship skills and competencies while working on real-world projects. Additionally, the TCA creates a temporary hub of activity around which stronger ties to partners in our entrepreneurship ecosystem are cultivated. Throughout the program, students evaluate multiple patents to identify promising new market applications. They must then professionally interview customers to acquire early users, build partnerships with local manufacturers and distributors in a regional entrepreneurship ecosystem, pitch their product ideas to seasoned seed capital and angel investors, and learn to work with alumni mentors to form preliminary boards.

THE EXPERIENCE

Once student teams have developed potential commercial applications for the technology, the top ideas are selected and students form work teams of three–four persons based on their disciplinary expertise, interest in the licensed

IP and proposed application, and the personal strengths each student brings to the project.

Once formed, teams have access to a small development fund that supports customer interviews and early prototype development and iteration. These development funds fall outside the general operating budget, forcing us to rely on donations to enhance real-world testing and development of ideas. Fortunately, we have found area businesses—especially banks—to be enthusiastic in support of this type of program. Once the TCA concept was proven in year 1, the pool of funds available to teams grew from $1000, to $10,000 in year 2. This fund will grow again in year 3, to at least $16,000. This support demonstrates an additional benefit to this program: building new relationships, and strengthening existing relationships with key stakeholders in the entrepreneurship ecosystem.

Throughout the eight weeks of the program, students meet four days per week (Monday through Thursday), for four hours per day. These sessions are used to help student teams understand weekly benchmarks and expectations, to provide project mentoring, and to bring in relevant speakers. Additionally, students work on their own outside the scheduled hours. In order to support development of the companies, and the students' mindsets, we partner with a local incubator space on a two-month student membership.

The program proceeds as follows:

- Weeks 1–3: Customer discovery interviews, ideation, application development, and getting approval of application for IP license.
- Weeks 4–6: Product research and additional customer interviews. This is the period for prototype iteration, refinement, and pivoting.
- Week 7: Pitch deck development, pitch practice, specialty mentoring (emphasis on "pre-investment pitch") (Teague, Gorton, & Liu, 2019).
- Week 8: Make final pitches to investment caliber judges, award EWU Technology Commercialization Fellows standing in university, and program debrief.

GETTING STARTED

The management of the TCA experience proceeds in phases. The pre-academy phase involves vetting potential IP. This phase begins at the start of winter term. Since our institution does not produce significant IP, we partner with local research universities in order to procure access to the technologies. We work based on a two-stage licensing agreement. When students enter the academy, they sign a development license that allows them to research potential commercial applications for the IP. This license lasts for one year and also allows the teams to enter their ideas in student business plan competitions.

Upon reaching the end of the one-year license, or upon legally forming the business, students negotiate the final details for the second-stage, commercial license.

As with any new program, trial-and-error learning has played a large role in developing TCA processes. This was particularly true when it came to vetting IP for the program. In the first year, the IP vetting process was expert-driven. In other words, we relied heavily on the guidance of the technology commercialization office as we selected the IP that the students would be working with. While some excellent projects emerged from this process, student commitment to the projects was low.

Thus, in the second year, we switched to a student-centered vetting process. We began by bringing in four different patents, each of which fit two criteria: (1) the licensed patents must possess the qualities of a platform technology and have wide-ranging applications that stretch across multiple industries according to the assessment of IP experts; (2) the inventor and their lab must be willing to devote time to meeting and working with student teams. IP selected for year 2 of the TCA included a protein nanofiber, two patents related to an automated apple-picking robotic arm, and a data-driven activity prediction algorithm.

These four IP then were investigated by the students who selected the IP and the application thereof that they wanted to work with. In this way, we created a controlled marketplace in which IP competed for student interest. This process worked better and led to stronger business commitment beyond the end of the TCA. Our experience over the first two years of the TCA consistently show that technology experts/evaluators add incremental value to technology commercialization success.

Once the patents are selected student recruitment begins. We begin active program promotion solicitation of applicants ~3 months before the start of the academy. Selected students have the opportunity to be recognized as EWU Technology Commercialization Fellows, and are awarded a $1,500 fellowship. In contrast to the business development funds mentioned earlier, the fellowship stipends are built into the operating budget of the program, and have been grant-funded. Thus, the students are presented with four inducements to participate: (1) the opportunity to launch a business; (2) the chance to develop and hone real-world skills; (3) the chance to be recognized as a student fellow of the university; and (4) the $1,500 stipend.

Review of applications begins one month prior to the star of the TCA, and students are admitted on a rolling basis. Along with student interest, reasons for applying into the program, and other academic qualifications, diversity of student background is prioritized. This is to ensure teams have the opportunity to draw upon different backgrounds, experiences, perspectives, and skills that will be necessary to successfully commercialize their application of the technology.

Having completed the vetting of patents and the promotion and recruitment phase of pre-program development, we are ready to launch the TCA. We begin with our day 1 whirlwind experience. This helps students rapidly evaluate perceived opportunities associated with multiple IP while simultaneously acting as a program ice breaker. Here is how it works:

Day 1 whirlwind: (repeat day 2 with different patents)

- 30 minutes – introductions and networking
- 30 minutes – patent evaluation/application brainstorming
- Pitch presentations
- Group feedback
- Idea selection (student who pitched becomes team lead).

SUCCESS TIPS

As with any complex new program, there is a great deal of learning that takes place early on. In spite of this, we view the first two years of the program as successful. The first 24 technology commercialization fellows developed eight commercialization plans, five of which continued towards legal formation of the business. Two were accepted into the regional National Science Foundation's ICorp program and two competed in national business competitions.

These preliminary results support our belief that a diverse group of motivated and well-supported undergraduate student teams are capable of commercializing IPs when provided with opportunity, training, and adequate resources. Additionally, the TCA provides numerous opportunities to build stronger ties with important entrepreneurship ecosystem members.

Based on our early experiences, we have identified a number of success tips for those who wish to start their own technology commercialization academies. First, diversity is beneficial – make teams as diverse as possible. We specifically recruit students from all areas of the university in order to ensure teams would be diverse in knowledge, skills, and abilities. Over the first two years, participants have included students majoring in marketing, accounting, finance, entrepreneurship, music, electrical engineering, mechanical engineering, computer science, psychology, and economics. In the 2019 program, approximately two-thirds of students came from outside of the business school. However, while diversity can enhance the quality of ideas developed by the teams, it can also create challenges as students learn to communicate from their different starting assumptions and experiences.

Second, building a diverse pool of applicants requires capturing the attention and interest of students across the campus. In our experience, short, in-class presentations have proven the most effective way to grow the applicant pool. Student employees of the EWU Center for Entrepreneurship schedule appointments to visit classes across campus. We find that our students lack an existing mental model for a summer fellowship program such as the TCA. The ability to ask questions immediately has resulted in (a) more requests for additional TCA information, and (b) more completed applications. Additionally, our student employees compile an email list of interested students from business, social sciences, and science, technology, engineering, and mathematics (STEM). This list allows the Center to follow up with students from a variety of backgrounds. At the same time, we have found this approach counters the tendency of some majors to assume this program is only for business and STEM students.

Third, we added an alternate opportunity for students to participate during our second year: student consultants. Student consultants are recruited based on specialized technical skills that may be useful to multiple teams, but typically are students who do not see themselves as entrepreneurs, or who are unwilling to make the full commitment required. Whereas the student fellows earn a fellowship stipend, the student consultants must offer value that is worth a portion of the development money the teams have received. Thus, TCA teams may propose using a portion of their development money to hire these student consultants. Student consultant services have included 3D design and printing, but could involve development of trademarks, website design, or any other specialized task that might be of value.

Fourth, we have found it beneficial to license multiple patents for each round of the program. Students complete multiple rounds of patent evaluation during the first week of the TCA. An advantage of this approach is that students are able to select an IP for which they feel their existing skills are a strong match. At the same time, this allows the students to practice separating technology from application as they brainstorm commercialization ideas. We find that student teams with intrinsic interest in their technology and application become more proactive in utilizing their own extended networks to access additional faculty mentoring from their home departments.

Fifth, when it comes to commercialization success, diversity of technology applications is even more critical than diversity of IP. Our students purposefully apply the brainstorming technique of S.C.A.M.P.E.R. (Substitute, Combine, Adapt, Modify, Put to another use, Eliminate, and Reverse) to find applications of licensed IPs (Schroeder, 2016). We provide descriptions of the licensed patents, and students apply S.C.A.M.P.E.R. to develop a large pool of possible applications around which businesses might be developed. This occurs during the "whirlwind" sessions that start the program.

Sixth, we found that providing a prototype budget – even a small one – along with access to technical consultants (e.g., programmers, 3D printing experts, etc.) for specialty knowledge proved to be necessary for program success. The TCA program provides ample opportunity to put lean startup principles into action, but the student teams require resources to iterate early prototypes that can be used during customer discovery. Also, as we found in the latter half of the TCA program, customers begin requesting working prototypes in order to offer adequate feedback. This has also played an important role in obtaining commitments from test sites and/or early product placement for testing demand. Customer discovery and prototyping are frequently intertwined. We find that very early in the program, student teams require low-resolution prototypes.

Seventh, if budget allows, we have found it beneficial to simulate a startup environment throughout the TCA. One way we do this is by keeping some relatively inexpensive food and beverages on hand during working sessions. This seems to offer several benefits. Among these, it seems to reinforce student perceptions that they are participating in an active startup environment rather than simply an extended classroom experience. Also, it minimizes disruption to worktime with teams. Our goal is to maximize the progress made during the four hours of seminar time so that teams have a plan for using their time outside of the TCA.

Eighth, we recommend designing the program curriculum around performance milestones. These clear milestones provide structure and a framework as student teams learn to manage a rapidly iterating process to complete their commercialization plans within the eight-week window. Student teams must conduct high-quality interviews with customers, manufacturers, and distributors, build a working prototype (minimum viable product), and create effective pitch decks and three-minute videos to pitch to a panel of outside judges. Milestones impose a linearity to the challenge of what is otherwise a recursive and non-linear experience. As they move from interviews to product evolution, and back again, these milestones provide a clear path that keeps them moving forward.

Ninth, we have found it valuable to leverage partnerships with key stakeholders across the local and regional ecosystems. For example, we utilize North Idaho College's Gizmo and Rapid Prototype Lab to help with prototyping. Our business faculty also use their contacts to arrange student tours at selected local companies. During tours, students pitch their ideas to business managers leading to valuable recommendations about prototyping, production, and distribution. To date, EWU TCA teams have visited several companies in our region, including KeyTronics in Spokane Valley, Washington State University, Altek/Minds-I, and Proto Technologies in Liberty Lake, Idaho.

Last, just like diversity on student teams is valuable, diversity in program instruction is also valuable. We have found it useful to "team teach" using one entrepreneurship professor and one STEM professor or tech entrepreneur. This structure allows for more customized advising when students run into inevitable challenges.

CONCLUSION

Our experience demonstrates that successful technology commercialization programs do not require that your university has an active technology commercialization office, nor that your university produces a significant volume of patents. In fact, we have found technology commercialization offices to be extremely willing partners in developing these programs. Similarly, we have demonstrated that technology commercialization need not be reserved solely for graduate students with advanced skills and experience. Undergraduate students can be quite successful working in this kind of program. Additionally, we believe certain elements of this program will prove effective at increasing deep learning by stimulating student iteration between trial-and-error learning in the face of uncertainty and ambiguity, and periods of reflective learning.

One of the advantages of a TCA co-curricular program is that students engage intensively in a real-world experience that requires action and reflection as they engage with high degrees of uncertainty, which should lead to heightened entrepreneurship capabilities and propensity (Kassean, Vanevenhoven, Liguori, & Winkel, 2015). Through this process, we simulate learning by offering the students a real, albeit contained, entrepreneurship experience. By working with undeveloped IP, brainstorming new applications for new potential markets, and working with industry experts to identify and develop a business opportunity, students are forced to deal with ambiguity and challenge their assumptions. This program develops an action orientation on the part of student participants, while encouraging them to engage in reflection at each step along the way.

Reflection is an important process if learning is to develop out of experience, and conditions of high uncertainty and ambiguity that require new problem solving are particularly effective at eliciting learning (Neck & Greene, 2011). This process of reflection leads to deep learning based on a rich understanding of both the problem and the environment in which the solution must work. Working on real-world problems has been found essential to encouraging this type of learning (Pittaway & Cope, 2007). Pittaway and Cope (2007) argue that real-world problems, combined with the independence to pursue working solutions, led to increased responsibility and attachment to the project, which has been our experience in the TCA.

For these reasons, a TCA program can be an exciting addition to the co-curricular learning opportunities offered at most universities. Students who complete the program advance their entrepreneurship skillsets, gain real experience, and practice commercialization skills.

REFERENCES

Kassean, H., Vanevenhoven, J., Liguori, E., & Winkel, D. E. (2015). Entrepreneurship education: a need for reflection, real-world experience and action. *International Journal of Entrepreneurial Behavior and Research, 21*(4), 690–708.

Neck, H. M., & Greene, P. G. (2011). Entrepreneurship education: known worlds and new frontiers. *Journal of Small Business Management, 49*(1), 55–70.

Pittaway, L., & Cope, J. (2007). Simulating entrepreneurial learning: integrating experiential and collaborative approaches to learning. *Management Learning, 38*(2), 211–33.

Schroeder, B. (2016). *Simply Brilliant: Powerful Techniques to Unlock Your Creativity and Spark New Ideas*. New York: AMACOM.

Teague, B., Gorton, M. D., & Liu, Y. (2019). Different pitches for different stages of entrepreneurial development: the practice of pitching to business angels. *Entrepreneurship and Regional Development, 32*(3–4), 334–52.

30. Film as an experiential medium: entrepreneurship education through *Door to Door*

Jeff Vanevenhoven, Josh Bendickson, Eric W. Liguori and Andrew Bunoza

INTRODUCTION

The demand for, and production of, entrepreneurship education research and resources continue to increase at near exponential levels (Loi, 2018). As educators we continue to long for engaging content that enables us to reach broad student audiences in scalable and meaningful ways. Similarly, we are seeing entrepreneurship classrooms beginning to offer online learning opportunities, a trend that was nearly unilaterally accelerated on campuses globally during the 2020 COVID-19 virus pandemic (Liguori & Winkler, 2020). Students today are seeing more and more video content integrated into entrepreneurship classrooms. For example, one entry in this volume stresses the pedagogical value of using interactive video vignettes to students learning effective customer discovery techniques (viz., Dominik & Cliver, Chapter 28). The use of film is a scalable, effective, and experiential educational technique. While some prior work has explored the use of film in entrepreneurship education, there is room for additional theoretical and experiential exploration, as well as a need for continuous development of new instructional support materials.

Accordingly, this chapter presents one such resource – a toolkit for the use of the television film *Door to Door* in the classroom. *Door to Door*, released in 2002, is based on a true story and features actor William H. Macy, who portrays Bill Porter, a door-to-door salesman with cerebral palsy. It was nominated for 12, and won six, Emmy Awards as well as a Peabody Award. For years, Porter had been told he was unemployable; that his condition made it impossible for him to work. Yet, it wasn't his doctors telling him this, it was the workforce. It took Porter incredible persistence to find a company willing to give him a chance, but finally he found an opportunity selling household items and baking products door to door for Watkins, one of America's oldest direct selling companies.

Through the story of Bill Porter, as portrayed in *Door to Door*, numerous entrepreneurship learning points (e.g., perseverance, persistence, passion, community and relationship building, and others) can be conveyed to students in a captivating and experiential manner via the film. In essence, the film serves as a Trojan horse, a surreptitious vessel to deliver impactful and meaningful content. Importantly, these learning points are based in fact, not fiction, with William H. Macy noting "It was elegant... we told stories about his customers. We fictionalized them so we could stick to the truth about what Bill had done."[1]

The use of film as a learning tool is a familiar and effective approach for many business school educators around the globe (Champoux, 1999). As entrepreneurship educators we are challenged to teach students to navigate the "unpredictable world of practice" (Downey, Jackson, Puig, & Furman, 2003: 401), and the use of film is uniquely positioned to help facilitate the translation of the complex and unpredictable into a digestible form that students can relate to at a cognitive level. Our goal here, however, is to offer a useful overview of *Door to Door* as a learning tool, rather than elaborate on the many cognitive benefits of film as an experiential medium (cf., Mallinger & Rossy, 2003; Medina, 2008; Wlodkowski, 1999).

DEBRIEFING *DOOR TO DOOR*: SELECT ENTREPRENEURSHIP LEARNING POINTS

Passion and Commitment

- Bill Porter displays incredible commitment selling Watkins products and would not let anything stop him. This is a reoccurring theme throughout the movie, especially from the start when he tried to get the job, even if that meant offering to take the worst route they had. This is also seen towards the end when he was trying to convince Peter to let him continue to sell door to door, even in the era of phone sales.
- One way to show passion is through emotions. Bill portrays this by always having a smile on his face and always trying to remain positive on his route. This can especially be seen through his use of humor throughout the film. Showing your passion through happiness will make others happy as well.
- Good fortune will follow when you genuinely love what you do. Bill Porter was completely devoted to the Watkins company and what they sold. By religiously following his passion, Bill achieved many accomplishments, such as Salesman of the Year for 1989.

- Bill was always passionate and committed to making a sale. He even did this when he was not going door to door. Examples in the film include when he was selling products to the waitresses at the diner or to his room-mate at the hospital.

Patience and Persistence

- Always think outside of the box and be patient with the new strategy. Sometimes, new plans may not be effective at first, but may succeed in the future. Bill witnessed this multiple times, such as with the one customer who filed the complaint or when confronted by a reluctant potential customer, Bill tried a new tactic, making the son laugh via a puppet. The mother had a change of heart and allowed him in.
- Even though some people would turn him away for a variety of reasons, Bill was persistent. He would be persistent (but kind) on his first stop at a house, and would continue to return no matter the result. This can be seen multiple times whether successful or not, no matter what, he still tried.
- Always be patient with yourself and with others. Your own stress may limit your success right away and deter others from following your cause. Show patience, just like Bill did. This can be seen throughout the movie. For example, on his first day of work, he was not making many sales, but his mother reminded him to be persistent. You also never know what situation others may be in, so it is best to be patient with them as well.

Building Relationships/Community

- Building relationships will take you far in life, whether in your personal life or professional life. This can be seen with all the customers and business relationships Bill formed over the course of his career. Many of the customers appreciated Bill for what he did and helped him out over the course of his career.
- Always remember to take care of your community. Take care of your community and the community will take care of you. Bill continuously did this throughout his career with many of his customers. Examples include taking care of customers and trying to help them out while also always going to other people for their services and treating them nicely. Note how he always took the bus and created a bond with the bus driver. Even though he was injured at one point, he refused to go after the bus company.
- Even if a situation did take a turn for the worse, Bill would make amends to maintain that relationship. He would even help others do the same. This

could be seen when he made amends with Shelly and helped the two neighbors make amends, which also made them closer.

Sample Discussion Questions for Online In-Class Use

1. Grit can be defined as passion and perseverance for very long-term goals and many thought leaders have suggested grit to be a key trait of most successful entrepreneurs. Having watched *Door to Door*, where do you see examples of grit? Please explain.
2. Imagine you were the chief executive officer of Watkins. What does your business model look like? How do the distribution channels and key resource boxes differ from a traditional retailer? Does the value proposition get conveyed differently, and if so, how?
3. What obstacles, real or perceived, did Bill have to overcome? Even though he had to overcome physical limitations, what made him one of the best salesmen for Watkins products?
4. Even though Bill found wonderful success during his career, what risks did he take by attempting this job?
5. What other strategies or tactics could Bill have tried to expand his business even though he did not want to sell over the phone or online?

CONCLUSION

Unquestionably, film has the ability to help transcend learning in ways textbooks cannot. *Door to Door* is the engaging adaptation of a true story about a man of remarkable spirit who overcomes what life throws at him and changes his and others' lives. This noted, we make no presumption to be the first to posit film as a powerful and effective pedagogical tool, nor do we posit that *Door to Door* is the only or even the best film to use. What we do proffer is *Door to Door* is a useful option to introduce students to the direct selling business model, to facilitate the "experiencing" of what passion and perseverance look like, to illustrate relationship building, and to simulate what to expect when undergoing rejection therapy. We acknowledge there are drawbacks and limitations to the use of film in the classroom, many of which Liguori, Muldoon, and Bendickson (in press) list and discuss, noting that context is everything and entrepreneurship education cannot be considered one-size-fits-all. Moving forward, we hope this summary is helpful to educators looking to integrate these topics in new and novel ways in their classrooms and that it helps inspire others to share tools they develop for use in their classrooms with our wider community of entrepreneurship educators.

NOTE

1.   https://interviews.televisionacademy.com/interviews/william-h-macy

REFERENCES

Champoux, J. E. (1999). Film as a teaching resource. *Journal of Management Inquiry*, 8(2), 206–17.
Downey, E. P., Jackson, R. L., Puig, M. E., & Furman, R. (2003). Perceptions of efficacy in the use of contemporary film in social work education: an exploratory study. *Social Work Education*, 22(4), 401–10.
Liguori, E., & Winkler, C. (2020). From offline to online: challenges and opportunities for entrepreneurship education following the COVID-19 pandemic. *Entrepreneurship Education and Pedagogy*. https://doi.org/10.1177/2515127420916738
Liguori, E. W., Muldoon, J., & Bendickson, J. (in press). Experiential entrepreneurship education via US films: why and how. *Journal of Small Business and Enterprise Development*.
Loi, M. (2018). Dealing with the inconsistency of studies in entrepreneurship education effectiveness: a systemic approach to drive future research. In Alain Fayolle (ed.), *A Research Agenda for Entrepreneurship Education* (pp. 38–61). Cheltenham, UK and Northampton, MA, USA: Edward Elgar Publishing.
Mallinger, M., & Rossy, G. (2003). Film as a lens for teaching culture: balancing concepts, ambiguity, and paradox. *Journal of Management Education*, 27(5), 608–24.
Medina, J. (2008). *Brain rules: 12 principles for surviving and thriving at work, home, and school*. Chichester: Wiley.
Wlodkowski, R. J. (1999). *Enhancing adult motivation to learn: A comprehensive guide for teaching all adults*. San Francisco, CA: Jossey-Bass.

31. Developing a strategic (entrepreneurship) mindset in engineering graduates

Robert S. Fleming

INTRODUCTION

The need for a comprehensive engineering program in South Jersey was recognized by entrepreneur, engineer, and industrialist Henry Rowan and his wife Betty, leading to their designated gift of $100 million, the then largest gift ever to a public college or university. This generous gift was designated to establish a college of engineering with the stipulation that the curriculum should address the shortcomings of engineering education. In reality the Rowan Gift enabled the institution not only to establish a well-respected engineering college whose programs address the earlier shortcomings of engineering education, but also served as a catalyst in its pilgrimage to achieve its full potential as the respected teaching and research institution that Rowan University is today.

This chapter reports on our experience in delivering an innovative course called *Strategic Engineering Management* over the past two decades. This graduate course was the first course offered in the newly established College of Engineering. It was designed in response to the specific shortcomings of engineering education that were identified by our academic consultants and an engineering development advisory group comprised of contemporary leaders in engineering education. These experts were challenged to envision what engineering education should look like, unconstrained by traditional or existing curricula.

One of their primary findings was that engineering graduates typically lacked an understanding of the business world and the role of engineering in determining organizational success. That was to be expected, given that most courses in engineering programs were discipline-specific and taught by engineering faculty. Our *Strategic Engineering Management* course was developed by a business faculty member in consultation with our newly hired engineering program chairs. The first course delivery was team taught by a business and engineering faculty member.

COURSE EXPERIENCE

Each summer a group of 20–30 graduate students embark on a pilgrimage in search of a destination described by the course facilitator as developing a "strategic mindset." Interestingly, the travelers on this journey are not business students. Rather, the travelers are graduate engineering students who have not traveled to the destinations typically offered by business schools, but they sign up for the journey based on what they have heard about the experience from past travelers.

While many students initially underestimate the experience in terms of developing a "strategic mindset" prior to the journey, most discover that at some point in the adventure they actually begin to develop their own "strategic mindset" often without realizing that they were doing so. Each year they tell others about their journey, and their friends and colleagues commit to this pilgrimage the following summer.

COURSE OVERVIEW

The objectives of the course include: developing a strategic mindset, understanding the role and responsibilities of engineers in strategic entrepreneurship and business model innovation, and demonstrating the ability to enhance an organization's competitive advantage and success by leveraging the entrepreneurial knowledge, skills, and innovation of its engineers. The course introduces graduate engineering students from the various engineering disciplines to the world of strategic entrepreneurship through traditional strategic management tools and business model innovation, an outlook we've taught for two decades but has just recently begun to get more traction in the academic literature (Anderson, Eshima, & Hornsby, 2019; Mazzei, Ketchen, & Shook, 2017).

The importance of a proactive approach is emphasized throughout the course, as is the need for organizations operating in today's fast-paced competitive environment to be prepared to recognize and embrace change. Their leaders, both traditional business professionals and their engineering counterparts, need to become change agents capable of ensuring that their organizations have the agility and adaptability to build on organizational strengths while minimizing organizational weaknesses as they pursue environmental opportunities while avoiding the threats of their task and general environments.

Students learn about the roles that an organization's business vision, mission statement, and core values play in an informed articulation of the future direction of an organization. Throughout the course they develop the ability to determine the core competencies of an organization, to align these competencies with the expectations of customers and other stakeholders, and to articulate an appropriate value proposition and necessary supporting strategies. The role of engineering and resulting product and process innovation in gaining and sustaining a competitive advantage is a theme considered throughout the course, as is the importance of developing diverse network connections when taking products and processes to market (Laudone, Liguori, Muldoon, & Bendickson, 2015).

COURSE METHODOLOGY

The first session of the course is devoted to an orientation of the contemporary business world, beginning with a discussion of the systems approach to viewing an organization, which proves to be an effective "ice breaker" topic with which engineering students feel extremely comfortable, given their education and orientation. The course is conducted as a seminar that, in addition to the normal content of a course in strategic management or entrepreneurship, incorporates interesting discussions of the engineering implications of each topic examined. A focus of these insightful discussions is always the role of engineering and entrepreneurship as building blocks of a sustainable competitive advantage.

Students learn how to perform a comprehensive analysis of an organization and its environment in order to formulate strategies designed to provide value to the organization's stakeholders that contributes to a sustainable competitive advantage, as well as fulfillment of the organization's mission. At appropriate points in the course, case studies are utilized to enhance and reinforce learning. Students prepare a written analysis of each case and deliver presentations during the class.

Students also select a contemporary organization and conduct research on that organization and the role of engineering within its strategic management and business model innovation, as well as the role of engineering and innovation in gaining and sustaining a competitive advantage. Each student is required to share the "lessons learned" through his or her course research project with other course participants through the delivery of an executive briefing and to submit a comprehensive written report on their research project. This approach leverages the learning experience of each student through sharing it with others in a facilitated discussion. Rather than learning about just one organization, course participants thus typically learn about 20–30 organizations. Students have routinely commented on the value of this approach.

COURSE EVOLUTION

Over more than 20 years the course has evolved in a number of meaningful ways. These enhancements have been based on the recognition that, just like organizations, courses should not remain static. The practice of continuous process improvement advocated in the course as an appropriate strategy to maintain an organization's competitive advantage has been similarly practiced throughout the history of this course. While the initial delivery of the course took place during the fall semester, we decided to move the course to a summer delivery to afford more students the opportunity to take this course. The course has been offered each summer since then with sizeable enrollments each year. This shift permitted a more diverse student group to share their differing academic and professional experiences with the other members of the class. The course instructor's knowledge and insights regarding engineering were similarly enhanced through the facilitated engineering implications discussions during each class session and through the course research project reports and executive briefings.

The initial focus of the course was on the development of strategic planning skills in environmental scanning, strategy formulation, and strategic implementation. Course enhancements over the years have refocused the course coverage and projects to incorporate strategic entrepreneurship, engineering entrepreneurship, and business model innovation. These beneficial enhancements further contribute to the development of a strategic mindset in each of the engineering students.

Several years ago we introduced an assignment that requires students to interview an executive from the industry in which they aspire to work. The focus of these interviews is on the role that engineering plays in contributing to competitive advantage and the degree of involvement of engineers within that organization's strategic planning activities. While the intended purpose of these interviews was to learn about the involvement of engineering personnel in organizational planning processes and the role that engineering can and should play in an organization's present and future success, many of the executives who have been interviewed subsequently became mentors to our students.

We implemented an online version of the course several years ago in order to permit students from other engineering programs and engineering professionals to take this course. This change has also proven beneficial to our students in that it allowed them to participate in the course while engaging in professional travels to conferences and work assignments during the course. This will also enable us to continue to offer this course during the current pandemic.

For many years, a highlight of this innovative course was having the unique opportunity to invite the benefactor who made establishing the engineering program possible to join the class for an invaluable evening of exchanging ideas with the course participants. During this session the teaching faculty member interviewed this distinguished corporate executive and facilitated his telling of the story of how he started his business and the various experiences and challenges that he, as an engineer, faced in his business pilgrimage. The spirited discussions that always ensued for several hours were designed to integrate the various concepts covered in the course and to reinforce the role and responsibility of engineering in contributing to a sustainable competitive advantage.

COURSE OUTCOMES

Various assessment tools have been utilized in the interest of ensuring that the course learning objectives are being met. The specific learning objectives assessed align with the course objectives and incorporate both cognitive and psychomotor measures. Rubrics are used in evaluating student performance and learning with respect to the established learning objectives.

While various outcomes assessment measures have routinely indicated that the course is succeeding in meeting these learning objectives, the most meaningful and affirming feedback has been from past participants who periodically report on how this course prepared them for the many challenges they have faced as engineering professionals in an entrepreneurial world. These graduates routinely have used the term "strategic mindset" to describe the value proposition of this innovative course.

CONCLUSION

While the course has come a long way since its initial offering, we have no intention of resting on our laurels. We continue to seek ways to further enhance this course in the interest of more fully preparing what some have come to consider a generation of "entrepreneurial engineers." These graduates and their organizations will realize the benefits of their ability to understand the role of engineering in gaining and sustaining a business competitive advantage. Their related knowledge, skills, and confidence will serve them well as they face the increasing challenges of the competitive business environment.

REFERENCES

Anderson, B. S., Eshima, Y., & Hornsby, J. S. (2019). Strategic entrepreneurial behaviors: Construct and scale development. *Strategic Entrepreneurship Journal*, 13(2), 199–220.

Laudone, R., Liguori, E. W., Muldoon, J., & Bendickson, J. (2015), Technology brokering in action: Revolutionizing the skiing and tennis industries. *Journal of Management History*, 21(1), 114–34. https://doi.org/10.1108/JMH-03-2014-0068

Mazzei, M. J., Ketchen, D. J., & Shook, C. L. (2017). Understanding strategic entrepreneurship: A "theoretical toolbox" approach. *International Entrepreneurship and Management Journal*, 13(2), 631–63.

32. Entrepreneurship education and the arts: designing a commercial music production major and entrepreneurship minor

Thomas Haines and Charles H. Matthews

INTRODUCTION

By all accounts, over the past quarter century, fueled in part by a digital transformation of unprecedented proportions, the music industry has and continues to experience a disruptive process that reshaped nearly every aspect of the industry's value chain. That value chain includes, but is not limited to, how music is created, produced, distributed, and sold (Tschmuck, 2016); to crowdfunding and social networks in the music industry (Martinez-Cañas, Ruiz-Palomino, & Rubio, 2012). Including the evolution in do-it-yourself music production (Walzer, 2017); to how the next generation of musicians, producers, and managers are educated and prepared for the future (White, 2013). It is a brave new world for commercial music production and entrepreneurship education.

This chapter focuses on (1) an overview of the critical issues facing music and entrepreneurship education; (2) a brief overview structure and goals of the recently minted major in commercial music production with an entrepreneurship minor (CMP/EMinor); (3) an outline of the specific curricula design for the CMP/EMinor program; and (4) a summary and future directions.

As part of the ongoing debate, one critical area that has been identified is the need for musicians to augment their training with business and entrepreneurship education – understanding not only how to build and commercialize their musical skills, but more fully consider the pros, cons, and process of starting a new business. Given the often technology-driven cottage industry music business model of scalable growth, it is a particularly compelling idea to bring together musicians and entrepreneurship curricula in an effort to address this need for today's arts students, as well as education and curricular opportunity for colleges and universities.

Similarly, while there is consensus surrounding the importance of traditional music education at all levels in general and higher education in particular, there is little agreement surrounding best practices on implementation in the classroom. To address this issue, a team of educators in the College Conservatory of Music and Lindner College of Business at the University of Cincinnati came together in 2011, to propose a unique four-year education program solution centered on the nexus of modern music education and entrepreneurship. In order to attack this problem, three key issues were simultaneously addressed: issues outside the academy; issues inside the academy; and the lack of music and business acumen.

Issue 1: Outside the Academy

In the twenty-first century, the traditional music education model is viewed as unnecessary for most young adults wanting to make music. The digital revolution has transformed musical instrument skills in some positive and less positive ways. That is, when musical instrument skills are acquired, the computer has supplanted the need for formal music education through personalized and self-directed internet study. There is general agreement that this personalized self-study model has sidestepped many of the important music theory and professional practices needed for most to become a well-rounded and successful professional musician. Moreover, evidence also suggests that many professional arts training programs may be failing to prepare students to be professional artists (White, 2013).

Issue 2: Inside the Academy

As music making has become increasingly computer-centric, so much so, a music maker needs little to no traditional music-making skills to craft professional-level music. This is due in part to generation Z's music consumption practices. The traditional music education process is one that demands a thorough grounding in every aspect of Western music traditions. Nearly half of this educational model is formatted to deliver an historical perspective that builds a knowledge base that, in the best sense, perpetuates the support for this centuries-old tradition. In the twenty-first century, our digital native students have become ill-equipped to easily assimilate to this highly structured environment. Additionally, with the advent of internet "training" and online music master classes, the traditional model has direct competition inside the classroom. Moreover, entrepreneurship education has traditionally been the domain of business schools and where offered these courses are often available outside of an arts training context (White, 2013).

Issue 3: Lack of Music and Business Acumen

In general, higher education in Ohio has been mandated to provide education that prepares its graduates with the ability to find gainful employment in their chosen field of study. In the new music "gig economy," a firm grasp of current and future business trends are needed to launch a new business venture. Additionally, a professional-level online presence is expected in the vast majority of cases. It should be noted that most music schools do offer a modicum of "real-world" business skills, typically as an afterthought.

Solution: Career-Based Entrepreneurship Music Training Education Curriculum

Rethinking the information flow used in traditional music education models was necessary to address the above concerns. Chief among them was creating an experiential course structure based upon current and future music business trends. The entrepreneurship aspect of this structure became the sea-change ideation and key structural element of the commercial music production program that includes a minor in entrepreneurship (CMP/EMinor). Joining forces of the internationally regarded and highly ranked College Conservatory of Music and Lindner College Business at the University of Cincinnati created a benchmark program that addresses the needs of music, business, the university, and community.

WHAT IS COMMERCIAL MUSIC PRODUCTION?

Commercial music production can be defined as music that is produced for the commercial market. Production music is frequently used as theme or background music in radio, film, television, and episodic internet series. Performance income is generated when music is publicly performed on radio, television, or streamed. Production music libraries are typically constructed to meet the demand for high-quality music in a broad range of musical styles and genres, enabling producers and editors to find what they need in a prepackaged format.

THE "NEW" MUSIC BUSINESS ECONOMY

The economics of the music industry has been radically changed in the past two decades. The entire industry faced the negative effects of web technology where music can be downloaded for free. Many internet users have essentially stopped paying for their music since the mid 1990s. With this music consumption dilemma, new revenue streams were needed.

New Sources of Revenue

The music industry discovered new ways to monetize their product to take advantage of the current consumer trends. The following outlines several of these new revenue streams.

Streaming
Music streaming has become a popular choice by many consumers. Apps like Spotify provide consumers with access to songs for free, adding advertisements between songs. Consumers are urged to pay for ad-free services.

Product placement
Music videos have also become an important part of the revenue strategy. When songs become popular, they are viewed almost as much as they are heard. Music producers often team up with brands for video product placement.

YouTube monetization
It is not uncommon for songs to have millions of views. YouTube allows creators to monetize their content. More and more, this is becoming an important source of revenue for music producers.

Licensing
Song producers can license their songs for use in advertisements. This revenue stream is highly unpredictable but can be profitable in most situations.

Touring
Popular artists and music companies can make a majority of their money on concert tours. Music companies negotiate contracts wherein they get a percentage of the revenue generated from ticket sales. Touring remains the primary source of revenue for music performers.

Merchandising
Music companies often have merchandise sales at their concerts. Additionally, it is not uncommon for music producers to collaborate with professional merchandising firms to sell their products online.

Royalties
Artists and music producers receive royalty fees from their content if it is played on air. Radio, television stations, and internet streaming services routinely pay royalties.

PEDAGOGICAL OVERVIEW

As preparation for traditional music careers has become less important, education has been forced to reevaluate its purpose. One method to address this change is to bring ambiguity and uncertainty into the classroom. Future work environments will not have a syllabus and worksheets with example problems showing people what to do. Work tasks will likely be vague, emergent, and approachable through multiple solution pathways. To prepare for such conditions, students need to experience uncertainty, ambiguity, risk, and failure in ways that strengthen their ability to ask questions, make reasoned approaches, and seek help. Students also need to balance self-confidence and humility and become skilled at emotion regulation so that they can navigate the ups and downs of an uncertain cottage industry business environment. The more prescriptive learning activities are, the less likely they will contribute to students' ability to navigate ambiguity and uncertainty at work, in further learning, and in their lives. In contrast, looking for ways to bring passion-driven, open-ended projects, peer-based collaboration, and play-centered experimentation and creation into learning environments will help foster productive approaches to ambiguity and uncertainty (Vander Ark & Vander Ark, 2017).

The changing nature of work in the music industry is shortening the shelf life of job-specific skills related to the music industry, transforming the nature of the production processes in ways that shift the focus of training and preparation for work. Post-secondary education institutions will continue with responsibility for helping students to prepare for their initial career opportunity but can no longer be viewed as the final stage in the transition to work. As key contributors to lifelong learning, post-secondary education institutions can play an important role in preparing students to develop strategies to guide their choices in the rapidly changing music industry. Individuals need support in strategizing for career and life options and choices rather than for current career paths that may not endure.

Implementing Twenty-First-Century Education Models

The main shift in our commercial music educational model was to adapt competency-based teaching and learning pedagogies in the curricular coursework. In order to create fulfilling and successful careers, musicians will need to continue to discover their own personal and professional strengths, weaknesses, passions, and emotional patterns. Self-discovery will also help students develop visions for their lives and will fuel creativity. This shift was additionally supported by the following student-centered goals.

Navigating through uncertainty
The rapidly changing music market and its associated new service niches can leave music producers with ever changing professional goals and vague work tasks. This can be challenging for those without the necessary skills to manage themselves and who lack the ability to figure it out with little guidance. The new music professional will need to be able to create fluid structures to organize, plan, and prioritize work. They will need to develop their adaptability and resourcefulness, and balance confidence with humility.

Problem-based learning
One variant in problem-based learning uses real-world scenarios allowing the student to define their own learning objectives. Having students approach problems as learning opportunities will be commensurate with professional opportunities and growth. Understanding what you don't know then gathering new tools to solve problems will become the new norm.

Unconventional thinking
Teaching students to use unconventional ways of looking at a problem or idea can yield unexpected results. Using cognitive frameworks and disciplinary models can be important for creativity and innovation. Diverse outside-the-box thinking will be expected in all facets of the new music business. Using entrepreneurial approaches to create novel ideas, then expanding them and building off of others' ideas, and synthesizing these diverse ideas into deeper understanding is the beginning of many new startups in the twenty-first-century economy.

BACHELOR OF MUSIC IN COMMERCIAL MUSIC PRODUCTION

This degree offers a comprehensive education in professional commercial music studies. This unique program combines core training in music theory, composition, arranging, and musicianship combined with recording studio techniques, commercial music, and media technologies. The commercial music production degree includes an additional emphasis on startup business acumen by inclusion of a minor in entrepreneurship. This creates a vibrant and exclusive educational experience that will provide graduates numerous opportunities for meaningful employment in the music industry.

The graduates will possess skills in these areas:

- Music composition for television, commercial media, and film
- Music business in entrepreneurship
- Career management

- Music and related technologies
- Studio production techniques
- Producing, mixing, running live sound
- Scoring music to picture
- Songwriting and arranging.

ENTREPRENEURSHIP MINOR FOR COMMERCIAL MUSIC PRODUCTION: COTTAGE INDUSTRY MODEL

Partnering with Lindner College Business was critical in establishing the linkage to providing our students with real-world business-based education (Figure 32.1). The entrepreneurship aspect of our cottage industry business model perfectly aligns with launching new commercial music product and services businesses. Many modern cottage industries serve a market that seeks out original, handcrafted music products as opposed to mass-produced, highly capitalized music service entities. These "at home" business offerings can include a wide variety of "custom music" services geared toward a more customizable and personalized solution.

Required Courses
   Foundational

ECON 1001	Microeconomics	3 Credit Hrs
FIN 3080	Business Finance	3 Credit Hrs

   Minor Courses

Course	Name	Credit Hrs
ENTR5070	Entrepreneurship: New Venture Creation	3
ENTR5098 (22-FIN-408)	Capstone in Entrepreneurship	3
CMP6061 and 6062	Music Business I and II	6

Figure 32.1   Entrepreneurship minor for commercial music production

CMP students are routinely asked to identify successful niche market leaders as personal benchmarks in an effort to understand these entities through the lens of innovative startup companies (Figure 32.2). Furthermore, they begin their freshman year by attending music performances and critically assessing the ensemble stage presentations, merchandise marketing, collateral product distribution efforts, etc. These findings are presented in class as pseudo-case studies as examples, good and bad, of live music event business strategies.

Core Relationships

Studio Training and Production consists of a thorough grounding in commercial studio operations on both sides of the glass is at the heart of the CMP program. It is where the craft is learned and ideas are brought to life.

Professional Practice is expressed not only in musicianship but is extended into career development through various program benchmarks. Theory in practice for the commercial musician is a multifaceted mix of music, craft and business acumen.

ePortfolio consists of managing a collection of digital artifacts that display the students growth in the program. This program content will have a range and scope that is predictable yet unique for each student. The continual process of building a program portfolio supplies a firm foundation for a successful capstone project.

Web Presence is an on line presence that highlights the students educational experiences as they journey through the curriculum. This will create a sense of ownership for the student as they put their curricular content on line for their family, friends and colleagues to see.

Entrepreneurship is interwoven throughout their college career in a wide range of formal and informal academic experiences. Each student will be trained to excel in variety of professional practice environments throughout the CMP program. Formal business education comes from a tightly integrated curricular plan as they earn a minor in Entrepreneurship from the College of Business.

Capstone Projects are the formal development of their capstone project culminates in creating a "cottage industry" business entity through the launch of a professional web site, populated with their most successful CMP content. These sites will vary in style and substance, each according to their individual entrepreneurial plans. Industry professionals will review and critique these projects at mid and final stages of development.

Figure 32.2   Commercial music production

CREATING A SOLID FOUNDATION: THE COMMERCIAL MUSIC PRODUCTION FRESHMAN EXPERIENCE

The freshman experience was first launched as a University of Cincinnati initiative where a summer reading requirement was given prior to incoming freshmen's first fall term. This effort was then bolstered by the development of learning communities or cohorts where diverse student groups would share their experiences within the common freshman coursework. Subsequently, we build our freshman course sequence to expand upon this framework by cultivating a deeply integrated coursework flow that builds a fluid connection between course instruction and the overall program goals. Figure 32.3 illustrates the course flow.

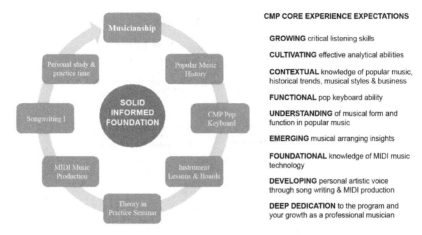

*Figure 32.3   Commercial music production program: freshman year core
program process model*

CMP CURRICULUM: FOUR-YEAR PLAN COURSE CHANGES AND CONFIGURATION

As with every new curriculum, the CMP program has enacted several substantial curricular changes over the last eight years (Figure 32.4). Most notably have been changes in course sequencing, additional music production course creation, and focus in core course offerings and those courses offered by partner content deliverers. Most noteworthy are:

• Desktop music production 2, course creation designed to extend technology foundational studies.
• History of American popular music, aligns with freshman music theory in coordinated content delivery.
• Music business courses using entrepreneurship business models for business plans and website creation.
• CMP collaborators corner, a course designed to create cohorts from freshman and junior CMP students.
• History of Creative American music, aligns with the film scoring course coordinating content delivery.
• Song writing and film scoring track creation, tailoring the program to better suit students' career paths.
• Music engraving course adoption, to prepare students for the professional music publishing market.

- Studio ensemble course creation, to prepare students for the professional studio production market.
- CMP senior capstone alignment with professional music production of commercially focused content.

CMP --- 4 YEAR PLAN

FRESHMAN YEAR

Fall	Course	Credits
English Composition	ENGL1001	3
Commercial Keyboard Skills I	CMP1001	1
History of American Popular Music	CMP2063	3
Desktop Music Production I	CMP1011	3
Theory 1	THRY1011	2
Musicianship1	THRY1015	2
CMP Applied Lessons	CMP1010	2
CCM Collaborators Corner	CMP1081	1
Freshmen Experience Seminar	FAM1005	1
Semester Total		18

Spring	Course	Credits
The Musician in Society	MUHS1001	1
Commercial Keyboard Skills II	CMP1002	1
Songwriting I	CMP2071	3
Desktop Music Production II	CMP1012	3
Theory 2	THRY1012	2
Musicianship2	THRY1016	2
CMP Applied Lessons	CMP1010	2
CCM Collaborators Corner	CMP1081	1
Semester Total		15

SOPHOMORE YEAR

Fall	Course	Credits
Intro to Microeconomics	ECON1001	3
History of Creative American Music I	CMP2041	2
Jazz Theory I **OR**	JZST2011	2
Theory 3 **AND**	THRY2011	
Musicianship3	THRY2015	
Songwriting II	CMP5172	3
Sound Reinforcement and Recording	JZST5151	3
CMP Applied Lessons	CMP2010	2
CCM Pop Ensemble	CMP2081	1
Semester Total		16

Spring	Course	Credits
Digital Entrepreneurship	ENTR3015	3
History of Creative American Music II	CMP2042	2
Jazz Theory II - **If taken Jazz Theory I**	JZST2012	2
Film Scoring I	CMP5131	3
Digital Recording and Editing	JZST5152	3
CMP Applied Lessons	CMP2010	2
CCM Pop Ensemble	CMP2081	1
Semester Total		16

CMP --- 4 YEAR PLAN

JUNIOR YEAR

Fall	Course	Credits
Intermediate Composition	ENGL2089	3
Music Business I	CMP3061	3
Studio Music Production I	CMP3053	3
Jazz Arranging I **OR**	JZST5121	3
Lyric Songwriting **OR**	CMP3071	
Orchestration - **If taken Theory 3**	COMP3011	
Beginning Music Engraving (Fall or Spring)	Comp5001/5003	3
Studio Ensemble	CMP2084	1
Semester Total		16

Spring	Course	Credits
Contemporary Topics (DC/SE)	****	3
Music Business II	CMP3062	3
Studio Composition	CMP3025	3
Non-Music Elective	****	3
Non-Music Elective (Fall or Spring)	****	3
Studio Ensemble	CMP2084	1
Semester Total		16

SENIOR YEAR

Fall	Course	Credits
Business Startup Experience OR	ENTR3071	3
Essential Entrepreneurship Skills	ENTR4005	
Film Scoring II **OR**	CMP5132	3
Songwriting III	CMP4071	
Music Elective	****	3
Non-Music Elective	****	3
Studio Ensemble	CMP2084	1
Semester Total		13

Spring	Course	Credits
General Education (NS/HP/HU)	****	3
Entrepreneurship: New Venture	ENTR5070	3
Studio Music Production II (Capstone)	CMP4054	3
Music Elective	****	3
Studio Ensemble	CMP2084	1
Semester Total		13

CMP BM Degree	*TOTAL CREDITS*	123

Figure 32.4   Four-year plan course changes and configuration

DEEPER LEARNING: KEY CMP INSIGHTS

Moving to a competency education model provides tangible benefits in and outside the classroom environment. This competency framework seeks to create dynamic learning environments that help students foster deep personal understanding of core content. Crafting a skills and knowledge base to solve problems, think critically, communicate effectively, and be self-reflective may be their greatest asset upon graduation. Through the development of cohorts, productive academic relationships among students, between students and faculty, and between students and other professionals strengthen highly valuable intangible assets and people skills that oftentimes determine the long-term success.

SUMMARY AND MOVING FORWARD

Given the trend of the shortening shelf life of music production skills, post-secondary institutions can support students' ongoing success by helping them create learning strategies that support them over their lifetimes. When in school, these learning ecosystems include faculty, industry experts, social networks, digital content, learning experiences, and will be instrumental for students' lifelong personal and professional growth. When training students to navigate the rapidly changing employment landscape, they need to learn how to identify their strengths and weaknesses, professional goals, and pathways for career mobility. It is our belief that through the development of competency-based course content and activities, and offering clear pathways for tangible growth, professional development, and preparedness in the digital age of music business, we are supplying our students the best opportunity for success.

REFERENCES

Martinez-Cañas, R. & Ruiz-Palomino, P., & Rubio, R. (2012). Crowdfunding and social networks in the music industry: Implications for entrepreneurship. *International Business and Economic Research Journal*, 11, 1471–6. 10.19030/iber.v11i13.7449

Tschmuck, P. (2016). From record selling to cultural entrepreneurship: The music economy in the digital paradigm shift. In P. Wikström & R. DeFillippi (Eds.), *Business Innovation and Disruption in the Music Industry* (pp. 13–32). Cheltenham, UK and Northampton, MA, USA: Edward Elgar Publishing. doi: https://doi.org/10.4337/9781783478156.00007

Vander Ark, K., & Vander Ark, T. (2017). The rise of AI demands project-based learning. *Getting Smart*, March. www.gettingsmart.com/2017/03/rise-of-ai-demands-project-based-learning

Walzer, D. A. (2017) Independent music production: How individuality, technology and creative entrepreneurship influence contemporary music industry practices. *Creative Industries Journal*, 10(1), 21–39. doi: 10.1080/17510694.2016.1247626

White, J. C. (2013) Barriers to recognizing arts entrepreneurship education as essential to professional arts training. *Artivate*, University of Arkansas Press, 2(1), 28–39. www.jstor.org/stable/10.34053/artivate.2.1.0028

33. Weaver's Social Enterprise Directory: a tool for teaching social enterprise and entrepreneurship

Rasheda Weaver, Maimouna Mbacke and Katie Gallagher

INTRODUCTION

An increasing number of students are seeking the knowledge and skills needed to create businesses that advance social change. As such, the number of educational programs related to social enterprise and entrepreneurship have skyrocketed since the Millennium (Mirabella & Eikenberry, 2017; Wiley & Berry, 2015; Murdock, Tekula, & Parra, 2013). Universities and colleges typically use courses, business competitions, and certificate programs to teach students about social entrepreneurship (Wiley & Berry, 2015). However, engaging students in new initiatives and networking opportunities can enhance students' entrepreneurial skills and mindset (Lee, Kreiser, Wrede, & Kogelen, 2018). This conceptual chapter introduces a new resource called Weaver's Social Enterprise Directory (WSED) that does just that.

WSED is a public, online directory that provides information for over 1,200 social enterprises operating throughout the United States. It was created in April 2018 by Dr. Rasheda L. Weaver, an assistant professor at Iona College's Hynes Institute for Entrepreneurship and Innovation. The directory is currently the largest informational resource on the social, economic, and legal activities of social enterprises in the United States. While it has various uses, including academic and market research, this chapter focuses on its use as a pedagogical tool for training students interested in pursuing careers in social enterprise and entrepreneurship.

WHAT IS WEAVER'S SOCIAL ENTERPRISE DIRECTORY?

WSED is a public, online resource for locating and acquiring information about social enterprises throughout the United States. It outlines information regarding the name, goods and services, legal structure, and social activities of social enterprises. The directory also provides business information such as the name and email addresses of the top executives in social enterprises, along with their mailing addresses and company email addresses. It is free for anyone to use, however, a small payment is required to download a database that contains information in the directory. The download may be used in academic and market research, as well as for other purposes. The goal behind fees is to foster the sustainability of the directory over time, as databases are costly to manage and curate (Bloom & Clark, 2011). In the last year, the directory has started to generate revenue and qualitative interest from leading social enterprise organizations, social entrepreneurs, and the media.

The goal of the directory is to facilitate the identification of social enterprises in the United States, as this has been a major issue affecting empirical research and partnerships in the field. It was developed as an outcome of Dr. Weaver's dissertation research study entitled *Social Enterprises and the Capability Approach: Examining the Quest to Humanize Business* (Weaver, 2017). The study is the first large-scale study on the social, economic, and legal activities of social enterprises based in the United States. In order to conduct the study, Dr. Weaver researched information from social enterprise membership organizations and government offices to obtain the contact information of self-identifying social enterprises.

After examining information on more than 3,000 social enterprise websites, she developed a database with 942 company and executive email addresses for social enterprises. The goal was simply to use the email addresses to disseminate her dissertation survey. After defending her dissertation and starting a tenure-track assistant professorship, she decided to make the information public for other people seeking knowledge on this growing field. She then developed WSED and has raised approximately $100,000 in financial and human resources to launch it.

Today, the directory is almost two years old. So far, a diversity of leaders, students, and people have used the directory. However, it can also be used by social entrepreneurs, civic-minded consumers, job seekers, educators, researchers, and anyone seeking to work with social enterprises (e.g., business accelerators, foundations, government) (WSED, 2019).

ENTREPRENEURSHIP EDUCATION THEORY

WSED is itself a socially conscious business and a resource for education and research related to social enterprise and entrepreneurship. As such, this chapter focuses on how it can be used to teach students about and prepare them to run social enterprises. One way the directory is used to prepare students to become entrepreneurs is by involving them in its development and promotion as a form of experiential education. Lee et al. (2018) argue that including students in new university (and college) initiatives may help them develop the proactiveness, confidence, and network to advance their entrepreneurial mindset and capabilities. In addition, there is a need to train students *how* to practically run businesses (Smith & Holcomb, 2018) and how to use research to inform business operations (Zhang, 2018).

Students working on this directory gain such experiences by literally aiding in the development of the website, conducting research on social enterprise needs, and then using the information for digital product development (e.g., online workshops and communities). Lastly, Mirabella and Einkenberry (2017) emphasize the need to strengthen the "social" aspect of social enterprise and entrepreneurship educational programs. Most of these programs focus on traditional business planning and management skills. Developing WSED gives students a chance to understand why it is important to track the development of a field focused on using business to address social problems. Students literally get to learn about the variety of business models that are being used to address social issues.

USING WSED IN TEACHING AND RESEARCH

WSED can be used to teach students how to run a social enterprise, to educate them on the field in general, and to engage them in research on the field. The following paragraphs discuss this in detail and Table 33.1 summarizes the expected learning outcomes of the three educational strategies.

Practically Training Students to Run a Social Enterprise

Students working on the development of the directory gain knowledge about how it was created, how startup funds and resources were acquired, and how consumer feedback can be used to develop products. The directory is in its second year of operation. So far, the five students that have helped develop the directory have learned how Dr. Weaver saw a need in the social enterprise community that the directory was used to meet. They have also learned how she utilized her position as an assistant professor to acquire startup funds and

Table 33.1   Expected learning outcomes

Use	Expected student learning outcomes
Practically training students to run a social enterprise	- Experience actually employing business concepts such as opportunity identification, bricolage (pulling resources from diverse places), bootstrapping, market research, and product development - Practical work experience developing a new college initiative for their resume
Teaching students about social enterprise and entrepreneurship	- Experiential learning opportunities that enhance student learning and experience - Networking opportunities with social entrepreneurs - Experience actually visiting social enterprises - Understanding the strengths and weaknesses of different social enterprise business models
Engaging students in research on social enterprise and entrepreneurship	**Students developing the directory** - Teaches students about how the directory itself is a business that uses evidence-based knowledge to develop its services and products **Students using the downloadable database** - Increasing knowledge about social enterprises in one's local, regional, and national area - Having a deeper understanding of various social enterprise business models - Conducting large-scale empirical studies on social enterprise that contribute to career development

assistants that helped take the directory from an idea into a business. In year 3, Dr. Weaver will launch a Social Enterprise Needs Survey that will capture the evolving business needs of social entrepreneurs. Students working on the survey will use the results to develop digital products (e.g., budget templates, webinars) and a training institute that will strive to meet the identified needs. The directory may also delve into working with government to foster social procurement (intentional government purchasing from socially beneficial businesses) in the social enterprise sector. The goal is to start generating revenue that sustainably finances the directory while also meeting consumer needs.

Given all of these activities, the expected experiential educational outcomes of students developing the directory relate to entrepreneurial concepts such as opportunity identification, bricolage and bootstrapping, market research, and product development.

Teaching Students about Social Enterprise and Entrepreneurship

In addition to being a tool for practical business education, WSED can also be used by educators to teach students about social enterprise and entrepreneurship. Educators may use the directory to help students identify social enterprises within and outside of their geographic community. This may improve their understanding of different social enterprise models and the impact that social enterprises have on society, which may help students design their own social enterprises. In addition, educators may use the directory to identify service-learning sites, field visit sites, case studies (e.g., social enterprise profiles), guest speakers for classes and events, socially conscious businesses, and employment and internship opportunities.

The expected learning outcomes from using the directory to teach students about social enterprise and entrepreneurship will differ in relation to how it is used by educators. Nevertheless, it presents many learning and networking opportunities.

Engaging Students in Research on Social Enterprise and Entrepreneurship

Students may learn about using the directory for research by working on its development or using the data download to conduct empirical research on social enterprises. Students working on the development of the directory itself have the opportunity to send email surveys to social entrepreneurs that will help us design future products and services. In doing so, these students will learn about market research and how to run an online business.

Most students that use the directory for research, however, will be downloading the social enterprise database from the website to use for individual research projects. These students will have access to data on a large number of social entrepreneurs and social enterprises that many of their advisors did not. Given the past difficulties associated with identifying and recruiting social entrepreneurs and enterprises for empirical study (Granados, Hlupic, Coakes, & Mohamed, 2011; Hoogendoorn, Pennings, & Thurik, 2010), WSED gives students today the opportunity to conduct large studies on social enterprises. The expected learning outcomes from this include increasing knowledge about social enterprises in one's local, regional, and national area and having a deeper understanding of various social enterprise business models. In addition, students that successfully conduct large-scale empirical studies on social enterprises may make major contributions to knowledge in the field, which will ultimately advance their career development. This benefit to their career development is particularly true if they are seeking careers as faculty. Given the growth of social enterprise education programs (Mirabella & Eikenberry,

2017), we need more faculty with expertise in both the social and entrepreneurial aspects of this field.

CONCLUSION

As educational programs related to social enterprise and entrepreneurship grow across the world (Murdock et al., 2013), so will the need to develop experiential learning projects that prepare students to understand and run social enterprises (Weaver, 2020). This chapter outlines three ways that WSED may be used as an educational resource. First, engaging students in new initiatives housed in colleges and universities gives them confidence, proactiveness, and an increased network that enhances their entrepreneurial capabilities (Lee et al., 2018). As a revenue-generating social business, WSED offers students the practical experience of running a business that Smith and Holcomb (2018) argue they need. Students receive practical training related to product design, marketing, bricolage, and more. While this work occurs with Dr. Weaver at this time, there is potential to collaborate with faculty and students across campuses.

The second way WSED is an educational resource for social enterprise and entrepreneurship education is through the examples it provides related to learning about the social mission of social enterprises. Mirabella and Eikenberry (2017) suggest there is a need to emphasize the social aspect of social enterprise in college and university curricula, as they tend to focus on the managerial and commercial aspect of social enterprise. Lastly, WSED engages students in empirical research on this evolving field. Numerous studies emphasize the need for more empirical studies on social enterprises as organizations (Granados et al., 2011; Hoogendoorn et al., 2010). As one of the only publicly accessible databases on social enterprises, it provides students and all researchers the opportunity to generate important research that informs a diversity of initiatives and opportunities in the field.

REFERENCES

Bloom, P. N., & Clark, C. H. (2011). *The challenges of creating databases to support rigorous research in social entrepreneurship.* Durham, NC: Center for the Advancement of Social Entrepreneurship, Fuqua School of Business Duke University.

Granados, M. L., Hlupic, V., Coakes, E., & Mohamed, S. (2011). Social enterprise and social entrepreneurship research and theory: A bibliometric analysis from 1991 to 2010. *Social Enterprise Journal,* 7(3), 198–218.

Hoogendoorn, B., Pennings, E., & Thurik, R. (2010). What do we know about social entrepreneurship: An analysis of empirical research. *Erasmus Research Institute of Management,* 8.

Lee, Y., Kreiser, P., Wrede, A. H., & Kogelen, S. (2018). Examining the role of university education in influencing the development of students' entrepreneurship capabilities. In C. Matthews and E. Liguori (Eds), *Annals of Entrepreneurship Education and Pedagogy – 2018* (pp. 134–61). Cheltenham, UK and Northampton, MA, USA: Edward Elgar Publishing.

Mirabella, R. M., & Eikenberry, A. M. (2017). The missing "social" in social enterprise education in the United States. *Journal of Public Affairs Education*, 23(2), 729–48.

Murdock, A., Tekula, R., & Parra, C. (2013). Responding to challenge: Comparing nonprofit programmes and pedagogy at universities in the United Kingdom, Spain, and the United States. *NISPAcee Journal of Public Administration and Policy*, 6(2), 69–96. https://doi.org/10.2478/nispa-2013-0007

Smith, B. R., & Holcomb, T. R. (2018). Innovating on and beyond the campus: Entrepreneurship at Miami university. In C. Matthews and E. Liguori (Eds), *Annals of Entrepreneurship Education and Pedagogy – 2018* (pp. 264–73). Cheltenham, UK and Northampton, MA, USA: Edward Elgar Publishing.

Weaver, R. L. (2017). *Social enterprise and the capability approach: Examining the quest to humanize business* (Doctoral dissertation, Rutgers University-Camden Graduate School).

Weaver, R. L. (2020). Using experiential education to teach social enterprise and entrepreneurship: A teaching guide. White Paper published by the Association for Research on Nonprofit and Voluntary Associations (ARNOVA).

Weaver's Social Enterprise Directory (WSED) (2019). About. Retrieved June 17, 2019 from: http://socialenterprisedirectory.com/about/

Wiley, K. K., & Berry, F. S. (2015). Teaching social entrepreneurship in public affairs programs: A review of social entrepreneurship courses in the top 30 US public administration and affairs programs. *Journal of Public Affairs Education*, 21(3), 381–400.

Zhang, Y. (2018). Business and educational entrepreneurship: Purpose and future. In C. Matthews and E. Liguori (Eds), *Annals of Entrepreneurship Education and Pedagogy – 2018* (pp. 58–78). Cheltenham, UK and Northampton, MA, USA: Edward Elgar Publishing.

34. Implementing data analytics into the entrepreneurship curriculum: a course overview

Xaver Neumeyer

INTRODUCTION

Entrepreneurship educators have come a long way to recognize that entrepreneurship is not about innate personality traits, but the development of cognitive and affective competencies that help them identify new opportunities and turn these into new ventures. It involves gaining and developing a number of skills that are specific to entrepreneurial behavior. And, as entrepreneurial behavior is primarily related to a unique set of knowledge structures (both heuristic and scripted) and to decision-making processes (assessment and judgment), understanding the interplay between external information sources and opportunity identification and creation is crucial to enhancing student learning about entrepreneurship. This is particularly pertinent for novice entrepreneurs, whose personal experience with finding viable and attractive opportunities is limited.

With the emergence of the World Wide Web, entrepreneurship has become increasingly digital and new tools have emerged that challenge some of the preconceived notions of how opportunities are identified and assessed. The vast amount of digital applications and platforms have led to a surplus of customer data on purchasing behaviors, disposable income, influencers, and others that can help entrepreneurs to better compare the market performance of different products and services. With that comes the ability to conduct affordable and quick customer experiments and surveys, enabling the entrepreneur to customize his/her product and/or service offerings.

Therefore, the ability to gather, analyze, and act on data is becoming a critical skillset for future entrepreneurs that warrants more attention. In this chapter, I will provide a perspective of how the emerging field of business analytics can contribute to entrepreneurship education, adding to current debates about digital entrepreneurship (Nambisan 2017; Richter, Kraus, Brem, Durst, & Giselbrecht, 2017). First, I analyze the literature and provide an approach incorporating insights from entrepreneurship cognition, education, and business analytics research. In doing so I discuss the areas of analytics that could be most impactful for, and/or to be integrated into, entrepreneurship education.

THE EMERGENCE OF ANALYTICS IN BUSINESS AND ENTREPRENEURSHIP

The rapid proliferation of digital applications and platforms precipitated a rapid increase in the volume, velocity, and variety of data on how customers are purchasing and using new products and services. Empowered by "smart" devices (e.g., smartphones) nearly anyone can capture information (e.g., videos and photos) and quickly distribute the content. Over 500 hours of video are uploaded to YouTube every minute (YouTube, 2019) and Facebook generates over 4 new petabytes of data per day (Facebook, 2019). IBM estimates that 90 percent of all available data were generated in the past two years and the trend is expected to continue with more data being generated in the coming years (IBM, 2019).

This abundance of large datasets provides entrepreneurs with an opportunity to identify emerging trends in the market or new customer segments as well as a better utilization of their existing customer base. The new data sources also create opportunities for business process optimization and development (Davenport, 2006). For example, customer feedback, one of the most valuable sources of information for businesses, has been historically difficult and expensive to obtain. Social reviews posted on Yelp, TripAdvisor, and other services provide vast amounts of customer feedback information for interested entrepreneurs and small business owners.

Extracting even marginal improvements from data insights can lead to meaningful gains in business efficiency, which in turn can have a strong impact on business profitability (Soteriou & Zenios, 1999). The increasing amount of data also poses some questions about privacy and how entrepreneurs can balance information richness while protecting the often very personal data of users.

INTEGRATING BUSINESS ANALYTICS INTO ENTREPRENEURSHIP EDUCATION

The emergence of business analytics has led to an increase in curricular offerings, ranging from individual classes to new undergraduate and graduate programs. Although no uniform definition of "business analytics" exists, Holsapple, Lee-Post, and Pakath (2014) have found that business analytics has been described by the literature as: (1) a movement, (2) a collection of practices and technologies, (3) a transformation process, (4) a capability set, (5) a set of activities, and (6) a decisional paradigm. Borrowing from this diversity of perspectives I define entrepreneurship analytics as the ability to "access, aggregate, analyze, and construct data from diverse sources to bring value to entrepreneurial activities."

With respect to curricular activities, over 130 academic programs in business analytics have been launched between 2007 and 2012 (Wixom et al., 2014). Due to the early stage of business analytics as a discipline, studies on pedagogical approaches are still scarce, with some exceptions. Mamonov, Misra, and Jain (2015) presented a curricula approach that lies at the intersection of specialized business expertise, technical data management and programming as well as applied statistics. They further identified a set of key skill sets that include: (1) the ability to locate, extract, and prepare data for analysis, (2) the ability to apply data visualization techniques, and (3) the ability to communicate complex information.

With respect to entrepreneurship education, several observations can be made. Large datasets containing relevant information for entrepreneurs are scarce. As pointed out in the effectuation literature, opportunities are often co-constructed by different stakeholders, rather than planned on the drawing board. Second, learning to access and examine large datasets to the degree that one can discern different opportunities requires a level of knowledge and practice that is often hard to achieve for non-business analytics majors. As a result, integrating analytics into the entrepreneurship curriculum poses some challenges that prevent its widespread adoption as of yet. To address this shortcoming, an entrepreneurship analytics course for undergraduate business students was developed and implemented at the University of North Carolina at Wilmington. The following sections provide a description of the course, its contents, and outcomes.

COURSE OVERVIEW

The Entrepreneurship Analytics course is offered as an elective for the Entrepreneurship and Business Development and Management and Leadership concentration, offered by the Department of Management at the University of North Carolina at Wilmington. The course has two underlying goals: (1) learning to apply data analytics/big data tools in the context of new venture creation; and (2) execute an entrepreneurship analytics project for an entrepreneurial firm or one's own business idea. The primary learning objectives for the course are:

- Practice analyzing different types of datasets and formats and provide decision recommendations.

- Demonstrate the ability to understand privacy concerns and generate appropriate response policies for entrepreneurial ventures.
- Develop the capacity to use data insights to inform different parts of the entrepreneurship process such as opportunity recognition and creation, competitive analysis, customer segmentation, business modeling, etc.
- Learn how to find different monetization paths for data.

COURSE MATERIALS AND FORMAT

Currently, there are two versions of the course. In the 16-week face-to-face version, the emphasis is placed on establishing and strengthening students' data analysis and interpretation skills through a series of Excel labs. In contrast, the online five-week course focuses on understanding and creating data-driven business models. The following two textbooks are utilized: *Competing on Analytics: The New Science of Winning* by Thomas Davenport as well as *Business Analytics: Data Analysis and Decision Making* by Christian Albright and Wayne Winston. In addition, a selection of case studies from Babson and Harvard are assigned. Course topics include:

- Data-driven business models and monetization
- Data privacy
- Making decisions under uncertainty
- IT infrastructure
- Sampling techniques
- Hypothesis generation and testing
- Advanced analysis methods
- Data triangulation for secondary market research.

With respect to the final projects, students are given two options. The first option includes the development of a business idea with a focus on data monetization. Proposed business ideas have to pass through several checkpoints, after which they receive feedback from the instructor. Deliverables include an executive idea summary, a business model canvas, a competitive and market analysis, a business concept write-up, and presentation slides. The second option requires students to conduct a data analytics consulting project for an entrepreneurial venture or small business of their choice. The consulting project is conducted in three phases:

- Phase 1: Identification and selection of potential clients. Students are asked to utilize their personal network as well as use existing university partners such as the Small Business Development Technology Center or the Center for Innovation and Entrepreneurship to identify startups or small businesses that could support a student team.

- Phase 2: Project identification and planning. After the client has been selected, potential data projects are selected and a project timeline with a set of milestones is determined. A "contract" is drafted between the students and the client to specify the deliverables and expectations. Students sign confidentiality agreements as needed.
- Phase 3: Execution and presentation. Student teams conduct a comprehensive analysis based on the information provided by the client as well as their own research. Subsequently, the recommendations and discoveries are presented to the client. Based on the client's feedback a written report is generated.

The project deliverables for the client will vary. They may include Excel spreadsheets, data visualizations, primary and/or secondary datasets collected throughout the project, and analyses of the client's direct and indirect competitors. Furthermore, confidentiality agreements are signed if requested by the client. Progress reports and peer reviews are submitted to the instructor on a regular basis and subsequent feedback is provided.

COURSE OUTCOMES

To date, the course has engaged 35 students with concentrations in entrepreneurship and business development, management and leadership, as well as marketing. All students get the opportunity to watch their peers' presentation, whether it is in class or online. Several benefits for students have been recorded. Some of the business ideas developed in the course have been submitted and presented at university-level business idea competitions, leading to additional learning and expertise in a rapidly growing field. Students have also found the course to be helpful in job interviews, where recruiters are frequently gauging students' expertise in data analytics/big data as well as general digital literacy skills (Neumeyer et al., 2020). From a faculty perspective, the course has been very insightful with respect to necessary content development as well as student learning in an area that will see growing interest in the future. As a result, the course has been made a requirement in the entrepreneurship and business development concentration with additional sections to be added in subsequent years.

CONCLUSION

In this chapter, we proposed entrepreneurship analytics as an area that requires more attention from entrepreneurship educators and scholars. Entrepreneurship analytics aims to understand how entrepreneurs collect and use data to engage in startup activities. We see analytics as an enhancement of typical startup decision processes, helping students to expand their opportunity horizon (Morris, Santos, & Neumeyer, 2018) as well as reducing typical cognitive biases such as overconfidence, self-serving and confirmation biases (Simon, Houghton, & Akino, 2000). Moreover, we contend that experiential learning can play a key part, but requires the redesign of learning activities and experiences to meaningfully mesh principles of entrepreneurship and business analytics, so as to change knowledge structures and reasoning processes. Despite the fact that this chapter advocates for the formation of entrepreneurship analytics content, programs need to coordinate and learn from existing business analytics programs to make sure that analytics elements fit within the overall goal of their entrepreneurship curriculum. Thinking like an entrepreneur involves imagination, critical and divergent thinking, and seeking continuous improvement. Therefore, entrepreneurship analytics should not lead to "paralysis by analysis" but provide entrepreneurship students with meaningful options to make better and faster decisions.

REFERENCES

Albright, S. C., & Winston, W. (2015). *Business Analytics: Data Analysis and Decision Making*, Boston, MA: USA: Cengage Learning.

Davenport, T. H. (2006). Competing on analytics. *Harvard Business Review, 84*(1), 98.

Davenport, T., & Harris, J. (2017). *Competing on Analytics: The New Science of Winning*. Boston, MA: Harvard Business Press.

Holsapple, C., Lee-Post, A., & Pakath, R. (2014). A unified foundation for business analytics. *Decision Support Systems, 64*, 130–41.

Mamonov, S., Misra, R., & Jain, R. (2015). Business analytics in practice and in education: A competency-based perspective. *Information Systems Education Journal, 13*(1), 4.

Morris, M., Santos, S., & Neumeyer, X. (2018). *Poverty and Entrepreneurship in Developed Economies*. Cheltenham, UK and Northampton, MA, USA: Edward Elgar Publishing.

Nambisan, S. (2017). Digital entrepreneurship: Toward a digital technology perspective of entrepreneurship. *Entrepreneurship Theory and Practice, 41*(6), 1029–55.

Neumeyer, X., Santos, S. C., Morris, M. H. (2020). Overcoming barriers to technology adoption when fostering entrepreneurship among the poor: the role of technology and digital literacy. *IEEE Transactions on Engineering Management*, 1–14. https://doi.org/10.1109/TEM.2020.2989740.

Richter, C., Kraus, S., Brem, A., Durst, S., & Giselbrecht, C. (2017). Digital entrepreneurship: Innovative business models for the sharing economy. *Creativity and Innovation Management, 26*(3), 300–10.

Simon, M., Houghton, S. M., & Aquino, K. (2000). Cognitive biases, risk perception, and venture formation: How individuals decide to start companies. *Journal of Business Venturing, 15*(2), 113–34.

Soteriou, A., & Zenios, S. A. (1999). Operations, quality, and profitability in the provision of banking services. *Management Science, 45*(9), 1221–38.

Wixom, B., Ariyachandra, T., Douglas, D. E., Goul, M., Gupta, B., Iyer, L. S. et al. (2014). The current state of business intelligence in academia: The arrival of big data. *CAIS, 34*(1), 1–13.

Websites

Facebook. (2019). Facebook statistics. Retrieved from https://about.fb.com/news/.
IBM. (2014). Performance and capacity implications for big data. Retrieved from http://www.redbooks.ibm.com/redpapers/pdfs/redp5070.pdf.
YouTube. (2019). Youtube viewership statistics. Retrieved from http://www.youtube.com/yt/press/statistics.html.

35. Rapidly responding to the Covid-19 pandemic impact on small businesses: the GetVirtual Local Business Assistance Course at the University of California Santa Cruz

Nada Miljkovic and Robert D'Intino

INTRODUCTION

We describe an agile entrepreneurship education solution to help small businesses retain their customers and revenues in the face of the current social environment. The Covid-19 pandemic has permanently changed how businesses operate. The effects of social distancing have created an unprecedented global economic crisis (cf. Atkeson, 2020; McKibbin & Fernando, 2020). Immediately after California's shelter-in-place order in March 2020, businesses relying on face-to-face customer interactions suffered significant revenue reduction. Many without an eCommerce presence and corresponding revenue stream may never recover. The new Covid-19 environment requires many of the 30 million United States small business firms to rapidly learn how to communicate online to current and future customers. Marketing, sales, and customer support must now be conducted virtually. Presented here is the development of a new course (viz., Crown 1995) to help businesses go virtual. The course was developed as a partnership between a local serial entrepreneur, the City of Santa Cruz, and the University of California, Santa Cruz (UCSC).

UCSC/CITY OF SANTA CRUZ PARTNERSHIP WITH GETVIRTUAL.ORG

With redwood forests and ocean surf breaks located close to Silicon Valley, Santa Cruz is a popular location for serial entrepreneurs including Steve Blank, Reed Hastings, and Philip Kahn. Local entrepreneurs provide significant mentoring to UCSC students. Serial entrepreneur Toby Corey comprehended the disruptive threat to small business survival and responded quickly with an innovative education partnership with UCSC. Corey co-founded USWeb and Novell, worked with Elon Musk building SolarCity and Tesla, is a Stanford engineering lecturer, and lives in Santa Cruz. To help address the Covid-19 economic crisis, he created GetVirtual.org as a non-profit community partnership to connect local industry experts and mentors with UCSC students and the City of Santa Cruz economic development program. The primary goal is to assist brick-and-mortar retail businesses to rapidly become virtual within the new Crown 199 course described here. This course is designed as an education prototype.

Corey first invited participation with local entrepreneurs, programmers, philanthropists, and UCSC educators with the skills to add value, collaborate, and co-create the new GetVirtual organization. GetVirtual.org[1] was registered and a Google Drive document was created to develop an organization to help local businesses survive by rapidly learning to go online. After several iterations to improve this idea, it was shared with the City of Santa Cruz economic director and the business council director. In these conversations, the city economic director explained a rapidly unfolding small business collapse. Brick-and-mortar human-centric service-based retail shops not currently online were going to fail and fail fast. The Santa Cruz problem involved 1,000 local businesses. Only those already online could potentially survive the Covid-19 crisis. How could many businesses not already online be immediately helped? This was the problem needing contributions from all relevant stakeholders including UCSC.

Corey previously interacted with UCSC students through symposiums and as a Crown college lecturer. He understands two maxims: in a crisis people want to help each other, and the transformational power of student energy. The idea was to directly connect digitally literate students with local businesses online.

RAPIDLY PROTOTYPING A NEW COURSE CONCEPT

As the first week of UCSC's spring quarter began during a time of great academic uncertainty (Liguori & Winkler, 2020), Corey reached out to connect UCSC with GetVirtual. At the same time, a group of students running an "Effectivity Website" business called Kahzum approached the Provost of Crown College at UCSC asking how they could help local businesses while also getting course credit. On the same day, the Provost was asked by one of the co-authors for permission to create the new Crown 1995 course incorporating GetVirtual.

The Kahzum student team offered programming, marketing, design, and strategic support. Several Kahzum student team members were the first to enroll in Crown 1995, the same students who approached the Crown provost to offer help. The founders of Kahzum formed their team and company while enrolled in fall 2017 Crown 90 Startup Entrepreneurship which the authors co-taught. Since then the Kahzum student company had pivoted from a digital marketing platform to a growing website consulting company.

GETVIRTUAL COURSE STUDENT RECRUITMENT

Conversations leading to course decisions happened on the fly. The course needed to enroll students and start quickly. Student recruitment is one key to rapid course prototyping. The Kahzum student team was already formed and functioning. Three enrolled for credit and the rest were willing to participate and contribute. Recruitment for the remaining seven students was accomplished by reaching out to recent outstanding students from the author's undergraduate honors entrepreneurship courses Crown 90-Startup Entrepreneurship and Crown 92-Social and Creative Entrepreneurship and also Crown 90-Startup Entrepreneurship Summer Academy, a hybrid course for PhD and undergraduate students supported by the National Science Foundation to prepare students through the Partnerships for Innovation program to apply for grants to address problems in technology translation.[2] All three courses provide the education scaffolding for students to grasp necessary entrepreneurship knowledge, values, skills, business model canvas, and most importantly, lean startup agile methodology including the customer discovery process. With students ready and willing we were able to move this pilot course forward to serve small business clients and help them rapidly Get Virtual.

GETVIRTUAL COURSE DESCRIPTION

The City of Santa Cruz economic director and the director business council selected the first two businesses: a woman's apparel store and a comic book novelty retail store. Corey was informed and communicated the businesses to the course instructor. Crown 1995 began on March 28, 2020 with students tasked to research both businesses, their specific niche markets, create a business model canvas, and present their team member strengths assessment. The first course session was on April 6 via web conferencing. Prior to the second meeting, students were tasked to create two Google documents presenting a draft schedule of the scope of work and a draft specifying student roles and responsibilities, including a list for the tasks they wanted to own.

Students use Google Team Drive for document control, Slack for communications, and Trello for task assignment and tracking. Teams were divided into the two businesses, schedules were discussed and approved, and roles and responsibilities were assigned. Several team members accepted leadership task roles.

Moving forward in this spring 2020 course, students received weekly instruction to help guide the team and manage the client projects. Students had already learned processes for communication, collaboration, and document control fundamentals in their previous entrepreneurship classes. Skills learned included agile iterative design development, team building, and qualitative customer data discovery. Additionally, students were introduced to project documentation including proposal questions, straw documents, mission and vision statements, and meeting minutes. They began using these examples and customizing them for their businesses' needs. Weekly progress project meetings were established with clients.

The student teams began their work with a diagnosis of their business client's digital literacy, then visualizing and designing a virtual strategy, and planning and managing the GoVirtual implementation. Student teams knew to prepare weekly slide presentations from previous Crown entrepreneurship classes and consequently were proficient in presenting their findings, analysis, strategy, and implementation plan to their clients.

As the students interacted with the clients and each other, they learned which specific skill sets they possessed and which skills they needed to learn. Students sought out industry mentors to provide ongoing support for the student's GetVirtual course endeavors. For example, their first request was to talk to a search engine optimization and search engine marketing professional, whom they met within the third class web-conferencing meeting.

Student teams designed and built initial prototypes for both the GetVirtual. org and client websites with detailed service descriptions and recommendations for software and online technology acquisitions. Students proposed company-specific virtual solutions to clients and with their client's input and efforts, and with help from local professional mentors, student teams implemented and accomplished solutions to get their business clients online.

The multiplicity of stakeholders presented communication challenges and thus the students established formal communication protocols and designated client leads to minimize mistakes in messaging and avoid overwhelming clients with too much technical information given that the client businesses were already in dire straits.

When the course concludes later in the spring, the student team's final task will be to write a highly detailed close-out project report and also create a map and directions for on-boarding the next cohort. In this case, the class will be handing off the projects to a summer course at California State University Monterey Bay, as well as on-boarding the student teams enrolled in the fall 2020 course section.

KEY COURSE STEPS

- City business development selects business clients.
- Students form teams and perform assessments of client businesses.
- Students decide communication, document control, task management, and customer discovery software.
- Students research the selected businesses and learn the lay of the land with local entrepreneurship mentors and industry experts.
- Students create a Business Model Canvas for the business in its current state.
- With the help of mentors, students assess their client's business needs for a new online business model that can survive and thrive in the post-Covid-19 world.
- Students develop and present their strategy and implementation proposals to clients.
- With the help of professional mentors, students implement and execute the proposed solutions.
- Students document and develop project close-out reports for follow-on tasks to on-board the next student cohorts.

CONCLUSION

The Covid-19 pandemic is devastating and disrupting the world's economies. Entrepreneurship mindsets comprehend opportunities for new business solutions and unique and unexpected partnerships. Through entrepreneurship education, UCSC is providing students with real experiences to use their knowledge and skills to support local businesses to survive and thrive in a virtual environment. Where the previously taught entrepreneurship classes were considered "startup simulations," Crown 1995 is helping local businesses in crisis. This course is designed as a prototype solution with the goal to scale and roll out to United States universities. Already at this early stage, California State University Monterey Bay has fast-tracked a summer 2020 class based on this pilot and Stanford is also employing the GetVirtual concept to pilot-test a new course.

NOTES

1. www.getvirtual.org
2. www.nsf.gov/funding/pgm_summ.jsp?pims_id=504790

REFERENCES

Atkeson, A. (2020). What will be the economic impact of COVID-19 in the US? Rough estimates of disease scenarios. No. w26867. *National Bureau of Economic Research.*

Liguori, E., & Winkler, C. (2020). From offline to online: Challenges and opportunities for entrepreneurship education following the COVID-19 pandemic. *Entrepreneurship Education and Pedagogy.* https://doi.org/10.1177/2515127420916738

McKibbin, W. J., & Fernando, R. (2020). The global macroeconomic impacts of COVID-19: Seven scenarios. Centre for Applied Macroeconomic Analysis working paper series, Australian National University.

Index

Printed and bound by CPI Group (UK) Ltd, Croydon, CR0 4YY